TRACES OF A JEWISH ARTIST

DIMYONOT דמיונות
Jews and the Cultural Imagination

Samantha Baskind, General Editor

EDITORIAL BOARD
Judith Baskin, University of Oregon
David Biale, University of California, Davis
Katrin Kogman-Appel, University of Münster
Kathryn Hellerstein, University of Pennsylvania
Laura Levitt, Temple University
Ilan Stavans, Amherst College
David Stern, Harvard University

Volumes in the Dimyonot series explore the intersections, and interstices, of Jewish experience and culture. These projects emerge from many disciplines—including art, history, language, literature, music, religion, philosophy, and cultural studies—and diverse chronological and geographical locations. Each volume, however, interrogates the multiple and evolving representations of Judaism and Jewishness, by both Jews and non-Jews, over time and place.

OTHER TITLES IN THE SERIES:
David Stern, Christoph Markschies, and Sarit Shalev-Eyni, eds., *The Monk's Haggadah: A Fifteenth-Century Illuminated Codex from the Monastery of Tegernsee, with a Prologue by Friar Erhard von Pappenheim*
Ranen Omer-Sherman, *Imagining the Kibbutz: Visions of Utopia in Literature and Film*
Jordan D. Finkin, *An Inch or Two of Time: Time and Space in Jewish Modernisms*
Ilan Stavans and Marcelo Brodsky, *Once@9:53am: Terror in Buenos Aires*
Ben Schachter, *Image, Action, and Idea in Contemporary Jewish Art*
Heinrich Heine, *Hebrew Melodies*, trans. Stephen Mitchell and Jack Prelutsky, illus. Mark Podwal
Irene Eber, *Jews in China: Cultural Conversations, Changing Perspectives*
Jonathan K. Crane, ed., *Judaism, Race, and Ethics: Conversations and Questions*
Yael Halevi-Wise, *The Multilayered Imagination of A. B. Yehoshua*
David S. Herrstrom and Andrew D. Scrimgeour, *The Prophetic Quest: The Windows of Jacob Landau, Reform Congregation Keneseth Israel, Elkins Park, Pennsylvania*
Laura Levitt, *The Objects That Remain*
Lawrence Fine, ed., *Friendship in Jewish History, Religion, and Culture*
Hassan Sarbakhshian, Lior B. Sternfeld, and Parvaneh Vahidmanesh, *Jews of Iran: A Photographic Chronicle*
J. H. Chajes, *The Kabbalistic Tree / האילן הקבלי*
Alan Mintz, edited by Beverly Bailis and David Stern, *American Hebraist: Essays on Agnon and Modern Jewish Literature*
Oren Kroll-Zeldin and Ariella Werden-Greenfield, *This Is Your Song Too: Phish and Contemporary Jewish Identity*

Traces *of a* Jewish Artist

THE LOST LIFE AND WORK OF RAHEL SZALIT

Kerry Wallach

THE PENNSYLVANIA STATE UNIVERSITY PRESS
University Park, Pennsylvania

Library of Congress Cataloging-in-Publication Data

Names: Wallach, Kerry, author.
Title: Traces of a Jewish artist : the lost life and work of Rahel Szalit / Kerry Wallach.
Other titles: Dimyonot (University Park, Pa.)
Description: University Park, Pennsylvania : The Pennsylvania State University Press, [2024] | Series: Dimyonot : Jews and the cultural imagination | Includes bibliographical references and index.
Summary: "Explores the life and career of Rahel Szalit (1888–1942), among the best-known Jewish women artists in Weimar Berlin"—Provided by publisher.
Identifiers: LCCN 2023038847 | ISBN 9780271095592 (hardback)
Subjects: LCSH: Szalit, Rahel, 1888–1942. | Artists—Germany—Berlin—Biography. | Jewish women artists—Germany—Berlin—Biography. | Jews, Lithuanian—Germany—Berlin—Biography. | Berlin (Germany)—Biography. | LCGFT: Biographies.
Classification: LCC N6888.S925 W35 2024 | DDC 700.92 [B]—dc23/eng/20230825
LC record available at https://lccn.loc.gov/2023038847

Copyright © 2024 Kerry Melissa Wallach
All rights reserved
Printed in China
Published by The Pennsylvania State University Press,
University Park, PA 16802–1003

The Pennsylvania State University Press is a member of the Association of University Presses.

It is the policy of The Pennsylvania State University Press to use acid-free paper. Publications on uncoated stock satisfy the minimum requirements of American National Standard for Information Sciences—Permanence of Paper for Printed Library Material, ANSI Z39.48–1992.

Contents

List of Illustrations vii

Acknowledgments xi

Introduction 1

PART 1   FROM THE SHTETL TO THE CITY (1888–1919)

1 The Markus Family in Eastern Europe 15

2 Munich, War, and Marriage 29

3 Berlin Expressionist Circles 46

PART 2   INFLATION-ERA ILLUSTRATIONS (1920–1923)

4 Classic World Literature 67

5 Grotesque Yiddish Figures 88

6 "Hebrew Melodies" 110

PART 3   THE WILD SIDES OF WEIMAR (1924–1933)

7 Newspaper Artist 129

8 Sexuality and the Bible 153

9 The Jewish Käthe Kollwitz 166

PART 4   EXILE IN PARIS (1933–1942)

10 From Berlin to the School of Paris 189

11 Holocaust Fates 204

Epilogue: Remembering Rahel Szalit 215

Chronology 221

CONTENTS

Appendix 1: Rahel Szalit's Known Exhibitions and Works 223

Appendix 2: Translations of Short Stories by Rahel Szalit 229

Notes 237

Selected Bibliography 265

Index 273

Illustrations

FIGURES

1. Photograph of Rahel Szalit, date unknown 2

2. Rahel Szalit, *Perk Number Two*, illustration from Sholem Aleichem's "Chickens on Strike: A Humorous Yom-Kippur Story," in *Israelitisches Familienblatt*, 1931 7

3. Rahel Szalit, *Self-Portrait*, in *Menorah*, 1926 10

4. R. Szalit, *Jewish Neighborhood*, in *B'nai B'rith Magazine: The National Jewish Monthly*, 1931 17

5. Jakob Steinhardt, *Dorfstrasse mit Frau* (Village Street with Woman), ca. 1922 18

6. Rahel Markus's birth record in Russian and Hebrew, 1888 23

7. R. Szalit-Marcus, *Jahrmarkt* (Annual Fair), 1922 25

8. Photograph of Julius Szalit, ca. 1916 35

9. Marriage record of Rahel Marcus and Julius Schalit, 1915 37

10. Rahel Szalit-Marcus, *Leipziger Platz*, 1917, in *Ost und West: Illustrierte Monatsschrift für das gesamte Judentum*, nos. 3–4 (1920): 77 40

11. Rahel Szalit-Marcus, *In der Kälte* (In the Cold), in *Ost und West: Illustrierte Monatsschrift für das gesamte Judentum*, nos. 3–4 (1920): 74–75 41

12. Rahel Szalit-Marcus, *Interieur*, in *Ost und West: Illustrierte Monatsschrift für das gesamte Judentum*, nos. 3–4 (1920): 79 47

13. Rahel Szalit-Marcus, *Der Rabbi und sein Schüler* (The Rabbi and His Pupil), 1920 56

14. Jakob Steinhardt, *Portrait of Rahel Szalit-Marcus*, 1921/22 60

15. Guestbook entry by Rahel Szalit-Marcus in Guestbook of the Steinhardt Family from 1920 to 1927, September 1920 61

16. Rahel Szalit-Marcus, *Peering into the Crocodile's Mouth*, illustration from Fyodor Dostoyevsky's *The Crocodile*, 1921 71

17. Rahel Szalit-Marcus, *Elena Ivanovna Studies the Monkeys*, illustration from Fyodor Dostoyevsky's *The Crocodile*, 1921 72

18. Rahel Szalit-Marcus, *Watching the Crocodile*, illustration from Fyodor Dostoyevsky's *The Crocodile*, 1921 73

19. Rahel Szalit-Marcus, *Three Monkeys*, illustration from Fyodor Dostoyevsky's *The Crocodile*, 1921 74

20. R. Szalit-Markus, *Two Men Surrounded by Women*, illustration from Leo Tolstoy's *The Kreutzer Sonata*, 1922 76

21. R. Szalit-Markus, *Wife Anticipating Her Murder*, illustration from Leo Tolstoy's *The Kreutzer Sonata*, 1922 77

22. R. Szalit-Markus, *Vasya Pozdnyshev Sitting by His Wife's Coffin*, illustration from Leo Tolstoy's *The Kreutzer Sonata*, 1922 78

ILLUSTRATIONS

23. Rahel Szalit-Marcus, *The Three Briggs Sisters*, illustration from Charles Dickens's "The Steam Excursion" in *Londoner Bilder*, 1923   80

24. Rahel Szalit-Marcus, *Cymon Tuggs and Belinda Waters*, illustration from Charles Dickens's "The Tuggses at Ramsgate" in *Londoner Bilder*, 1923   81

25. Rahel Szalit-Marcus, *Mrs. Tibbs Faints*, illustration from Charles Dickens's "The Boarding-House" in *Londoner Bilder*, 1923   82

26. R. Szalit, *Benjamin Rathery and His Sister on a Donkey*, illustration from Claude Tillier's *My Uncle Benjamin*, 1927   84

27. R. Szalit, *The Narrator's Grandmother*, illustration from Claude Tillier's *My Uncle Benjamin*, 1927   85

28. R. Szalit-Marcus, *Arabella Minxit, Benjamin's Intended*, illustration from Claude Tillier's *My Uncle Benjamin*, 1927   86

29. Rahel Szalit-Marcus, *In the Emigration Office / Miss Zaichik from "Ezra,"* illustration from Sholem Aleichem's *Motl, the Cantor's Son* in *Milgroym* and *Menshelakh un stsenes* (People and Scenes) portfolio, 1922   90

30. Rahel Szalit-Marcus, *The Drive to the Rabbi*, in *Milgroym*, 1922   92

31. Rahel Szalit-Marcus, *Woman Sitting with Children*, title page of *Menshelakh un stsenes* (People and Scenes) portfolio, illustration from Sholem Aleichem's *Motl, the Cantor's Son*, 1922   95

32. Rahel Szalit-Marcus, *We Say Goodbye to Our Loved Ones at the Ship*, illustration from Sholem Aleichem's *Motl, the Cantor's Son*, 1922   97

33. Rahel Szalit-Marcus, *Moishe the Bookbinder Whacks the Children with a Board*, illustration from Sholem Aleichem's *Motl, the Cantor's Son*, 1922   98

34. R. Szalit, *Prügelpädagogen* (Abusive Pedagogues), illustration from Magnus Hirschfeld's article in *Die Aufklärung*, 1929   99

35. Rahel Szalit-Marcus, *A Street Sneezes*, illustration from Sholem Aleichem's *Motl, the Cantor's Son*, 1922   100

36. Rahel Szalit-Marcus, *We're Going to America*, illustration from Sholem Aleichem's *Motl, the Cantor's Son*, 1922   101

37. Rahel Szalit-Marcus, *Reb Mendele and the Moon*, illustration from Mendele Moykher Sforim's *Fishke the Lame*, 1922   104

38. Rahel Szalit-Marcus, *Fishke the Lame*, illustration from Mendele Moykher Sforim's *Fishke the Lame*, 1922   106

39. Rahel Szalit-Marcus, *The Traveling Band of Beggars*, illustration from Mendele Moykher Sforim's *Fishke the Lame*, 1922   107

40. Rahel Szalit-Marcus, *Reb Mendele and the Innkeeper's Son / Erste Talmudprüfung* (First Talmud Examination), illustration from Mendele Moykher Sforim's *Fishke the Lame*, 1922   108

41. R. Szalit-Marcus, *Sabbath*, illustration from Heinrich Heine's "Hebrew Melodies," 1923   114

42. R. Szalit-Marcus, *Havdalah*, illustration from Heinrich Heine's "Hebrew Melodies," 1923   115

43. R. Szalit, *La prière dite "Havdalah"* (The Prayer Called Havdalah), in *Le Judaisme Sepharadi*, 1935   116

44. R. Szalit-Marcus, *Jerusalem*, illustration from Heinrich Heine's "Hebrew Melodies," 1923   117

ILLUSTRATIONS

45. R. Szalit-Marcus, *Jehuda Halevi in Heaven*, illustration from Heinrich Heine's "Hebrew Melodies," 1923 118

46. R. Szalit-Marcus, *Disputation*, illustration from Heinrich Heine's "Hebrew Melodies," 1923 119

47. Rahel Szalit-Marcus, *Blowing a Sailboat*, title page of Hayim Nahman Bialik's *Ketina kol-bo*, with lithographs by Rahel Szalit-Marcus, Ernst Böhm, typography: Franziska Baruch (Berlin: Rimon-Verlag, 1923) 122

48. Rahel Szalit-Marcus, *Group of Boys*, last page of Hayim Nahman Bialik's *Ketina kol-bo*, with lithographs by Rahel Szalit-Marcus, Ernst Böhm, typography: Franziska Baruch (Berlin: Rimon-Verlag, 1923) 124

49. R. Szalit, *Entlassen!* (Laid Off!), in *Lachen links: Das republikanische Witzblatt*, p. 529, 1924 133

50. R. Szalit, *Kostümball* (Costume Ball), in *Ulk*, supplement to *Berliner Tageblatt*, p. 68, 1930 134

51. R. Szalit, *Portrait of Johannes Becher*, 1928 136

52. R. Sz., *Portrait of Herbert Ihering*, in *Berliner Börsen-Courier*, 1924 137

53. Rahel Szalit, *Kinder beim Frühstück* (Children Eating Breakfast), pastel, in *Blätter des jüdischen Frauenbundes*, 1930 138

54. R. Szalit, *Cats*, drawing in *Der Querschnitt*, 1927 140

55. R. Szalit, *Bird*, drawing in *Der Querschnitt*, 1931 141

56. R. Szalit-Marcus, *Ritt auf dem Kamel* (Riding on the Camel), illustration from Alphonse Daudet's *Tartarin of Tarascon*, in *Die Schaffenden* 4, no. 3 (1923) 142

57. R. Szalit, *Elephant Pedicure*, in *Zeitbilder*, supplement of *Vossische Zeitung*, 1930 143

58. R. Szalit, *Brunnenkur im Zoo* (Spa Cure at the Zoo), in *Ulk*, supplement of *Berliner Tageblatt*, p. 130, 1930 145

59. R. Sz., *Sport Schild* (Sport Shield), in *Der Schild*, 1925 146

60. R. Szalit, *Vacationers*, in *Jüdische Rundschau*, 1928 147

61. R. Szalit, *I also Took My First Walk with Mr. Stone*, illustration from Shemarya Gorelik's "A Jewish Writer Goes to Canada," in *Jüdische Rundschau*, 1928 148

62. R. Szalit, *At the Front is Queen Esther, Riding Proudly on a Billy Goat*, illustration from Rahel Szalit's "Purim in a Small Town," in *Jüdische Rundschau*, 1930 150

63. R. Szalit, *Before the Purim Festival Ends, Think of Your Purim Donation*, advertisement in *Jüdische Rundschau*, 1928 150

64. R. Szalit, *Leibe Slid the Matzahs in the Oven*, illustration from Rahel Szalit's "Baking Matzah in a Small Town," in *Jüdische Rundschau*, 1930 151

65. R. Szalit, *The Drunk Chickens*, illustration from Rahel Szalit's "Baking Matzah in a Small Town," in *Jüdische Rundschau*, 1930 151

66. R. Szalit, *Dina*, illustration from Thomas Mann's "Dina," in *Die Aufklärung*, 1929 159

67. R. Szalit, *The Rape of Dina*, illustration from Thomas Mann's "Dina," in *Die Aufklärung*, 1929 160

68. R. Szalit, *Men Joined the Dance as Well*, illustration from Thomas Mann's "Dina," in *Die Aufklärung*, 1929 161

69. R. Szalit, *Sichem on a White Donkey*, illustration from Thomas Mann's "Dina," in *Die Aufklärung*, 1929 162

ILLUSTRATIONS

70. R. Szalit, *Because of Morality*, illustration from Magnus Hirschfeld's article in *Die Aufklärung*, 1929 164

71. R. Szalit, *The Convicts' Walk*, illustration from Hermann Nöll's poem in *Die Aufklärung*, 1929 165

72. Rahel Szalit, *Fahrt zur Hochzeit* (The Ride to the Wedding), 1927, postcard from the 1928 Calendar of the Jüdischer Frauenbund (League of Jewish Women) 172

73. Photograph of *Die Frau von heute* (The Woman of Today) exhibition organized by the Verein der Künstlerinnen zu Berlin, 1929 176

74. Rahel Szalit, *Portrait*, in *B'nai B'rith Magazine: The National Jewish Monthly*, 1931 177

75. Rahel Szalit, *Die Emigrantin als Bardame* (Emigrant Woman as Barmaid), 1929 179

76. Rahel Szalit, *Die Fechterin, Selbstbildnis* (The Fencer, Self-Portrait), in *Die Dame*, 1930 181

77. Rahel Szalit, "Parade Riposte," in *die neue linie*, 1930 182

78. Rahel Szalit, *Increasing-temperature Footbath*, illustration from Alfred Brauchle's *Lexikon für Naturheilkunde* (Lexicon for Natural Medicine), 1931 184

79. R. Szalit, *La leçon du Talmud* (The Talmud Lesson), in *Le Judaisme Sepharadi*, 1935 200

COLOR PLATES (AFTER P. 186)

1. Rahel Szalit-Marcus, *Die Dorfmusikanten* (The Town Musicians), 1920

2. Marc Chagall, *The Fiddler*, ca. 1913

3. Szalit's Berlin studio apartment, ca. 1921–33, Stübbenstrasse 3, Schöneberg

4. Cover of Hayim Nahman Bialik's *Ketina kol-bo*, with lithographs by Rahel Szalit-Marcus, Ernst Böhm, typography: Franziska Baruch (Berlin: Rimon-Verlag, 1923)

5. Cover of *Milgroym*, issue no. 1, 1922

6. Ernst Böhm, *Crew of the Nutshell Boat*, illustration from Hayim Nahman Bialik's *Ketina kol-bo*, with lithographs by Rahel Szalit-Marcus, Ernst Böhm, typography: Franziska Baruch (Berlin: Rimon-Verlag, 1923)

7. Szalit's Paris studio apartment, late 1930s, 6bis rue Lecuirot, Montparnasse

8. Szalit's last known Paris address, 7 impasse du Rouet, Montparnasse

MAPS

1. Rahel Szalit's Europe, from Telz, Lithuania (then Russian Empire), to Paris, France, ca. 1910 4

Acknowledgments

Finding sources for this book was like solving a mystery. Who was Rahel Szalit, and where were the traces of her life and work hiding? What remained in the wake of destruction? I started searching for material on Szalit when I first discovered her work, but it took years of research to be satisfied that I had found enough. Every time a new detail came to my attention, it felt like a breakthrough. This was especially true for documents that surfaced during the COVID-19 pandemic, the first year of which coincided with my sabbatical to write this book. But I could not have completed this project alone. Colleagues and institutions in seven countries helped make this book possible, and I am beholden to everyone who was a part of the Szalit recovery team.

I am particularly grateful to Gettysburg College for granting me a full year of leave as well as significant funds to support this book's publication. My research was generously funded by a Hadassah-Brandeis Institute Research Award and by a Sharon Abramson Research Grant from the Holocaust Educational Foundation of Northwestern University. The Association for Jewish Studies Women's Caucus Cashmere Subvention Award contributed additional funds to support publication. Thanks to Samantha Baskind, this project found its rightful home at Penn State University Press, where Patrick Alexander, Josie DiNovo, and other fantastic team members, along with copy editor John Morris, worked tirelessly to produce a book that could do justice to Szalit's art.

Two private collectors from Germany deserve special recognition for their generous contributions of sources, time, and expertise. Eva-Maria Thimme, a Berlin-based scholar, donated five books illustrated by Szalit that eventually will find their way to the Leo Baeck Institute, New York. Gerd Gruber of Wittenberg, who uncovered much in his own research on Szalit, shared wonderfully rich material including biographical information and many of Szalit's works in periodicals.

I was fortunate to work with several brilliant and persistent research assistants, most notably Catherine Ellsberg (in Paris) and Joshua Shelly (in Berlin and Jerusalem). Gettysburg College students Madeleine Neiman and Jack Herr provided additional research assistance and offered important feedback as readers. Other Gettysburg students and alumni supported this project in different ways, including Elizabeth Topolosky and Sophie Gelling. Karolina Hicke provided translation assistance with Polish; Asaph Levy translated Bialik from Hebrew; and Catherine Ellsberg and Esther-Lilith Melchior assisted

ACKNOWLEDGMENTS

with French. Eva and Wolfgang Luber helped decode old German handwriting. Genealogists Stanley Diamond (JRI-Poland) and Petje Schroeder in Lodz graciously assisted with research on the Markus family.

Some of the most exciting sources turned up in unexpected locations. I am especially grateful to Anna Dżabagina for sharing her research on Eleonore Kalkowska. Many others have helped me track down sources: Ralf Dose at the Magnus-Hirschfeld-Gesellschaft e.V.; Volker Landschof at Akademie der Künste, Berlin; colleagues at Jüdisches Museum Berlin; Erik Riedel and Eva Atlan at Jüdisches Museum Frankfurt; Annette Sasse and Kerstin von der Krone at University Library J. C. Senckenberg Frankfurt am Main; Pascale Samuel (and Rachel Koskas) at MahJ, Paris; David Mazower at the Yiddish Book Center; Ute Luise Simeon; and Nadine Nieszawer. At the Leo Baeck Institute, Renate Evers, Tracey Felder, Lauren Paustian, and Michael Simonson assisted tremendously with digitization and permissions. In addition, I could not have completed this book without the wonderful library staff at Gettysburg College, especially Clint Baugess, Betsy Bein, Amy Lucadamo, and Vanessa Sanjuan-Miranda.

I am indebted to valued colleagues for kindly serving as readers and helping to shape this project. Daniel Magilow, Celka Straughn, and the Editorial Committee at PSU Press offered incredibly helpful feedback. Darcy Buerkle, Lisa Silverman, and Abigail Gillman sustained me with invaluable input and extended support over many years. Tahneer Oksman deserves heartfelt thanks for her careful reading of the full manuscript at an early stage—this book would have looked very different without her comments. Samuel Spinner, who has encouraged me to work on Szalit since the beginning, read draft upon draft and helped with difficult Yiddish passages.

Many other colleagues provided feedback on parts of the manuscript, often pointing me to sources as well. Daniella Doron, Aya Elyada, Marion Kaplan, Ellie Kellman, and Sven-Erik Rose generously read chapter drafts. Sonia Gollance, Iris Idelson-Shein, Paul Lerner, Curtis Swope, and Lea Weik commented on proposals and early drafts. I am grateful to art historians Paula Birnbaum and Rachel Perry for sharing their knowledge of artist networks in France. I would like to thank the following colleagues for comments offered in response to presentations or in conversation: Ofer Ashkenazi, LaNitra Berger, Sara Blair, Vance Byrd, Michael Figueroa, Ian Fleishman, Jay Howard Geller, Evan Goldstein, Atina Grossmann, Rebekka Grossmann, Ruth HaCohen, Matt Handelman, Kathryn Hellerstein, Sarah Imhoff, Noah Isenberg, Mariana Ivanova, Eric Jarosinski, Sheila Jelen, Matthew Johnson, Dov-Ber Kerler, Yuliya Komska, Zachary Levine, Catriona MacLeod, Guy Miron, Kenneth Moss, Pamela Potter, Simon Richter, Na'ama Rokem, Mark Roseman, Javier Samper Vendrell, Jonathan Skolnik, Frank Trommler, Liliane Weissberg, Caroline Weist, Daniel Wildmann, Sarah Wobick-Segev, Sunny Yudkoff, and Lisa Zwicker. Both Sharon Gillerman (*z"l*) and Jonathan Hess (*z"l*) encouraged me to pursue this project in its early days. In Gettysburg, Tres Lambert, Bill Bowman, Christiane Breithaupt, Henning Wrage, Robin Oliver, John Cadigan, Caroline Ferraris-Besso, Florence Jurney, Nathalie Lebon, Jack Murphy, Radi Rangelova, Richard Russell, Jack Ryan, Stefanie Sobelle, Luke Thompson, Beatriz Trigo, Mike Wedlock, Chris Zappe, Rachel Lesser, and Elana Nashelsky all stood behind this book in countless ways. Several friends also deserve mention here: Mitch Rotbert assisted with copyright questions, and Ben Magarik helped search for lost works.

Short sections of this book were first published as part of the chapter "Art Without Borders: Artist Rahel Szalit-Marcus and Jewish Visual Culture," pages 149–70 in *German-Jewish Studies: Next Generations* (New York: Berghahn Books, 2023), which I coedited with Aya Elyada. I am grateful to Berghahn Books for the permission to reprint this material here.

Finally, my family was instrumental in supporting my dedication to telling Szalit's story. I enjoyed discussing translations from French and German with my mother, Happy Wallach, who once lived near Montparnasse. Regular visits to the Cleveland Museum of Art with my father, Mark Wallach, inspired my love of art at a young age. Karla Bell shared valuable feedback on the scenes that open each chapter. Philip Wallach, Vera Krimnus, and the Firsheins all listened to many a Szalit story. No one is more deserving of thanks than my amazing wife, Jess Firshein, who recently became a painter in her own right. This book is dedicated to Jess and to Zev and Rafael, who have all made space in their lives for Rahel Szalit.

Introduction

Berlin, April 1923: A woman in her mid-thirties with dark hair and dark eyes walks from her studio apartment to the famous Romanisches Café, where she joins fellow artists and skims the newspaper headlines. What news? The German mark has just collapsed again. Rahel leaves the café and strolls through the nearby Zoologischer Garten, pausing to sketch a few animals: a panther, a giraffe. Her next stop is the women's fencing academy, where she spars with a more advanced opponent. Though she still has much to learn, she wields the fencing foil with the same precision and control she uses for drawing fine lines. "En garde. Ready? Fence!"

That evening she attends a gathering to celebrate Expressionist artist Ludwig Meidner's birthday. The host greets Rahel with a friendly nod but remains immersed in his conversation, gesturing animatedly. Looking around, she sees that this is an unreasonably festive celebration, tables piled high with meats, cheeses, rolls, and drinks that are not easy to come by during these hard times. But anything is possible when one has friends with foreign currency or access to other markets, and Meidner has many such friends.

Among the guests at Ludwig Meidner's party are prominent artists and writers from Germany and beyond. Rahel is thrilled and proud to be part of such an illustrious crowd. Different languages can be heard: German, French, Yiddish, and Russian. In conversation with writer Arthur Holitscher and painters Karl Hofer and Marc Chagall, Rahel describes her work: "Last year, I finished two portfolios of prints illustrating Yiddish literature. Then stories by Bialik and Dickens. Right now I am immersed in German poetry: Heinrich Heine's 'Hebrew Melodies.'" When an acquaintance from the party visits her studio apartment the next day to see her recent work, the modern, career-oriented Rahel seems worlds apart from the soulful faces of eastern Europe that look out from the drawings and paintings on her walls.[1]

FIGURE 1 | Photograph of Rahel Szalit, date unknown. Courtesy of the Musée d'art et d'histoire du Judaïsme, Paris. Photo © mahJ.

One could easily spend hours looking at Rahel Szalit's powerful images, transfixed by the characters they portray. Until now, however, it was not possible to find many of her works in one place. Like their creator, they were largely forgotten. Many are still lost and may remain forever absent from the record. This is the story of an extraordinary artist, told here for the first time at length.[2] These pages recover Szalit's life and assemble a collection of notable, representative works of her art.

Rahel Szalit (1888–1942; pronounced *Sha-leet*; née Markus) was once a sought-after illustrator and portraitist. Toward the beginning of her career, she used the hyphenated last name Szalit-Marcus, though she later shortened this to Szalit (initially her husband's last name). We follow her lead and give preference to the short form with which she signed most works produced after 1923. Today there is only one known photograph of Szalit (fig. 1). Though she hailed from eastern Europe, she was counted among Weimar Germany's most prominent Jewish artists, alongside very few other women. But she was not only Jewish in terms of background and upbringing: she also consistently made art with Jewish subjects. Her work appeared in numerous newspapers and magazines read by both Jews and non-Jews. In 1926, she was praised in the German-Jewish press as "quite simply the best modern female illustrator" and the "first female illustrator of Jewish literature."[3] At times, her illustrations made a stronger impression than the literary works they depicted. By 1929, when she was just over forty years old, Szalit achieved international acclaim as a painter, and her star was rising. But Hitler and the Nazi Party brought her life in Berlin to a sudden halt. Forced to start again in Paris as a refugee from Nazi Germany, she struggled and was fortunate to find a modest amount of success, though this, too, was soon cut short. When she was arrested and murdered in 1942, her Paris studio was plundered, and most of her paintings were destroyed or went missing. Since then, Szalit has largely fallen into obscurity.

Another reason Szalit was erased from history is that her life and work spanned several countries and artistic movements, making it difficult to classify her. Was she Lithuanian? Russian? Polish? German? French? Art history often emphasizes an artist's nationality—but, for Szalit, citizenship and national belonging were complex matters, complicated by such factors as migration, shifting borders, war, and marriage.[4] Like many East European Jewish émigrés, Szalit was driven westward by the quest for personal and artistic freedom. On some level, hers is a familiar story of Jewish migration. She was born into a traditional Jewish world in Lithuania, then part of the Russian Empire. When she was young, her family moved within the Russian Empire to Congress Poland, where they remained. Even though Szalit never lived in independent Poland, and Polish was not her strongest language, she possessed Polish citizenship during the final decades of her life. Yet Szalit chose to spend most of her adult life in Germany and later France (map 1).

The porous boundaries of eastern, central, and western Europe, as well as complexly intertwined ethnic and linguistic identities—Russian and Polish; Yiddish, German, and German-Jewish—become increasingly blurred as we examine the works of this artist. Different national, social, and political contexts play key roles in helping us understand and analyze Szalit's work. Szalit lived at an exciting time for modern art. Like many of her contemporaries, she experimented with new styles and forms, often with a focus on Jewish subject matter. The cities of Berlin and Paris and their thriving communities of artists are also at the heart of this story. Berlin was Szalit's chosen home; Paris was a good backup plan (until it wasn't).

Today we think of Szalit primarily as a literary illustrator because many of these works survive. We associate her with the Yiddish, Hebrew, and German books she illustrated (including German translations of English, Russian, and French literature). But Szalit also painted and drew landscapes, Berlin city scenes, animals, and portraits of women, children, and contemporary public figures (writers, critics, actors). She produced numerous lithographs and worked in pen and ink, pencil, pastel, chalk, oil paint, and watercolors. Women figured prominently in many scenes, from small-town Jewish life to snapshots of the metropolis. Some images employ currents of exaggeration in line with Expressionism, a movement that encouraged expression of the individual's inner experiences

MAP 1 | Rahel Szalit's Europe, from Telz, Lithuania (then Russian Empire), to Paris, France, ca. 1910. Map by Kate Blackmer.

through intense colors and unusual perspectives. Others offer more realistic, unsentimental portrayals. Jews constituted a significant portion of her audience, but her work appealed to those beyond Jewish circles as well.

Internationally, the field of illustration provided many women artists with opportunities. Some found it possible to earn a living as book illustrators already in the late nineteenth century. By the 1920s, the profession expanded to include fashion illustration and other work for magazines. Yet only a few women became known for illustrating German books. Szalit's name is included on multiple lists of noted literary illustrators in early twentieth-century Germany, suggesting that she made a considerable impact in this realm.[5] Still, Szalit's illustration work did not stop with books: she continued to publish drawings in magazines after Expressionist-style lithographic illustrations fell out of favor.

Szalit was a remarkably talented artist who created visually arresting, unforgettable scenes. Her story demonstrates that exceptional women artists gained simultaneous access to both the Jewish Renaissance and mainstream movements (Expressionism, New Objectivity) by engaging with different media and genres. As an artist of great breadth and versatility, Szalit followed broader cultural trends to meet the artistic demands of the moment, from printmaking to portraiture. Her work intersected with literature and journalism in exciting ways. In these male-dominated fields, she often went against the grain by featuring female subjects and perspectives. Many images appeared in periodicals as eye-catching illustrations, and she authored a few short stories for newspapers as well.

Major art critics and art historians in Germany and France took note of Szalit's work and included her in discussions of contemporary Jewish art. Several lent her a great deal of support throughout her career. They, too, are protagonists in her story, especially Karl Schwarz, Adolph Donath, Rachel Wischnitzer-Bernstein, Max Osborn, and Jacques Biélinky. Szalit's renown in her own day shows us that female artists could earn a place in both mainstream and Jewish art circles. Since 1945, however, Szalit's work has been largely neglected by scholars and is usually omitted from broader discussions of both Weimar and interwar Jewish visual culture.[6] Even today, relatively few women artists are represented in European Jewish art history. Including Szalit's work in the canon expands our understanding of what constitutes Jewish art—and art by women—and centers images that were previously only on the margins.

A Feminist Jewish Artist

Szalit unquestionably thought of herself as a Jewish artist.[7] Asked to elaborate on her relationship to Judaism as part of a 1930 survey of artists, she wrote: "I am comfortable as a Jewish woman—I love my people.... I am an Eastern Jewish woman [*Ostjüdin*], and I feel closest to Eastern Jews."[8] For Szalit, the label *Ostjüdin* was not a stigmatized one but rather an identity that fit and was highly relevant for her work. Various Jewish artists from eastern Europe were active in Germany (Jankel Adler, Joseph Budko, Leo Michelson, Abraham Palukst, Lasar Segall), but Szalit was the only woman to leave a mark on Weimar culture. Many other East European Jewish women artists spent time in or passed through Germany (for example, Regina Mundlak), but very little is known about their work and contributions.[9] Most Yiddish-language periodicals in Berlin did not even mention women artists, with the exception of *Milgroym*, which had a female art editor.[10] Indeed, few women artists were successful in foregrounding Jewish subjects in the context of avant-garde movements.

As the only woman artist, besides Else Lasker-Schüler, usually mentioned in conjunction with Expressionism and German-Jewish culture, Rahel Szalit arguably made more significant contributions to the Jewish Renaissance than any other female artist in Germany. Proclaimed by Martin Buber in 1901, this renaissance was initially linked to a cultural Zionist agenda of creating a national Jewish art. Buber and others called for modern Jewish artists and writers to take up Jewish subject matter in the face of antisemitism and assimilation, thereby creating new Jewish traditions based on culture.[11] Ephraim Moses Lilien, for one, contributed well-known images in this vein to the cultural Zionist journal *Ost und West*; Hermann Struck, Joseph Budko, and Jakob Steinhardt also portrayed Jews in their art. Szalit, too, met this task with enthusiasm. Furthermore, at a time when women were often sidelined in artistic representations of Jews, Szalit went out of her way to make women the focus of her art, thereby establishing herself as a feminist Jewish artist.

With Rahel Szalit, we have someone who was at once talented at capturing specific scenes and had a special connection to her Jewish subjects. As journalist Moritz Goldstein observed in 1924, Szalit's perspective as an eastern Jewish "insider," not an outside observer, put her in the rare position of being able to relay and visually translate these experiences without promoting them as idyllic.[12] Nevertheless, it was Szalit's distance from the East, along with the experimental license granted by such movements as Expressionism and later the more realistic and socially conscious New Objectivity, that enabled Szalit's work to upend expectations for how Jewish subjects and experiences should be depicted. By representing Jews as striking, absurd, or grotesque (that is, deformed, exaggerated, the "inverse of beauty and rationality"), Szalit confronted viewers with an ironic and sometimes humorous form of criticism that invited both sympathy and repulsion.[13] Jacques Biélinky, a Paris-based art critic, called her characters "outwardly grotesque and inwardly moving," noting that Szalit created "visions of ghettos where grimaces distort faces but not souls."[14] This was especially perceptible in her illustrations of Yiddish literature, which highlight and respond to suffering.

Consider, for example, Szalit's illustrations of a short story by Yiddish writer Sholem Aleichem (pen name of Sholem Rabinovich), best known for his Tevye stories, which later inspired *Fiddler on the Roof*. Under the title "Chickens on Strike: A Humorous Yom-Kippur Story," the story appeared in German translation in the best-selling newspaper *Israelitisches Familienblatt* (Israelite Family Paper) in 1931. In one of Szalit's images, a rabbi swings a chicken above his head to symbolically transfer his sins to the animal before Yom Kippur (fig. 2).[15] The story pokes fun at this ancient Jewish tradition, known as *kapores*, by having the rabbi offer the chickens several ridiculous "perks" if they cooperate. Szalit draws the actual ritual in action, illustrating the second perk: the chicken is swung around carefully and slowly rather than wildly and quickly. Szalit focuses our gaze on the chicken in midswing, who regards the scene with a bewildered look, as implied by the Yiddish idiom *kukn vi a hon in bney-odem*, meaning "to peer like a rooster during the 'children of man' prayer," recited as part of this ritual.

This visual commentary complements literary works by such authors as Joseph Roth, who was at times ironic or mocking in his treatment of East European Jews and their customs.[16] It further calls our attention to the perspective of the overlooked or oppressed

FIGURE 2 | Rahel Szalit, *Perk Number Two*, illustration from Sholem Aleichem's "Chickens on Strike: A Humorous Yom-Kippur Story," in *Israelitisches Familienblatt*, 1931. Digitized by the University Library J. C. Senckenberg Frankfurt am Main.

„Vergünstigung Nummer zwei . . ."

"other" in the story, in this case an animal. Szalit may have gained personal empathy for chickens by keeping them as pets or by participating in this ritual as a child—in some Lithuanian families, every child performed *kapores*.[17] Within her larger body of work, Szalit generally privileged the viewpoint of women, children, and others who lacked representation and whose viewpoints might have otherwise remained hidden.

Szalit was one of many eastern Jewish émigré artists, writers, performers, and other cultural figures who migrated westward to such booming cultural centers as Berlin and Paris. They did so to flee armed conflict, to pursue artistic and economic opportunities, and to create, publish, perform, and exhibit their work alongside similar artists. Would Marc Chagall have been able to achieve such renown had he stayed in Vitebsk? Who would have had access to Joseph Roth's satirical wit if he had published only in local newspapers in Brody or Lemberg? Works by Chagall, Roth, Szalit, and others became known in the West precisely because they depicted a supposedly authentic version of the East.

In fact, much of what is considered "Jewish art" from the early twentieth century was connected in some way to imaginings of authentic eastern Jewish folk traditions. By the broadest definition, Jewish art encompasses works that incorporate biblical or Jewish themes or that connect in some way to experiences from the Jewish past and present, including the notion of living in the Diaspora in a state of perpetual wandering.[18] Much of Szalit's work meets one or more of these criteria, including many of her literary illustrations, and she contributed to the creation of Jewish art in interwar Europe in numerous ways.

Weimar Berlin provided a home to many East European Jews in the 1920s, and Jewish culture and avant-garde culture flourished. However, the rise to power of the Nazi Party in 1933 created a new class of émigrés-turned-refugees who urgently sought asylum in France, Great Britain, the United States, Palestine, and elsewhere. France, which had no anti-immigration statute, absorbed a good number of these refugees, and Paris offered a thriving, if temporary, cultural haven.[19] Despite the growing presence of antisemitism and xenophobia, many Jews did not believe that France, too, would eventually turn on its Jewish population. Some prominent Jewish artists and writers (among them Chagall, Eugen Spiro, Hannah Arendt, and Lion Feuchtwanger) later managed to escape Nazi-occupied France for the United States. Many of their rescues, for example those organized by Varian Fry and Hiram "Harry" Bingham, are by now quite well known.[20] These refugees found escape routes in the early 1940s through Marseille, Spain, North Africa, and Portugal, as popularized by the film *Casablanca*, which featured European émigré actors.[21]

But many less fortunate refugees could not escape, and their stories need to be told. Szalit was murdered in the Holocaust along with over eighty other Jewish artists associated with the School of Paris, most of whom were foreign.[22] Citizenship often played a critical role: foreign or stateless Jews, and especially East European Jews, were among the first targeted in France. We must ask whether Szalit would have met this fate had she been able to find more support for her work, and in what ways gender and Jewishness mattered. What level of success or connections would have brought Szalit to the attention of international rescue committees? If Szalit had been a man, would she have had more opportunities through proximity to other male artists? Could she have become as well known as her male contemporaries Jakob Steinhardt, Ludwig Meidner, and Marc Chagall (who escaped to Jerusalem, London, and New York, respectively)? Certainly Szalit would be better known today if she had survived, or if more of her works had been smuggled out of Nazi-occupied Europe.

Finding Evidence of Rahel Szalit

I first stumbled upon Szalit while conducting research in Berlin archives in 2008, and I was immediately struck by how many of her images appeared in the Weimar Jewish press. Once I started looking for her name, I seemed to find it everywhere. Her images enchanted and haunted me; I could not stop wondering about the person who created them. I felt an affinity for Rahel Szalit that I could not explain, and this, coupled with a sense of moral obligation, led me to want to tell her story at length. No one else was able or motivated to do so. But it soon proved very difficult to find out more about the artist herself. I stumbled upon a few seemingly credible articles from the 1920s, yet details were scarce. The information that has circulated about Szalit's biography is limited, error-filled, and sometimes contradictory, and there are still countless gaps and unknowns. Many questions will always remain unanswered.

For the last fifteen years, I have searched everywhere imaginable for sources that could help reconstruct her life. Drawing on thirty-five archives in seven countries, I tracked down public records, a handful of Szalit's letters in German and Polish, dozens of newspaper articles, and other archival materials, including those of artists' organizations. The extensive 1951 account from Hersh Fenster's Yiddish memorial book for Jewish artists who lived in France remains one of the richest sources of information.[23] Several journalists profiled Szalit during her lifetime, including three who interviewed her and described her personality. One even wrote about Szalit for American Jewish publications.[24] Szalit herself published an autobiographical essay and two short stories in Jewish periodicals, as well as an article about fencing in the Bauhaus lifestyle magazine *die neue linie* (the new line).[25] Many articles by and about Szalit appeared around 1930, when her star shined its brightest after her painting *Die Emigrantin als Bardame* (Emigrant Woman as Barmaid, 1929; fig. 75) won a prize.

Still, no diary or memoir survives that would allow us to hear more of her voice. We have precious few surviving letters, each one worth its weight in gold. On top of that, accounts of Rahel Szalit by people who knew her are surprisingly rare. Even though she circulated among well-known artists, writers, and other prominent figures, very few of them immortalized her in their own writings. It bears repeating that there is little evidence to be found, and it is thus necessary to speculate at times to create a fuller picture. I have made every effort to gather accurate information that sheds new light on this artist's story and body of work.

Though it might sound strange, I have greatly enjoyed the painstaking work of piecing together Szalit's story and the countless hours spent with her and her work. I feel closest to her when I walk the streets of Berlin-Schöneberg that she called home. Twenty-first-century Berlin is alive with Jewish history; visitors to her former neighborhood near Bayerischer Platz cannot miss the many memorials and commemorative markers, though none of these memorials remember her. Still, Szalit is as present as many others of her day. It is an honor to reintroduce her almost exactly one hundred years after the publication of her best-known literary illustrations.

So: who was Rahel Szalit? The only known photograph of the artist is a passport-style photo that tells us little about her personality (fig. 1). We also have several self-portraits; one shows her with a friendly smile and eyes downcast (fig. 3).[26] The line-focused sketch captioned *Das bin ich selbst* (This is me myself) magnifies her eyes and adds exaggerated eyelashes. From these and other images, including one of Szalit as a fencer (fig. 76), we know she had high cheekbones and cut a poised, athletic figure. Described as modest,

FIGURE 3 | Rahel Szalit, *Self-Portrait*, in *Menorah*, 1926. Digitized by the University Library J. C. Senckenberg Frankfurt am Main.

RAHEL SZALIT / SELBSTPORTRÄT

unpretentious, generous, kind, and good-natured, she had a way of relating to people that inspired confidence.[27] Her undeniable magnetism drew others to her; she thrived when among people. She became melancholic when she felt lonely, which occurred often toward the end of her life. Something powerful drove her from within. Like many women of her time, she faced an uphill battle in realizing her career ambitions. It was no small feat to convince male artists and critics that she was capable and should be taken seriously as an artist, and especially as a Jewish artist; this was an ongoing struggle and ultimately a major triumph on her part.

At once determined and vivacious, Szalit was a perceptive visual chronicler and commentator on the world around her. In the absence of accounts of her life, her artwork provides us with insight into who she was as a person and how she styled herself as an artist. Her art reflects the weight she placed upon her eastern European background and Jewish identity, and it also shows her deep engagement with women's circles and the image of the modern woman as resilient, self-sufficient, and athletic. Through Szalit's hand, we gain access to her unexpected sense of humor and the lighthearted approach she used at times to overcome adversity—her own form of "laughter through tears" (see chapter 5). We are surrounded by the warm glow that emanated from the works of many European Jewish artists right up until their world collapsed.

INTRODUCTION

Key to This Biography

A brief overview of Szalit's biography helps us understand the different places and phases of her life, which generally align with the four parts of this book. Rahel Markus was born in the summer of 1888 in Telz (Telšiai), a market town in Russian Lithuania, to a family of modest means. Like nearly all Jews living in the Pale of Settlement, the region of the Russian Empire where Jews were permitted to settle permanently, she was a native Yiddish speaker.[28] Early on, Rahel learned Polish, German, and French. Although she became remarkably fluent in German, it is almost possible to hear a Yiddish accent behind the minor errors and imperfections in her letters written in German and other languages. While she was growing up, the Markus family lived in Lodz, and they eventually acquired Polish citizenship. Rahel maintained contact with her family long after she left eastern Europe. The Markus family's origins and fates are explored in depth in the first and last chapters.

The first place Rahel (now Marcus) lived on her own was Munich. Though we know little about the phase that started in 1910, this was the beginning of her studies and career as an artist. She also studied briefly in Paris and London. As a foreigner, she was expelled from Germany as an enemy alien following the outbreak of the First World War in August 1914, and she fled to Austria with actor Julius Szalit (1892–1919), whom she had met in Munich. They married in Vienna in 1915, though the pair separated before Julius's suicide in 1919. Rahel never remarried, but she had romantic relationships with both men and women after Julius's death. Her story fits into LGBT and queer history on several levels, as discussed in chapters 2 and 8.

From 1916 until soon after the Nazis took power, Rahel Szalit made her home in Berlin. Her Berlin years can be divided into two phases. Leading up to and during the early 1920s, Szalit experienced initial success, especially in Jewish circles; she painted, made lithographs as illustrations, and participated in a few exhibitions. Part 2 takes a close look at her illustrated books and print portfolios, nearly all of which were published by 1923. The second Berlin phase began in 1924, a year that marked both the end of hyperinflation and the decline of Expressionism. Szalit began regularly placing portraits, cartoons, and illustrations in periodicals, and her career became entangled with journalism by the middle of this decade. Starting in 1927, she participated in events and exhibitions of the Verein der Künstlerinnen zu Berlin (Association of Women Artists in Berlin, or VdBK), and through this organization she achieved international renown as a painter. She continued to be active in Berlin's Jewish community; one critic regarded her as a Jewish counterpart to Käthe Kollwitz.[29] Yet despite Szalit's relative success, she was never well-off financially, and she augmented her artist's income by giving lessons in drawing, painting, and fencing. Chapters 3 and 9 offer the most insight into how Szalit fit into Berlin's art scenes.

Szalit fled Germany in 1933 for Paris, where she took up residence near Montparnasse and began the final phase of her career. Despite experiencing tremendous hardship in exile, she was able to exhibit her work in Paris from 1935 to 1939. In Paris, as she had in Berlin, she spent time at well-known cafés frequented by émigrés and built connections to other artists. She tried unsuccessfully to flee to Switzerland. As a foreign Jew, Szalit was considered stateless and was arrested as part of the Vel d'Hiv roundup in Paris on 16 July 1942. After a month in the internment camp at Drancy, she was deported to Auschwitz and murdered, as discussed in chapters 10 and 11.

Among Rahel Szalit's surviving works are lithographic book illustrations, drawings and short texts printed in periodicals, photographs of oil and watercolor paintings, and a few oil paintings that have been floating around France for decades. One oil painting was exhibited in 2005 (plate 1); another, of a woman in a garden, resurfaced at a flea market in 2021; and a third, a landscape that also includes a small figure of a woman, turned up in Paris in 2022.[30] In addition, Szalit's original graphite-and-ink illustrations of Israel Zangwill's *The King of Schnorrers*, long presumed lost, suddenly reappeared in a New York auction of Judaica in 2023 and sold for the impressive amount of twelve thousand dollars. That several works have only just been found suggests there may be more waiting to be discovered, especially in France, Germany, and perhaps Israel. Indeed, all of Szalit's other paintings remain at large if they were not destroyed, as many certainly were. Rather than dwell on what is missing, we will focus on the somewhat miraculous fact that many works have managed to come down to us in one form or another. More than seventy of Szalit's works are reproduced here. Even small, grainy, black-and-white photographs of paintings that appeared in magazines hold some of the answers to our many questions. The images tell a story that was not preserved in any other form.

At the beginning of each chapter, a fictional scene (such as the one about Ludwig Meidner's birthday party above) expands upon historical facts to imagine what Rahel Szalit's days might have looked like in a particular period. Like reenactments in a documentary film, these invented scenes begin to fill in the gaps where insufficient evidence survives. They are designed to help bring Szalit to life. The work of scholar Saidiya Hartman serves as a model for how imagined scenes can tell the histories of marginalized individuals for whom there is limited archival material.[31] Fictional scenes are set off with italics; the rest is a true story firmly rooted in historical sources and art. Let us now follow Szalit on her journey from eastern to central and western Europe.

PART 1

From the Shtetl to the City

(1888–1919)

CHAPTER 1

The Markus Family in Eastern Europe

Telz, Russian Lithuania, August 1901: With her parents and younger sister, thirteen-year-old Rahel Markus mourns the death of her grandfather, Yankel Markus. He has died of old age at eighty-five; his wife, Leah, of blessed memory, died a few years earlier.

Expenses for Yankel's burial are covered by the Jewish community. Everything takes place in accordance with traditional Jewish custom; the khevre-kadishe (burial society) recites the proper psalms in a religious ceremony. After the funeral, the family spends seven days sitting shiva at home. A large wall clock with weights hanging down marks the hours. All the mirrors stay covered.

Rahel's mother, Tsipa, sweeps the wooden floors and lights the kerosene lamps several times each day. They're joined in the evening by relatives and friends—at least ten men must be present to pray for the dead. The rhythmic chanting of the mourners echoes throughout the crowded rooms of the small wooden house. Rahel and her sister bring hot tea and plates of rolls, berries, and sweets from the kitchen to the living room.

With Yankel Markus's death, the family's long-time connections to the small towns of northwest Lithuania are severed. A few months after Yankel's death, his son Yudel—Rahel's father—decides that it's finally time to leave Telz and try their luck in a bigger city with a larger Jewish population, farther away from the pogroms. They have cousins who settled in Lodz, and they make arrangements to do the same. "We must leave before winter," Yudel reminds them.

Tsipa goes to market to trade larger household items for linens and other things that can be transported in a horse-drawn coach. Young Rahel goes with her to study the faces, foods, and animals on display. They walk along cobblestone streets toward the center of town, where the market is surrounded by two-story houses with shops. Women bustle about in shawls, colorful *kerchiefs on their heads, their baskets laden with potatoes, cabbage, rye bread, and smoked fish. Children at play appear and then disappear among the crowd. Cattle, goats, chickens, and horses contribute loudly to the constant movement of the marketplace. Rahel takes in as much as she can, knowing she may never see this place again.*

To understand the life and artistic practice of Rahel Szalit, we must first understand the East European worlds in which she was raised. The shtetls and communities in Russian Lithuania and Poland that Szalit engaged with as a child made a profound and lasting impression on her. She depicted the shtetl itself in various forms in her work. Like many other artists who worked in an Expressionist style, which aimed to upend social norms by emphasizing distorted, angular shapes and powerful colors (think of Franz Marc and Ernst Ludwig Kirchner), Szalit found this approach particularly suited to her early aesthetic aims.

One of only a few of Szalit's paintings known to have survived, *Die Dorfmusikanten* (The Town Musicians, 1920), uses this style to depict a shtetl scene in oil on canvas (plate 1).[1] The painting is small enough that it could fit easily in a suitcase. In it, two men stand while playing string and woodwind instruments, likely a bass and a wooden flute, as was common among small-town musicians. Szalit's subject matter and bold use of green, blue, brown, and black hues parallel contemporary works by such painters as Marc Chagall, Mané-Katz, and Jakob Steinhardt. Chagall's painting *The Fiddler* (1913), among others, depicts the Jewish folk musicians that inspired the musical version of *Fiddler on the Roof* (plate 2).[2] More realistic musicians appeared in illustrations by Jakob Steinhardt, one of Szalit's friends and influences in Berlin, for a 1920 German translation of stories by Yiddish author I. L. Peretz.[3] Szalit draws on these folkloric motifs, though with a greater sense of melancholy. In paintings by both Szalit and Chagall, the featured musicians have sallow, green faces. The backgrounds show cluttered clusters of single and two-story houses with slanted roofs, wooden fences, and quirky inhabitants of small East European towns.

Yet whereas Chagall's subjects are often lighthearted or whimsical, as shown through their airy gestures and body positions, Szalit's figures struggle to get their bearings on narrow roads lined with closely packed houses. *Die Dorfmusikanten* was likely exhibited under the short title *Musikanten* in 1928; critic Ruth Morold observed that one of its musicians' heads could have come from a colored wooden sculpture, noting that these Jewish musicians "had the weightiness [*Schwere*] of poetry rooted in reality."[4] These houses, and especially their sharp-angled roofs, are visible in multiple images of small-town life. Szalit's protagonists crowd the foreground of these works, as if moving out of the frame toward the viewer.

FIGURE 4 | R. Szalit, *Jewish Neighborhood*, in *B'nai B'rith Magazine: The National Jewish Monthly*, 1931. Courtesy of B'nai B'rith International.

In Szalit's painting *Jewish Neighborhood* (original title and date unknown), reproduced in a photo in the American Jewish *B'nai B'rith Magazine* in 1931, the lamppost looms at an angle that lends perspective but also disorients (fig. 4).[5] A woman with a covered head looks out, coyly inviting the viewer to identify with her position. Her large shawl covers her body entirely and perhaps also conceals a basket if she is headed to market. Behind her, several men in long coats walk in different directions; it is possible that they have emerged from the same nearby building with a partially open door. The streets and roofs look like they are covered in snow, and the sky appears dark. Such complex and quietly unsettling imagery of Jews in traditional settings can be found in many of Szalit's works from the early 1920s.

The subject matter and composition of this painting recall several of Jakob Steinhardt's works. Similar motifs can be found in Steinhardt's oil painting *Auf dem Weg ins Bethaus* (On the Way to the Prayer House, 1921) and his woodcuts *Litauisches Dorf* (Lithuanian Village, 1918) and *Winter* (1919). One woodcut by Steinhardt, *Dorfstrasse mit Frau* (Village Street with Woman, 1922), likewise shows slanted roofs and a lone woman with a covered head in the foreground (fig. 5). The woman depicted here seems older and directs

FIGURE 5 | Jakob Steinhardt, *Dorfstrasse mit Frau* (Village Street with Woman), ca. 1922. Woodcut, 25 × 15.8 cm. Jüdisches Museum Berlin, Inv.-Nr. GDR 93/8/36, acquired with funds from the Stiftung Deutsche Klassenlotterie Berlin. Photo: Jens Ziehe.

her gaze downward. Steinhardt's print draws the viewer's eye to patterns on the street and rooftops; the woman adds perspective, but she plays a secondary role to the street itself.

In such East European Jewish neighborhoods and villages, Yiddish was a central part of daily life. According to the first comprehensive census of the Russian Empire in 1897, nearly 97 percent of Jews (over five million) in the Russian Empire spoke Yiddish as a first language.[6] As a child, Rahel likely heard stories by the classic Yiddish authors whose works she would one day go on to illustrate, particularly those of Mendele Moykher Sforim and Sholem Aleichem, and she later immersed herself in this literature while living in Berlin. Indeed, cultural traditions and sensibilities accompanied many Yiddish speakers in their migrations well beyond eastern Europe, making Yiddish a transnational and even a global phenomenon. Yet Yiddish culture remained heavily tied to its East European origins, including shared experiences of oppression and hardship. Many writers integrated references or allusions to other Jewish texts in their work.[7] So, too, did Szalit continue to engage with East European Jewish culture in much of her work, which drew on both her personal experiences and those recounted in works she illustrated.

Modest Origins

Rahel Markus was born into a working-class Jewish family. There are no known Markus family papers or archives, which makes it difficult to picture exactly how they lived. Far fewer stories are told of families with little influence and limited means, particularly when the Holocaust severely ruptured or destroyed the family line. Even so, using public records and genealogical research, the Markus family can be traced back several generations to the early nineteenth century. We can presume that they lived like other Jewish town dwellers in northwest Lithuania. During the worst of times, they may have experienced the extreme poverty and persecution that affected many Jews in that region. Rahel's father was a brushmaker (*bershter*), and his livelihood seems to have kept the family afloat. The Markus family's story is not one of great economic prosperity but rather a story of modest upward mobility as a result of migration, hard work, acculturation, and relatively good fortune until the 1930s.

The history of the Markus family also teaches us much about migration patterns within Europe in the late nineteenth and early twentieth centuries. Jews made up most of the westbound migrants from the Russian Empire. Within the Pale of Settlement, the adjacent provinces where Jews were permitted to settle in the Russian Empire, Jews moved from rural areas to small towns and big cities, and the Jewish urban population grew rapidly in the early twentieth century.[8] Rahel's parents, Yudel and Tsipa Markus, both hailed from small towns in the province of Lithuania known in Yiddish as Kovno (Kaunas). Rahel and her younger sister Sheina Machla (Szejna Michla) were also born in this region. The family moved to Lodz around 1900, during a period when the city was experiencing rapid growth. Most of Rahel's immediate family members spent the rest of their lives in Poland. Rahel was the only one who left for central and later western Europe, initially to gain access to major art scenes.

Many stories of Jewish migration are interwoven with accounts of exclusion and persecution, and this was certainly the case for Rahel later in her life. The Markus family, however, moved westward within eastern Europe (from Lithuania to Poland) largely because of the promise of economic opportunity. To be sure, all of the countries where members of the Markus family lived prior to 1945 would actively discriminate against, persecute, and eventually murder or contribute to the mass murder of Jews. But oppressive laws, growing antisemitism, and anti-Jewish violence largely impacted the Jews of Lithuania after the Markuses had already left that region. From around the turn of the century until war broke out in 1939, Poland provided the family with a better home, though it, too, saw an uptick in antisemitism during these years and was at best an "uncertain haven."[9] A closer look at the history of the Markus family's eastern European origins will help us get a better sense of Rahel Szalit's background and sources of inspiration, as well as the types of persecution that confronted Jews in the Russian Empire.

Small-Town Jews in the Pale of Settlement

From the late eighteenth century until the First World War, Lithuania was part of the Pale of Settlement under tsarist rule and was subject to constant anti-Jewish rulings and violence. Jews in the Russian Empire were tolerated by their non-Jewish neighbors but considered inferior, useless (because of their disproportionate involvement in trade and not agriculture), or even harmful. Most Jews in Lithuania lived in cities or small towns and earned a living from crafts and trade.[10] Many smaller towns could be considered traditional Jewish shtetls, where Jews constituted a large proportion or majority of the inhabitants and where religious belief remained strong. Jewish artisans and traders served as economic middlemen who traded goods for agricultural produce from Christian peasants.[11] The Markus family was part of this category as well: they were town dwellers who eventually made their way into the artisan sector.

The town of Užventis in the Šiauliai district of Lithuania was the hometown of both Rahel's father and paternal grandfather. Užventis is located about thirty miles from the town of Šiauliai on the bank of the Venta River; its name means "beyond the Venta." In the eighteenth century, it was granted the right to exist as a town and to engage in commerce such as weekly market days and three annual fairs. Jews first settled in Užventis around this time as well. By 1897, the Jewish population of Užventis consisted of 330 people, or 35 percent of the total population.[12] Its name was spelled and recorded differently in other languages—for example, as Ushvent (Yiddish) and Użwenty (Polish)—and for years was listed in public records as the Markus family's place of origin and permanent residence. This likely explains why, though Rahel was not born in Užventis, her birthplace is listed as "Ichjenty" or "Ischgenty" on many official documents.

Different ways of writing place, family, and given names complicate the family history on several levels. Some of these spelling choices were made to help local populations pronounce names more accurately, or to align with local spelling conventions. The family's surname is "Markus" in Lithuanian and Polish records but becomes "Marcus" in German. Another spelling of Rahel's name in Yiddish is "Rokhl." In French, Rahel becomes "Rachel"; Szalit becomes "Schalit" ("Schalit" is also the original Polish/German spelling). She signed letters written in Polish as "Rachela Szalitowa," where the suffix "-owa" denotes that Szalit was her married name. Additionally, many East European Jews had two versions of their given names: a Jewish name (Yiddish or Hebrew) and another version that varied depending on language, alphabet, and region. Rahel's father, referred to as "Yehuda" in Hebrew, went by "Yudel," sometimes spelled "Judel" or "Iudel"; her mother, whose given name was "Tzipora," went by "Tsipa" or "Cypa."

Rahel's grandfather, Yankel Markus, son of Leyb, was born in Užventis in the second decade of the nineteenth century. Nothing is known about Yankel's line of work, but he was able to support his family. Yankel married a woman named Leah, and they had at least four children in the 1840s and early 1850s.[13] The children were presumably all born in Užventis: Pese (born around 1842), Leyzer (1844), Rokhl (1850), and Yudel/Yehuda (1851). The family omitted Yudel's name when they completed the 1858 census; they may have omitted the names of other sons as well. It was common for Jewish families to conceal the existence of young boys to protect them from conscription into the Russian army. Jews were initially exempt from military service, but this changed under Tsar Nicholas I in 1827.[14] Although the Markus family remained officially registered in Užventis, Yankel Markus owned a house in Telz, about twenty miles away, which was valued at two hundred rubles in 1855. This meant that the Markuses were classified as real estate owners and were not in the lowest tax bracket. Though not middle-class, they were also not the poorest. Leah died of old age in 1895. Yankel was living in Telz in 1897 (when he paid taxes amounting to ten rubles), and he died there in 1901.

In general, things improved for Jews in the Russian Empire after 1855 under Tsar Alexander II, who repealed many oppressive measures and instituted Russia's Great Reforms.[15] Yet life was still far from ideal. Most Jews were confined to the Pale of Settlement and had restricted mobility. In Lithuania in the 1860s, some Jews were threatened in the wake of the 1863 Polish uprising, and famine followed a poor harvest in 1867–68.[16] A cholera epidemic also hit toward the end of the decade. The late nineteenth century saw both tremendous population growth and massive impoverishment among Jews in the Russian Empire.[17] Perhaps to avoid some of these hardships, or simply to live and work among larger Jewish communities, the Markus family moved around within the adjacent Šiauliai and Telšiai districts.

With the assassination of Alexander II in 1881 and the pogroms that ensued, life became significantly more difficult for Jews in the Russian Empire. The "Storms in the South" and pogroms of the early 1880s represent a turning point in anti-Jewish violence in terms of scale and mass participation. Rioting mobs attacked and beat Jews and robbed, looted, and destroyed their property. In northwest Lithuania, where local authorities did not permit pogroms, there were more recorded incidents of arson than usual in the 1880s. A major wave of anti-Jewish violence spread through northern Lithuania in the summer of 1900. Other violent conflicts, including one in Telz, occurred during the 1905 Revolution.[18]

But it was not only fear of this violence that made life harder for Jews in the Russian Empire. The May Laws of 1882 further restricted Jewish rights of trading and residence. Jews were not permitted to resettle in peasant villages within the Pale and were in constant danger of losing their homes. Further measures included fines imposed for evading military service, a *numerus clausus* or quota of 10 percent for Jewish students at high schools and other institutions of higher education, and the loss of the right to participate in municipal elections.[19] Responses to these pogroms and restrictive measures varied. Some Lithuanian Jews recommended that local Jews go out less in public; others prepared to defend themselves or appealed to local authorities for protection.[20]

Emigration was a common solution for Jews who sought a better life. In addition to the 1880s, another emigration peak occurred between 1903 and 1907, prompted by the Kishinev pogroms in 1903 and anti-Jewish outbreaks in nearly seven hundred locations in 1905, including in Lodz.[21] Another wave of migration followed a terrible series of pogroms that took place in Ukraine from 1918 to 1920. Artist Issachar Ber Ryback, whose father was murdered in one of these violent attacks, immortalized the Ukrainian pogroms in a series of complex, fantastical watercolor paintings that show the destruction of Jewish shtetls. Victims of violence are at the center of these images; smaller scenes in the margins narrate the course of events, with attackers wielding swords, men lying buried under Torah scrolls, and towns going up in flames.[22]

Overall, some 2.3 million Jews left the Russian Empire between 1880 and 1930. About 1.75 million Jews went to the United States, many through Germany. Others settled in West and Central European cities such as London and Berlin. Yet many Jews also migrated internally from small towns to cities within the Russian Empire, with large concentrations in Odessa, Warsaw, Lodz, and Vilna. In many of these cities, Jewish artisans were active in the production of consumer goods such as clothing and shoes.[23] For new arrivals, cities like Lodz seemed like a kind of promised land.

Family Records and Rituals

In April 1886, during this period of upheaval, Yehuda (Yudel) Markus (1851–1915) married Tsipa (née Gerszonowicz, 1869–1938) in the slightly larger town of Varniai, about thirteen miles west of Užventis.[24] Tsipa came from the same Šiauliai district in Lithuania where Užventis was located. Her parents, Shimel Girsh and Rokhl, may have arranged Tsipa's marriage to Yudel, who was a promising craftsman from a local family. Rabbi Benjamin Merber performed the ceremony. In the marriage registry, Yudel's age was listed as twenty-eight and Tsipa's age as twenty, though other records suggest he was thirty-five and she was only seventeen at the time. By 1888, the year Rahel was born, Yudel had established himself as a brushmaker and was listed among craftsmen working in Telz. It is possible that he became involved with the Bershter Bund, the large bristle workers' union in Poland and Lithuania, founded in 1898.[25] Tsipa was a homemaker and a beloved mother who was devoted to her children. Given the Jewish custom of naming children after a deceased family member, we can surmise that Rahel Markus was named for her maternal grandmother or her father's sister, if one or both died before she was born. Rahel's

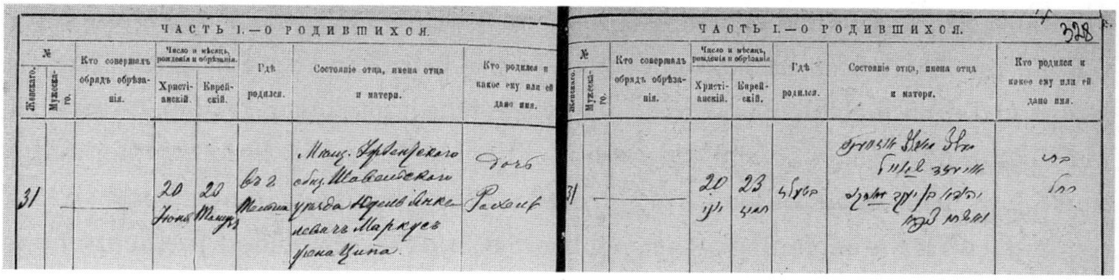

FIGURE 6 | Rahel Markus's birth record in Russian and Hebrew, 1888. Courtesy of the Lithuanian State Historical Archives.

younger sister, Sheina Machla, was born around 1894.[26] The Markus family left Lithuania for Poland not long after this—possibly shortly after Yankel's death in 1901, and well before 1910.

Exactly when and where Rahel Markus was born have long been matters of dispute. Actual birthdates were sometimes obscured or falsely recorded in eastern Europe out of the superstitious belief that this would trick the evil eye, keeping young children safe from harm. Birth records for girls were considered far less important since girls did not have bar mitzvahs and their birthdays were not always celebrated.[27] But original birth registries, if they exist, can provide information thought lost to history. While researching the Markus family, I found the handwritten, bilingual Russian and Hebrew birth record for Rahel Markus among the records for Jewish communities of Kovno Province (Kaunas Gubernia) in the Lithuanian State Historical Archives for 1888 (fig. 6). One reason this registry entry was so difficult to locate is that her birthdate is usually given as 1892, 1894, or later. Rahel may have wished to make herself seem younger by claiming to have been born a few years later than her actual birth year, as many of her female contemporaries did, or she may not have known the exact year of her birth. In one interview, Szalit added to her mystique by avoiding the question of her age, responding instead, "I was born in Lithuania. . . . Does it really matter how many years ago?"[28]

Determining Rahel's actual birthdate is even more complicated: today we would say that she was born on 2 July 1888. The Kovno birth registry indicates that she was born on 23 Tammuz (5648) on the Hebrew calendar, or 20 June on the Russian (then Julian) calendar. After moving to Europe, which used the Gregorian calendar, many people born in the Russian Empire (including Marc Chagall) calculated their birthdates by adding thirteen days, which explains why Rahel's birthday is often given as 3 July.[29] However, the difference between the calendars was only twelve days in the nineteenth century: in 1888, 23 Tammuz corresponded to 2 July on the Gregorian calendar. Rahel's actual European birthdate was thus 2 July 1888, even though 3 July 1892 is the date that appears on most state records, and she likely considered her birthday to be 3 July.[30]

Rahel Markus's birth record lists her birthplace as Telz, the Yiddish name for Telšiai (Tel'shi), the capital city of both the Telšiai district and the Samogitia (Zamet) region. In Telz, Rahel might have lived in or visited the house owned by her grandfather Yankel Markus. Perhaps several generations of the Markus family lived together in this house. Jews first settled in Telz in the fifteenth century, and it was home to over sixteen hundred Jews at the beginning of the nineteenth century. Several blood libel accusations were leveled against Jews in Telz, as in other towns in this region, around this time.[31] By the end of the century, Telz had a Jewish population of 3,088, or just over half of the town's residents. It was home to the Great Yeshiva and was known as a center of Jewish learning. Poet Yehuda Leib Gordon founded a girls' academy in Telz in 1866.[32] Numerous Zionist organizations also emerged in Telz toward the end of the century. Little is known about the Markus family's relationship to Zionism, but Rahel would go on to have several connections to the Zionist movement in Germany, and Israel would later serve as a home for the Markuses' descendants.

As a child, Rahel got to know her small Lithuanian town while accompanying her mother on errands to the marketplace to buy what was needed for the weekly Sabbath and other household needs. There and elsewhere in the small town, including at annual fairs, she witnessed amusing situations that she later reproduced in her art, including many characters who could only be found in the shtetl. One striking lithograph of such a market scene, *Jahrmarkt* (Annual Fair, 1922), was exhibited and became part of the Berlin Jewish community's collection; it eventually made its way to Warsaw (fig. 7).[33] This print shows a throng of people and animals gathered by a fence; the faces of two women with covered heads have the most charismatic expressions. Men wearing hats and other head coverings go about their business. At least three people look out toward the viewer playfully, questioningly.

Szalit described going to market in her interview with Austrian-American journalist David Ewen, which Ewen wrote about in English for two American Jewish magazines in 1930 and 1931. The following appeared in the *American Hebrew*:

> Fortunately, I was something of a favourite daughter to my mother and so she took me everywhere she went. When she went to the market, or to the synagogue, or to the baths, or even just to pay a neighbor a friendly visit, she had to take me along with her. I say that this is fortunate because it gave me a most enviable insight into the Jewish milieu of our little Jewish-Lithuanian town. Again and again, I came across the most unique and interesting Jewish personalities; again and again, I saw unique Jewish scenes—either in the marketplace or in the synagogue.... These people, these scenes you will find in all of my Jewish drawings.[34]

FIGURE 7 | R. Szalit-Marcus, *Jahrmarkt* (Annual Fair), 1922. From the collections of the E. Ringelblum Jewish Historical Institute in Warsaw.

This passage reflects how much her early years in Lithuania inspired her Jewish art, far more, even, than the years she later spent in Poland. Ewen's framing further suggests that Szalit's Lithuanian background was of interest to Jewish American readers.

Religious observance was an integral part of Jewish life in Lithuanian small towns, and the rhythm of life revolved around Jewish holidays and traditions. According to Szalit, the attachment to Jewish texts is what served to uplift Jews during hard times. In an autobiographical article published in the newsletter of the Jüdischer Frauenbund (League of Jewish Women) in 1930, Szalit wrote: "The whole misery—pogroms and hunger—is forgotten when the holy Torah is opened. 'Ah, how wonderful, how good it is to be a Jew' sing the poor and poorest of my Lithuanian home [*Heimat*]. They sing and firmly believe, 'since what can hunger and persecution do to us when we have the Torah,' one hears there from every Jewish mouth."[35] Interesting is the way Szalit distances herself from religiously observant Lithuanian Jews; "they" are the ones who firmly believe. Nonetheless, the Markuses, too, maintained a traditional Jewish home, and Rahel remembered watching her father studying the Talmud and praying in synagogue and at home.[36] But their level of religious observance declined over the generations and with moves to larger cities, as often occurred. We have no evidence that Rahel Szalit was observant as an adult or that she attended synagogue services in Berlin, though she often depicted Jewish holidays and rituals in her art, and she maintained strong ties to other Jews in the various cities where she lived. Her family, too, remained connected to the Jewish community of Lodz after moving to Poland.

A Jewish Daughter in Lodz

Like many other Jews from Lithuania, the Markus family relocated to Lodz around 1900 because of the social and economic opportunities it provided. Jews could move freely within the Russian Empire, and many chose to migrate westward as anti-Jewish violence put their safety in jeopardy. From 1815 until 1918, when Poland regained its independence, Lodz was part of the Kingdom of Poland under the Russian Empire. Because the separate legal system in Poland afforded Jews more rights than they had in the Pale of Settlement—Jews were granted legal equality in Poland in 1862—many Jewish craftsmen and merchants moved to Lodz in the late nineteenth century.[37] Lodz grew to have the second-largest Jewish community in Poland. By 1900, roughly one-third of its population was Jewish; by 1915, Jews made up 36 percent of Lodz residents.[38]

Lodz quickly became a booming center of textile production; factories filled the air with smoke. The city's rapid economic growth attracted many new settlers, including a large number from German-speaking lands. German entrepreneurs had settled in

Lodz and established wool and linen mills in the early nineteenth century. The population of Lodz grew from 50,000 to 459,000 in the four decades before the First World War, making it the second-largest city in Poland, after Warsaw.[39] The addition of new rail and tram lines around 1900 helped make Lodz an urban-industrial center known as the "Polish Manchester" and the "promised land." It employed over half of the workers in the Polish textile industry.[40] About 40 percent of the city's textile production was under Jewish ownership, as were other commercial and financial enterprises. Jews were also well represented in the arts and publishing.[41]

It is easy to see why Lodz was an attractive destination for the Markus family. As an artisan and brushmaker, Yudel Markus would have found many opportunities there, such as employment in a factory or small textile business. One account suggests that Yudel wore his hair long to show solidarity with the activists in the Jewish labor movement, known in Yiddish as *akhdes*, who sought to make change for workers in Lodz. Young Rahel, too, presumably derived inspiration from this city's atmosphere of "dreams, ambitions, and bright hopes for a better tomorrow."[42]

Like many Jewish women (and other women artists), Rahel was successful in part thanks to her supportive father. Yudel Markus, reportedly artistic at heart, avidly supported his daughter's artistic inclinations. The brushes he crafted may well have been among the first used by the budding painter. Yudel first encouraged Rahel to study with a cousin in Lodz, from whom she learned German, Polish, and a little French.[43] But there were not many places for women to study art in Lodz. To live among Europe's finest avant-garde artists, Rahel would need to follow other artists who left Lodz for Munich, and from there she could travel to Paris and other cities. Yudel finally agreed to send Rahel to Munich to study art in 1910. He surely supported her financially or at least sent her with the resources to make a start in this new city; her indebtedness to her family affected the way she presented herself to the world.

There is no question that Rahel Markus saw herself as a Jewish woman, and she would go on to identify as a Jewish artist above all else. In her autobiographical article titled "Ich bin eine jüdische Künstlerin" (I Am a Jewish [Woman] Artist), Rahel described how when she left home, her father's final parting words were "Don't forget that you are a Jewish daughter."[44] These words apparently had a great influence on the young artist and the work she would go on to produce. She never distanced herself from Judaism or gave preference to any other identification, including national identity. On the contrary: she viewed herself as a representative, even public (Eastern) Jewish figure. David Ewen, who argued that Szalit portrayed the "soul of Israel" in her work, described her as a "charming, lovable Jewish young lady."[45]

The rest of the Markus family began to identify more strongly with Polish-Jewish culture in the coming decades. Lodz was their home—they did not migrate westward, as Rahel had. Instead, they learned Polish and acquired Polish citizenship. Both Rahel and her sister would go on to marry Jews who spoke Polish, among other languages. Yudel Markus would die in Lodz in 1915, just two months after Rahel got married. Tsipa and Sheina Machla Markus would both live in Lodz through the interwar years; Tsipa would die in 1938. Sheina Machla and her family would be interned in the Lodz ghetto during the Second World War; we will come back to their stories later. But now we turn to Rahel and her new life in Germany and beyond.

CHAPTER 2

Munich, War, and Marriage

Berlin, August 1919: One sunny afternoon, Rahel Szalit sits on her bed in the small furnished room of her boardinghouse and opens a letter with no return address. The street outside is quiet, the blue bedspread is simple but soft; here she finds respite from the chaos of the metropolis. As she reads the words penned by Moriz Seeler, one of her husband's friends, her heart begins to race. His news is shocking: Julius Szalit has been found dead in Munich, by his own hand. Rahel rocks on the bed, devastated. She has never stopped caring for him.

She thinks back to the last time she saw Julius—the last time, she now knows, that she will ever see him. The war had ended, and he'd just recovered from the Spanish flu. They met at a café near Nollendorfplatz. There wasn't much to order, so they only drank bad ersatz coffee. He was polite as always but seemed distracted. Rahel listened patiently as he bragged about his current acting jobs ("No one will forget my Raskolnikov!"), his upcoming plays, his socialist meetings. His monologue was frenzied, joyless. As she finally began to speak, Julius looked at his watch, stood abruptly, apologized, and said he needed to leave for a meeting with his director.

Rahel ruefully remembers how Julius had always been more obsessed with his stage appearances than with showing up for people. Even on their wedding night, he'd left her, rushing off to play a minor role at a Vienna theater while still wearing his formal suit.

Were they ever happy? She had loved him fiercely and fled with him to Austria when the war broke out. When he was in town, he would rehearse and perform all day, and she would paint and draw. They would sometimes lunch together and walk the city streets. Then things had fallen apart not long after they moved to Berlin. This city brimmed with temptations, ambition, and infidelity.

The outbreak of the First World War found Rahel Marcus studying art in Munich, her primary home from 1910 to 1914. But when Germany declared war on Russia in August 1914, in a nationalistic campaign to defend itself from the dangers of the backward East, foreigners and especially citizens of the Russian Empire such as Rahel were expelled as "enemy aliens" and forced to live abroad.[1] Mass migration of East Europeans to the German Empire prior to the war had already begun to threaten the position of those who considered themselves ethnic Germans. The number of resident foreigners had tripled between 1890 and 1910, and Germans increasingly defined citizenship according to descent and genealogy to protect an ethnocultural sense of Germanness.[2] Jews and others from the Russian Empire were considered "speakers of inferior languages and elements of subversion."[3] Further, East European Jews, so-called *Ostjuden*, constituted an increasingly visible presence in Germany. As a result, the war was tied to new hostilities and xenophobia directed toward these foreigners and especially toward eastern Jews. Rahel was made acutely aware of the fact that she was a foreign Jew on more than one occasion, not least by the abrupt end to her budding artist's life in Munich. It would be several years before she found a way to return to Germany.

Antisemitic sentiments were only exacerbated by the Jewish census of 1916, which set out to prove that Jews were shirking their military duty to serve Germany. Although this census had a demoralizing effect on German Jews, it also resulted in a renewed interest in Jewish culture that set the stage for Szalit's work to find an audience. Philosopher Martin Buber had called for a return to Jewish culture, a Jewish Renaissance, and the year 1916 marked a turning point when Jews began to heed his call.[4] Many German-Jewish soldiers stationed on the eastern front returned with a fascination with their eastern Jewish counterparts. This is evidenced by Hermann Struck's lithographs of Jews and others from Lithuania, Belarus, and Latvia (1916), as well as Struck's images in Arnold Zweig's book *Das ostjüdische Antlitz* (The Face of East European Jewry, 1920), among others.[5] That Szalit had origins in these eastern worlds and was able to depict them authentically, as an insider, lent her work great appeal in the coming years.

Munich, Paris, London

Rahel Marcus lived and studied art in Munich for four years, but she also made noteworthy short visits to Paris and London in the early 1910s. Official police records show that she first arrived in Munich in June 1910 with a Russian-language passport from Petrikau near Lodz. The Munich police records give her birth year as 1892, which would have made her only eighteen years old, though the Lithuanian birth registry from 1888 suggests she was twenty-two. She changed addresses often, relocating four times within Munich's bohemian Schwabing district during her first year.[6] Perhaps she had unfriendly landladies or difficulty paying her rent, or perhaps she moved to improve her situation as she broadened her networks and became more familiar with the city.

Rahel's Munich residences were not far from the beautiful Englischer Garten, a much-frequented public park with ample space to stroll and find inspiration. The first place she stayed was on the Feilitzschstrasse, the very street where Thomas Mann had finished his masterpiece *Buddenbrooks* ten years earlier. Her later addresses in Munich inched closer toward Josephsplatz in the Maxvorstadt, the cultural heart of the city, just blocks away from the city's theaters, the Munich Art Academy, the Damenakademie, where women could study art, and some of Munich's best art collections, including the Alte Pinakothek.

Living and studying in major cities was expensive. We can guess that Rahel rented simple, sparsely furnished rooms and worked one or more jobs to sustain herself. Women were limited in their options for paid work at this time. She might have found part-time work in a tavern, *Konditorei* (pastry shop), or clothing shop, or as a domestic servant or governess. A job in an art supply shop would have served her especially well, or she might have worked as an artists' model. With her still-developing, nonnative German-language skills, it is unlikely that she could have secured one of the newer and more prestigious white-collar positions available to women, such as bookkeeper, stenotypist, or clerk. Many eastern Jewish immigrants worked in garment production, but this would have left little time for studying or making art.[7]

From July 1911 until March 1912, Rahel Marcus traveled beyond Munich, making at least one return visit to Lodz. Railway networks were quite extensive and offered multiple travel routes between major cities. She traveled to Paris and London either during this period or the following year, in 1913. These trips were formative experiences for the young artist, who, regardless of what she accomplished there, used the fact that she had visited these capital cities to enhance her credentials as an artist. She would choose Paris as an exile destination two decades later, and she always longed to return to London. Szalit once wrote, "I was astonished by London. . . . It's the only city in the world where I'd wish to spend my entire life."[8] Her visit to London would inspire her illustrations of stories from Dickens's *Sketches by Boz*, published as *Londoner Bilder* in 1923.

Around the fin de siècle, Paris was nearly unrivaled as the cultural capital of Europe. Fauvism, Cubism, and other modern art movements were quickly gaining momentum. Henri Matisse, Pablo Picasso, and Auguste Rodin were among the luminaries who drew artists to the City of Light. Even more importantly, Paris was one of the few places in Europe where women could formally enroll in art academies, though these courses of study were very expensive. Most women artists came from middle-class families and relied on their parents or husbands for financial support. A significant number of well-known women artists from Germany studied or lived in Paris. Julie Wolfthorn studied at Académie Colarossi. Maria Slavona moved to Paris in 1890, having already studied in Munich together with Käthe Kollwitz. For her part, Kollwitz studied at the Académie Julian in 1904, and Augusta von Zitzewitz followed suit. Paula Modersohn-Becker also spent time in Paris before her untimely death in 1907.[9]

Rahel Marcus would have learned from her art contacts in Munich that she, too, ought to make her way to Paris. There she likely encountered some of the artists she would work alongside in Berlin in the 1920s or in Montparnasse in the 1930s. Some critics would later refer to Szalit as having been trained according to Parisian models, implying that her short time in France in the 1910s made a strong impression on her artistic style.[10] Still, it was in Munich, her primary home during her early twenties, where she forged the most significant connections for her immediate future and personal life.

An Exciting Time to Study in Munich

The founding of the artists' group Die Brücke (the Bridge) in 1905 in Dresden and later Berlin is widely considered the birth of German Expressionism. But Munich was another hot spot in the art world, particularly around 1910. At this point, Munich was home to more artists than all other German cities with art schools and thus held great appeal for foreigners.[11] Artists from Russia, Poland, France, Switzerland, and other countries gravitated toward Munich, with the result that it became a major center for the international avant-garde. It was in 1911, shortly after Rahel Marcus arrived from Lodz, that Wassily Kandinsky, Franz Marc, Gabriele Münter, August Macke, Paul Klee, and others joined together in Munich to form Der Blaue Reiter (the Blue Rider).[12] This influential Expressionist group notably welcomed women to its ranks and embraced a range of styles and media.[13]

Founded as a rejection of the bourgeois social conventions and realistic representations associated with nineteenth-century movements including Naturalism and Impressionism, Expressionism focused on an artist's repressed thoughts, feelings, and energies to achieve a heightened awareness of what it was to be human.[14] The emotional and spiritual aspects of color and form were crucial for members of Der Blaue Reiter, who mixed media to produce everything from abstract compositions paired with music (Kandinsky) to blue horses and yellow cows (Marc). The animals that featured prominently in Marc's works and in other modernist art, including in Chagall's paintings and illustrations of French fables, may have inspired Szalit to incorporate animals into her own works. Russian-born painter Marianne von Werefkin, whose circle included many women artists, was also active in Der Blaue Reiter. Among those in close contact with Werefkin and Marc was the German-Jewish poet and artist Else Lasker-Schüler, who dubbed Werefkin the "blaue Reiterreiterin" (female rider of the Blue Rider).

Else Lasker-Schüler and Szalit certainly knew of each other later, in Berlin, though they would not necessarily have gotten along despite having many mutual friends. Lasker-Schüler was nearly twenty years older and liked to command attention, whereas Szalit had a more unassuming character. Even so, Lasker-Schüler, Werefkin, and others paved the way for women artists to engage in gender-bending activities such as the performance of male personas and other types of creative play.[15] Lasker-Schüler's illustration of her alter ego Prince Jussuf of Thebes, a play on the biblical Joseph, graced the cover of her 1913 book of poems *Hebräische Balladen* (Hebrew Ballads), and she was known for dressing up as Jussuf. Szalit must have known of this book, and she was no doubt inspired by Lasker-Schüler's success.

Munich also attracted several other Jewish artists from Lodz who left eastern Europe to pursue avant-garde art movements. Henri (Chaim) Epstein and Marcel Słodki went to study at the Munich Art Academy around 1910, and Rahel Marcus befriended them during her early years in Munich. Both were born in 1892 and were thus of the same generation as Szalit; together, they constituted a small colony of Lodz artists based in Munich.[16] Szalit would be reunited with both again after leaving Munich. Epstein was based in Paris for many years, and Słodki lived in Berlin in the early 1920s and then in Paris.

Several sources report that Rahel Marcus, too, studied at the Munich Art Academy, though the school did not admit women until 1920, and there is no record of her matriculation at the Damenakademie. Given her working-class background and migrant status, she probably could not afford the Damenakademie's high annual enrollment fee of four hundred marks, an exorbitant sum compared to the fee of seventy marks that men paid at other institutes.[17] We can guess that she would have enrolled if this had been an option for her financially, as it would have further enhanced her credentials. Kollwitz, Münter, and many other renowned artists were among those who studied at the Damenakademie in the early 1900s; this may have led Szalit to claim that she did as well. It is possible that she found a way to audit classes or simply studied informally in private studios.[18] Perhaps she received training through Epstein and Słodki.

Philology is often cited as another interest of Rahel's, and we can assume that she used these years to hone her language skills in German and French. Painting dominated her art studies, though she also trained in the graphic arts and especially lithography. Soon Berlin would replace Munich as Germany's largest artistic center—a kind of collection point for art from across Germany, especially for Jewish artists and others from eastern Europe—and she was ready to discover a new metropolis upon her return to Germany.[19] Berlin would also call to her for personal reasons.

The Untold Story of a Marriage

It was in Munich that Rahel met Jewish actor Julius Szalit, likely in the spring of 1912, when Julius was almost twenty years old. Julius wasn't conventionally good-looking, but he was nevertheless attractive, with piercing eyes, blondish-brown hair parted on the side, wide lips, and a strong nose that might have helped directors typecast him in "Slavic" roles (fig. 8). He was described as slender, with "more sinews than flesh; and more bones than sinews.... Nothing soft in his physical presence."[20] Perhaps Rahel saw him perform at a Munich theater, or they could have met through friends or at a café or tavern in the Maxvorstadt. Their relationship was serious enough that Julius stayed at the Munich boardinghouse where Rahel lived (Görresstrasse 4, proprietress: Elise Gensheimer) for about eight months beginning around October 1912, though Julius also maintained an address in Vienna during that period. The boardinghouse was located two blocks from the Schellingstrasse, a major street lined with cafés frequented by artists and writers including Wassily Kandinsky, Franz Marc, Thomas Mann, Frank Wedekind, and Stefan George.

Originally from Tarnopol in eastern Galicia (today Ukraine), then part of Austria-Hungary, Julius Szalit spoke German and Polish, and possibly also Yiddish. He was born on 8 June 1892, the same year that Rahel's documents claimed was her birth year. Julius was the fifth of six children born to Abraham Schalit, a merchant, and Anna Schalit, née Birnbaum. Although "Schalit" was the spelling used on most official records, Julius always used "Szalit" as his stage name. This spelling was less common and gave his name a more readily apparent Polish or eastern sensibility.

Like the Markuses in the Russian Empire, the Schalits moved around freely within Austria-Hungary. Julius's mother was originally from Krakow, and members of the Schalit family eventually left Tarnopol for Krakow and later Vienna. Tarnopol was a small town with a large Jewish community; Krakow, an important city in western Galicia, had modern conveniences such as running water and an electric tram, and Jews made up one-quarter of its population. Vienna was the fourth-largest city in Europe, after London, Paris, and Berlin, and had a population of close to two hundred thousand Jews. Whereas Regina, Julius's eldest sibling, got married in Tarnopol in 1898, his oldest brother Dawid married in Krakow in 1907, and both Julius and his younger sister Augusta celebrated their weddings in Vienna, in 1915 and 1917. Abraham and Anna Schalit, too, eventually made their way to Vienna. They might well have been among the seventy-seven thousand Jewish refugees who fled from Galicia and Bukovina to Vienna soon after the invasion of the Russian army in 1914.[21]

As a theater actor, Julius found work in different German-speaking cities—primarily Munich, Vienna, Innsbruck, and Berlin—and he moved between them frequently for acting and occasional directing roles. Julius first came to Munich in 1911 with an Austrian

FIGURE 8 | Photograph of Julius Szalit, ca. 1916. Photo by Karl Schenker via Getty Images.

passport that had been issued in Berlin. When supplying information for his Munich registration card, he identified himself as a religious "dissident," meaning that he had distanced himself from the Jewish religious community but had not converted.[22] Like Rahel, he changed addresses often in Munich, though nearly all were in the Maxvorstadt, not far from Munich's major theaters. Yet as of June 1912 Julius was registered as permanently living in Vienna, and his stays in Munich and Innsbruck were temporary and mainly linked to short-term acting jobs. Vienna became his base, and he never spent more than a few weeks at a time in Munich after 1913.[23]

Newspaper reviews from this period allow us to follow Julius from city to city. As part of a Munich-based acting ensemble, he performed in a few plays at Vienna's Deutsches

Volkstheater in May 1913. Several performances featured such well-known actors as Albert Steinrück and Rosa Valetti.[24] Soon Innsbruck, a small town about three hundred miles west of Vienna and only ninety miles south of Munich, offered Julius Szalit several professional opportunities. In fall 1913, Julius was engaged as a character actor to play youthful roles at the Innsbrucker Stadttheater. That winter he directed two plays there: *Die Zarin*, about Catherine the Great, and *Der Teufel* (The Devil), in which he also played the title role. But Vienna, Munich, and Berlin continued to tempt the young star. Julius was living in Vienna in spring 1914 when he was called back to Munich to codirect a pantomime at the Münchner Künstlertheater (Munich Art Theater) together with Eugen Robert.[25] Several years later, Robert would go on to become the stage manager at the Residenz-Theater in Berlin and would become an essential connection for Julius. Even before that, Julius would join the Lessing-Theater in Berlin, and his roles with a touring Berlin acting ensemble would take him to Vienna, Prague, and Budapest.

Rahel, on the other hand, became a refugee from Germany for the first time in 1914. Munich records indicate that Rahel left for Innsbruck on 4 August 1914, though she must have lived there under cover, as Austria-Hungary, too, declared war on Russia just a few days later. Did Rahel flee to Innsbruck together with Julius, or did she reunite with him there? If her route was similar to the path taken by others, she would have traveled by train to the official exit point of Lindau, and from there gone on to Innsbruck. Other Munich-based Russian artists and their partners, including Kandinsky, Münter, Werefkin, and Alexej von Jawlensky, fled via Lindau to Switzerland. Werefkin later wrote: "I arrived on 3 August 1914 as a refugee, without possessions, without money, without luggage."[26] Rahel was fortunate to have Julius's connection to Innsbruck in the Tyrolean Alps, far removed from the violence of the war. If she stayed there for a significant amount of time and was able to move about freely, she might have spent her days painting landscapes, walking around the idyllic town, or hiking in the mountains. But there were only about five hundred Jews in Innsbruck in 1914, and no proper synagogue. And amid rising antisemitism, with small towns providing little anonymity during wartime, Innsbruck served as a mere way station between major cities. There is in fact no record of Rahel Szalit having ever stayed in Innsbruck.[27] This is not surprising, given her enemy alien status.

By December 1914, the couple had moved on to Vienna, the "Paris of Austria." Vienna city registration records state that Rahel was in Antwerp before coming to Vienna, though this seems like false information provided to mislead the authorities. We have no other information about Rahel ever visiting Belgium, nor is it apparent what she would have been doing there while the city was under German occupation. But it is clear from these records that she lived in Vienna for an extended period of time, from December 1914 until at least May 1915, and likely longer.[28] Her first address in Vienna was in the same building—though, presumably for the sake of keeping up appearances, as the two were not yet married, in a different apartment—where Julius had maintained a residence for several years: Stuwerstrasse 15, a five-story building located in the Leopoldstadt or second district. This was only a few blocks from the Danube River and the Prater, a large public park known for its amusement park and Ferris wheel. The Leopoldstadt was nicknamed the *Mazzesinsel* (matzah island) and was home to most of Vienna's Jews, including many Galician and other East European refugees.[29] Joseph Roth famously called it a "voluntary ghetto" for eastern Jews.[30] In February 1915, Rahel officially moved into a new apartment at Auersbergstrasse 19, a narrow building in the heart of the Josefstadt or eighth district, Vienna's theater district. From there, Julius could walk to the nearby Deutsches Theater in five minutes. It would have taken him a bit longer to get to the Wiener Bürgertheater, where he played the role of Captain Riebel in Richard Wendriner's play *Der Marschall* (The Marshal) that April.

Records from the Jewish community of Vienna confirm that Rahel Marcus and Julius Schalit were married on Friday, 16 April 1915, one week after Passover ended (fig. 9).[31] They were married in the Leopoldstadt at the Tempelgasse Synagogue (Leopoldstädter Tempel), a majestic Moorish-style building and Vienna's largest synagogue until it was destroyed in 1938. Three days before their wedding, Julius returned from a stint in Berlin to join Rahel at the theater district apartment. He might well have performed in *Der Marschall* on Friday evening after getting married that same day—advertisements for the play's run that weekend included his name. Jewish weddings rarely occur on Friday evenings, and their ceremony would have taken place in the morning or afternoon before

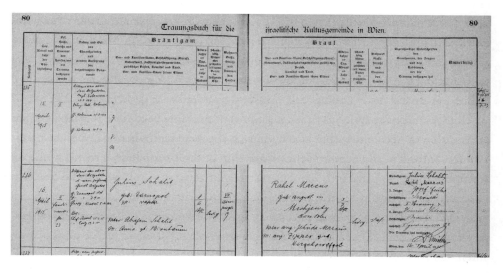

FIGURE 9 | Marriage record of Rahel Marcus and Julius Schalit, 1915. Courtesy of the Archive of the Jewish Community of Vienna.

the Sabbath began at sundown. Given Julius's "dissident" status, it may have been Rahel who preferred to get married in a synagogue. That they had a Jewish ceremony attests to some level of identification with their upbringing and family background.

Rahel and Julius probably had a small ceremony, with at most a few friends in attendance and possibly some of Julius's fellow actors or family members who were based in Vienna. It is extremely unlikely that members of the Markus and Schalit families would have traveled hundreds of miles from Lodz or Krakow to attend, especially because the wedding took place at a time when the German army occupied much of eastern Europe. The two witnesses who signed the Jewish community's marriage registry book were Josef Fuchs, a secretary, and Heinrich Schramm, a clerk, suggesting that the couple did not provide their own witnesses. If the bride and groom wore the formal attire typical for Vienna in that period, Julius would have donned a frock coat and a top hat, with a stiff white shirt and a white bow tie. Rahel would have worn a white dress with long sleeves and white gloves, and a white headpiece or veil, though wartime fashions were often minimalist. Unable to afford this kind of finery, the young couple might have borrowed or rented outfits or opted for less formal attire, particularly given wartime austerity. Did anyone think to take a photograph of the wedding couple? Did they celebrate afterward at a restaurant or in someone's home?

It is difficult to picture Rahel Szalit in a traditional wedding dress, as later images of her suggest that she embraced the tomboyish, athletic fashions of the New Woman as they became more popular in the 1920s. She also took up fencing, for which she wore pants—and she might have occasionally worn pants outside the fencing studio, though knee-length skirts with stockings were still the norm for most women. By 1929, Szalit's sleek, short hairstyle would match that of the androgynous *garçonne*, a type often associated with masculine dress and lesbians. But she also wore earrings and delicate scarves, and we can assume that she, like many women of the time, experimented with styling herself in both more feminine and more masculine ways. A journalist once described Szalit's personal style by noting, "She dresses simply and with good taste."[32]

Rahel's marriage to Julius Szalit is significant not only because it formalized their relationship to one another but also because it absolved her of her enemy alien status. Women automatically acquired the citizenship of their husbands.[33] By marrying an Austrian citizen, she instantly gained Austrian citizenship—and with it the freedom to move around within Austria and Germany. However, there are no surviving official records that list Rahel as an Austrian citizen, and it is unknown to what extent this temporary change impacted her life. It would have relieved any pressure to live under cover, and it made travel possible again, even during the war. The fact that this marriage drastically improved Rahel's legal situation raises the question of whether it was a marriage of convenience.

After their wedding, the newlyweds spent a few weeks together in Vienna. Julius's acting ensemble continued performing there through late April before moving on to perform in Prague and Budapest in May. Rahel might have accompanied him on this tour, or perhaps she preferred to stay behind in Vienna. Later that year, Julius took an engagement at the Albert Theater in Dresden, which brought him closer to Berlin.[34] The Vienna city records do not include Rahel's departure date, but she likely lived there for another year or so. If she was not busy working to support herself, she might have spent this time visiting museums, galleries, or cafés, though many still excluded women. With luck, she could have joined a *Stammtisch* of artists who met regularly at a café.[35]

At this time, Vienna was also a major center for art. Gustav Klimt had mentored many of the city's younger artists, including Expressionists Oskar Kokoschka and Egon Schiele, who experimented with printmaking. Rahel Szalit must have encountered works by these artists in Vienna, if she had not already done so in Munich, and might well have been inspired by their styles. In some of her works we see resonances of the contorted positions and angular outlines found in Schiele's drawings. It is also possible that Szalit continued her education in Vienna, for example at the Kunstschule für Frauen und Mädchen (Art School for Women and Girls), which had relatively low tuition. She might have found her way to some of the many women artists active in Vienna, though the Radierklub der Wiener Künstlerinnen (Print Club of Viennese Women Artists) had disbanded just before she arrived.[36]

The Artist and the Actor in Berlin

Finally, in 1916, an Austrian citizen thanks to her marriage, Rahel Szalit returned to Germany and made a new home in Berlin, where she would live until the Nazis came to power. The timing of her move to Berlin was likely related to Julius's career: in late 1916, he replaced stage manager Eugen Robert at Berlin's Residenz-Theater when Robert was called up to serve in the Hungarian army.[37] However, most sources suggest that Rahel and Julius separated at some point, probably by 1918. Because their Berlin registration cards are missing from the city's official record file (which, like many German archives, experienced significant losses during the Second World War), it cannot be confirmed whether or how long they lived together after relocating to this quickly growing metropolis.[38] What is certain is that both Szalits were living and working primarily in Berlin by the end of 1916.

Julius eventually rented an apartment in his name on the ground floor of Nymphenburger Strasse 10 in Schöneberg.[39] This was close to the Bavarian Quarter, a part of Berlin's artists' district that was home to many German Jews, and where Rahel would later have

FIGURE 10 | Rahel Szalit-Marcus, *Leipziger Platz*, 1917, in *Ost und West*, nos. 3-4 (1920): 77, *Illustrierte Monatsschrift für das gesamte Judentum*, Berlin: Verlag von S. Calvary; Jüdisches Museum Berlin, XI. Ost 69 Jg.20 H.3/4. Photo: Roman März.

her own studio. It was just south of the newly built Rathaus Schöneberg, the city hall where US president John F. Kennedy would declare "Ich bin ein Berliner" over four decades later, and which in 2005 came to house *Wir waren Nachbarn* (We Were Neighbors), an exhibition commemorating Schöneberg residents who were persecuted and murdered in the Holocaust. Julius's apartment was also located only about a mile from Nollendorfplatz, another part of Schöneberg, which served, and still serves, as a center of gay nightlife in Berlin.

Rahel Szalit's early paintings of street scenes helped her build a reputation as a Berlin-based artist in Jewish circles. Photographs of five paintings, including several Berlin scenes, were featured as part of an early profile of Szalit by art historian Karl Schwarz in the magazine *Ost und West* in March/April 1920.[40] Like Szalit and her work, this respected periodical attempted to serve as a bridge for Jewish culture across European lands. Szalit's inclusion in it also marked her grand entrance into Jewish cultural circles in Germany. As art historian Celka Straughn has shown, the German-Jewish press played a central role in establishing a canon and community of Jewish artists.[41] Szalit's painting *Leipziger Platz* (1917, fig. 10) shows electric trams running through a major square in the city center, which at that time was rapidly developing and was home to two major department stores, Wertheim and Tietz. Shining multistory building facades are interspersed with trees as people hurrying about their business wait to cross the street. Schwarz noted that the droning sounds of the surging metropolis emerged from this painting.

Unfortunately, there is no way to tell from newspaper images what the paintings looked like in color, or to get an exact sense of Rahel Szalit's painting techniques. But we

FIGURE 11 | Rahel Szalit-Marcus, *In der Kälte* (In the Cold), in *Ost und West*, nos. 3-4 (1920): 74-75, *Illustrierte Monatsschrift für das gesamte Judentum*, Berlin: Verlag von S. Calvary; Jüdisches Museum Berlin, XI. Ost 69 Jg.20 H.3/4. Photo: Roman März.

can tell that she was beginning to experiment with Expressionist forms of rendering city scenes, from bright and bustling centers to frigid winter days. Her painting *In der Kälte* (In the Cold, fig. 11) shows a hunched older woman wrapped in a cloak, shivering next to a building and reflected in its surface. This painting perfectly captures the hardships that overwhelmed many Berliners during the postwar years, which coincided with the final waves of the 1918 influenza pandemic and growing inflation. Actress and screenwriter Salka Viertel later commented about this period: "*Hunger* is what I remember most from those years, 1919, 1920. I was always hungry, and cold. And sometimes slightly drunk, because that was the one thing you could always get if you had any money at all."[42]

Meanwhile, Julius was very successful at finding work in Berlin, and his career took off in new directions. He acted in several silent films while remaining heavily involved with Berlin's Residenz-Theater, where he was responsible for the staging of many contemporary plays from eastern Europe in German translation.[43] In several instances, Julius translated dramatic works from Polish to German and then performed them. This was the case for Gabriela Zapolska's five-act play *Die Warschauer Zitadelle* (The Warsaw Citadel), which Julius Szalit starred in with Rudolph Schildkraut, a known supporter of Jewish art.[44] Together with Stefania Goldenring, Julius Szalit also translated Zapolska's play *Sibirien* (Siberia), which was performed in 1917 with Fritz Kortner in a lead role. Critic Curt Moreck observed that in Berlin Julius Szalit's image had become a commodified part of a mass culture routine that no longer prioritized artistic quality.[45] Indeed, Julius found himself in the thick of Berlin's mass celebrity culture. Postcards with his likeness were created by well-known photographers, and his image was distributed widely in magazines and other media.

While in Berlin, Julius met with and resisted pressure to enlist and fight in the First World War. He saw it as his right to be spared from military service, and he was fortunate to be protected from serving by his directors. When a military consul general finally called him up toward the end of the war to discuss the matter of conscription, Julius turned red as a beet and protested indignantly, repeatedly crying out, "And my future—?"[46] Ambitious and fearful, Julius seems to have evaded combat to focus on his acting craft, which often included playing the roles of soldiers.

In his final years, Julius's stage performances were memorable, unsettling, and even shocking. He played highly dramatic, nervous characters that drew on his eastern background and relied on stereotypes about Jewish or Russian ethnic difference. One of his most famous roles involved showcasing the "macabre agitation" of Raskolnikov in a play by the same name based on Dostoyevsky's *Crime and Punishment*. Critic Siegfried Jacobsohn, founder of the theater magazine *Die Schaubühne*, later *Die Weltbühne*, praised the "ethnically authentic" way Szalit enacted the "torturous upheaval of his [character's] nerves."[47] Respected theater critic Alfred Kerr described another one of Julius Szalit's impressive performances in March 1919: "Herr Szalit, as the dying soldier, showed the dread of numbness; the pain of the victim; the resentment of the rebel; the broken-radiant gaze of the feverish."[48] Like this character, the talented young actor met a tragic end.

On 27 July 1919, Julius Szalit shot and killed himself in Munich: suicide by coup de grâce (*Fangschuss*). His body was found at 8 o'clock in the evening in the garden of the Nymphenburg villa owned by wealthy Dutch musicologist Anthony van Hoboken, known as "der Holländer" (the Dutchman). This was a popular gathering spot for poor artists and an "undisturbed island" during the days of the revolution and short-lived Bavarian Soviet Republic, which came to a dramatic end in May 1919. Some of the Dutchman's friends even took up residence at his villa, including painter Heinrich Maria Davringhausen and writer and socialist revolutionary Oskar Maria Graf, who held many extended drinking sessions there.[49] Julius Szalit's presence at this villa suggests he was visiting artist friends when he decided to take his own life. His death record indicates that the first name of his wife was unknown, implying estrangement.[50] In the days immediately preceding his death, Julius stayed at a grand house in Vienna's eighteenth district, Türkenschanzplatz 7. Records suggest that Julius arrived in Vienna on 22 July after a trip to Tarnopol, then departed Vienna on 26 July—only to die in Munich one day later. It is unknown what he learned or who might have contacted him in the days leading up to his suicide. Though some would blame Rahel, Julius's suicide may always remain a mystery.

Julius Szalit was mourned in major Berlin newspapers as a mysticism-inclined ecstatic who had embodied fanatic and ascetic figures.[51] One socialist journal described him as super slender and feverish while also praising his extraordinary artistic creativity.[52] Alfred Kerr wrote that Szalit was a rare type, a consummate performer with no inhibitions: one could never tell he was acting.[53] Director and writer Moriz Seeler similarly praised the actor's unforgettable talents in an open letter to the recently deceased Julius Szalit, whom Seeler described as a "flickering, rebellious, youthful revolutionary saturated with endless Slavic melancholy."[54] Julius's early death at age twenty-seven naturally came as a shock to many. If his life and career had not been cut short, he would surely have gone on to become a leading actor in Weimar silent films, or an even more successful theater actor. But perhaps there are more factors to consider.

A Queer Story

If we look closely at the circumstances of Julius Szalit's suicide, especially within the broader context of Rahel's life, another story begins to unfold. Rumor had it at the time that Julius's suicide came in response to an unhappy marriage.[55] They were certainly separated at the time of his death. Some sources go so far as to attribute Julius's death to an affair that Rahel allegedly had with another artist, painter Iser Weissberg, though there is no convincing evidence for this claim.[56] Alfred Kerr alleged that Julius had shot himself due to a *Liebesgram*, or a telegram-like notification about someone he loved, lamenting, "What the war could not accomplish [in terms of destroying Julius Szalit's future], a woman was able to do." Kerr further described having seen Julius Szalit circa 1918 at a social gathering on a boat, where he sat next to a "dark dame" who referred to him as "Bubi" (presumably not Rahel), though Kerr later determined that this was not the person responsible for Julius's demise. Yet Kerr never mentioned Rahel and stopped short of naming or implicating anyone specific.[57]

All of this points to a more complex backstory that may never reveal itself in full, but which bears striking similarities to other stories of the late 1910s. Although we have no way of verifying the motivations behind Julius's suicide, it is possible that his death was connected to his own sexuality. Many suicides occurred among individuals whose desires did not fit traditional heterosexual norms and expectations. German-Jewish sexologist Magnus Hirschfeld's research from this period shows that homosexual men sometimes killed themselves when faced with the prospect of being trapped in marriages to which they were not well suited; this despair could be compounded by antisemitism.[58] Suicide was further associated with "Jewish nervousness," and suicide rates were exceptionally high among Jews in Germany at the time.[59] Given what we know about Rahel and the circles they both moved in, it would not be surprising if Julius Szalit's suicide was linked to closeted homosexuality, though this remains unconfirmed.

When it comes to Rahel's brief marriage to Julius, there is much we do not know. We have none of their correspondence, though they must have exchanged dozens or even hundreds of letters while Julius was on the road. What would these letters reveal? It seems that his Austrian connections and eventually his citizenship saved her when she desperately needed a plan for wartime. He was her "entrance ticket" back into Germany. Financial reasons, too, might have driven them to live together. Perhaps they had an open marriage or the kind of marriage of convenience sometimes called a "lavender marriage." During the early years of their relationship, Julius's acting schedule kept him on the road so much that the two essentially lived separate lives. The rumors of Rahel's affair could have served as an additional way of disguising the true reasons behind Julius's suicide. It is telling that such rumors proliferated, as if there was something important to conceal. Perhaps Rahel in fact had an affair with a woman?

Rahel Szalit's own story is indeed a queer story: we have evidence that she later had relationships with both men and women. Today we might classify Szalit as bisexual, though we don't know if this is a label she chose for herself. Bisexuality, lesbianism, homosexuality, and other forms of sexual nonconformity were common among free-spirited Berliners and Parisians in the interwar years, from German actors Marlene Dietrich and Conrad Veidt to such American expatriate writers in Paris as Gertrude Stein and Natalie Barney. The sexually free atmosphere and the company Szalit kept likely impacted her own sexual fluidity. Among Szalit's friends in Berlin were several women who had romantic relationships with both men and women, notably painter Julie Wolfthorn, who was married to a man but was widely known as a *Hosendame*, a woman who wore trousers long before it was accepted; and writer Eleonore Kalkowska, who left her husband and lived openly with a female partner in Berlin.

Szalit's correspondence with Kalkowska reveals that the two women confided in each other about their love lives. In one of Rahel Szalit's only surviving personal letters, written to Kalkowska in Polish years later from Paris, Szalit casually referred to breakups with both male and female love interests. At that time, Szalit felt deeply hurt: her female partner brought a man home to their shared apartment and stayed up all night drinking wine with him. Unrelatedly, Szalit's male lover turned out to already have a wife and another fiancée. Suffering greatly, Szalit lamented, "For the heart, I got nothing.... Tell me, how much meanness can there be in the world?"[60] Though we know very little about Szalit's relationships and affairs, what we do know suggests that she had a good number of lovers during her years in both Berlin and Paris.

This and Rahel Szalit's other surviving letters, largely German-language professional correspondence, reveal that the multilingual artist consistently used punctuation in dramatic ways across languages. It was then common among Polish speakers to use exclamation marks in opening greetings. Expressionist writers, too, made heavy use of exclamation marks, question marks, and dashes; Szalit was inspired by the lyrical style that was in vogue while she was perfecting her German. A nonnative speaker of both Polish and German, Szalit also relied on these extralinguistic details to communicate her enthusiasm. Every letter opens with a respectful salutation and honorific followed by an exclamation mark: "*Moja droga Pani!*" (My dear lady!), "*Hochgeehrte gnädige Frau!*" (Highly honored madam!), "*Sehr geehrter Herr Professor!*" (Dear Herr Professor!). Szalit thus imparted a sense of energy and urgency. To further emphasize key words, she underlined them. She sprinkled dashes liberally throughout, often in place of commas or as crutches to help with awkward formulations. The letters that have survived are all written in sprawling, hastily scribbled cursive that quickly filled her small, plain stationery. In many pages but relatively few words, Szalit's letters conveyed that she had people to see and things to do. Regardless of the addressee, each letter hinted that she was going places—and she found companions of both sexes to prevent her from going it alone.

Rahel reportedly suffered greatly from the trauma of her husband's suicide, and she is said to have carried this tragedy with her for the rest of her life. She kept Julius's last name, and by 1923 began shortening the longer, hyphenated last name of "Szalit-Marcus" to "Szalit." She never married again, and she may not have had any other long-term relationships. Despite the loss of Julius (and with him her claim to Austrian citizenship), Rahel Szalit was poised to enter the most exciting and prolific stage of her career. It was in Berlin, the "Athens on the Spree," that she would make a name for herself as a graphic artist and illustrator among both mainstream and Jewish artists.

CHAPTER 3

Berlin Expressionist Circles

Berlin-Wilmersdorf, September 1920: In the cozy home of Jakob Steinhardt, Rahel is surrounded by artists from Germany, Poland, and elsewhere. They talk, drink tea, coffee, and wine, and enjoy a delicious fruit torte made with ingredients obtained on the black market. She has met fascinating people here: Bruno Krauskopf, an up-and-coming graphic artist; Arno Nadel, a musician and painter from Vilna; and Abraham Palukst, another Lithuanian artist who depicts shtetl life and teaches Hebrew.

This apartment is a microcosm of Berlin itself, bringing together East and West in new ways. Many in Steinhardt's circle are Jewish and draw their eastern towns or shtetls in his guestbook. Steinhardt and others served on the eastern front, and now they are obsessed with portraying eastern Jews.

And here is Rahel: she too knows Lithuania and Poland firsthand. These places appear in her work and inform her worldview. To Steinhardt and others, she is both an authentic eastern Jew and a Jewish artist. But—she's also a woman. She has never worn a prayer shawl, and she doesn't know how to lay tefillin. Aside from basic prayers, she hasn't learned much Hebrew. She only went to synagogue on a few occasions. Her mother kept a kosher home, but this is not important to Rahel, who cannot afford much meat anyway, let alone extra dishes. Holidays mattered more when she was a girl; now she is aware of them but rarely celebrates.

Still, she remembers all this vividly. Rahel tells stories about her childhood, her father and her grandfather, about those who rigidly adhered to Jewish law. Her listeners are most interested in hearing about the men, the "real" observant Jews. They also want to see more of her art, taking inspiration from her recent lithographs.

BERLIN EXPRESSIONIST CIRCLES

Rahel Szalit's career took off around 1920, at the exact moment when women artists and many Jewish artists found solid footing in Germany. The constitution of the newly founded Weimar Republic granted equal rights to women and minorities, and more women began to enroll at art academies. The Bauhaus, also founded in 1919, stipulated that women must be permitted to enroll, though women were not always treated equally as promised.[1] The city of Berlin was the home of such great Jewish painters as Max Liebermann, Lesser Ury, Eugen Spiro, and Julie Wolfthorn, as well as printmaker Hermann Struck. All were involved with the Berlin Secession, a modernist countermovement founded by Liebermann and others in 1898. Having reached a critical mass of galleries, dealers, and exhibition opportunities, Berlin also called to younger Jewish artists. Painter Julius Rosenbaum described the burgeoning "Jewish artist proletariat" of the city already in 1910.[2] By 1923, critics observed that there were a great number of Jews working as visual artists in Berlin, notably many graphic artists.[3]

Widespread interest in Jewish art made it possible for Szalit to break into this scene. She supposedly had her first artistic success when a painting she exhibited of an elderly Jew immediately met with critical acclaim.[4] In addition to landscapes and scenes of Berlin, her early oil paintings included portraits, flowers, and still life interiors. She also painted with watercolors and gouache, opaque pigments ground in water.[5] One of Szalit's paintings, *Interieur* (ca. 1920), shows a child sitting by a window, eating an ice cream cone. Outside is a view of other windows in a back courtyard, a central part of many Berlin buildings. Next to the child is a small table with flowers; a water pitcher and vase stand on nearby shelves (fig. 12). In his description of the original color painting, Karl Schwarz

FIGURE 12 | Rahel Szalit-Marcus, *Interieur*, in *Ost und West*, nos. 3–4 (1920): 79, *Illustrierte Monatsschrift für das gesamte Judentum*, Berlin: Verlag von S. Calvary; Jüdisches Museum Berlin, XI. Ost 69 Jg.20 H.3/4. Photo: Roman März.

commented that the sunlight flooding in from the window covered the room with warmth, lending it a cozy and calm feeling.[6] Much of Szalit's graphic art would appeal to viewers in a different way.

Graphic works, including woodcuts, etchings, and lithographs, played a key role in German Expressionism, and it was in this context that Szalit turned her attention to lithography. Printmaking was less expensive than painting and thus better suited to the economic crisis of the postwar years. Individual original prints and portfolios (*Mappenwerke*) became popular among collectors. Many artists (Max Beckmann, Otto Dix, George Grosz) turned to print media to respond to the trauma of World War I. Others such as Käthe Kollwitz would come to rely on the sharp contrasts of black-and-white printmaking as a form of social or political commentary. The period from 1918 to 1922 saw unprecedented social engagement, including new radical literary journals filled with Expressionist prints.[7] As art historian Hans Tietze predicted in 1922, "The prints of our time will give evidence of [the Expressionists] to a later generation as the truest document of the fever that agitates us."[8] Szalit, too, took advantage of the starkness of this medium and became known first and foremost as a graphic artist, though she would later return to painting. She began several illustration projects around 1920, and nearly all of her best-known illustration work was completed by 1924 during this prolific early phase of her career.

Berlin attracted many artists and intellectuals from abroad at this time. Szalit became acquainted with and circulated among Yiddish, Polish, Russian, and even Hebrew speakers—and many German speakers, too, of course. Unsurprisingly, many of Szalit's contacts during these years were Jewish, and she exhibited mainly in Jewish spaces with other Jewish artists, which gave her a much needed but limited platform and may have held her back from the mainstream success she would later achieve. But Szalit ultimately thrived as a Jewish and Expressionist artist working in Berlin during these years of exaggerated, emotional glory. As a female artist, she fought hard to earn a place among the male Expressionists contributing to Jewish Renaissance.

Making Ends Meet in Berlin West

By 1921, Szalit had moved into a small apartment that doubled as her home and studio until 1933.[9] This apartment at Stübbenstrasse 3, just around the corner from Bayerischer Platz in the Bavarian Quarter of Berlin-Schöneberg, was not far from the apartment that had been registered to Julius a few years earlier. Rahel must have struggled financially and sacrificed other luxuries to afford her own apartment in this central location, which provided easy access to different Berlin artist scenes. While in Paris, London, and New York eastern Jewish migrants gravitated to only one area, in Berlin they were dispersed throughout the city.[10] It was not eastern Jews that brought Szalit to Schöneberg but rather its location and the fact that it was a center of Jewish life more generally. The Bavarian Quarter was known as "die jüdische Schweiz" (Jewish Switzerland).

Szalit lived quite close to many prominent German Jews who made their homes in Schöneberg. Albert Einstein and Erich Fromm both lived steps from Szalit's building. Billy Wilder, Else Lasker-Schüler, Egon Erwin Kisch, and Lesser Ury all lived within a mile or so. Other well-known writers, artists, and performers also resided in this part of town. Arno Holz lived next door to Szalit; Marlene Dietrich, Kurt Tucholsky, and Christopher Isherwood (whose Berlin stories inspired the musical and film *Cabaret*) were not far away. From her home, Szalit could walk to the Romanisches Café on the Kurfürstendamm in less than thirty minutes. Many of her Schöneberg neighbors were also regulars there. To be sure, there were buses, an underground subway, and other forms of public transportation, but starving artist types did not always have money left over for bus fare.

Szalit's studio apartment was located five flights up in a white building on the narrow, quiet, residential Stübbenstrasse (plate 3). This beautiful building from 1908 still stands today, complete with its original interior wooden wall paneling and carved, decorative wooden banisters and door frames. The small apartment Szalit occupied was most likely in one of the building's side wings, meaning that her windows looked onto a peaceful back courtyard. There the sounds of the city would not have been audible; only occasionally would Szalit have heard a neighbor coming and going.

Since 1993, a sign located almost directly across from the arch-adorned main entrance of Stübbenstrasse 3 has reminded passersby that Jews were prohibited from pursuing doctoral degrees at all universities in Germany beginning in April 1937. This sign is part of a larger memorial called *Orte des Erinnerns* (Places of Remembrance), which consists of eighty such signs about Nazi persecution distributed throughout the Bavarian Quarter.[11] Other signs in the nearby Grunewaldstrasse recall that Jews were forbidden to swim at the Wannsee public beach in 1933, and that Jews could only sit on designated yellow benches at Bayerischer Platz beginning in 1939.

Thanks to descriptions by several journalists who interviewed Szalit in her home studio, we can easily imagine her at work there. This space was occupied by Szalit and her many artworks, both completed and in progress. An article in the magazine *Die jüdische Frau* (The Jewish Woman) by a journalist writing under the pseudonym Ger Trud described Szalit's "narrow, ascetic, sparse studio," its walls adorned with bright landscapes, an easel holding a child's portrait, and "the spell-binding power and the suffering of innumerable Jewish faces, which greet and plaintively follow visitors from all corners."[12] Journalist David Ewen described Szalit and her studio in detail for an American magazine about ten years after she moved in, when she was far better known. His descriptions would still have applied to her earlier self, with the exception of her hairstyle:

> There is something irresistibly magnetic about her. She is very dark, with hair combed straight backwards, with deep black eyes, prominent brow and straight aquiline nose; obviously a Jewish girl in all her features.... The study-room in which we were sitting was covered with her artworks. Remarkable works, each one of them! Rahel Szalit has succeeded in placing upon the canvas the sensitive face of the Jew, with soft, delicate strokes. Her characters are sometimes pale mystics, with eyes which seem (like in El Greco's paintings) to peer not only outward but inward, too—and in their faces can we find an expression of the soul of the Jew.[13]

This detailed description aligns with the portraits and one known photograph of Szalit. In some of these images, her pitch-black hair is pulled back to reveal a low brow and strong gaze, also a characteristic of some of her subjects. That many faces surrounded the artist at work should not surprise us. The "soul of the Jew" that Ewen references will become more relevant as we follow Szalit's career. A mystical sense of soul was considered central to Jewish art.

Even though Szalit often worked in her home studio, she spent many of her days and nights out and about in Berlin. Like other artists, she went to cafés to meet up with friends and expand her networks. She gave lessons in fencing, painting, and drawing to offset her insufficient and inconsistent artist's income; these lessons helped pay for her rent and art supplies. According to advertisements for her art lessons that Szalit placed in Jewish newspapers, her students could choose to focus on painting or drawing landscapes, portraits, or figures (potentially including nudes). One advertisement suggests she could be reached at home by phone (at "Nollendorf 6673") only until 10 o'clock in the morning.[14] We can assume she offered art instruction in such locations as cafés or private homes, or perhaps even in her own studio.

When Szalit was not making art, she was fencing. Her fencing lessons took place at a local fencing club, perhaps the women's fencing academy located near the Zoologischer Garten. Szalit herself learned to fence in such clubs, and she practiced for years before gaining the skills to become an instructor. Fencing gained popularity in the 1920s as more women began to participate in athletics, and women fencers appeared regularly in popular culture and art from this period. After German-Jewish fencer Helene Mayer won the gold medal in fencing at the 1928 Olympics, images of women fencers were suddenly everywhere. Julie Wolfthorn's portrait of a woman fencer helped her become well known in the Berliner Secession.[15] Szalit would later paint a memorable self-portrait in a fencing uniform (fig. 76). She would also write and illustrate an article in which she, as a "distinguished fencer, recommended the artful sport of fencing to the elegant lady" (fig. 77). In this 1930 article for *die neue linie*, Szalit observed that "there is hardly any type of sport that requires as many years of training as fencing.... But it is a wonderful distraction from the daily grind. To sit in the evening in a brightly lit fencing salle, relaxing after a bout by watching the business, brings great joy."[16] Here Szalit offers us a rare glimpse into how she spent many an evening.

In her roles as fencer and artist, Szalit lived like the emancipated New Woman type that she sketched and painted. She supported herself with a career and did not shy away from activities, such as sport and art, that had historically been gendered male. In fact, the supposedly masculine activity of fencing was believed to coincide with homosexual desires among women.[17] Perhaps Szalit even learned that she was attracted to women while practicing at a fencing club. Berlin provided no shortage of opportunities and surprises.

Russians and the Romanisches Café

The versatile Szalit moved in numerous Berlin circles. She eventually became acquainted with many well-known artists and writers, including some women writers who were members of the German PEN Club.[18] Several women's organizations, including the Jüdischer Frauenbund and the Verein der Künstlerinnen zu Berlin, facilitated introductions to prominent women as well as access to the opportunities that these friendships provided.

In the early 1920s, Russian emigrants, too, welcomed Szalit among their ranks. In the wake of revolutions and war, hundreds of thousands of Russians and other East Europeans moved through Germany, and some stayed for years. Of these, tens of thousands were Jews, who helped make up a sizable Yiddish-speaking Diaspora in Berlin, particularly from 1918 to 1925.[19] Some knew Hebrew as well, and others spoke Russian; those who stayed eventually learned German.[20] But Berlin also had Russian publishing houses, newspapers, theaters, shops, cafés, restaurants, and a slew of Russian associations and aid organizations.[21] Café Leon, a Russian literary café that served as a gathering point for Russian writers and artists, was located at Nollendorfplatz.[22] Marc Chagall, El Lissitzky, Ilya Ehrenburg, and Vladimir Nabokov were among those active in Russian émigré circles.[23]

Familiarity with Russian artists suggests that Szalit, too, was part of these circles, though we have no evidence as to whether she spoke any Russian. In a letter to German art historian Hans Hildebrandt, who was compiling information for his book on women artists and wished to include more Russian artists, Szalit first listed her own accomplishments and then named several Paris-based artists, including Xenia Boguslawskaja, wife of painter Iwan Puni, who had done theater decorations for the Berlin Russian cabaret Der Blaue Vogel. Another Russian artist Szalit mentioned was Zinaida Serebriakova, known for her self-portrait *At the Dressing Table* (1909), whose works were reproduced in the German magazine *Die Dame* (The Lady). How well Szalit knew these artists is unclear, though she generously reached out to friends in Paris and contacted the Russian embassy in an attempt to locate them for Hildebrandt.[24] Perhaps Szalit, like other prominent German writers and artists (Alfred Polgar, Kurt Tucholsky, Else Lasker-Schüler), was among those who frequented Der Blaue Vogel and other Russian venues in Berlin.[25]

Further, Szalit was acquainted with Maria Lowenstein (née Baetge; from 1914 to 1925: Maria Steinberg), a Russian/Estonian-born artist based in Berlin who often hosted artist salons. Several of Rahel Szalit's original lithographs from the early 1920s can be found among Lowenstein's papers, suggesting that Lowenstein either purchased them or received them from Szalit as a gift.[26] Szalit likely attended some of Lowenstein's gatherings; they had mutual artist friends such as Karl Hofer. Even if Szalit did not spend much time amid Russian circles, she was certainly familiar with them.

Berlin's famous Romanisches Café gave Szalit access to a wide range of cultural figures who would become important for her career. In the twenty-first century, the café has come to symbolize the complex world of Weimar culture and politics; it features prominently in the hit television show *Babylon Berlin*, set in the late Weimar period. In the early 1920s, however, it was home to an international, bohemian artist scene. It nurtured encounters between mass culture and the avant-garde, and between the major figures of Berlin modernism and Yiddish and Hebrew writers and artists. The café was quite large, with over one hundred tables, and it functioned as a meeting and networking place for artists and writers of all kinds. Among those Szalit could have encountered there were Else Lasker-Schüler, Joseph Roth, Alfred Döblin, Hermann Kesten, Walter Benjamin, Erich Kästner, Bertolt Brecht, Arnold Zweig, Stefan Zweig, Ludwig Meidner, and Abraham Palukst, as well as Yiddish and Hebrew writers Avrom Nokhum Stencl, Dovid Bergelson, Moyshe Kulbak, and Uri Zvi Greenberg.[27]

Alongside the many East European Jewish writers, artists, and intellectuals who gathered there, Szalit felt at home in familiar surroundings and immersed herself in the Yiddish literature she would come to illustrate.[28] If Berlin was the spiritual threshold between East and West, as Franz Kafka believed, then the Romanisches Café was the place where many of these paths crossed.[29] Yiddish writer Daniel Charney suggested that the Yiddish corner of the Romanisches Café was "the transit point for the whole of Yiddishland." It was reportedly also where the ideas for YIVO (the Yiddish Scientific Institute) and for the *General Jewish Encyclopedia* were first proposed.[30] Marc Chagall commented on the "crowds of Constructivist artists" that could be found at this café circa 1922, suggesting that Russian artists too were well represented.[31] Just as young writers such as Mascha Kaléko were effectively discovered in the Romanisches Café, so too did Rahel Szalit find valuable networks in this setting.

Jewish Paths into the Art World

In the early 1920s, Szalit established herself as a graphic artist and illustrator. She was initially known mainly in Jewish circles, though her Russian background also made her the perfect candidate to illustrate works by Dostoyevsky and Tolstoy. Most group exhibitions in which Szalit participated before 1925 were Jewish exhibitions: they either took place in such venues as the B'nai B'rith fraternal lodge or they offered the opportunity to show her work alongside other Jewish artists, as in two exhibitions held in Breslau and Wiesbaden (near Frankfurt am Main). One exception was a special "Black and White" exhibition of graphic artwork at the Academy of the Arts that helped publicize her work beyond Jewish circles.[32] In general, though, Szalit was more limited in her reach during these years, and the fact that she exhibited mainly with male Jewish artists and faced an ongoing uphill battle to be taken seriously kept her from fully breaking through into mainstream Weimar art scenes.

Nevertheless, Szalit attracted the interest of three key art historians and critics during these years, and their support had a tremendous impact on her career. As we have seen, prominent art historian Karl Schwarz was the first to intervene on behalf of Szalit by publishing a lengthy article about her and her work in *Ost und West* in 1920. He continued to follow her career closely and profiled her several times in the following decade.[33] As an editor of *Der Cicerone*, a magazine aimed at art scholars and collectors, Schwarz ensured that Szalit's publications and exhibitions were included in reports about graphic art in the early 1920s.[34] Later, Szalit's works would be among those that Schwarz cited as exemplary in a lecture on "The Jewish Family in Art."[35]

Art historian Rachel Wischnitzer-Bernstein likewise helped build Rahel Szalit's reputation in other Berlin Jewish circles, including those that operated outside of the German language. The two Rachels were born around the same time in the Russian Empire and were both native speakers of Yiddish. Perhaps their common backgrounds and gender predisposed Wischnitzer to lend her support to Szalit. Originally trained as an architect, Rachel Wischnitzer is best known for her work as art editor of the highbrow *Milgroym* (Pomegranate), subtitled in English as *A Yiddish Illustrated Magazine of Arts and Letters*, and its Hebrew counterpart *Rimon*. Both magazines were published by the Rimon Jewish Art and Literature Publishing Company, which Rachel and her husband Mark Wischnitzer established in 1922 to print books and periodicals in Yiddish and Hebrew. It was dually based in Berlin and London and financed with foreign currency.[36] As art editor of *Milgroym/Rimon*, Rachel Wischnitzer oversaw the inclusion of two of Szalit's lithographs in a feature article on graphic art in the second issue. She discussed Szalit's work again in her "Art and Letters" summary updates in the third and sixth issues of

Milgroym. Although none of their correspondence survives, we know that Wischnitzer would again support Szalit at later stages of her career in both Berlin and Paris.

Either Wischnitzer or the mentions in *Milgroym/Rimon* helped Szalit find additional work illustrating Yiddish, Hebrew, and German-language books; several of Szalit's illustrated books were published by the Rimon Publishing Company. Having images reproduced in *Milgroym/Rimon* was a tremendous opportunity, and it meant that Szalit's name was associated with these journals and at times included in promotional materials. Readers of the *Soncino-Blätter*, the journal of the Soncino Society of the Friends of the Jewish Book, for example, would have come across Szalit's name in conjunction with *Milgroym/Rimon*.[37] Members of this Jewish bibliophile society, which aimed for a revival of the "beautiful Jewish book," were later given the chance to purchase six signed original graphic works by Szalit and other Jewish artists for only thirty marks (about $125 in today's dollars).[38]

Finally, Austrian-Jewish art critic and poet Adolph Donath also proved to be a long-time supporter of Szalit's work. He published art criticism primarily in mainstream outlets. Donath first mentioned Szalit in his preeminent art journal *Der Kunstwanderer* (The Art Wanderer) in 1921, when her work appeared in an exhibition of Jewish artists held at the B'nai B'rith lodge at Kleiststrasse 10 in Schöneberg.[39] There was even talk of Donath doing a special issue of *Der Kunstwanderer* with an essay on Szalit by art historian Hans Hildebrandt, though these plans never materialized.[40] Such enthusiastic support from Donath, who published on Jewish artists including Herrmann Struck and Lesser Ury and who remained active in Berlin's Jewish art world, would prove key to the success of Szalit's emerging career. Donath also highlighted Szalit's work in numerous exhibition reviews in the *Berliner Tageblatt* and other papers and can be credited with spreading news of her work beyond Jewish circles.

In fact, Donath and his journal may well have influenced the positive reception of Szalit's two Weimar-era solo exhibitions. The first, discussed further in the next chapter, had the title *Szenen aus dem jüdischen Kleinstadtleben* (Scenes of Jewish Small-Town Life). It took place at the Gutenberg Buchhandlung (bookstore) in Berlin from roughly September to November 1922. On view were individual images and portfolios (*Blätter und Mappen*) of Szalit's illustrations of literary works by Buber, Daudet, Dickens, Dostoyevsky, Tolstoy, and Zangwill.[41] Notable among the exhibited works were those about motherly love, according to one review by Donath.[42]

Strangely, only the works by Buber and Zangwill dealt with Jewish subjects. Szalit's illustrations of Buber's works are still lost, so we can only imagine what they might have shown. Although Szalit presumably created her Zangwill illustrations for a German-language edition of Zangwill's *The King of Schnorrers* (first published in English in 1894), there is no evidence that they were ever reproduced or published in book form. This picaresque novel set in eighteenth-century England revolves around two Jewish beggars. Several of Szalit's recently rediscovered original drawings feature Zangwill's two beggar protagonists (Manasseh da Costa, who has Sephardic lineage, and Yankele ben Yizchok, who despite his Ashkenazic origins wishes to marry da Costa's daughter), who wear different head coverings, and a miserly rabbi they encounter whose name refers to a herring he regretted not purchasing. Unsurprisingly, Szalit's image titled *Rabbi Pöckelhering* bears some resemblance to other traditional Jewish characters depicted by Szalit, such as those in her illustrations of *Fishke the Lame*.[43] In addition to these scenes of Jewish life, some of her best illustrations of Dickens and Tolstoy must have been on display at the bookstore. Critic Willi Wolfradt concluded that her thrilling graphic works conveyed a great deal through depictions of conflicts, fears, and scorn.[44]

Another anonymous review in the *Berliner Tageblatt* of Szalit's Gutenberg bookstore exhibition compared Szalit's work to that of Jakob Steinhardt. The reviewer argued that whereas Steinhardt focused on the "pathos" of eastern Jews, Szalit drew these figures and their lives as unstable or trembling (*schlotterichte Gestalten*). The reviewer noted, "She has the exact stroke suitable for this phenomenon.... This life cannot be depicted in correct [straight] lines, just as it cannot be told in correct High German."[45] The comparison to Steinhardt, a firmly established artist known for his images of Jews, was a sign that Szalit had earned a place in the Berlin Expressionist scene, one of very few Jewish women to do so. At the same time, this reviewer subtly implied that Szalit's images gave form to eastern Jews as only a Yiddish speaker could—and that these subjects naturally lent themselves to the distorted shapes of Expressionism.

Among the Expressionists

Was there such a thing as "Jewish Expressionism"? Szalit was certainly surrounded by Expressionists in Berlin, and there were many Jewish artists working in an Expressionist style in Germany and beyond. To name but a few: Moissey Kogan, Arthur Segal, Lasar Segall, and Irma Stern. But some of these artists did not always—or ever—depict Jewish subjects. Instead, their works focused on expressions of feelings and the quest for identity more broadly. Modern urban spaces were a key theme; this also extended to rural life and the tension between the city and nature.

Some scholars believe that artists who worked on Jewish subjects and drew on intense mystical or religious feelings contributed to a specifically Jewish style. Art historian Małgorzata Stolarska-Fronia has argued that there was such a thing as Jewish Expressionism, defining it as "the specific emotional, convulsive, biomorphic language of expressionistic art forms ... combined with mystical themes," including praying Jewish figures and

FIGURE 13 | Rahel Szalit-Marcus, *Der Rabbi und sein Schüler* (The Rabbi and His Pupil), 1920. Courtesy of the Beck Archives, Special Collections, University of Denver Libraries.

Hasidic and other exotic eastern subjects.[46] To be sure, Szalit created many works in this idiom. Take, for example, her lithograph *Der Rabbi und sein Schüler* (The Rabbi and His Pupil, 1920, fig. 13), which was printed individually and reproduced in the satirical magazine *Schlemiel*.[47] Both men in this image wear head coverings and *peyes* (sidelocks). The rabbi's elongated nose, eyelids, beard, and crooked fingers, gesturing above an open book, seem eastern and otherworldly. Szalit further commented about her own knowledge of

Judaism: "With respect to religion, only the lines of thought of Hasidic mysticism are especially familiar."[48]

Yet rather than consider such Jewish artists and their artworks as representative of a formal subset of Expressionism, it would be more accurate to consider Szalit as one of the Jewish artists who engaged with Expressionism in different ways, both in and beyond Germany. Expressionist artwork with Jewish themes could be found across Europe, from the Yung Yiddish avant-garde movement, founded in Lodz in 1918, to the works of Chagall and Mané-Katz in Paris.[49] These artists generally considered themselves both Jewish and Expressionist, but they were not always interested in being categorized as both at the same time. Even as they worked to create specifically Jewish art in some cases, they also participated in modern German and European art more broadly. One 1929 study by art historian Ernst Cohn-Wiener identified Jakob Steinhardt and Ludwig Meidner as the two foremost Jewish representatives of German Expressionism, noting that they approached expression through "an ecstasy of pain and piety." Cohn-Wiener also mentioned Szalit briefly in a list of illustrators.[50] Steinhardt and Meidner served as important contacts for Szalit in the early 1920s, introducing her to other artists and shaping her approach to Expressionism. A close look at their worlds gives us a sense of how Szalit interacted with major Jewish artists of her generation.

Steinhardt and Meidner were both born in the 1880s in Silesia, an eastern region of the German Empire now in Poland, and they trained with the great Jewish printmaker Hermann Struck around 1908. In fact, Struck's studio is where they first met. An observant Jew, Struck produced many etchings and lithographs of eastern Jews, contributing to the broader notion of eastern Jewish authenticity. Struck was considered a master of graphic art, and such artists as Max Liebermann, Lovis Corinth, and Lesser Ury went to him for advice.[51] Other Jewish artists were inspired to take up graphic art because of Struck. Many artists, writers, and musicians gathered at his studio along with rabbis, Zionists, and eastern Jews. Chagall, too, learned techniques from Struck in the early 1920s before Struck immigrated to Palestine. Fewer women studied with Struck in Berlin, though both Regina Mundlak and Else Lasker-Schüler referred to him as their teacher.[52] Szalit may also have visited Struck's studio, but we have no record of her presence there. Still, her proximity to Struck by way of other artists suggests she benefitted from his expertise, if only indirectly.

Szalit must have known of Struck's technical handbook *Die Kunst des Radierens* (The Art of Etching, 1908), which went through many editions. This book instructed readers in "the beautiful art of black and white," outlining different approaches to printmaking throughout art history, from engravings by Albrecht Dürer to etchings by Rembrandt and Goethe. It also included Struck's detailed instructions for carrying out various methods. Drypoint etching (*kalte Nadel*) involved using needles and other tools to cut or scratch an image out of a metal printing plate, then inking the plate to prepare it for the printmaking press. For other etchings, an "etch" made from a chemical mixture with fuming nitric acid would set the scratched image for the printing press. Examples of work by French and German masters (Manet, Pissarro, Renoir, Rodin; Liebermann, Corinth, Slevogt) appeared in the 1920 edition of Struck's book; Joseph Budko, Meidner, and Steinhardt merited short entries as well. Käthe Kollwitz was the lone female artist to make the cut.[53] In other publications about Jewish artists working in the graphic arts, no women's names appear at all, though Charlotte Berend-Corinth and Lene Schneider-Kainer had both published portfolios by that time.[54]

As she entered the world of printmaking and lithography, Szalit had few female role models aside from the well-known Kollwitz, and it is thus not surprising that she associated with many male artists during this period. But there is nothing to suggest that Szalit was trained in the etching techniques that her contemporaries used or that she used needles or other such engraving tools in her work. Whereas Steinhardt and Meidner both experimented with different forms of etching and woodcuts, Szalit worked mainly with lithography, also known as *Steindruck* (literally: stone printing).[55] To make her lithographs, Szalit brushed ink (*Tusche*) or used special oil-based pencils, crayons, or chalk (*Kreide*) to create a reverse image on stone or on a metal plate. She then used a solvent to fix the image and make it ink-receptive for a printer's press.

Together with non-Jewish artist Richard Janthur, Steinhardt and Meidner founded an Expressionist group called the Pathetiker (Pathetic Ones, or Artists of Pathos) that focused on the use of pathos in art, of suffering to invoke compassion. The short-lived group formed in 1911 (not long after Martin Buber used the term "pathos" to denote a Jewish sense of being torn between two worlds) and notably exhibited in Herwarth Walden's modern art gallery, Der Sturm, before disbanding.[56] In their November 1912 exhibition, all three showed paintings and drawings, and Steinhardt also exhibited lithographs. As Pathetiker, they treated apocalyptic and biblical themes, including the spiritual torment of Cain, Lot, and Job, as well as prophets such as Jeremiah, and were influenced by El Greco, Cubism, and Italian Futurism. Meidner's *Apokalyptische Landschaft* (Apocalyptic Landscape, 1912), a frenzied scene of fire engulfing a city while two men flee toward the viewer, is one of the most famous paintings to come out of this era. Steinhardt and Meidner continued to focus on similar themes in the decade that followed. They were known for trying to convey in Expressionist terms a "very sincere and profound mysticism" inspired by their encounters with eastern Europe.[57]

Jakob Steinhardt came into Szalit's life as she entered the Jewish art scene. She visited Steinhardt's home in 1920, when both were producing graphic works illustrating Jewish literature; their work appeared in some of the same exhibitions around this time. Steinhardt had kind eyes, a warm smile, hair parted on the side, and a clean-shaven face that reflected his distance from the bearded, religiously observant men he sometimes depicted. Many of Steinhardt's woodcuts, etchings, lithographs, oil paintings, and other works showed eastern Jews and Jewish subject matter. His figures of Job and others embodied eastern Jewish suffering and lamentations, which critics described as "authentic Jewish art."[58] Steinhardt was strongly influenced by his experience serving on the eastern front in Lithuania during the First World War, which he describes in his memoirs:

> Just before a small town, we stopped to rest, weary and dying of thirst. I see on the path a small wooden house, shlep myself over to get a drink. A dimly lit room. Hidden in a corner sits an old woman, and next to her a girl at a sewing machine. From where do I know the old woman? She is wearing a wig like my great-grandmother, whose picture hangs in Zerkow in our apartment. I have never seen this woman before in my life—and yet I know her, this old Jewish mother, and she knows me and gives me tea and takes from a hiding place a few small cakes, and we speak like old, age-old acquaintances, and I feel as if I am at home in this poor little room.[59]

Steinhardt's recollections of his time in Lithuania, including such encounters with Jewish women, may well have driven his cultural interactions with Szalit. Around 1921, Steinhardt painted a remarkable portrait of Szalit with a melancholic expression (fig. 14). This portrait suggests that even Szalit's sadness took the form of a determined gaze and loose, wild hair. Steinhardt amplified Szalit's dark eyes with dramatic shadows above and below the eye that recall the makeup used in such Expressionist silent films as *The Cabinet of Dr. Caligari* (1920). It was common for artists to exchange work as a sign of friendship; perhaps Steinhardt gave Szalit the portrait he painted of her, just as Szalit left a drawing in his guestbook.

The entry by Szalit in Jakob Steinhardt's guestbook in 1920, a pencil-and-ink drawing, confirms that she was one of many artists who gathered at his home.[60] The drawing shows an impoverished family seated on the floor, with a breastfeeding mother caring for both a baby and an older child, and a man with an outstretched arm, perhaps a beggar, seated just behind them (fig. 15). Even when signing a guestbook, Szalit highlighted the struggles of the lower classes, and especially impoverished mothers. Taken in its broader context, the drawing also reveals that Szalit chose to focus on women's issues within Jewish art circles. This is one of several images Szalit created of breastfeeding mothers. Her mothers and children recall artworks by Berthe Morisot, Mary Cassatt, Paula Modersohn-Becker, Käthe Kollwitz, and Chana Orloff, who were among the first women artists to highlight women's very personal parenting experiences.

FIGURE 14 | Jakob Steinhardt, *Portrait of Rahel Szalit-Marcus*, 1921/22. Jüdisches Museum Frankfurt, used with permission from Josefa Bar-On Steinhardt.

Szalit might have met Ludwig Meidner at Jakob Steinhardt's house, or perhaps at the Romanisches Café. Meidner loved cafés and often depicted them. He was short of stature, bald, and mustached and had an impish grin. Known for his dynamic city scenes and his turn to Orthodox Judaism and religious subject matter beginning in 1924, Meidner brought intense, ecstatic fervor to his work.[61] He was explosive and chaotic; some of his friends found his eruptive manner difficult to tolerate. Chagall once said about Meidner, "He is very talented, but crazy!"[62] Meidner, for his part, described Chagall as "neither 'interesting'

BERLIN EXPRESSIONIST CIRCLES

FIGURE 15 | Guestbook entry by Rahel Szalit-Marcus, drawing, black ink over pencil, lower right: Rahel Szalit-Marcus / September 1920, in Guestbook of the Steinhardt Family from 1920 to 1927, Berlin. Cardboard, embossed paper, various writing and drawing media, 31.5 × 25.5 × 2 cm. Jüdisches Museum Berlin, Inv.-Nr. DOK 95/525/870, donation by Josefa Bar-On Steinhardt, Nahariya, Israel.

nor witty, he uttered nothing that was unusual, eccentric, or even 'fashionable,' but showed himself a sensible man—although one could feel that he was inwardly burning with unrest."[63]

Meidner encouraged many artists to depict the metropolis of Berlin; he could well have inspired Szalit on both a thematic and a formal level.[64] Meidner's and Szalit's Expressionist street scenes use similar vertical, angular lines to show cityscape contours. Meidner's numerous portraits of everyone he encountered—including such figures as Bella Chagall, artists Martel Schwichtenberg and Willy Jaeckel, writers Jakob van Hoddis and Joachim Ringelnatz, actors Lotte Lenya and Alexander Granach, and Rabbi Leo

Baeck—could have inspired some of Szalit's portraits as well, particularly since she would go on to draw several of the same individuals Meidner portrayed.

A man about town who enjoyed city nightlife and slept until one o'clock in the afternoon, Meidner liked to organize regular gatherings and parties, and he knew many kinds of people. During his years in Paris (1906–7), he visited every bar and café in Montmartre with his friend Amedeo Modigliani, who painted him twice. Later, in Berlin, Meidner organized and hosted colorful gatherings of artists, writers, and actors at locations including restaurants and his various ateliers, most notably his fifth-floor attic studio at Motzstrasse 55, where he lived from 1920–27, only half a mile from Szalit's apartment. Among the many writers who visited Meidner's studio were Franz Werfel, Arthur Holitscher, Alfred Döblin, Mynona, Hugo Ball, Emmy Hennings, Johannes Becher, and Max Herrmann-Neisse; artist George Grosz and publisher Wieland Herzfelde were also regulars.[65] We know that Szalit, too, attended some of his parties and likely made important contacts there. Meidner further grappled with his own homosexual inclinations, and one might also wonder if Meidner and Szalit ever ran into each other while visiting gay bars or parties in Schöneberg.[66]

Szalit's friendship with Meidner was in full swing by 1923, when their lives and careers intersected in several ways. Both contributed to the mainstream literary journal *Der Feuerreiter* (The Fire Rider) and took part in a Wiesbaden exhibition of graphic works by Jewish artists, suggesting that Szalit's success as a Jewish artist had begun to extend beyond Berlin.[67] Meidner was briefly affiliated with the Novembergruppe, a group of radical socialist artists founded after the November Revolution of 1918. Many claim that Szalit, too, was part of the Novembergruppe, though this remains unconfirmed: Szalit is not listed among its members or exhibition participants, though she certainly knew many of them.[68] It is possible Szalit informally attended meetings; a few other women artists, including Irma Stern and Hannah Höch, were active in the Novembergruppe.[69] A document later penned by Meidner describes a celebration for his thirty-ninth birthday in April 1923, which Szalit attended along with Marc Chagall, painter Karl Hofer, and writer Arthur Holitscher, among others.[70] Karl Hofer would soon come to play a more significant role in Szalit's life.

This description of Meidner's party confirms that Rahel Szalit and Marc Chagall encountered each other at least once when Chagall lived in Berlin in 1922–23 before returning to Paris. If Szalit and Chagall conversed at length, their conversation might have made a stronger impression on Szalit than on Chagall. They would have spoken together in Yiddish, for despite the fact that several of his artworks contain German words, Chagall did not speak much German but rather Yiddish, Russian, and French.[71] In addition to having Russian, working-class backgrounds in common, Szalit's and Chagall's biographies and careers overlapped on many levels, and they had quite a few mutual friends. Chagall was good friends with Yiddish critic Bal-Makhshoves (Isidor Eliashev), who wrote a text to accompany Szalit's *Motl* illustrations, and Chagall later got to know Hebrew writer Hayim Nahman Bialik, whose book *Ketina kol-bo* included two illustrations by Szalit.[72] Several German critics compared the work of Szalit and Chagall, noting that both used humorous types to depict Jewish folklife.[73] Their works were also included in many of the same exhibitions over the years. Even if Chagall did not consider Szalit more than an insignificant acquaintance, it is unlikely that he had no idea who she was. The two may have encountered each other again when Szalit, too, lived in Paris in the 1930s.

When the German economy stabilized at the end of 1923, the popularity of both printmaking and Expressionism began to decline. As a result, Szalit began to widen her networks beyond the Jewish artists who had played a key role during her first years in Berlin. These other artists, too, soon branched out in new directions. Steinhardt would make his first trip to Palestine in 1925 and would end up fleeing to Jerusalem eight years later. Ludwig Meidner would marry Else (née Meyer), a student in his drawing class who was seventeen years his junior, in a 1927 ceremony performed by Rabbi Leo Baeck, bringing an end to the parties at the Motzstrasse atelier. According to one source, Szalit was good friends with both Ludwig and Else Meidner.[74] The Meidners would wait until 1939 to leave Germany for an extended exile in England, though Ludwig would return to Germany in 1953.

From both her many social contacts and the artwork she produced, it is evident that Szalit was immersed in Weimar culture and Expressionism in the early 1920s. This was also when she focused mainly on literary illustrations ranging from Dostoyevsky and Dickens to Sholem Aleichem, Heine, and Bialik. Like other artists associated with Expressionism, Szalit experimented with different emotionally evocative forms in her illustrations and brought characters to life in exciting and sometimes unsettling ways.

PART 2

INFLATION-ERA ILLUSTRATIONS

(1920–1923)

CHAPTER 4

Classic World Literature

Berlin-Charlottenburg, October 1922: Solo exhibitions are hard to come by, so Rahel is overjoyed about her first, a small exhibition of her graphic works at the Gutenberg Buchhandlung, a respected bookstore and gallery. She knows of several other artists planning exhibitions here. It helps that many of her works are literary illustrations. The bookstore's location is perfect: right on the Tauentzienstrasse, a busy shopping street near the Kaiser Wilhelm memorial church and the KaDeWe department store. This makes it simple to persuade friends and Berlin notables to visit, and this afternoon she takes a short walk with others from the Romanisches Café to the gallery.

The exhibition's official title is somewhat misleading: Scenes of Jewish Small-Town Life. But there are far more images than just those of Jewish life, and she is proud of them all. Karl Buchholz, an ambitious young bookstore employee with a charming smile, has helped her select which images to include. He has an eye for display. The final exhibition includes illustrations for works by Dostoyevsky, Tolstoy, Dickens, and Daudet; the Jewish scenes are of Zangwill's The King of Schnorrers, tales of Reb Nachman of Breslov, and children's stories by Martin Buber.

The exhibition is written up in major papers. Reviewers praise her original perspective. They see her as a skilled artist with a spirited temperament and sense of humor. She is pleased with the reviews; they see her for who she is.

Rahel is not too disappointed when only two people inquire about purchasing her prints. This is a crazy time. Bread is so expensive one must use stamps to buy the cheaper, rationed amounts. The only ones who can afford luxuries like art are rich or foreign collectors. Right now it's far more important that people know her work.

INFLATION-ERA ILLUSTRATIONS

The inflation period of the early 1920s saw a flurry of illustration and publishing activity by Rahel Szalit and other artists. Printmaking was less expensive than other art forms and was thus very common. Publishers and artists alike sought to contribute to the surge in bibliophilic book production. In fact, nearly all of Szalit's major literary illustrations were completed during this time, including six books (two of which are now lost), one set of unpublished drawings, and three print portfolios. Only one book with lithographs appeared later, in 1927, and another full set of illustrations (drawings) appeared in a magazine in 1929.

Aside from the widespread popularity of printmaking, there are two explanations for Szalit's high productivity as a lithographic illustrator during inflation. First, artworks were considered safe investments, and both individual prints and print portfolios of graphic art were in demand because they resembled a form of stable currency when the German Papiermark became increasingly worthless in late 1922 and 1923. When Szalit's solo exhibition closed in November 1922, the exchange rate was over seven thousand marks to the dollar. It fell to one hundred sixty thousand by July 1923. By the end of that year, it averaged more than two million marks to the dollar and peaked in the trillions. Second, publishers from other lands flocked to Germany to take advantage of relatively low costs for those paying with foreign currency, which resulted in the publication of Yiddish and other foreign-language books. Hyperinflation ended with the reform to curb currency devaluation in November 1923 via the Rentenmark and finally the introduction of a new Reichsmark on 30 August 1924. But before then, Szalit was able to take advantage of numerous publishing opportunities to launch her career as a graphic artist and illustrator of key works by well-known authors of world and Jewish literature.

Szalit's career as an illustrator arguably began with exhibitions of individual prints. She benefitted from several exhibitions at the B'nai B'rith lodge that were held with the express goal of supporting Jewish artists during tough times, though they also served to educate the Jewish public about art.[1] Her first known exhibition took place there in December 1920, earning Szalit glowing reviews. One noted that whereas her paintings were done capably and well, she "found her own language in her satirical prints of Jewish life."[2] Lavishing even more praise upon the young artist, a critic for the Zionist newspaper *Jüdische Rundschau* (Jewish Review), Paul Zucker, extolled Szalit as the "born illustrator for the books of a new generation." But Zucker notably evaluated Szalit separately from German artists. Instead, he compared Szalit with another Lithuanian-born artist, Feiga Blumberg, further suggesting that Szalit's talents were on par with those of nineteenth-century French printmaker Honoré Daumier. Zucker also pointed out that Szalit's grotesque humor was always accompanied by a "spooky undertone." Hesitant to use the term "Expressionist," he concluded that Szalit's illustrations struck the right balance between naturalistic representation and abstract principles of form.[3]

On the heels of such reviews, Szalit quickly became the best-known Jewish woman illustrator in 1920s Germany. Some considered her the best female illustrator overall, though she was initially better known within Jewish circles. To be sure, there were not many women who illustrated German-language books in the early twentieth century, but it was still no small accomplishment to make it to the top tier. Many of Szalit's male contemporaries were known for their book illustrations, including Hermann Struck, Joseph Budko, Jakob Steinhardt, Marc Chagall, and Eugen Spiro. Rosy Lilienfeld, who illustrated *The Legend of the Baal-Shem* and Joseph Roth's *Job* in the 1930s, deserves to be mentioned here as well, though there were few other Jewish women illustrators active in Germany for long periods.[4]

Exactly how Szalit came to illustrate specific works of world literature is not clear, but her East European background made her an ideal candidate to illustrate Russian literature in German translation. Her periods of study in London and Paris enhanced her qualifications as an illustrator of Charles Dickens and Claude Tillier. Still, national origin could play a significant or controversial role in matching an illustrator with a text. When Chagall, a foreign Jewish artist, was first commissioned to illustrate classic French fables by Jean de La Fontaine, he was unprepared for the backlash from xenophobic and nationalistic French critics.[5] No such responses to Szalit's illustrations have been noted, however, and German-Jewish circles along with some mainstream German critics were generally welcoming of this newcomer with international connections.

Szalit as Literary Interpreter

"To give visual form to the thoughts of great writers is a wonderful feeling for me every time," Szalit once wrote.[6] Her illustrations reflect this creative enjoyment. Yet the choices that illustrators make as interpreters of texts are often overlooked. An illustrator such as Szalit must first read and engage with a written text, then select isolated moments to render in realistic or at least believable two-dimensional images. In addition, what illustrators decide to show is sometimes just as important as what they do not show. Illustrations can provide rich detail and offer a smaller-grained description of a situation; in other instances, they put forth an argument or narrative that differs from that of the written text.[7]

As an illustrator, Szalit had her own kind of authorship and ability to influence readers. Whereas some illustrations primarily depict a written text in image form, others extend and augment it, thereby creating something new. The latter applies to Szalit, whom we might understand as an "augmenting illustrator."[8] Szalit's illustrations do not purely retell but rather generate a dialogue between text and image, producing another layer of content and interpretation. Translation also played a role in this process. Szalit most likely read the foreign works she illustrated in German translation, except for the Yiddish texts. Many of her illustrations were thus doubly removed from the original texts, operating as new renderings of translations that were themselves already interpretations.

Szalit consistently adhered to several core principles or strategies for illustrating written texts. The remarks that she published about her approach to illustrating apply specifically to illustrations of Jewish subjects, but it is possible to draw more general conclusions about her artistic approach based on a broad overview of her work. In short, Szalit's illustrations tend to show moments or scenes from a story that seem significant, absurd, provocative, or especially memorable. Most focus on an action carried out by at least one central character. Many emphasize women and girls by placing them in the center or foreground of the image, or by enhancing their overall visibility. Animals, too, appear whenever marginally relevant, adding universal appeal. In some cases, Szalit implicitly references interactions between humans and certain animals (horses, goats, chickens) in eastern Europe, as well as power structures between people and animals. Szalit's illustrations of Jews form a separate category and are discussed in later chapters. Let us first turn to world literature to see how Szalit retold stories through a feminist lens.

The Russian Greats: Dostoyevsky and Tolstoy

Beginning in the nineteenth century, and especially in the wake of the First World War, Germans were fascinated with Russian culture. Russia served as a source of inspiration and hope. Many believed that Russian writers had the ability to reach into the deepest layers of the soul. Dostoyevsky in particular was regarded as a sign of postwar renewal and was read even more widely than Tolstoy; "Dostoyevsky cults" popped up all over Europe.[9] Szalit was one of countless artists and illustrators in Germany who participated in "Dostoyevsky fever." In 1920, *Die Schaffenden*, a quarterly periodical for collectors published by Paul Westheim, devoted a whole issue to Dostoyevsky, including graphic works by Otto Gleichmann, Erich Heckel, Karl Hofer, Paul Holz, Richard Janthur, and Alfred Kubin.[10] That same year saw lithographs by Heinrich Maria Davringhausen illustrating *The Brothers Karamazov* and by Bruno Krauskopf for *A Gentle Creature*. Dietz Edzard illustrated a different version of this story several years later. Hermann Struck published illustrations of *A Weak Heart*, and Karl Rössing created woodcuts for *White Nights*.[11]

Szalit's 1921 illustrations of Fyodor Dostoyevsky's *The Crocodile* marked her debut as a published literary illustrator. Although she had sold, exhibited, and given away individual lithographs in the preceding years, these were the first she published in book form. She also created more illustrations for this story by Dostoyevsky than for any other work, with twenty-one original lithographs made to accompany Edith Ziegler's slim German translation, *Das Krokodil*. This was the seventh volume of Gustav Kiepenheuer Verlag's illustrated series Graphic Books, which introduced original works by new artists to readers of classic literature. The book's price ranged from thirty-five to fifty marks, and one journal advertised it as a possible Christmas gift.[12] Although "Rahel Szalit-Marcus" was credited prominently on one of the book's opening pages, the individual illustrations were not signed. With this first set of published illustrations, Szalit established her reputation as an artist invested in depicting both satirical wit and animals.

Dostoyevsky's story *The Crocodile*, first published in Russian magazine installments in 1865, is set in January of that year. Its simultaneously parodic and hauntingly absurd tale recounts how Elena Ivanovna (in German: Jelena Iwanowna), a friend of the first-person narrator, watches as her husband, Ivan Matveitch (Iwan Matwejewitsch), is eaten by a German showman's crocodile. But Ivan does not die; rather, he offers advice and makes demands from inside the crocodile's stomach. A fight ensues, and the showman refuses to harm or sell his crocodile. Ivan decides to take advantage of his new eminence by reporting from within the crocodile while his wife hosts a salon outside. Yet the newspapers get the story wrong, and some even sympathize with the crocodile. The narrator is frustrated that he must play a kind of secretary for Ivan. The story concludes without a resolution, and we are left to wonder what will become of Ivan inside the crocodile (fig. 16).

FIGURE 16 | Rahel Szalit-Marcus, *Peering into the Crocodile's Mouth*, illustration from Fyodor Dostoyevsky's *The Crocodile*, 1921.

FIGURE 17 | Rahel Szalit-Marcus, *Elena Ivanovna Studies the Monkeys*, illustration from Fyodor Dostoyevsky's *The Crocodile*, 1921.

Most of Szalit's illustrations of *The Crocodile* are small character studies, portraits of one or two characters and their reactions at specific moments in the story. About one-third feature Elena Ivanovna, the most important female character. In the first few images, Elena is easily recognized by her fashionable hat and giant eyes, even when she stands in a crowd studying the monkeys and other animals presented by the showman (fig. 17). Just as the monkeys entertain the crowd, Elena is the star of Szalit's show: from the foreground, she watches the monkeys on the other side of the glass, perhaps considering the situation of these caged animals. Szalit's Elena is as charming and aspirational as Dostoyevsky describes her. The final image of Elena shows her laughing, welcoming the idea of buying new dresses in which to host salons.

Animals, of course, are central to this story: the crocodile appears in five of Szalit's illustrations, including the first and final images. Human characters are separated from the crocodile by cage bars in two instances, including one that positions the viewer on the side of the crocodile (fig. 18). Monkeys appear in another illustration that coincides with the narrator's dream on this subject. Here the three monkeys are not behind glass or

FIGURE 18 | Rahel Szalit-Marcus, *Watching the Crocodile*, illustration from Fyodor Dostoyevsky's *The Crocodile*, 1921.

INFLATION-ERA ILLUSTRATIONS

FIGURE 19 | Rahel Szalit-Marcus, *Three Monkeys*, illustration from Fyodor Dostoyevsky's *The Crocodile*, 1921.

bars but simply peer out from a branch inquisitively (fig. 19). The reader cannot help but marvel at the peculiar relationships between humans and animals in this story, where it is never clear who is benefiting or profiting the most from the other.

Overall, Szalit's drawings, like Dostoyevsky's text, alienate the reader from the foreign German showman and his mother, who are concerned only with the welfare of themselves and their crocodile. Some of the Russian male protagonists also seem exotic, with long beards and heavy brows, but Szalit's depictions of the narrator, Elena, and Ivan all offer something with which German readers could have identified. Little is known about the reception of Szalit's Dostoyevsky images, but it speaks highly of this first illustrated book that she was soon asked to illustrate others.

One year later, seven illustrations by Szalit accompanied a new German edition of Leo Tolstoy's controversial 1889 novella *Die Kreutzersonate* (The Kreutzer Sonata). This edition appeared in print while Szalit's works were on display at the Gutenberg Buchhandlung in fall 1922, and some critics associated the Tolstoy book with Szalit's exhibition.[13] As with the Dostoyevsky book, the individual Tolstoy illustrations did not bear Szalit's signature. Rather, they were attributed to the gender-neutral "R. Szalit-Markus" on the title page. Translated by August Scholz, the book was published by the Sebastian Löwenbuck Akademischer Verlag in Berlin as part of Tolstoy's collected works. This elegant, standard-sized, leather-bound volume opens with a few bars of Beethoven's sonata dedicated to Rudolf

Kreutzer, a photograph of Tolstoy, biblical passages from the Gospel of Matthew, and a brief foreword by German author Gerhart Hauptmann. Praising Tolstoy, Hauptmann wrote, "Let us celebrate his artistic and his human greatness! His struggle with himself was humanly great." The book further includes an afterword written by Tolstoy in 1900 to explain how the book should be interpreted.

Szalit was one of many artists who interacted with Tolstoy's work.[14] Her illustrations may have been inspired by the Expressionist silent film *Die Kreutzersonate*, released in cinemas in February 1922. Whether or not she saw this film, she might have encountered film posters on advertising columns all over the city. One poster showed the story's female protagonist listening attentively to the music of a green-faced violinist with an evil expression. The story remained wildly popular, and artist Bruno Krauskopf—whose studio at Bülowstrasse 34 near Nollendorfplatz was a gathering point for Expressionist artists and actors from Max Pechstein to Ernst Deutsch and Paul Wegener—would go on to create Impressionist-inspired illustrations for another version of the book only a few years later.[15]

Anyone familiar with *The Kreutzer Sonata* will recall that it is psychologically disturbing on several levels. The work was initially banned in Russia in 1890 for its explicit sexual content. While conversing with passengers on a long train ride, the main character, Vasya Pozdnyshev, narrates in the first person his story of flying into a jealous rage and brutally murdering his wife after hearing her play Beethoven's sonata on the piano together with a male violinist. But it is not only his violent response to suspected adultery that upset critics. The work was most controversial due to its overall attacks on romantic love: Pozdnyshev's extreme calls for total celibacy and chastity, a position adopted after committing murder, scandalized Tolstoy's contemporaries. This prompted Tolstoy to clarify in his afterword that he agreed with Pozdnyshev about the concept of celibacy as an ideal, if not a realizable, goal.

The first three of Szalit's illustrations accompany the beginning part of the novella, in which Pozdnyshev and his fellow train riders engage in a philosophical discussion about love and marriage. One image shows two men surrounded by women in a crowded room (fig. 20). If this image illustrates the passage next to which it was printed, it shows the tavern or brothel that Pozdnyshev described visiting and being sexually corrupted by at the age of sixteen. The women in this image all have somewhat vapid expressions; their eyes are large, with exaggerated star-shaped eyelashes, and in some cases shoulders and bustlines are visible.

Szalit's final four illustrations of Pozdnyshev, his wife, and the violinist Trukhachevsky are by far the most memorable. In keeping with the broader Expressionist focus on feelings, Szalit illustrated this story with a series of images that each express a specific emotion: jealousy, anger, fear, and regret. The first sets up the love triangle, with Pozdnyshev and

INFLATION-ERA ILLUSTRATIONS

FIGURE 20 | R. Szalit-Markus, *Two Men Surrounded by Women*, illustration from Leo Tolstoy's *The Kreutzer Sonata*, 1922.

his wife casting meaningful glances at each other about the messy state of their marriage while the violinist looks on. The next image portrays Pozdnyshev as a man disturbed, listening to Trukhachevsky's violin play in the background and absorbing the power of the sonata.

Given Szalit's approach to centering female characters, it is not surprising that the most dramatic image—the one that comes closest to depicting the story's awful climax—offers insight into Pozdnyshev's wife's perspective (fig. 21). This illustration shows the terrified wife in front of her piano, clutching at her breast and covering one eye as she watches her murderous husband approaching, knife in hand. But we see only her body and facial expression; he does not appear in the frame, nor do we see the ferocious act of murder.

Tolstoy's story as told through Szalit ends on a note of regret. Instead of following Pozdnyshev on his subsequent train journey, the last we see of Pozdnyshev is decidedly not his finest moment. The final illustration shows Pozdnyshev sitting at the side of his wife's coffin, head mournfully in his hand (fig. 22). The dark background of this scene,

FIGURE 21 | R. Szalit-Markus, *Wife Anticipating Her Murder*, illustration from Leo Tolstoy's *The Kreutzer Sonata*, 1922.

FIGURE 22 | R. Szalit-Markus, *Vasya Pozdnyshev Sitting by His Wife's Coffin*, illustration from Leo Tolstoy's *The Kreutzer Sonata*, 1922.

with candles eerily and dramatically lighting the pale face of the deceased, recalls other candlelit interiors that Szalit depicted. Szalit's Pozdnyshev has no chance for redemption, and the visual reminder of his ghastly deed gives posthumous voice to Pozdnyshev's nameless, murdered wife. From her coffin, the wife's corpse reminds the reader of the dangers of infidelity, jealousy, and marriage. The central place of the wife in Szalit's Tolstoy illustrations reflects her own sympathies toward women being able to engage in modern love affairs and lifestyles.

The reception of Szalit's Tolstoy illustrations was excellent. Writing about Szalit's oeuvre several years later, journalist Ger Trud noted that the Tolstoy illustrations possessed a strong, incisive power of interpretation. This writer observed that Szalit's illustrations of French author Alphonse Daudet's novel *Tartarin of Tarascon* and Dickens's short stories were equally compelling.[16] Indeed, the illustrations Szalit created for Dickens would become some of her best-known works.

Images of Dickens's London

In the spring of 1923, as Germany neared the peak of hyperinflation, the Hans Heinrich Tillgner Verlag in Berlin published a special edition of three stories by Charles Dickens. Translated by Ernst Sander, it was the fifth book in the publishing house's series Das Prisma and contained sixteen illustrations attributed to Rahel Szalit-Marcus. The three stories in this book are from Dickens's *Sketches by Boz* (first serialized in 1833–36), but the German title is more readily comprehensible: *Londoner Bilder*, or images of London. It is easy to see why this impressive book would have been considered a valuable object by those who sought to invest in artwork. The first hundred numbered copies have hardbound, gilded goatskin covers and delightfully thick handmade paper with rough edges. Other, less expensive copies have paper covers.[17] Ten of Szalit's illustrations are smaller, quarter-page illustrations. Each of the three stories is accompanied by two larger illustrations. In the numbered, leather-bound editions, the artist herself signed full-page lithographs in pencil: some as "R. Szalit-Marcus," and others simply as "R. Szalit," suggesting that she began using a more concise signature around the time this book was published.

The first of the three short stories in *Londoner Bilder*, "The Steam Excursion," deals with a grand party on a steamship. Led by law student Percy Noakes and his friends, members of London's high society embark on a day-long voyage on the *Endeavor*. Szalit avoided drawing much of the boat, choosing instead to show Percy taking note of the initially sunny weather, two children who join the party uninvited, the three Briggs sisters singing while playing a new Spanish composition on their three guitars, several guests becoming seasick as they and a vibrating table covered with dishes all pitch forward when a sudden storm hits, and three members of the party in final disarray. Here as elsewhere, the moments Szalit depicts are among the most entertaining and memorable. The singing women bear a strong resemblance to the women in her Tolstoy illustrations; the women wearing bonnets in the background of this image could be mistaken for women in her later Tillier images (fig. 23).

In "The Tuggses at Ramsgate," which opens near London Bridge, Joseph Tuggs and his family learn that they have come into a significant amount of family money. Though they are not explicitly labeled as Jews, the ways members of the Tuggs family immediately begin to style themselves as more aristocratic call to mind forms of Jewish assimilation in the nineteenth century. For example, their son Simon becomes Cymon (or Rimon, in German). The unfavorable depiction of this family is also in line with Dickens's problematic depictions of Jewish characters in other works.[18] The newly wealthy Tuggses prove easy targets. On their way to the seaside town of Ramsgate, the Tuggses befriend Captain Waters and his alluring wife, with whom they spend the next six weeks. The

INFLATION-ERA ILLUSTRATIONS

FIGURE 23 | R. Szalit-Marcus, *The Three Briggs Sisters*, illustration from Charles Dickens's "The Steam Excursion" in *Londoner Bilder*, 1923.

Captain and his wife, Belinda, are the subject of two of Szalit's illustrations; the donkeys that the ladies ride, and the chaotic ride that ensues, are depicted in several others.

The most picturesque of Szalit's images depicts a peaceful, romantic seaside scene featuring Cymon Tuggs and Belinda Waters (fig. 24). This calm moment occurs just before Captain Waters comes home to find Cymon hiding behind a curtain, as we see in another image. The Tuggs family, now obviously the dupes of the story, must pay hush money to Captain Waters to avoid a scandal. Interestingly, Szalit's images hardly focus on the Tuggses. Aside from Cymon's long nose shown in profile, which is not overly striking, there is nothing visual to suggest that Szalit interpreted them to be Jewish.

The final story in *Londoner Bilder*, "The Boarding-House," has two parts and is the longest in the book. Boardinghouse keeper Mrs. Tibbs and her hapless husband arrange for elegant dinners for their boarders, which leads to the planning of multiple surprise weddings of the Maplesone sisters and their mother to male boarders. Szalit notably did not take the bait Dickens laid for an illustrator with his remark "It would require the pencil of Hogarth to illustrate—our feeble pen is inadequate to describe—the expression which the countenances of Mr. Calton and Mr. Septimus Hicks respectively assumed, at this unexpected announcement [of a third planned marriage]." Instead, Szalit

FIGURE 24 | R. Szalit-Marcus, *Cymon Tuggs and Belinda Waters*, illustration from Charles Dickens's "The Tuggses at Ramsgate" in *Londoner Bilder*, 1923.

illustrated this story with one small image of the Tibbses and one full-page image of the boarders heading into dinner together.

In the second part of "The Boarding House," Mrs. Tibbs loses her initial Coram Street boarders to marriage, but new ones emerge. Szalit's image of Mrs. Bloss, a recently widowed and wealthy new boarder in Mrs. Tibbs's house, depicts this character in an unflattering way that remains faithful to Dickens's description of her as "fat and red-faced." When the antics of Mrs. Bloss's servant, Agnes, prompt Mrs. Tibbs to spy on Agnes in the middle of the night, confusion ensues and Mrs. Tibbs faints upon becoming an object of suspicion. This preposterous moment finds expression in Szalit's final illustration of London life, which shows angry and suspicious men, crying women, plotting servants, and generally hysterical boarders (fig. 25). Szalit depicts some of these figures comically, as Dickens also portrays them, but none are particularly surprising or outrageous in appearance.

FIGURE 25 | R. Szalit-Marcus, *Mrs. Tibbs Faints*, illustration from Charles Dickens's "The Boarding-House" in *Londoner Bilder*, 1923.

Journalist Moritz Goldstein observed that Szalit's Dickens illustrations, like her illustrations of Jewish literature from this same period, contained unforgettable folkloric characters that reflected her joy in creating vivid human figures.[19] The London milieu that Szalit captured nearly a century after Dickens envisioned it holds a prominent position among her contributions to world literature.[20] It was also her last limited-edition book to appear during a time when art and books were prized for their ability to retain value in tumultuous markets.

Tillier as Outlier

The only known published book that Szalit illustrated after the inflation period was French writer Claude Tillier's novel *My Uncle Benjamin* (1842/43; German title: *Mein Onkel Benjamin*). The best-known work by this non-Jewish author, it was translated from French into German by Ludwig Pfau in 1866 and was reprinted many times. Szalit illustrated a 1927 edition of Pfau's translation published by the Volksverband der Bücherfreunde (National Association of Bibliophiles) in its own Berlin publishing house, Wegweiser-Verlag. Founded in 1919, this bibliophile organization aimed to make German and world literature affordable for readers who were struggling economically after the First World War. This highly affordable book was thus the opposite of the valuable limited-edition books and portfolios that Szalit illustrated several years earlier.

We can venture a guess as to how Rahel Szalit came to illustrate Tillier's book. Literary scholar Hugo Bieber, who wrote the introduction to Szalit's 1923 portfolio of Heine illustrations (see chapter 6), was responsible for determining the Association of Bibliophiles' literary program beginning in the mid-1920s. He likely sought out Szalit as an illustrator based on his previous experience with her work. Bieber's choice was logical insofar as Szalit had already illustrated numerous other classic works of nineteenth-century literature, some of which were similarly humorous or satirical.

Set in the late eighteenth century, Tillier's tale follows the first-person narrator's great-uncle Benjamin Rathery, a country doctor who earns little, through halfhearted attempts to pay his debts. His main side occupations consist of searching for wine and women. Szalit also might have been chosen to illustrate this book because of a ruse in which Benjamin passes himself off as the Wandering Jew, pretending that his sister (the narrator's grandmother) is the Holy Virgin. Yet Szalit's illustration of this scene merely shows Benjamin together with his sister, who is wearing fancy clothes and riding a borrowed donkey (fig. 26). It is unclear whether this is meant to be Benjamin's performance of the Wandering Jew. Instead, the animal features prominently. Another, strikingly similar donkey would appear several years later in one of Szalit's illustrations of Thomas Mann's "Dina," set in biblical times.

FIGURE 26 | R. Szalit, *Benjamin Rathery and His Sister on a Donkey*, illustration from Claude Tillier's *My Uncle Benjamin*, 1927.

Although the story largely centers around the interactions of male characters with one another, half of Szalit's eight illustrations focus on the women in Tillier's novel. In addition to a pretty image of Manette, the rosy-cheeked peasant owner of a wine shop, Szalit's illustrations call the reader's attention to two central female characters: the narrator's grandmother, depicted by Szalit as surrounded by her many children (fig. 27), and Arabella Minxit, Benjamin's intended, who looks down mournfully at a flower (fig. 28). The grandmother surrounded by six small children vying for her attention is a timeless image of motherhood that could be from any century and country; only the woman's style of dress and hat and the number of her children suggest an earlier period. Szalit's depiction of Arabella as a stylish and elegant lady, in contrast, is strikingly modern in appearance. It illustrates the scene when Benjamin asks Arabella to confirm that she cannot marry Benjamin because she already loves another, yielding a woman the power of refusal, which was also a relatively modern concept. Indeed, Szalit's rendering of Arabella has more in common with images of women in twentieth-century fashion magazines and works that Szalit did in the late 1920s than with the other female characters in this novel.

FIGURE 27 | R. Szalit, *The Narrator's Grandmother*, illustration from Claude Tillier's *My Uncle Benjamin*, 1927.

Several of Szalit's illustrations in *My Uncle Benjamin* do not line up perfectly with the passages they depict, making them seem somewhat random and out of place. They also suggest that the locations of Szalit's images were determined by where the publisher wanted to insert high-quality image paper rather than by their correlation with the text. For example, Szalit's image of Old Sergeant Duranton sitting on the ground with his poodle, an illustration of a scene in the third chapter, appears in the book's twentieth and final chapter. The image of the narrator's grandmother is included one chapter later than the initial description of her large family, just as she has given birth to her seventh child. This disconnect between text and image leaves the reader curious as to whether Szalit's illustrations were intended to be read as part of the book, or whether they were more of an afterthought.

Today, Tillier's *My Uncle Benjamin* is among the least known of Szalit's surviving illustrated books. The title page contains no reference whatsoever to Szalit, all but erasing her contribution. Each of her illustrations is signed (six as "R. Szalit," two as "R. Szalit-Marcus"), however, and a separate loose insert explains that the illustrations are all original drawings by Rahel Szalit. This small piece of paper could easily have fallen out

FIGURE 28 | R. Szalit-Marcus, *Arabella Minxit, Benjamin's Intended*, illustration from Claude Tillier's *My Uncle Benjamin*, 1927.

of most copies, which perhaps explains why Szalit is not credited in any current library records of this edition. There was also little to no reception of the illustrations when the book was first published. Present-day readers can therefore acknowledge Szalit's overlooked contribution for the first time.

Szalit's illustrations of world literature (Dostoyevsky, Tolstoy, Dickens, Tillier)—which, with the exception of Tillier, were published between 1921 and 1923—appear distinct in some ways from the eastern Jewish subjects she portrayed using similar artistic techniques during these years. The facial features of non-Jewish characters are notably less exaggerated: noses are long and straight, not rounded and protruding; men's heads are bald and uncovered; women reveal their necks and shoulders and gaze through large, vapid eyes. Protagonists of Russian literature, though perhaps depicted comically, are undeniably human. Even where Szalit sketches a pivotal, if parenthetical, moment in world literature, such as when Dickens's Mrs. Tibbs faints and causes a scene, Szalit's renderings of non-Jewish subjects and their circumstances are more subdued and realistic. They are a far cry from the dreadful sneezing fits, apelike beggars, and ominous "Jewish gypsies" in her illustrations of Yiddish literature printed in 1922.

CHAPTER 5

Grotesque Yiddish Figures

Berlin-Mitte, May 1922: At the recently founded Klal-Farlag publishing house at Markgrafenstrasse 73, Rahel meets with esteemed literary critic Dr. Isidor Eliashev, who uses the pen name Bal-Makhshoves (Man of Thoughts). Like Rahel, Eliashev is originally from the Kovno region of Lithuania. He served as a physician in the war and is partly paralyzed. He strikes Rahel as melancholic, with sad eyes. Having recently returned to Berlin after many years in eastern Europe—in fact, he once shared an apartment with the Chagalls in Petrograd—he is now head of Klal-Farlag's Yiddish department. He and Rahel speak Yiddish together; she is honored to have the chance to meet with such a great man of letters. He, too, has heard tell of her work—Berlin is buzzing about her lithographs.

Rahel makes her case: "I have been working on illustrations for Sholem Aleichem's *Motl, the Cantor's Son* for several years now. The individual prints have been popular with collectors and have sold well. But now I would like to publish them together as a book. Would Klal-Farlag like to publish a new, illustrated edition of the Yiddish novel, or perhaps a German translation?"

Eliashev lights a cigarette while he considers these suggestions, but he makes Rahel a different offer. He responds thoughtfully: "There are already many Yiddish editions of *Motl*, and others are translating Sholem Aleichem into German. Besides, we can do better than just another book. What if we were to make a special limited-edition portfolio of your prints with a short introduction in Yiddish? I myself could write the introduction. This would be well received in the art world and the international Yiddish book market. It would be more accessible to collectors than a book, and it will let the images shine." Rahel thinks this over; print portfolios are indeed very popular. She has seen some by Hermann Struck and George Grosz.

Her eyes sparkle as she signs the contract drawn up by Eliashev's assistant. Rahel believes this will become a great work.

Berlin was home to a thriving East European Jewish culture in the early 1920s. About thirteen thousand Jews from the former Russian Empire and Austria-Hungary lived in Berlin by 1920, or roughly 10 percent of the city's Jewish population. By 1925, one quarter of Berlin's one hundred and seventy-two thousand Jews were immigrants, most from eastern Europe, creating a "Yiddish cultural microcosmos" that had a great impact on the broader Yiddish-speaking world.[1] Even the renowned Vilna theater troupe performed in Yiddish in Berlin in the early part of the decade.[2] Foreign publishers sought to take advantage of the inflation of the German mark, and Yiddish book production flourished at publishing houses such as Klal-Farlag.[3] Not coincidentally, this was also when Rahel Szalit's best-known illustrations of Yiddish literature were published.

At the same time, the highly visible presence of some eastern Jews brought unwanted attention to Jewish difference. The term used for eastern Jews, *Ostjuden*, had derogatory connotations, and many German Jews looked down on them while simultaneously mythologizing East European traditions as more authentic.[4] Depicting eastern Jews within this context was thus a precarious undertaking, as audiences were easily critical of these subjects and sensitive to the ways they were portrayed. Szalit's personal connections to eastern Europe gave her a distinct advantage in depicting these worlds for wider audiences—it was very unlikely that anyone would accuse her of prejudice against eastern Jews. Still, Szalit did not hesitate to portray some of her Jewish subjects in visually critical or parodic ways that underscored the distance between Jews in Germany (herself included) and Jews in the East. Her commentary on the differences and tensions between eastern and western Jews is particularly illuminating in light of her experiences in locations across Europe.

Laughter Through Tears

In late 1922, which was also when she held her first solo exhibition and her Tolstoy illustrations were published, Szalit was becoming increasingly well known among Yiddish speakers. Her print portfolios of Yiddish literary illustrations, *Motl* and *Fishke*, both hit the market that fall: *Fishke* in September 1922, *Motl* toward the end of the year. It is curious that these works did not make it into her solo exhibition in November, or at least they were not advertised, and we must wonder why Szalit would have refrained from exhibiting individual lithographs in the months after the portfolios appeared. Nevertheless, news of Szalit's work spread rapidly.

FIGURE 29 | Rahel Szalit-Marcus, *In the Emigration Office / Miss Zaichik from "Ezra,"* illustration from Sholem Aleichem's *Motl, the Cantor's Son* in *Milgroym* and *Menshelakh un stsenes* (People and Scenes) portfolio, 1922.

In October, the Yiddish arts-and-letters magazine *Milgroym* spotlighted Szalit in its second-ever issue in an article with the English title "The Lithograph, A Chapter from the History of Graphic Art" (Yiddish title: *Di antviklung fun der moderner grafik: di litografye*). This article took Szalit as its primary representative of modern Jewish lithographers, claiming that she was an heir to such masters of this technique as Francisco Goya and Honoré Daumier. (Several years later, Max Osborn would pronounce Abraham Palukst a "Jewish Goya" because Palukst "translates into black-and-white language the dreams of a harassed soul that longs imploringly for rescue.")[5] The *Milgroym* article's author, one R. Inbar, offered close readings of Szalit's two lithographs that appeared with the article. The sobering scene in *In the Emigration Office* (fig. 29; titled *Froyleyn Zaichik fun "Ezra"* in Szalit's *Motl* portfolio) uses a backdrop of shadows to highlight the struggles of a haggard, distraught-looking emigrant woman and her young child interacting with a female clerk, who gives a "terrible grimace-smile."[6] But in Sholem Aleichem's novel, Froyleyn Zaichik at the Antwerp "Ezra" office is a compassionate Yiddish-speaking girl who keeps meticulous records and gives Motl gifts such as candy and shoes. Szalit's interpretation of this scene is much darker; compassion is distorted through the trauma of upheaval. If Froyleyn Zaichik appears at all helpful, she also symbolizes the arduous and unpleasant endeavor endured by many Jews seeking to relocate around this time.

Most notably, the *Milgroym* article suggested that Szalit's work exemplified the Jewish approach to lithography. About *The Drive to the Rabbi* (fig. 30), Inbar wrote: "The parched horse also hovers like a shadow, the Jewish horse [*dos yidishe ferd*], skin and bones. A collective scene with a national scope, as in Goya's *Bullfight*, only on a lesser scale. The [*pafos/pathos*], expressed with Jewish folk character (*yidishen folkskharekter*)."[7] Here we can guess that *pafos* (fodder) is a typo and might instead refer to *pathos*. This would constitute a broader claim, perhaps hinting at Szalit's affiliation with Steinhardt and Meidner, the Pathetiker. Either way, Inbar alludes to connections between Szalit's subjects and East European folk art. Szalit's heavy lines depicting the withered horse and weary-looking men further prompted Inbar to comment on the "gallows humor" present in Yiddish culture but absent from the lively works of Daumier. In other words, the style expressed in Szalit's lithographs conjured up a specifically Jewish/Yiddish form of humor and emotion that reflected the tragic, desperate plight of many eastern Jews.

In the case of the men and horse traveling to see the rabbi, Szalit approached her subject from a distinctly Jewish angle: like the Yiddish language, the group enters the frame from the right and moves toward the left.[8] The hats and beards of these men arguably mark them as Jewish; their goal of visiting a rabbi helps the viewer see them as part of a Jewish collective. It is the reluctance of the horse and the general awkwardness of leading him to the rabbi that evoke eastern folklore. The "Jewish horse" represents the

FIGURE 30 | Rahel Szalit-Marcus, *The Drive to the Rabbi*, in *Milgroym*, 1922. Courtesy of the Leo Baeck Institute, call number q N 8 M5.

everyday struggle of East European Jews to engage with their surroundings, including animals.

Indeed, the qualities with which Rahel Szalit imbued her eastern Jewish subjects tell of a long history of affliction while also pointing out the comical or absurd nature of individual moments. But distorting these subjects had the potential to alienate viewers who did not understand how to find beauty in ugliness. Many who viewed her images of eastern Jews saw them as grotesque, often referring to their bizarre, exaggerated misshapenness. When aligned with French poet Charles Baudelaire's notion of caricature, the grotesque can be a form of satire that is "at once laughable and troublingly recognizable."[9] Szalit herself freely adopted the term "grotesque." In a description of her strong connection to her childhood, Szalit wrote:

> I have the feeling that my whole childhood world lies dormant somewhere within my soul, always ready to appear before my eyes at the right moment.

This requires only a mood, music, poetry—a faraway song, and an indefinable longing comes over me, something rings out within.... I feel the urge to represent what I perceive. Obstacles, suffering, and joy join together—I just need to draw them. I experience all of this so deeply that often the abject misery to which I give shape leaves me severely shaken. I suffer—suffer almost physically with them, and out of a drive for self-preservation I reach for my instinctive humor and bestow my figures with grotesque ideas [*mit grotesken Einfällen*] that mitigate their tragedy. But it is a laughter through tears. This is how my ideas are born.[10]

Szalit evidently wanted audiences to engage with the ways humor served Jewish artists as a strategy for dealing with hardship. Her work was built on the principle of overcoming misery.

The concept of "laughter through tears" is often associated with Yiddish literature. Along with many others, Szalit attributed this phrase and its particular form of "self-irony" to Sholem Aleichem.[11] The 1928 Soviet silent film based on *Motl* also had the title *Laughter Through Tears*. Literary scholar Jeremy Dauber has pointed out that "how to turn trauma into joy" is a key theme of *Motl*, noting that Motl shouts, "Hurray—I'm an orphan!" to rewrite his own misery.[12] In a similar vein, Jewish humor and jokes in German contexts have long been perceived as a direct response to the oppression of the Jews as a people, an attempt to find relief from suffering.[13] The notion of laughter through tears takes on new dimensions when given visual form by Szalit: her art is not only about finding moments of happiness but also about the process of working through times of affliction.

In Szalit's lithographs, pain, discomfort, extreme poverty, misfortune, and even disability become sites for envisioning the eastern Jewish experience. Szalit's efforts to attenuate or distract from suffering, or to underscore its horrors, result in images that walk the line between humor and caricature, at times reproducing stereotypes about eastern Jews. Illustrations of classic Yiddish works provide the clearest examples of her use of exaggerated or grotesque features to make Jewishness legible; as a rule, we do not find these same exaggerations in her representations of non-Jews or of Jews in other contexts. But what does it mean for a Jewish artist to call attention to the Jewishness of her eastern subjects by making them appear stereotypical or unattractive? How can we sympathize with the plight of eastern Jews if we are also mildly shocked by their appearance?

The answer, in short, is that Szalit's complex representations provide both a window onto eastern experiences and critical commentary on them. There is little sense of pure nostalgia in these images, despite the poetic assertion in Hersh Fenster's memorial lexicon that Szalit's works expressed warm remembrances for her childhood.[14] (We find something that more closely resembles nostalgia in Szalit's Heine illustrations.) Instead, her often ironic visual accounts of eastern Jews respond to aspects of cultural experiences that Szalit wishes to highlight as absurd or untenable. In this way, Szalit engaged with the same kind of othering gaze present in the ethnographic techniques of much of Yiddish realism, as well as with works by Jews in and around Germany that similarly treated East European Jews as other.[15] Her satire adds layers of playfulness and sophistication, rendering them worthy of careful analysis and interpretation. One must be both clever and in on the joke to interpret ugliness and hardship as tragically humorous.

By entering the realm of the bizarre, Szalit's Yiddish illustrations also set Jewish difference in dialogue with avant-garde modernist movements such as Expressionism and even Dadaism. Here we find additional similarities between her work and the exaggerated, jagged subjects portrayed by Ludwig Meidner. Contemporary German artists such as Otto Dix and George Grosz, who often worked in a satirical, grotesque style, may have influenced Szalit as well. Of course, there were other Jewish artists known especially for their grotesque representations, but the best example—Chaim Soutine, a Yiddish-speaking artist who made his way from the Russian Empire to Paris in 1913—did not depict overtly Jewish figures, though some argue that hints of Jewishness can be found in his work.[16] In Szalit's work, though, there was no shortage of Jews, Jewish traditions, and Jewish suffering and resilience.

Suffering, Spanking, and Sneezing in Sholem Aleichem

It was with her illustrations of Yiddish literature that Szalit truly established herself as a Jewish artist. Her two surviving sets were published in Berlin in 1922 as print portfolios, each with sixteen images designed to accompany well-known novels by major Yiddish writers: *Motl, the Cantor's Son*, the unfinished final work by Sholem Aleichem (written from 1907 to 1916, first part published in 1911), and *Fishke the Lame* (1888) by Mendele Moykher Sforim. Both showcase Szalit's Expressionist style to a T. Many who saw these illustrations did not gain access to the most valuable original portfolios, which were printed in limited editions of numbered copies, but instead encountered less valuable versions or individual lithographs in periodicals or exhibitions.

Though she was likely commissioned to illustrate other works of literature, in this case the story goes that Szalit first took it upon herself to read and engage with the Yiddish classics. These works held different potential for her as an artist. She later described what made Yiddish literature unique: "The greatest experience for me is illustrating Jewish literature. To delve into a book by Sholem Aleichem or Mendele Moykher Sforim, to follow everything that his characters do, is a high artistic measure. The language is unbelievably vivid, full of Talmudic sayings. To draw the figures who masterfully wind their way through a hard life with humor and self-irony—is superb."[17] Szalit's own words suggest that she was inspired by this type of humor, that it infused her drawings. We can only imagine how Szalit managed to get these two sets of prints published as portfolios. Other opportunities, such as her illustrations of the tales of Reb Nachman of Breslov, of which no copies have survived and about which we know very little, may have come to Szalit via Rachel Wischnitzer and the Rimon Publishing Company.

Of Szalit's two surviving Yiddish portfolios, only the *Motl* illustrations were published with Yiddish captions and text and were thus intended for Yiddish speakers. This portfolio, titled *Menshelakh un stsenes* (the full title translates as *[Little] People and Scenes: Sixteen Illustrations to Sholem Aleichem's Work "Motl, Peysi the Cantor's Son"*), was attributed to "Fr. Markus-Szalit," though the images are signed "Rahel Szalit-Marcus." The Yiddish-Hebrew publishing house Klal-Farlag printed fifty numbered, leather-bound copies, as well as additional paperbound copies; many of the paperbound copies survive today. The title page image shows a sad, unidentified woman sitting with her children and what appear to be suitcases, presumably in transit (fig. 31). The portfolio included a short essay by critic Bal-Makhshoves (Isidor Eliashev), head of Yiddish literature for Klal-Farlag, as well as an eight-page summary text that explained the plot in some depth, presumably also written by Eliashev. In fact, Eliashev was one of the first critics to take Sholem Aleichem seriously, making him the perfect person to contextualize Szalit's images.[18] In his

FIGURE 31 | Rahel Szalit-Marcus, *Woman Sitting with Children*, title page of *Menshelakh un stsenes* (People and Scenes) portfolio, illustration from Sholem Aleichem's *Motl, the Cantor's Son*, 1922.

introductory essay to Szalit's portfolio, Eliashev concluded that of all modern graphic artists, only Szalit had attempted illustrations of *Motl*, making them part of her life's work. He further called Szalit's illustrations a "beautiful gift" for fans of Sholem Aleichem and concluded that her drawings would spark new interest in the *Motl* story.[19]

Though connected to Germany mainly through their place of publication, Szalit's *Motl* illustrations offer a "western" perspective insofar as they gain distance from their subjects and depict eastern Jews as other. These lithographs emphasize East European Jewish difference through their grotesque portrayals of both physical characteristics and behaviors. Scholar Sabine Koller, who has written about Szalit's *Motl* illustrations, has rightly observed that Szalit always depicts Motl and his friend Pinye in a hyperbolic fashion.[20] Minor characters, too, are exaggerated in every image. Faces and facial features are distorted, elongated, and sometimes even unrecognizable as human. Yiddish-speaking audiences in Berlin and beyond, many of whom also had origins in these eastern worlds, would easily have recognized the absurdity of the moments and figures Szalit depicted.

These illustrations give visual form to the trials and tribulations of nine-year-old Motl and his family, first at home in Kasrilevke (a fictional town invented by Sholem Aleichem) and then as they journey through various cities in Europe. In Sholem Aleichem's story, Motl narrates his family's travels from Kasrilevke to Brody, Lemberg, Krakow, Vienna, Antwerp, and London as they attempt to reach America. This mirrors the route taken by Sholem Aleichem and his family in 1905. In the second part of *Motl*, Motl's family eventually settles on the Lower East Side of New York. Szalit's illustrations, however, take them only as far as Antwerp, where they watch with envy as friends board a ship to America. Szalit's final illustration shows a heart-wrenching scene of Jewish men, women, and children weeping and embracing (fig. 32). Some board the ship, whereas others stand with their backs to the ship, facing the viewer, eyes downcast.[21] Szalit drew on firsthand familiarity to create her illustrations. But, like Szalit herself, who at a young age separated from her family in eastern Europe, her Jewish migrants make it only as far as central and perhaps western Europe.

We can assume that Szalit herself selected which parts of the story merited illustrations, and that her choices highlight what she considered to be especially interesting scenes from Jewish life in the Russian Empire. Since Szalit herself never left Europe for America, it is only fitting that the figures in her illustrations also do not cross the Atlantic. In fact, of the fifteen illustrations that appear in sequence, eleven portray scenes from Kasrilevke, and only four show the family as emigrants on the move. This stands in contrast to Sholem Aleichem's original text, in which over 40 percent of the first part deals with Motl's family's journey.[22]

In her other *Motl* illustrations, reminiscent of photographic snapshots, Szalit attempts to capture the immediacy of particularly absurd moments. In one illustration of life in

FIGURE 32 | Rahel Szalit-Marcus, *We Say Goodbye to Our Loved Ones at the Ship*, illustration from Sholem Aleichem's *Motl, the Cantor's Son*, 1922.

Kasrilevke, Moishe the bookbinder uses a board to whack a boy who made fun of Motl. Szalit captures him mid-whack, with either a scream or a very pained expression on the boy's face (fig. 33). Out of context, this image shows the brutality with which Jewish elders disciplined unruly youths. Although it is possible to interpret such inflicted pain as a reflection of Jewish childhood suffering, one might also take offense at its explicit content or the fact that it could have been considered representative of Jewish life. The composition of this lithograph—a grown man spanking a bare-bottomed, screaming young boy—anticipates another societally critical drawing that Szalit created several years later. This illustration accompanied a journal article by sexual reformer Magnus Hirschfeld titled "Prügelpädagogen" (Abusive Pedagogues), which addressed the dangers of corporal punishment in mainstream contexts (fig. 34).[23] Taken together, the two images suggest that Szalit's own stance on this issue was in line with Hirschfeld's, and that shocking visuals were needed to convey the trauma inflicted on children by way of beatings intended to teach them a lesson.

Several other *Motl* images render Jewish life in Kasrilevke as not only brutal but also ridiculous and pathetic. Motl's poor yet enterprising family embarks on escapades that lend themselves perfectly to such scenes. Szalit devotes four illustrations to the far-fetched

INFLATION-ERA ILLUSTRATIONS

FIGURE 33 | Rahel Szalit-Marcus, *Moishe the Bookbinder Whacks the Children with a Board*, illustration from Sholem Aleichem's *Motl, the Cantor's Son*, 1922.

moneymaking schemes of Motl and his brother Elyahu, thereby focusing on the folly of desperation. Two images show Elyahu preparing a drink called kvass and Motl trying to peddle the kvass from a jug at the marketplace. This works until Motl adds soapy water to the kvass. Another shows Elyahu and Motl mixing a huge supply of ink and pouring it into bottles. Their faces and hands are stained black from the ink, which no one wants to buy.

Another image of grotesque, sneezing figures attracted significant attention. Szalit's striking illustration of a scheme to drive away rats, *A Street Sneezes*, was later reprinted in the *Jüdische Rundschau* and exhibited independently (fig. 35).[24] Here, four people sneeze simultaneously because Motl accidentally bursts open a sack of fake rat poison that is actually sneezing powder (possibly pepper). Szalit depicts the characters midsneeze, but their expressions could easily be construed as animalistic howls. The faces of the sneezers are contorted beyond recognition, though it is still possible to make out traditional eastern attire. Their bodies are stooped, bent, and out of control. Upon seeing this image exhibited in 1928, critic Ruth Morold noted that it was reminiscent of "primitive Russian

FIGURE 34 | R. Szalit, *Prügelpädagogen* (Abusive Pedagogues), illustration from Magnus Hirschfeld's article in *Die Aufklärung*, 1929. Courtesy of the Magnus-Hirschfeld-Gesellschaft e.V.

grotesques."[25] This comparison reminds us that some viewers engaged in more politicized readings of Szalit's images, as we will see was the case with collector Eduard Fuchs.

In addition to her *Motl* illustrations, Rahel Szalit later illustrated a few short stories by Sholem Aleichem that highlight other comical adventures with Jewish traditions. Simple line drawings in the *Israelitisches Familienblatt* accompanied a German translation of "Chanukkah-Gelt: A Humorous Story." The father lights Hanukkah candles; he and an uncle quibble over moves in a game of checkers while tapping their feet to keep rhythm, as they would do while learning Talmud; and an aunt helps a young child blow his nose.[26] The preface to this story suggests it could teach German Jews about East European Jewish customs for celebrating Hanukkah. It thus comes as no surprise that Szalit's drawings show traditional Jewish scenes without adding much in the way of commentary.

The Hanukkah images stand in contrast to Szalit's illustrations of "Chickens on Strike: A Humorous Yom-Kippur Story," which make light of both the ritual and the rabbis' plan to try to negotiate with the chickens. As we saw in the introduction, Szalit's illustrations focus on the plight of the chickens (fig. 2). Because of the simplicity of these drawings, the characters do not appear grossly exaggerated, though their traditional or modest attire, men's long, pointy beards, and women's covered heads still help mark figures as East European Jews.

FIGURE 35 | Rahel Szalit-Marcus, *A Street Sneezes*, illustration from Sholem Aleichem's *Motl, the Cantor's Son*, 1922.

Caricatures of Jews

Some contemporary critics understood Szalit's work as sarcastic caricatures of Jews. The best example is German Marxist cultural historian and collector Eduard Fuchs's illustrated book *Die Juden in der Karikatur* (Caricatures of the Jews, 1921), which included two of Szalit's *Motl* illustrations, both with altered captions. One image, originally titled "We're Going to America," appeared in Fuchs's book as "The Sun Rises in the West."[27] As in other *Motl* illustrations, the Jewish figures in this image are frightening, ugly, and distorted (fig. 36). Their noses resemble those in antisemitic caricatures. The other image of a modestly dressed woman, "The Pious Jewish Woman," was retitled "The Agent" by Fuchs, suggesting that an image of an observant Jewish woman was highly susceptible to critique or misinterpretation.[28]

Fuchs's study of antisemitic and satirical representations of Jews concludes with a section on "Jewish self-mockery" that has ideological Marxist undertones. We see this especially where Fuchs corrects the title assigned to Szalit's image, arguing that the sun

FIGURE 36 | Rahel Szalit-Marcus, *We're Going to America*, illustration from Sholem Aleichem's *Motl, the Cantor's Son*, 1922.

does not rise in the West (America) but rather in the East (Soviet Russia).[29] But by and large, Fuchs viewed self-irony as a form of self-defense against antisemitism.[30] Finding the humor in one's own situation was better than merely being laughed at by others. Whereas Fuchs notes that Szalit's lithographs can be interpreted as satirical caricatures of Jewish figures, he also emphasizes the tenderness with which she created them as well as their favorable aspects. Fuchs observes that, like Chagall, Szalit portrays "the distinguishing characteristics of Jewish physiognomy" with scorn that is at the same time a positively inflected embrace of difference.[31] The fact that Fuchs took Szalit's images entirely out of context suggests he was more concerned with promoting his own messages than with offering a serious interpretation of her work. Still, the question remains: what, if anything, differentiates Szalit's images from other caricatures included in Fuchs's book? Why would Jews choose to reproduce stereotypical features and problematic situations?

The answer lies, in my view, in the shock value of stereotypes and how memorable Szalit could make them appear. That which is as repulsive as it is interesting may be the most difficult to forget. Fuchs's work on caricatures attracted the attention of cultural critic Walter Benjamin. In an essay from 1937, Benjamin argues that Fuchs stressed "the value of caricature as a source, as authority," and Benjamin further describes the grotesque as "a shocking reflection of the fact that for the times and individuals in question, the problems of the world and of existence appear insoluble."[32] While Szalit's illustrations bring some sense to the nonsensical, they also remind us that the truth can be grisly and despicable, and that maintaining a sense of humor can help us contemplate this reality. Szalit's works show the effects of oppression and antisemitism by depicting downtrodden Jews, leaving us at once mildly alarmed and commiserative. By confronting the viewer with eastern Jews in exaggerated forms, Szalit calls attention to the need to face grotesque realities head-on, and she does this from the perspective of one who had left some of them behind.

Fishke, the Repulsive Beggar

As in her illustrations of Sholem Aleichem's *Motl*, the subjects of Szalit's illustrations of *Fishke the Lame* are afflicted eastern Jews whose bodily otherness takes on radical dimensions. But in contrast to the Yiddish-language publication context of the *Motl* illustrations, Szalit's *Fishke* illustrations appeared in a portfolio printed by the German Propyläen-Verlag, a luxury imprint of Ullstein established in 1919. The *Fishke* portfolio appeared shortly before September 1922. The first twenty of the one hundred numbered copies of the *Fishke* portfolio are the most valuable: they were printed on highest quality "Japan" paper, bound with one leather cover, and during inflation originally priced at twenty-eight hundred marks each. (A few years later, with the new stable currency, the portfolio was priced at sixty Reichsmark.) The remaining eighty copies were printed on handmade paper, bound with one linen cover, and priced at only twelve hundred marks.[33] Lithographs are hand-signed by Rahel Szalit-Marcus. Each *Fischke der Krumme* portfolio contains annotations and a richly detailed plot summary in German by art historian Julius Elias, suggesting it was aimed at a German readership that might view eastern Jews through a somewhat different lens.[34]

Julius Elias was undoubtedly an important connection for Rahel Szalit. As an art historian, literary scholar, and art collector, he served as director of the Propyläen-Verlag's art program and commissioned many bibliophile editions of illustrated books and portfolios. Among the other portfolios he helped publish are Lovis Corinth's *Kompositionen* (Compositions, 1921–22), Max Pechstein's *Das Vater Unser* (The Lord's Prayer, 1921), and Emil Orlik's *Aus Ägypten* (From Egypt, 1922). Prior to this, Elias had published several books on Max Liebermann, including one on Liebermann's graphic works featuring the etching *Judengasse in Amsterdam* (Jewish Street in Amsterdam, 1906).[35] Elias may have served as a link between Szalit and the journal *Der Querschnitt* (The Cross Section), to which Szalit began contributing in 1925, after it moved to the Propyläen-Verlag. Szalit likely also knew Julius's wife, Julie Elias, a journalist and fashion writer who was involved with exhibitions of the Association of Women Artists in Berlin.

Fishke is one of the best-known novels by the "grandfather of Yiddish literature," Sholem Yankev Abramovitsh, who published under the pen name Mendele Moykher Sforim (literally: Mendele the Book Peddler). Literary scholar Dan Miron has suggested that Abramovitsh was known as "the first modern Jewish writer both in Yiddish and in Hebrew who accurately and poignantly described what his eye saw and his ear heard."[36] Abramovitsh's realistic and mimetic writing style indeed held strong appeal for his readers. The basic story of *Fishke the Lame* is simple: Reb Mendele and Reb Alter set out on their carts to sell books to Jews all over Poland. Along the way they listen to the intriguing life story of Fishke, a simpleminded "cripple" who is described as having crooked yellow teeth, a mild stammer, a heavy lisp, a hunchback, and a very bad limp.[37] A beggar himself, Fishke circulates among other unsavory characters.

Even before Szalit's illustrations, Abramovitsh's depictions of Fishke's encounters with the underworld of Jewish beggars were considered potentially problematic for some German audiences. In a review of Alexander Eliasberg's 1918 translation of *Fishke* into German, German-Jewish critic Ludwig Geiger expressed doubts "whether it is opportune to present the public at large with such atrocities" lest readers conclude that "those Jews are a filthy, dangerous kind of the worst criminals, the true scum of humanity."[38] Despite this fear, Geiger expressed personal sympathy with the character of Fishke. Geiger's review reveals a sense of embarrassment about eastern Jewish poverty—not

FIGURE 37 | Rahel Szalit-Marcus, *Reb Mendele and the Moon*, illustration from Mendele Moykher Sforim's *Fishke the Lame*, 1922. Courtesy of the Klau Library, Cincinnati, Hebrew Union College-Jewish Institute of Religion.

all German Jews wanted to be reminded of such realities, nor did they wish to provoke antisemitic responses to eastern Jewish otherness. We can only imagine how those who were embarrassed or disturbed by East European Jews might have viewed Szalit's work.

Szalit's *Fishke* illustrations provide an Expressionist counterpoint to Abramovitsh's realistic depictions of impoverished Jews by visually elongating, enlarging, and magnifying Jewish difference. Dark, haunting scenes of fenced-in wooden houses provide a backdrop for ghost-like figures. In one lithograph that perfectly recalls the angular architectural lines of Expressionist film imagery, Szalit portrays the character Reb Mendele pouring out his troubles to the moon while looking somewhat otherworldly (fig. 37). Julius Elias, in his German-language introduction, called the volume of Szalit's illustrations "a humorously viewed and tragically perceived conception of the world of extremely proletarian East European Jewry."[39] Yet the humor in Szalit's images is not only tragic but also bizarre and horrifying, and at times it crosses over into the realm of what under other circumstances might be construed as antisemitic.

Fishke is the ideal character for Szalit's hand. In her rendering, he appears animalistic and somewhat apelike (fig. 38). As we inquire into this symbolism, we recall that Szalit excelled at drawing animals. Szalit's images of Fishke stand in contrast to a contemporary rendering of Fishke by Austrian artist Uriel Birnbaum, who focused on Fishke's cane and thus emphasized his disability over his physical features.[40] Szalit's Fishke also appears somewhat childish, and in one image his stance parallels that of Motl peddling kvass. In addition to bearing markers of the afflictions Abramovitsh describes, Szalit's Fishke appears disheveled and wears tattered garments; he represents the wretched Jewish beggar one might encounter in any corner of eastern Europe. Though he tears at the viewer's heartstrings, he is also repulsive and even repellent.[41] With this image, Szalit challenges us to confront the pain and suffering of the beggar who repels us. Because Fishke is so off-putting, we must remember to consider his fate and be compassionate. At the same time, we are grateful to be viewing this character from afar.

Many of the Jewish characters in Szalit's *Fishke* portfolio appear tragically sympathetic in some way. Her illustrations exaggerate and call the viewer's attention to the noses of Fishke and other Jewish characters, which in her drawings are oversized, misshapen, and often end in a shaded point. Another image shows the marauding band of beggars that Fishke joins with his wife, a blind orphan (fig. 39). The traveling beggars, who at one point are referred to as "Jewish gypsies," unsurprisingly possess some of the most grotesque traits: one appears naked, several quarrel, and some have distorted or clown-like facial features.[42] This and other scenes of chiaroscuro interiors and exteriors that play with light and shadow point to tensions between an ominous impoverished Jewish existence and the search for light.

FIGURE 38 | Rahel Szalit-Marcus, *Fishke the Lame*, illustration from Mendele Moykher Sforim's *Fishke the Lame*, 1922. Courtesy of the Klau Library, Cincinnati, Hebrew Union College-Jewish Institute of Religion.

GROTESQUE YIDDISH FIGURES

FIGURE 39 | Rahel Szalit-Marcus, *The Traveling Band of Beggars*, illustration from Mendele Moykher Sforim's *Fishke the Lame*, 1922. Courtesy of the Klau Library, Cincinnati, Hebrew Union College-Jewish Institute of Religion.

As with the *Motl* images, several *Fishke* illustrations were reproduced out of context and came to serve as visual shorthand for authentic shtetl Jews and their daily lives and rituals. One image that appears to show a boy being quizzed on his knowledge of the Talmud was reprinted in the Viennese Jewish magazine *Menorah* with the caption "First Talmud Examination" without any reference to *Fishke*.[43] Taken on its own, the image supposedly depicts knowledge-sharing among generations of East European Jews, including an observant Jewish woman with covered head and a "teacher" complete with caftan and beard (fig. 40). Yet within the narrative of the original story, this image depicts a nonsensical conversation between Reb Mendele the Book Peddler and the innkeeper Chaje-Trajne's idiot son. The boy's teacher looks on from the sidelines while Reb Mendele attempts to make sense out of the boy's answers. This is hardly an examination in traditional Jewish texts. Rather, its Expressionistic use of shadowing and contour casts East European Jews as unknown and other.

FIGURE 40 | Rahel Szalit-Marcus, *Reb Mendele and the Innkeeper's Son/ Erste Talmudprüfung* (First Talmud Examination), illustration from Mendele Moykher Sforim's *Fishke the Lame*, 1922. Courtesy of the Klau Library, Cincinnati, Hebrew Union College-Jewish Institute of Religion.

Szalit's *Fishke* images were both unforgettable and accessible to a broad audience of German-speakers. In late 1922, the portfolio earned a mention in *Der Cicerone*, the German magazine for art collectors edited by Karl Schwarz, suggesting that it became a collector's item almost immediately.[44] Some critics writing about Szalit in the following decade referred to the *Fishke* illustrations as her best work, arguing that they conveyed the absurd "Jewish humor" unique to Jewish culture and Jewish artists.[45] Szalit effectively translated this Yiddish humor into Expressionist prints that held appeal far beyond Jewish circles—though they were undoubtedly upsetting to those who feared they might stoke the antisemitic fires.

Jews with distorted, exaggerated, or grotesque features constitute the main subjects of Szalit's interpretations of Yiddish literature. If we perceive Szalit's representations of Jews as more authentic because she was raised in eastern Europe, then we must also acknowledge the artistic license this personal proximity to her subjects gave her. It was only because Szalit was one of "them" that she could project visible difference onto eastern Jews at every turn. Her outsider status made her an insider in a privileged position.[46] The fact that her illustrations of characters in *Motl* and *Fishke*, among others, are mildly shocking is precisely what makes them compelling and memorable illustrations. Her use of humor made it easier for viewers to confront tragedy, hardships, and oppression.

When we contrast Szalit's illustrations of Yiddish literature with her images of Jews in German contexts, for example in Heine's "Hebrew Melodies," we can conclude that her characters from eastern Europe are nearly always more exaggerated. Szalit's appeal within Jewish circles in Germany certainly hinged on a broader fixation on eastern authenticity and difference. But Jewish readers and critics in and beyond Germany had a great appreciation for Szalit's ability to connect them to faraway worlds.

CHAPTER 6

"Hebrew Melodies"

Berlin, June 1923: The telephone rings loudly, waking Rahel early in the morning on Wednesday, 20 June. Her friend Maria asks, "Have you seen yesterday evening's Vossische Zeitung? Did you see the feuilleton 'below the line' on page two?" No, Rahel hasn't seen it yet—what does it say? Maria continues: "Why, it's a lovely article about your illustrations of Heine's 'Hebrew Melodies.' It's taken directly from Hugo Bieber's text. You should go out and get a copy as soon as possible!" Rahel is very pleased to hear that Dr. Bieber's text has made it into a major paper. This is excellent publicity—everyone reads "Tante Voss." The illustrations were interesting to create. She loved envisioning Heine's magical scenes. And, barring Goethe or Schiller, there's no better way to establish oneself in German literary and artistic circles than to illustrate Heine.

When Dr. Bieber first contacted Rahel about putting together a portfolio of Heine illustrations, he invited her to visit his family's home on a tree-lined street in Grunewald. Over coffee and cake prepared by Frau Bieber, they discussed Heine's Jewish identity, exile years in Paris, correspondents, as well as his final poetry collection containing the "Hebrew Melodies." They also talked about the status of Jews in Germany and the growing antisemitism directed at religious East European Jews in particular.

Dr. Bieber was proud to have served on the front lines in the German military, but he could understand why Heine had fled to France. Life was precarious for German Jews in the early nineteenth century; Heine took refuge in Paris for the last twenty-five years of his life. Dr. Bieber asked Rahel if she felt safe in Berlin as a Jew from eastern Europe. She responded that Berlin still felt safer to her than Lithuania or Poland, but, like Heine, she would relocate to Paris if the need arose.

The year 1923 was Rahel Szalit's year of Hebrew poetry. Among her publications facilitated by hyperinflation were illustrations of the "Hebrew Melodies" (1851) poetry cycle of German-Jewish poet Heinrich Heine and a children's book by celebrated Hebrew poet Hayim Nahman Bialik. Berlin was home to numerous Hebrew writers beginning around 1910, and Bialik's presence there from 1921 to 1924 (while waiting to emigrate to the Land of Israel) helped make Berlin the largest enclave of Hebrew culture in Europe. Many prominent Hebrew writers from eastern Europe and Palestine came to Berlin during this period. Like Yiddish publishing, Hebrew-language publishing flourished, largely financed by foreign currency. In fact, Bialik's own work as a publisher in Berlin was nearly as important to him as his literary production. Hebrew culture of course contributed to the Jewish Renaissance, though Hebrew writers were not always engaged with the German culture around them.[1] That Szalit had the opportunity to illustrate one of Bialik's books reflects her renown in Jewish circles. As an East European Jew who illustrated Yiddish, Hebrew, and German-Jewish literature, she also served as a bridge between Jewish groups.

Szalit's illustrations of Heine and Bialik had vastly different publication contexts and intended audiences. What unites them is that the Jews they depict are neither East European nor the subjects of grotesque satire. Instead of Jewish difference, these images emphasize traditional Jewish rituals, history, and youthful potential. With her Hebrew-themed images, Szalit conveys the reader to different settings, and especially to the Middle East. They offer a connection to medieval Spain and Jerusalem, to 1920s Zionism, and to other modernist works focused on Jews in such contexts. Taken together, and along with Szalit's illustrations of Yiddish literature and works with biblical themes, they reflect Szalit's breadth as an illustrator of Jews in a wide range of settings.

Modern Echoes of Heine

Heine's engagement, as a prominent German writer, with Jewish topics from Sabbath rituals to medieval Jewry laid the foundation for subsequent writers to take up similar subjects, often through references to Heine. Heine's novel fragment *Der Rabbi von Bacherach* (The Rabbi of Bacherach, 1840), for one, inspired such works as Else Lasker-Schüler's *Der Wunderrabbiner von Barcelona* (The Wonder-Working Rabbi of Barcelona, 1921).[2] This was not the modernist poet's first ode to Heine, nor her last; Lasker-Schüler's poetry collection *Hebräische Balladen* (1913) also referenced Heine's *Hebräische Melodien* through both its title and "oriental" subject matter. Beyond the German-speaking world, Heine was widely read and translated into Jewish languages. Bialik even contributed a translation of Heine's "Princess Sabbath" to a Yiddish edition of Heine's works in 1918. The

Zionist movement further debated considering Heine as a Jewish national poet, though there was some concern about appropriating him anachronistically for this cause.[3]

Just as Heine was beloved and widely known among Jewish readers, his works were extremely popular among Jewish illustrators in Germany. Joseph Budko published illustrations of Heine's *Der Rabbi von Bacharach* in 1921, the same year that El Lissitzky's "Chad Gadya" color lithographs were published as illustrations for a different edition of that work. Max Liebermann's illustrations of *Der Rabbi von Bacharach* appeared with the Propyläen-Verlag in 1923. Additionally, a new edition of *Romanzero* (1851), the poetry collection in which *Hebräische Melodien* first appeared, was published in 1923 with an introduction by Alfred Kerr. In fact, Kerr's introduction to *Romanzero* was reprinted in the *Jüdische Rundschau* only days before Bieber's essay on Szalit appeared in the *Vossische Zeitung*.[4]

It is therefore not surprising that Rahel Szalit chose to do a portfolio of twelve lithographs titled *Hebräische Melodien*. Like Szalit's other portfolios and several of her illustrated books, this stunning and valuable edition was designed specifically for collectors, with only 120 copies ever produced and every image hand-signed. The introductory text and lithographs were printed at two separate printing houses, the latter on special handmade paper. Unlike Szalit's previous portfolios, which include only short introductory materials, the Heine portfolio includes the full text of all three poems from his "Hebrew Melodies" poetry cycle: "Princess Sabbath," "Jehuda ben Halevy," and "Disputation."

Introducing the prints and poems is literary scholar Hugo Bieber's short text, which praises Szalit's initiative to interpret Heine's work anew and suggests that her imagination brings Heine's poetic fantasies to a state of perfection. Bieber is careful to point out that Heine's relationship to his Jewish background was fraught, and that Heine returned to these topics only while deathly ill. Compared with Heine, Szalit was "rooted more deeply in the life of the Jewish community" and was familiar with Jewish traditions from a very early age. Despite these differences, Bieber contends that Szalit was connected to Heine in many ways: "But the poet and artist are bound together through a commonality of experience that cannot be explained only by their ancestry. They both see in Judaism the sublime and the grotesque, the grandeur and the degradation, the beautiful primordial form and the enchantment known as reality. It is the same contradiction between emotion and irony, the same struggle between aggressiveness and romanticization, which take form in the language and in the drawings." To compare Szalit's aesthetic achievements to those of a poet of such stature was surely the greatest compliment Bieber could have paid Szalit. A significant portion of Bieber's text, including the favorable section about Szalit, was excerpted in the *Vossische Zeitung* in June 1923.[5] This offers further evidence of widespread interest in Heine; it may also reflect Szalit's efforts to win the favor of *Vossische Zeitung* editor Artur Michel, to whom she dedicated a signed print in December 1922.[6]

Szalit followed Heine in portraying the Sabbath as an illuminating respite from everyday life, though her illustrations notably do not bear the same ironic tone for which Heine is known. Heine's "Princess Sabbath" poem envisions the day of rest from the arrival of the mythical Sabbath bride at sundown on Friday to its close on Saturday evening. This Sabbath bride jokingly prohibits tobacco smoking, promising instead to deliver the delicacy of cholent, a long-simmering stew, "the food of heaven," for the midday meal. Szalit's illustrations do not engage this humorous tone but rather offer realistic portrayals of observant Jews listening to a cantor in synagogue, lighting the Sabbath candles, and making Havdalah (a ceremony involving wine, lighting a special candle, and smelling spices to mark the Sabbath's end and the start of a new week). These images are at once timeless and somewhat modern; only the head coverings and style of clothing hint at a particular period, but that era could just as well be the 1850s as the 1920s. The rituals themselves remain basically unchanged among observant Jews today, a full century after Szalit depicted them.

As per Jewish custom, a Jewish mother with a cloth-covered head is at the center of Szalit's first image, *Sabbath* (fig. 41, sometimes titled *Prinzessin Sabbat* or *Lichtbenschen*).[7] Hands covering her closed eyes, blessing the candles she has just lit, she ushers in the weekly holy day. Three children and their father watch the mother perform this ritual; they stand in the background, in shadow, and she is closest to the table with challah and two candlesticks, illuminated by their brightly blazing wicks. The father and son appear to have books tucked under their arms, whereas the other two children are marked as female by the absence of books and by clothing that seems to be an extension of the mother's patterned dress. This image holds particular significance because of Szalit's childhood memories of similar scenes; here it is possible to glean a sense of nostalgia. In an interview with journalist David Ewen, Szalit recalled "the sight of my mother weeping over her Sabbath candlesticks."[8] The light of these candles reaches across time and space to unite women of multiple generations and regions. Szalit's focus on the moment of candle lighting complemented representations of Sabbath rituals by her contemporaries Jakob Steinhardt and Joseph Budko. In some of their works, women are sidelined or play more passive roles. Yet with his prints *Schabbat* (Sabbath, 1921, lithograph) and *Lichtsegen* (Blessing the Candles, 1922, etching), Steinhardt also established a strong visual association between a woman blessing candles and the beginning of the Sabbath.

In Szalit's *Havdalah*, the father has taken the mother's place at the head of the table to perform the ritual that marks the end of both the traditional Sabbath and the "Princess Sabbath" poem (fig. 42).[9] Whereas Heine's poem is rife with such metaphors as the Sabbath princess and a prince named Israel, Szalit takes a much more literal approach in depicting the ritual Heine describes. In her version, it is simply an average father (not a prince) who pours wine into the Kiddush cup, and his son lifts the woven Havdalah

FIGURE 41 | R. Szalit-Marcus, *Sabbath*, illustration from Heinrich Heine's "Hebrew Melodies," 1923. Courtesy of the Department of Special Collections, Stanford University Libraries, PT2304.A2 H4 1923 FF.

FIGURE 42 | R. Szalit-Marcus, *Havdalah*, illustration from Heinrich Heine's "Hebrew Melodies," 1923. Courtesy of the Department of Special Collections, Stanford University Libraries, PT2304.A2 H4 1923 FF.

candle to be extinguished in the wine. A decorative spice tower stands on the table in front of them. A mother and a daughter clutching a doll watch from the sidelines, now more in shadow; another daughter's head appears to be hiding in her mother's skirt. A candle again illuminates this family's home, but this light falls differently and less brightly than at the beginning of the holy day. The composition of Szalit's *Havdalah* likewise mirrors Jakob Steinhardt's *Sabbatausgang* (The Departure of the Sabbath, 1921, etching), in which a son assists his father by raising the lit, woven candle and other family members look on. Both stand in contrast to Hermann Struck's *Hawdala* etching from this period, which features only a lone man performing the ritual.

Szalit would return to the Havdalah ritual over a decade later while living in Paris. Her work in exile continued to engage intensively with Jewish subjects, as we will see in chapter 10. A Havdalah-themed sketch with a strikingly similar composition but a sleeker, updated style appeared in a French-Jewish journal in 1935 (fig. 43).[10] Broad, airy

FIGURE 43 | R. Szalit, *La prière dite "Havdalah"* (The Prayer Called Havdalah), in *Le Judaisme Sepharadi*, 1935, Jacques Biélinky papers. From the Archives of the YIVO Institute for Jewish Research, New York.

strokes suggest this later version was made with pastels or chalk. This image focuses less on the faces of the subjects and more on the moment when the candle shines brightly, just before it is extinguished in the wine. Again, Szalit plays with ways of illuminating interior spaces. In contrast to the Heine *Havdalah* illustration, this father wears only a subtle head covering, and the mother doesn't seem to be wearing one.

Szalit's "Princess Sabbath" images show Jews playing traditional roles, suggesting that the classic stuff of Heine's poems provided Szalit with a platform for rendering religious Jews in a believable and sympathetic way in and for German contexts. Jewish difference is visible through traditional clothing, men's beards, and unambiguous symbolism such as a Star of David adorning the synagogue's pulpit. Such facial features as prominent noses could possibly support a reading of these figures as stereotypically Jewish, though none are as extreme or grossly exaggerated as those of Szalit's Jewish subjects in her illustrations of Yiddish literature.

"HEBREW MELODIES"

For the longest poem of the three, "Jehuda ben Halevy," Szalit created images that evoke the distant milieus of medieval Spain and Jerusalem. Heine's lyrical narrator uses an imagined encounter with the eleventh-century poet Jehuda ben Halevy as an opportunity to tell his story. This includes his education in the Torah and Talmud, his familiarity with biblical Hebrew and Aramaic, and his pilgrimage from Toledo to the Holy Land at the end of his life. Szalit chose to illustrate several aspects of this story: a simple portrait of Jehuda ben Halevy; ben Halevy surrounded by a "choir of angels" when he arrives in heaven; as a boy, listening to stories told by a pilgrim from the Orient; and the Jerusalem that this pilgrim describes. In one image, Szalit depicts a man in desert attire walking with a camel toward Jerusalem, though it is unclear if this is meant to be ben Halevy himself or the "servant of the desert" that Heine's narrator glimpses near tall grasses and gray ruins (fig. 44). Another image recreates the waters of Babylon referenced in this poem. Szalit's images, particularly the one of ben Halevy among the cherub or childlike angels (fig. 45), are far more fantastical than the illustrations of "Princess Sabbath" and allow the viewer to follow along with Heine's imagination.

FIGURE 44 | R. Szalit-Marcus, *Jerusalem*, illustration from Heinrich Heine's "Hebrew Melodies," 1923. Courtesy of the Department of Special Collections, Stanford University Libraries, PT2304.A2 H4 1923 FF.

FIGURE 45 | R. Szalit-Marcus, *Jehuda Halevi in Heaven,* illustration from Heinrich Heine's "Hebrew Melodies," 1923. Courtesy of the Department of Special Collections, Stanford University Libraries, PT2304.A2 H4 1923 FF.

For the third poem, "Disputation," Szalit created two images of the theological tournament that Heine offered as a way of criticizing historical conversations about Christianity and Judaism. Set in fourteenth-century Spain (Toledo), this spoken battle takes place between Caputian monks and Jews, led by Rabbi Judah of Navarre. For twelve hours, they debate the highly controversial topic of whether the Trinitarian Christian God or the unified Jewish God is the true one. Szalit depicts the monks squaring off against the rabbis. In both of her images, we see the king and queen in the background, though they are larger and the primary focus of the most striking image (fig. 46). Szalit's Queen Donna Blanka looks unamused. On her face we see the same long, star-shaped eyelashes found on some of Szalit's other non-Jewish female characters, especially in the Tolstoy and Dickens illustrations. This Spanish queen, as Heine also hints, may be equally vapid; expected to judge the disputation, she concludes simply that both opponents "stink."

Jewish figures portrayed in Szalit's twelve Heine illustrations are less exaggerated and contrast sharply with those in her illustrations of Yiddish literature. When the portfolio first appeared, a review in *Milgroym* interpreted Szalit's Heine illustrations as less

FIGURE 46 | R. Szalit-Marcus, *Disputation*, illustration from Heinrich Heine's "Hebrew Melodies," 1923. Courtesy of the Department of Special Collections, Stanford University Libraries, PT2304.A2 H4 1923 FF.

humorous but more deliberate and more grounded than her previous works. The review further suggested that Szalit's illustrations were like a Yiddish translation of works by a German poet who was more European than Jewish, one who felt foreign and for whom Jewishness was but a memory of the home he had been forced to leave.[11] In other words: Szalit brought a more authentic relationship to Jewish culture than Heine but in doing so may have lost some of the humor that she skillfully applied in her illustrations of Yiddish literature.

In general, Szalit's "Hebrew Melodies" illustrations were received favorably and continued to be reprinted and exhibited in German-speaking contexts for over a decade. A few images often stood alone as representations of scenes from traditional Jewish life or Jewish history. In the years following the publication of the portfolio, German newspapers and magazines reprinted individual images titled *Sabbat*, *Jehuda Halevi*, and *Disputation*.[12] Along with other works by Szalit, Heine images were included in the exhibition *Jüdische Künstler unserer Zeit* (Jewish Artists of Our Time) at Salon Henri Brendlé in Zurich, which coincided with the sixteenth Zionist Congress in July and August 1929. Critic Ruth Morold observed that the Heine illustrations displayed there were "rich in humor and well regarded."[13] In the mid-1930s, scholars included Szalit's images, along with those of Struck, Steinhardt, and Budko, in presentations about the Sabbath in Jewish art.[14] As depictions of classic, well-known poems by a beloved German-Jewish author, these images have endured the test of time and have been considered representative of Szalit's illustrations of Jewish subject matter.[15] Today, Heine's "Hebrew Melodies" poems remain internationally popular: American artist Mark Podwal recently illustrated a new English translation.[16]

Bialik's Fiftieth Birthday

Szalit's contributions to the colorful, rhyming Hebrew-language children's book by Hayim Nahman Bialik differ in several ways from her illustrations of Yiddish literature and works published in German. Most notably, she was not the sole artist. Her two illustrations of *Ketina kol-bo* reflect Szalit's engagement with up-to-the-minute cultural trends among living authors, artists, and publishers, many of whom knew Hebrew and were active Zionists. Szalit's collaboration on this project demonstrates her affiliation with cultural Zionism and the promotion of Hebrew culture, a key part of the Jewish Renaissance, which her later work for the Zionist newspaper *Jüdische Rundschau* also affirms.

It was no coincidence that *Ketina kol-bo* was published by the Rimon Publishing Company in January 1923, the same month in which Bialik celebrated his fiftieth birthday. The celebrations extended across the Jewish press and included numerous special book publications, including a Jubilee Edition of Bialik's complete works illustrated by

Joseph Budko, as well as a portrait of Bialik by Max Liebermann.[17] The book *Ketina kol-bo*, too, was part of this occasion, and Rahel Szalit was therefore among those who helped make the celebrations possible.

While there is nothing to suggest that Rahel Szalit knew Bialik personally, they had several mutual acquaintances in Berlin, and their lives overlapped for a short time. If they did meet, they might have spoken Yiddish—Bialik, too, hailed from the Russian Empire. Szalit worked on several projects for the Rimon Publishing Company in the months prior to Bialik's birthday, and we can guess that she was asked to illustrate this work of Hebrew literature because of her contributions to Yiddish-language projects. In any case, many of the people involved knew each other and could have recommended Szalit. Writer Moshe Kleinman, coeditor of *Milgroym* (a magazine to which Bialik also contributed), had traveled from Odessa to Moscow with Bialik one year before coming to Berlin.[18] Kleinman edited the Yiddish text of the Hasidic tales (*Sipure maysies*) by Reb Nachman of Breslov, for which Szalit created sixteen lithographic illustrations by 1923.[19] Bialik was also the chief Hebrew editor at Klal-Farlag starting in August 1922, around the time it published her *Motl* portfolio. Kleinman or someone at Rimon Publishing Company or Klal-Farlag likely suggested Szalit as an illustrator for Bialik's *Ketina kol-bo*.

The Hebrew-language book *Ketina kol-bo* was without question a product of the Rimon Publishing Company. For one, the magazines *Milgroym/Rimon* announced *Ketina kol-bo*'s publication to their readers.[20] But even more significantly, the two artists with whom Szalit collaborated on this book were known for their contributions to the stunning covers and title art of *Milgroym/Rimon*, supervised by art editor Rachel Wischnitzer. The cover of *Ketina kol-bo* bears some resemblance to the cover of *Milgroym* (plates 4 and 5). Calligrapher Franziska Baruch was responsible for both the Hebrew hand lettering in *Ketina kol-bo* and the chapter headings in the Jubilee Edition of Bialik's complete works. A student at the school attached to the Museum of Decorative Arts in Berlin, Baruch had already made a name for herself with the calligraphy for Jakob Steinhardt's bibliophile Passover Haggadah in 1921.[21] Painter and professor Ernst Böhm, one of Baruch's teachers (and briefly one of Charlotte Salomon's professors in the 1930s), created the cover illustrations and lighthearted, ornamental drawings surrounding the "ancient-looking" text of *Ketina kol-bo*.[22]

Thanks to the tremendous efforts of these three artists (Baruch, Böhm, Szalit), every page of this slim book is its own work of art and a true celebration of Bialik's whimsical text. The last page states that only fifty copies of *Ketina kol-bo* were printed using the stones on which Szalit, Baruch, and Böhm initially produced their contributions. However, if we compare the copies held today at various Jewish museums, it becomes apparent that two different versions of *Ketina kol-bo* were made: a luxury edition bound with linen (*Nessel*) and a slimmer, less expensive paperbound volume. Both include hand-colored pages, and some are signed by the artists. Whereas the paper edition has only four colored pages

FIGURE 47 | Rahel Szalit-Marcus, *Blowing a Sailboat*, title page of Hayim Nahman Bialik's *Ketina kol-bo*, with lithographs by Rahel Szalit-Marcus, Ernst Böhm, typography: Franziska Baruch (Berlin: Rimon-Verlag, 1923). Paper, bound, hand-colored, 30.50 × 23.5 × 1 cm; Jüdisches Museum Berlin, VIII.6. Biali 597. Photo: Jens Ziehe.

scattered throughout, including the first page, the final ten pages of the hardbound linen edition are in color. Further, the paper edition's color appears to have been added using pastel or crayon, but the linen edition was painted with brilliant watercolors. One internal page shows the cricket and grasshopper chosen by Ketina to serve as crewmembers of his nutshell sailboat (plate 6).[23]

Szalit's two black-and-white lithographic illustrations appear on the title page and the last page of *Ketina kol-bo*, and they are the only images in this book to depict human figures. All others show tiny insects, objects, and adornments. A casual reader might assume that Szalit's frontispiece, which shows a rosy-cheeked young boy blowing into the sails of a toy boat, depicts the book's protagonist (fig. 47). The protagonist's name is Ketina Kol-bo and thus remains the same in translation, though the book's title has been translated as "Tiny Collection," "Der kleine Alleskönner" (The Little Jack-of-All-Trades), and "The Little Boy Who Had It All Within Him." (Ketina comes from the word *katan*, meaning "small" in Hebrew. *Kol-bo*, which means "everything within," is the name of an anonymous Jewish law code from around the thirteenth century and a term used to describe certain prayer books.) Szalit's second image illustrates the final scene of the poem, in which a lively group of boys joyfully clusters together to sing the praises of Ketina's creations (fig. 48). The boys wear caps, one of which is waved in the air as they cheer for, surround, and even "crown" Ketina.

Bialik's poem is a playful adventure story about a miniature, thumb-sized character that draws on Jewish lore and invokes other fabled miniature characters. It opens: "There is a young boy, like a small lizard / his size as a thumb (*etzba*), and his spirit mischievous."[24] The tiny Ketina Kol-bo works adeptly with tools and makes mini-chariots for his insect companions, including ladybugs and mosquitoes. He makes a nutshell boat, *Noah's Ark*, which flies a Star of David banner and claims a dung beetle, cricket, and grasshopper as its crew (plate 6). In contrast to Szalit's drawings of people, Böhm's illustrations largely portray the tools, vehicles, insects, and other creatures for whom Ketina's tiny vehicles are designed. Böhm's drawings also include several Stars of David, whereas there is nothing overtly Jewish about the two images created by Szalit for this book. The children in Szalit's illustrations of Bialik are simply young boys at play.

Upon close examination of the text, it is perhaps surprising that Szalit's illustrations depict average human children despite Bialik's reference to a miniature, thumb-sized character. It is possible that this detail was lost on Szalit, who probably did not read Bialik's text in the original Hebrew. However, it seems more likely that Szalit made the artistic choice to portray average-sized children to whom readers could easily relate. In this way, her images of children stand alone and are not bound solely to the context of this story. One might also conclude that neither Böhm nor Szalit wished to depict Ketina as the "Tom Thumb" kind of figure that Bialik describes, or perhaps they were advised not to draw

FIGURE 48 | Rahel Szalit-Marcus, *Group of Boys*, last page of Hayim Nahman Bialik's *Ketina kol-bo*, with lithographs by Rahel Szalit-Marcus, Ernst Böhm, typography: Franziska Baruch (Berlin: Rimon-Verlag, 1923). Paper, bound, hand-colored, 30.50 × 23.5 × 1 cm; Jüdisches Museum Berlin, VIII.6. Biali 597. Photo: Jens Ziehe.

Ketina so as to leave room for the reader to imagine what he might look like. If Ketina is not pictured, Szalit's first image could be understood as a child (a reader?) recreating the scenes of the book while playing with his own toy boat. Yet Szalit's rendering of human figures further complicates the picture by adding a layer of ambiguity: because of Szalit's illustrations, the reader begins to question whether Ketina is the miniature character of Bialik's story or a human-sized boy who happens to be especially handy and creative. In either case, the reader gains new perspective on how to relate to Ketina Kol-bo and the other figures in the poem.

That Rimon printed a special limited edition, hand-painted, rhyming Hebrew children's book in Berlin in 1923 leaves us with questions about the book's intended audience. Was the hardbound book meant only as a collector's item to honor Bialik? Presumably, the less expensive paper version had a larger print run and could reach more readers. In 1924, *Ketina kol-bo* was offered to members of the newly founded Soncino Society for the discounted price of 27 Reichsmark.[25] To be sure, there were also some Zionist Hebrew enthusiasts who might have read *Ketina kol-bo* with their children or used it to teach them Hebrew. Yet the beautiful book could hardly have been given over to the care of the young children for whom it was supposedly written. One scholarly study of this rhyming poem by Bialik suggests it was not in fact intended for children but rather an apocalyptic satire and critique of various aspects of the Zionist movement.[26] Though plausible, this reading of Bialik's text would not have been apparent to Szalit or to other readers in the 1920s who did not possess an advanced knowledge of Hebrew and a sophisticated understanding of allegory. The way this book pairs illustrations with text suggests its intended readers included children and adults learning Hebrew, all of whom would have benefitted from the support of visually appealing illustrations on every page. Bialik was celebrated especially for creating children's stories that would help the next generation engage with Zionism.[27]

In 1920s Germany, Zionists advocated for displaying Jewish identity proudly rather than subverting it to blend in or be inconspicuous. Szalit's art, like that of such Zionist graphic artists as Ephraim Moses Lilien, Hermann Struck, Joseph Budko, and Jakob Steinhardt, demonstrates her unwavering commitment to portraying Jewishness in her work.[28] Her illustrations of Bialik's *Ketina kol-bo* further reflect her engagement with Hebrew culture in Germany. Szalit was not well-versed in Hebrew, nor are there any indicators that she ever seriously considered immigration to Palestine. Given her collaboration on this project and close ties to others with strong Zionist leanings, we may count her among those artists who embraced the cultural Zionist ideology that went hand in hand with the Jewish Renaissance.

Several years later, Szalit would respond to a survey of Jewish artists conducted by Felix Weltsch on behalf of the Prague-based Zionist journal *Selbstwehr* (Self-Defense), which asked directly about the artists' views on Judaism and the Zionist movement. Szalit wrote that she indeed "felt a sense of longing for Zion as well as for the land of my fathers—but I am thankful to every other land that takes in expelled Jews."[29] This prescient remark reveals that Szalit viewed the Land of Israel as one possible haven for Jewish refugees. Yet Szalit's declaration of her "longing for Zion" was more subtle and less politicized than the responses by other artists, for example Joseph Budko's unambiguous assertion "I am a Zionist."[30] In light of Szalit's position, we can read her other works with Middle Eastern or "oriental" themes as adjacent to, if not part of, the same Zionist project behind the Bialik publication. To some extent, this was the case for "Hebrew Melodies" and for her illustrations of Thomas Mann's biblical-themed "Dina," as we will see.

After 1923, Szalit largely turned away from book illustration and began to venture beyond Jewish circles. No longer restricted by the extreme conditions of the inflation years, she would join mainstream artists' circles and organizations and would reinvent herself as a newspaper artist, portraitist, and painter of Weimar Berlin. Whereas she was previously associated with Jewish and world literature, she would become known for her images of animals and the Berlin Zoo, works that engaged with fencing, and her drawings and paintings of women. Though still a "Jewish daughter," Szalit quickly became a woman of the world as well.

PART 3

The Wild Sides of Weimar
(1924–1933)

CHAPTER 7

Newspaper Artist

Berlin, Zoologischer Garten, 1929: *The Berlin Zoo is a popular attraction, and Rahel visits regularly when the weather is good. Couples and families stroll through the crowded zoo. She is not the only artist who sits with a sketchpad, observing as the creatures go about their daily routines.*

Sitting in front of the giraffe enclosure, a male artist she doesn't recognize makes small talk: "Don't you agree that animals have a way of speaking to everyone? They are the most universal subject of all." Rahel thinks about this for a while. For Jews in small towns, animals are part of everyday life and provide an entryway into local society: eggs, milk, a livelihood. Modern artists use animals to show off their different ways of seeing: Franz Marc had his colorful horses and cows; Soutine paints carcasses. Rahel empathizes with animals and tries to view the world through their eyes. She has always loved watching animals, even here, in their small, enclosed spaces, where they are somehow both wild and tame.

Rahel remembers how, not long after she moved to Berlin, she read a Kafka story about an ape who learned to talk by imitating his captors and eventually became just like a European. Martin Buber had published the story in his journal, Der Jude. It was certainly a story about how to win freedom; maybe it was about Jews.

The animals at the Berlin Zoo are far from free. (And what about people like her who sit and watch them all day?) But her drawings focus on the animals themselves, their lives, their constrained existence.

A journalist she knows from the cafés passes by and looks through some of Rahel's sketches while they chat for a few minutes. He encourages her: "Frau Szalit, your zoo drawings are quite good! You should send them to newspaper editors—I will give you some names."

Weimar Germany entered its "golden years" of relative stability and prosperity in the mid-1920s, and this was also the stage of Rahel Szalit's career when she successfully entered the Berlin mainstream through periodicals and paintings. In the years between the currency stabilization in 1924 and the end of the Weimar Republic in early 1933, Szalit's life took on a new pace in line with the city around her. Mass culture took off: there were around four thousand newspapers and magazines published during the Weimar period, and over thirty daily papers in Berlin alone. The best way for artists to reach a wide audience was through the press, even though this meant moving away from the highbrow literary illustrations and valuable collectors' items that Szalit had produced previously. Szalit's work as an illustrator thus followed the market and was driven by her own need to make a living: when bibliophilic books and Expressionist prints were out and newspapers were on the rise, she began contributing drawings to both mainstream and Jewish newspapers. Instead of having her lithographs printed, she now drew directly onto paper with ink, pencil, chalk, and pastels. She even published a few German-language short stories and articles of her own—which she also illustrated, of course.

In the first few years of this stage, from 1924 through 1926, Szalit became active as both a portraitist and a freelance *Pressezeichnerin* (newspaper artist), and she began showing work at major exhibitions. Her paintings and drawings appeared in exhibitions of the Berliner Secession and at the Preußische Akademie der Künste (Prussian Academy of Arts); she had another solo exhibition featuring her portraits. But no matter how many drawings and illustrations she produced, she never stopped painting. Szalit often painted with watercolors on paper; she less frequently used oil paint and the expensive canvases it required. Her work still found its way into Jewish circles, but they were no longer her only cultural foothold.

Illustrations for the Masses

In Weimar culture, illustration was part of a new emphasis on the visual, and artists such as Rahel Szalit possessed sought-after skills. Key developments in printing enabled more newspapers to include photographs and illustrations, and reading publics soon expected to see images alongside written texts. Illustrated weekly newspapers gained tremendously in popularity. Other newspapers stayed competitive by using outside publishing houses to produce attractive illustrated supplements.[1] This led to increased demand for commercial illustrators and graphic designers, and several institutions offered specialized courses in these subjects, from the Bauhaus to the Reimann School. Numerous women illustrators became known for their fashion sketches, including Lieselotte Friedlaender, Dodo (Dörte Clara Wolff), and Lissy Elder (later Alice Newman). Artists like Jeanne Mammen contributed to fashion magazines occasionally. Certainly, Szalit's training in fine art also lent itself to illustration. But perhaps because she was not formally trained in graphic design, she did only a limited amount of commercial illustration (as far as we know) and preferred to illustrate narratives or to draw subjects that interested her. We can guess that she took the initiative to pitch some illustrations to newspapers and was commissioned to do others.

The range of periodicals that featured Szalit's drawings is as broad as the spectrum of themes she covered. Her work appeared several times in the mass-circulated daily newspapers *Berliner Tageblatt* and *Vossische Zeitung*. Literary journals and popular magazines, including *Der Querschnitt* and *Ulk*, featured work by Szalit throughout the late 1920s and early 1930s. In addition, quite a few illustrations appeared in some of the largest weekly Jewish newspapers, *Jüdische Rundschau* and *Israelitisches Familienblatt*. It would not be an exaggeration to suggest that by 1930 the name Rahel Szalit had become a household name for readers of these German-Jewish papers. In fact, there were no Jewish women artists who contributed more to or received more attention in the Jewish press.

Many of Szalit's works in periodicals were stand-alone images that served as aesthetic decorations: they beautified the text-heavy space of the newspaper page. Some were not directly related to the adjacent texts, nor were they intended to illustrate them. In a few instances, Szalit was commissioned to create adornments for specific sections of Jewish papers. Other images took the form of caricatures or cartoons and bore their own original captions. The captions were presumably penned by Szalit, marking an important shift toward creating her own written content in addition to illustrating texts by others. Szalit was one of many artists who created images with captions; in some ways, her career paralleled that of Polish-Jewish artist J. D. Kirszenbaum, who drew cartoons for the *Berliner Tageblatt* and other papers under the pseudonym Duvdivani.[2]

Still other illustrations of Szalit's fulfilled a more traditional function by complementing short stories that appeared in Weimar periodicals. Especially in these instances, we see how text and image worked in conversation to send messages to the viewer. As the creator of eye-catching, thought-provoking images, Szalit engaged readers before they ever read a word. Her images brought characters and key moments of storylines otherwise buried among small lines of text to the attention of even the laziest reader. She quickly became one of many artists whose engaging visuals and pithy captions embodied the Zeitgeist of Weimar Berlin.

Capturing the Berliner Milieu

Periodical art by Rahel Szalit brought the Berliner milieu to life on several levels. Like Käthe Kollwitz, Otto Dix, and many other Weimar artists, Szalit often portrayed impoverished or down-on-their-luck members of the working class. Women were at the center of many images. Animals were also a central focus of her periodical illustrations, and Szalit returned to the Berlin Zoo as a setting and theme time and again. These and other images reflect Szalit's strong sense of connectedness to the culture of Weimar Berlin.

One of Szalit's earliest sets of newspaper illustrations appeared in the *Berliner Tageblatt* in December 1924. These drawings mark a clear departure from the Jewish subject matter in much of her work from the early 1920s: they illustrate an Advent-themed article titled "Golden Sunday" by feuilleton editor Fred Hildenbrandt.[3] Szalit's sketches of a Christmas tree, a person playing guitar, and a woman next to a glowing Advent candle provide a stark contrast to the Jewish Sabbath candle-lighting traditions in her Heine illustrations from the previous year. At the same time, they show how Szalit was able to move beyond the familiar and adapt her skills to what reading publics desired. There is, to be sure, a long tradition of Jews contributing to Christmas traditions in various ways, but this moment marks a kind of rebellion for Szalit, who sought to avoid being pigeonholed as a Jewish artist.

Images of women that Szalit placed in different journals addressed contemporary women's issues as well as social and economic concerns. We recall that her painting *In der Kälte* shows a haggard old woman shivering alone in the cold winter (fig. 11). Another drawing, *Entlassen!* (Laid Off!), done with pencil, pastel, or chalk, criticizes the poor treatment of employees (fig. 49). This cartoon published in the political satire magazine *Lachen links* (Laughter on the Left) in 1924 shows a dejected-looking young woman standing in the shadows in front of a bank. If authored by Szalit, the caption suggests that she was helping readers interpret her own work. The caption reads, "What was that again. . . ? We are giving you severance pay, Fräulein, said the director, so that you can be sure to buy yourself better clothes."[4] With such cartoons, Szalit's work became part of the discourse against the ill treatment and abuse of female employees. At the same time, the image's caption gestures toward the significance of both appearance and dress for German women in search of employment.

Women attending balls recur in many of Szalit's images, and we can assume that Szalit found inspiration for such characters by attending balls, clubs, and parties herself. Perhaps her work as a newspaper artist left her with enough spending money to enjoy Berlin's nightlife, or maybe she had friends who paid her way. Both partygoing and an interest in depicting this subject matter, and particularly costume balls, may have been facilitated by a friendship with painter Karl Hofer, whose circle she joined by the mid-1920s. Hofer had spent time in Paris and Rome and was inspired by Cézanne and Picasso.[5] This influence can be seen in Hofer's paintings of masquerade balls, such as *Maskerade* (1922) and *Großer Karneval* (Big Carnival, 1928), which, like Cézanne's *Mardi Gras* (*Pierrot and Harlequin*, 1888), incorporate figures in masks and costumes. Hofer held a professorship

FIGURE 49 | R. Szalit, *Entlassen!* (Laid Off!), in *Lachen links: Das republikanische Witzblatt*, p. 529, 1924. Universitätsbibliothek Heidelberg.

at the Vereinigte Staatschulen für Freie und Angewandte Kunst (United State Schools for Free and Applied Arts) in Charlottenburg, giving him access to broad networks of artists. Every Saturday, he hosted friends in his home; there, Szalit might have encountered sculptors Renée Sintenis and Moissey Kogan, painters Willy Jaeckel and George Grosz, and writers Joachim Ringelnatz and Alice Berend. Hofer also enjoyed having artists visit his studio, and he was known to go out dancing at Hotel Eden.[6] Did Szalit join Hofer and his crowd at the elegant Hotel Eden, which was visited by many celebrities and immortalized in artworks by Max Beckmann and others? Did Szalit, too, learn to dance the Charleston when it swept Berlin in 1925?

Szalit's drawings envision nightlife from women's perspectives, often taking costume parties held around Fasching (another name for Karneval or Mardi Gras) as a central theme. In an image titled *Kostümball* (Costume Ball) for *Ulk*, the weekly humor and satire magazine supplement of the *Berliner Tageblatt*, two women dance with tambourines in an affected, head-turning way (fig. 50).[7] One comments wryly: "If someone doesn't get hooked on this soon, I will start behaving completely naturally again." Another illustration

FIGURE 50 | R. Szalit, *Kostümball* (Costume Ball), in *Ulk*, supplement to *Berliner Tageblatt*, p. 68, 1930. Universitätsbibliothek Heidelberg.

of a Fasching story in *Lachen links* shows a woman fending off several men.[8] Weimar-era party scenes were apparently quite demanding, and Szalit's drawings helped readers understand that ball attendees might have tired of such contrived behaviors. Szalit's cartoons in satirical papers reflect her efforts to create witty images for broad audiences. In addition to unnamed female partygoers, Szalit also drew portraits of many well-known individuals, primarily men.

Portraits of Berliners

Commissions to draw portraits for newspapers brought Szalit into frequent contact with many prominent Germans by the mid-1920s. She may not have been personally acquainted with all of her portrait subjects, but she probably met most of them at least once. Among the best-known figures sketched by Szalit were writers Bertolt Brecht, Herbert Ihering, Walter von Molo, and Johannes Becher, and actors Heinrich George and Alexander Granach.[9] Several of these portraits appeared in the illustrated supplement of the *Berliner Börsen-Courier*. Access to certain playwrights and actors may have been facilitated by her earlier marriage to Julius Szalit and proximity to his theater contacts.

Szalit's connections to Ludwig Meidner might have yielded other portrait opportunities. Meidner knew Brecht and was close friends with both Ihering and Becher.[10] Plus, Meidner did portraits of nearly everyone he encountered. Meidner's portraits of Becher, Jakob van Hoddis, Alfred Wolfenstein, Franz Werfel, and other writers appeared as illustrations in the well-known Expressionist poetry collection *Menschheitsdämmerung* (Twilight of Humanity, 1920).[11] For Meidner, making a portrait was an intense journey into his subject's soul. He famously explained his approach to portraiture: "Like a burrowing animal, bore down into the inexplicable ground of the pupil and the whites of your sitter's eyes and do not let your pen rest until you have tied your sitter's soul to your own in a pathetic bond."[12] Szalit may have absorbed some of Meidner's portraiture strategies, though her portraits did not possess the same level of intensity. Her drawing of Johannes Becher, a poet and politician, bears a resemblance to one of Meidner's earlier chalk sketches of Becher. Both artists show Becher in a suit and tie with a serious expression and a penetrating yet distant gaze, looking out of the frame toward the viewer's left. Szalit's drawing emphasizes Becher's furrowed brow, portraying him as less gaunt than he appears in Meidner's images (fig. 51).[13]

When necessary, Szalit did not hesitate to make use of the professional connections she established by drawing portraits. Herbert Ihering, a film and theater critic for the *Berliner Börsen-Courier*, proved an important resource for Szalit. She corresponded with him after drawing his portrait in 1924; this work became part of a series of portraits of critics and actors that appeared in the *Börsen-Courier* (fig. 52). In one letter from April 1928, Szalit entreated Ihering to help an unemployed friend:

Dear Sir—dear Herr Doktor!
The bearer of this letter, Herr Stein, would like to find work at your newspaper.
And I should very much like to ask you to help him with this if possible.
This young man is a nephew of the poet Däubler and he—as well as his parents
belong to our circle of friends. (Circle of Professor Karl Hofer)
He himself is also a writer—but must absolutely find a job from which he can live.
It would be very kind of you, dear Herr Doktor, if you would employ this nice,
diligent person.
I hope that you will not mind my request and I thank you sincerely in advance.
I greet you—your wife and children all the best
Your Rahel Szalit.
It would be so lovely if we could see each other again—may I call you sometime?
If it is not possible, it would be very kind of you if you could recommend him
to the *Vossische Zeitung*.[14]

FIGURE 51 | R. Szalit, *Portrait of Johannes Becher*, 1928. Akademie der Künste, Berlin, Gerhard Pohl Archive, no. 293.4.

This letter gives us several additional clues about Szalit's friends in literary and art circles. She was clearly acquainted with Rolf Stein and his parents, painter Otto Th. W. Stein and Elena Däubler (a sister of Theodor Däubler), who remarried painter Willi Nowak around 1924. Szalit intervened to help find work for Rolf Stein precisely because his family had not been successful in this regard.[15] Several of Szalit's professional letters contain such requests for favors; professional and personal spheres merged in many cases. As an immigrant with few connections other than the ones she made for herself, this was how she made her way.

In July 1925, Szalit was fortunate to have a second solo exhibition that marked another turning point in her career. Not only was she was hailed for work on mainstream (non-Jewish) subjects, but she also became known for media other than lithographs. This exhibition took place at Zinglers Kabinett für Kunst und Bücherfreunde in Frankfurt am Main, a prestigious gallery that had previously shown Expressionist works by such artists as Paul Klee and Max Beckmann. As part of this exhibition, both her small, colorful landscapes and her "artistically strong, highly expressive portrait drawings" of children

FIGURE 52 | R. Sz., *Portrait of Herbert Ihering*, in *Berliner Börsen-Courier*, 1924. Akademie der Künste, Berlin, Herbert Ihering Archive, no. 12829.

and actors (Werner Krauss, Max Adalbert, Alexander Granach, Agnes Straub) found particular resonance.[16] Though we no longer have access to most of the works shown at this exhibition, we can assume that visitors to Zinglers Kabinett would have perceived Szalit as a portraitist of Berliners rather than strictly as an artist of Jewish or East European scenes. Szalit's portraits met with further success at a June 1926 exhibition at the Berliner Secession, *Berliner Bühnen-Bildner* (Berlin Stage Designers). She may also have had another solo exhibition (one article refers to a *Sonderausstellung*, or special exhibition) of this work in late 1926 in Berlin.[17]

Since Rahel Szalit never had any children of her own, we can consider other reasons why she often painted and drew children. Perhaps children provided alternative subject matter to the men and occasional women whose portraits she was commissioned to draw. Depicting young people connected Szalit to other modern artists who portrayed

FIGURE 53 | Rahel Szalit, *Kinder beim Frühstück* (Children Eating Breakfast), pastel, in *Blätter des jüdischen Frauenbundes*, 1930. Institut für die Geschichte der deutschen Juden, Hamburg.

children alongside mothers as a way of showcasing women's roles. Or maybe Szalit was inspired by friends' children or the births of her nephew and niece, her sister Szejna Michla's children, in Lodz in the mid-1920s. Szalit wrote that she enjoyed portraying the natural qualities of children playing, dancing, and eating. A pastel drawing accompanying this autobiographical article shows two children eating breakfast with what appears to be a squirrel perched behind them (fig. 53).[18] Another pastel reprinted in the *Berliner Tageblatt* shows children playing with a cat.[19] These and other works remind us that people were not Szalit's only subjects; many of her more humorous images used animals as a basis for commenting on relationships between people.

Animals and the Berlin Zoo

Animals always fascinated Szalit; she especially loved to portray their movements.[20] Prized for her good heart, Szalit was known for being tender and affectionate toward animals. Later, when she lived in Paris, she rescued stray cats and fed them in her studio.[21] Like many other Berliners, Szalit was a regular at the Zoologischer Garten, then located just behind the Romanisches Café. Here she observed the monkeys, camels, elephants, giraffes, and other animals that appeared in many of her images. The zoo recovered from the economic crisis of the early 1920s and continued to grow its particularly large collection. One guidebook boasted that the Berlin Zoo's fifteen hundred types of mammals and birds were housed in structures and against a backdrop artfully designed to be sightseeing attractions in and of themselves.[22] By the end of the decade, the zoo welcomed more than 1.5 million visitors per year, and many organizations held meetings and banquets there.[23] Szalit herself showed work in at least one exhibition at the zoo in 1931.[24]

Modernist writers and artists and those influenced by them used animals and zoos to different effect. Rainer Maria Rilke's "The Panther," a famous poem from 1902, describes a panther pacing behind bars at the Paris Zoo. Franz Kafka's *Metamorphosis* famously studies the unnerving experience of waking to find oneself transformed into a monstrous insect. Felix Salten's *Bambi* has been read as a metaphor for Jewish persecution.[25] Walter Benjamin wrote of extended encounters with the Berlin Zoo's otter in *Berlin Childhood Around 1900*.[26] H. A. Rey was inspired to sketch in every zoo everywhere he visited, and he later worked with his wife, Margret Rey, to create and illustrate the *Curious George* stories.[27]

Other artists who spent time in zoos, and especially at Berlin's Zoologischer Garten, produced animal-themed work that became very well known. Expressionist artist August Macke considered his *Zoologischer Garten* painting to be among his best works.[28] Uriel Birnbaum depicted a wide range of animals in their natural habitats.[29] Like Szalit, Richard Janthur was known for his illustrations of animals, especially of Rudyard Kipling's *The Jungle Book*. Jakob Steinhardt, too, portrayed the zoo in an etching (*Im Zoo*, 1925) and a landscape painting, *Brücke im Zoo* (Bridge in the Zoo, 1926). Rudolf Großmann's images of primates and bears at the Berlin Zoo appeared in *Der Querschnitt*. Renée Sintenis regularly visited the Berlin Zoo to study the animals she sculpted and drew. Erna Pinner illustrated books by Kasimir Edschmid with many exotic animals, and she also published her own book of animal drawings, *Tierskizzen aus dem Frankfurter Zoo* (Animal Sketches from the Frankfurt Zoo, 1927). The director of the London Zoo, Julian Huxley, later helped Pinner get commissions while in exile.[30] Finally, photographer Roman Vishniac, who lived in Berlin for many years, is known especially for one photograph, *People Behind Bars* (early 1930s), which positions the viewer alongside caged polar bears.[31]

Rahel Szalit's animal figures should not necessarily be understood as allegories of Jewish experience or persecution, or as a critique of Jewish assimilation, as some of Kafka's animal stories are often interpreted to be. Instead, Szalit's animals at times evoked her East European childhood or provided a common denominator between works. For example, we see strikingly similar donkeys in her illustrations of Tillier and Mann, stories set thousands of years apart. Animals held broad appeal and were sometimes used in humorous

FIGURE 54 | R. Szalit, *Cats*, drawing in *Der Querschnitt*, 1927.

ways, especially chickens. Rarely were they laden with bold political overtones. To the extent that Szalit's animals offer a commentary on Jews or Jewish life, they suggest that animals helped sustain Jews and provided small-town Jews with connections to local communities. Animals were often present as a regular part of Jewish life, as well as part of European life in general. But only the Yom Kippur chickens are persecuted outright; most of Szalit's animals either serve functional service purposes (horses pulling wagons, camels that can travel far in the desert) or provide a source of entertainment, as in zoo animals on display or chickens drunk on honey wine. In all instances, though, animals remain a step below humans and could be understood as lesser or downtrodden on some level.

Szalit's animal drawings were in demand and appeared frequently in Berlin papers, sometimes as illustrations for stories about animals. Many depict animals from the Berlin Zoo, including specific creatures who were known by name. Several spotlight human-animal encounters or interactions. Drawings of cats, a bird, and a camel appeared in the literary and art journal *Der Querschnitt*, which preserved the heritage of Expressionism

FIGURE 55 | R. Szalit, *Bird*, drawing in *Der Querschnitt*, 1931.

even as New Objectivity became the dominant movement.[32] In the context of *Der Querschnitt*, Szalit's work was part of a broader program focused on animals. Watched by a parrot in a cage, Szalit's two cats are shown in motion, playing with a ball, as an accompaniment to an unrelated story about cats (fig. 54).[33] Szalit's sketch of a bird, probably a white stork, illustrated an article about lions, parrots, and other animals worthy of a zoo display (fig. 55).[34] In this instance, too, there is a disconnect between image and text: the stork does not depict the talking parrot discussed in the adjacent paragraph but rather serves as a more universal signifier of birds in general.

A third, humorous image perhaps inspired by the zoo's *Kamelhaus* shows a disgruntled man in a ditch, nose to nose with a camel (fig. 56). This was one of Szalit's illustrations of Alphonse Daudet's *Tartarin of Tarascon*, which portray the hunter Tartarin planning and embarking on a hunting expedition. It was a popular lithograph that also appeared in *Die Schaffenden* (The Creators), a quarterly periodical for collectors with signed prints in each issue.[35] Although several of Szalit's Daudet illustrations appeared in *Der Querschnitt* and *Die Schaffenden*, they do not form a complete, surviving series. If they were

FIGURE 56 | R. Szalit-Marcus, *Ritt auf dem Kamel* (Riding on the Camel), illustration from Alphonse Daudet's *Tartarin of Tarascon*, in *Die Schaffenden* 4, no. 3 (1923). Gerd Gruber Collection, Wittenberg.

NEWSPAPER ARTIST

ever published in book form, Szalit was not properly credited. George Grosz also famously illustrated a book version of Daudet's *Tartarin* in 1921 that Szalit might have seen.[36]

By 1930, Szalit was closely associated with animals and the Zoologischer Garten. Both *Ulk* and the *Vossische Zeitung*'s supplement *Zeitbilder* ran full-page spreads of her zoo images. For *Zeitbilder*'s article "Zeichner im Berliner Zoo" (Artists in the Berlin Zoo), Szalit drew two scenes of animals being groomed, under the heading "Beauty Routines of the Animals."[37] Although the accompanying text is not clearly attributed to Szalit, we can guess that she penned this part of the article, especially as she was beginning to publish more of her own writing around this time. By comparing the care routines of animals to those of humans, Szalit personified and thereby called attention to specific animals: Toni, the female elephant, who gets a pedicure twice each year, and Betty, the giraffe, whose neck the zookeeper brushes in the morning. Szalit's memorable "Elephant Pedicure" scene shows an elephant through the cage bars, leg lifted high with chains and pulleys, while a zoo worker tends to her toenails (fig. 57). The text concludes with a story about

143

FIGURE 57 | R. Szalit, *Elephant Pedicure*, in *Zeitbilder*, supplement of *Vossische Zeitung*, 1930. Staatsbibliothek zu Berlin—Preußischer Kulturbesitz.

the preening routines of two birds on a chicken farm belonging to the author's friend; this could have been someone Szalit knew, and it offers insight into why she opted to include chickens in so many of her images. Szalit's childhood also provided plenty of opportunities to watch chickens living in or near Lithuanian homes.

In *Ulk*, Szalit's drawings of animals appeared as part of an eye-catching four-part cartoon titled "Brunnenkur im Zoo" (Spa Cure at the Zoo, fig. 58). All four images relate to the consumption of beverages. One pokes fun at the expensive water imported from spa towns; another comments on the romances that bloom between people named Marie and Karl over small talk about spa-themed drinks called Marienbader and Karlsbader. Apart from a giraffe, whose neck is compared to a straw, animals in these cartoons are largely in the background, including chickens as well as a monkey and lion in cages. The image on the lower left shows an artist sketching animals, but sitting in the foreground is a fur-clad, fashionable woman who asserts, "So what if he draws animals—I'm as beautiful and as wild as them every day."[38] This line recalls the foreign women, including some Jewish women, who were exoticized and sometimes even literally put on display in "human zoos."[39] In these cartoons, people and animals coexist harmoniously, but all are on public display for observers visiting the zoo.

The zoo continued to provide important subject matter for Szalit, and it is only fitting that a painting of the Zoologischer Garten was among her final contributions to mainstream German art exhibitions before Hitler came to power. In October 1932, Szalit's painting *Herbst im Zoo* (Autumn at the Zoo) was displayed in the exhibition *Rund ums KaDeWe*, which centered around and took place at the Kaufhaus des Westens department store.[40] Organized by the Association of Women Artists in Berlin, the exhibition included at least seven works featuring the zoo. Reviews described Szalit's now-lost painting as one that used "glowing colors" to depict "temperamentally drawn, wild flaming autumn."[41] We can imagine that this painting used such brilliant fall colors as orange and red to enliven what might otherwise be a somewhat banal setting. Szalit, too, expressed her delight in using color, especially for nature scenes such as spring and fall landscapes.[42]

Drawing for the Jewish Press: Boxers, Vacationers, and Everyday Life

As an illustrator who contributed to many newspapers, Rahel Szalit was also sought out by the Berlin Jewish press. She was commissioned to create decorative images as well as illustrations for stories in several Jewish periodicals. We have already seen that she was invited by the *Israelitisches Familienblatt* to illustrate short stories by Sholem Aleichem; this makes sense considering that she was an East European, Yiddish-speaking artist who had illustrated Sholem Aleichem's *Motl*. Szalit played the role of an authentic East

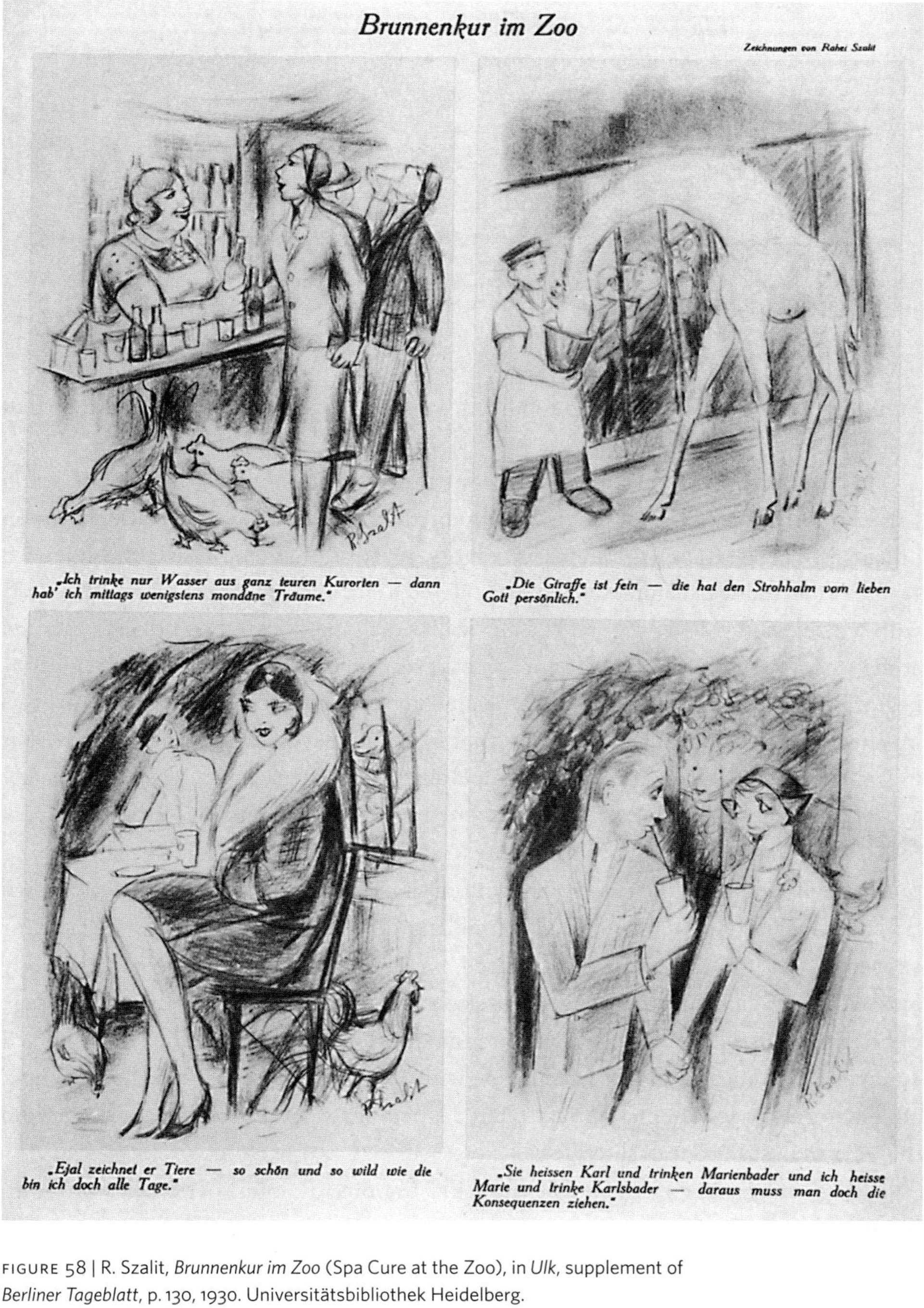

FIGURE 58 | R. Szalit, *Brunnenkur im Zoo* (Spa Cure at the Zoo), in *Ulk*, supplement of *Berliner Tageblatt*, p. 130, 1930. Universitätsbibliothek Heidelberg.

FIGURE 59 | R. Sz., *Sport Schild* (Sport Shield), in *Der Schild*, 1925. Courtesy of the Leo Baeck Institute.

European artist for other Jewish periodicals, too, but her overall range extended further than East European subjects.

In one exceptional instance, Szalit contributed decorative artwork to *Der Schild* (The Shield). This journal of the Reichsbund jüdischer Frontsoldaten (National Union of Jewish War Veterans), a Liberal Jewish organization that emphasized both Jewish ethnic pride and German national pride, offered a stark contrast to the Zionist agenda with which Szalit usually aligned herself. Szalit's drawing of two men boxing appeared at the top of the "Sport Schild" (Sport Shield) section of *Der Schild* for several months beginning in late 1924 (fig. 59).[43] The same drawing was reprinted each time, always bearing the tiny monogram "R. Sz.," a lesser-used signature that enabled Szalit to remove her full name and any reference to her gender. However, the magazine published a separate article announcing that Rahel Szalit was the artist behind these images.[44] The message of Szalit's bold image is in line with that of the Reichsbund itself: Jews could be athletic and practice self-defense in the face of antisemitism if needed. This organization was known for encouraging Jews to maintain a low public profile so as not to provoke negative or antisemitic reactions, yet it also encouraged members to use sports to prepare the body for military service. Read in the broader context of Szalit's life and oeuvre, this image of boxers gestures toward Jewish athleticism and strength as values that Szalit herself embraced as a fencer, and that were in line with Zionist ideals. For some Zionists, new, athletic forms of Jewish masculinity offered a path forward and a drastic change from the ways of East European shtetl Jews.[45]

To be sure, Szalit contributed far more illustrations to Zionist periodicals and exhibitions than to Liberal groups, though she was careful not to stake out a clear political position.[46] In 1928, Szalit contributed to the Zionist newspaper *Jüdische Rundschau* so many times that she was likely on its payroll. Her work must have been known to its editor, Robert Weltsch, who may have recommended Szalit for the survey of Jewish artists conducted by *Selbstwehr*, headed by Robert's cousin Felix Weltsch.

FIGURE 60 | R. Szalit, *Vacationers*, in *Jüdische Rundschau*, 1928. Digitized by the University Library J. C. Senckenberg Frankfurt am Main.

One of Szalit's header drawings for the *Jüdische Rundschau* shows vacationers in miniature. Some are boating and lying on the beach, as if in summer, whereas those across the page are skiing on a snowy mountainside, as in winter (fig. 60).[47] A hotel sits prominently in the center of the image, with travelers carrying suitcases and arriving or departing by car. This and similar images appeared in the *Jüdische Rundschau* on multiple occasions, always at the top above hotel and resort advertisements. Paired with advertisements that catered to a Jewish clientele through kosher cuisine and restaurants, Szalit's image takes on a distinctly Jewish quality, though without these ads it is merely an image of idealized vacations. It is also a fashionably modern depiction of travel and transportation methods, particularly if one contrasts Szalit's drawing of an automobile with the horse-drawn wagons and electric trams that appear in her previous works. Not long after these modern travel images appeared in a Jewish paper, Szalit contributed to a mainstream exhibition, *Das Auto im Bild* (Images of Cars, 1930), organized by the Berlin Artists Association. With her depictions of cars, Szalit had her finger on the pulse of the time, as envisioned by both Jewish and non-Jewish travelers.

Another set of Szalit's illustrations in the *Jüdische Rundschau* helped readers visualize the most memorable characters in Shemarya Gorelik's "Ein jüdischer Schriftsteller reist nach Canada" (A Jewish Writer Goes to Canada). This text, supposedly based on Gorelik's actual recollections of a trip to Canada, appeared in serialized installments from January through March, often printed just above Joseph Roth's novel *Hotel Savoy*. Three installments of Gorelik's story included distinctly modern illustrations by Szalit. One drawing shows Gorelik's first-person narrator visiting Montreal, where he takes a walk with Mr. Stone, the blond, rosy-cheeked "giant" of a man who serves as a *batlan*, an unemployed person who makes himself available to the Jewish community (fig. 61).[48] Although

FIGURE 61 | R. Szalit, *I also Took My First Walk with Mr. Stone*, illustration from Shemarya Gorelik's "A Jewish Writer Goes to Canada," in *Jüdische Rundschau*, 1928. Digitized by the University Library J. C. Senckenberg Frankfurt am Main.

the presence of female characters is not part of Gorelik's text, in Szalit's image we nevertheless see female passersby observing Gorelik's central characters. This offers a further example of how Szalit inserted women into her illustrations, even when unscripted.

Stories of Purim and Passover

As far as we know, Rahel Szalit wrote and illustrated only two German-language fictional stories. She penned these engaging short stories despite her belief that she was not an especially good writer.[49] Like many other Yiddish speakers outside of eastern Europe, Szalit lived between languages. Writing in a language other than one's mother tongue can be frustrating; visual art, on the other hand, largely transcends linguistic challenges and opens up new means of expression. Yet Szalit's German was good enough that she could compose her own original texts: for her writing for Berlin papers, German was her language of choice.

Szalit's two short stories, published in spring 1930 in Purim and Passover supplements of the *Jüdische Rundschau*, feature women and girls in poignant or absurd situations that could have occurred in small East European towns around these major Jewish holidays.[50] English translations of these two stories can be found in the second appendix. Although the stories were written in German, they use several unglossed Yiddish and

Hebrew terms that would have been familiar to only some Jewish readers. Even while recounting stories about traditional Jewish life, both stories bring underrepresented perspectives to the fore.

The Purim story is told through the eyes of a child; the first-person protagonist speaks on behalf of "we children" and offers insight into how children engage with amusing customs that invite their participation. In contrast, the Passover story narrates how Gitta, a strong woman with eight children to feed (and three more who already left for America), courageously stands up to the town mayor and fights for her right to bake and sell matzah. Through these stories, we see how both women and men of all ages find their place in small-town Jewish society. Many characters are poor and struggle to make ends meet by performing simple tasks. Children and others deliver Purim baskets and accompany Purim players for their evening performance; women workers help bake matzah in Gitta's home. The male characters include Schlojme, the poor but hardworking *Schalachmones* (Purim gift) carrier, and Jossel, the *badchen* (jester), who entertains the women baking matzah. Gitta's husband, Leibe, also receives a brief mention, though as an out-of-work carpenter, Leibe is but one of many who contribute to Gitta's matzah-baking enterprise. It is the women who direct the rhythm of life and move everything forward.

Like many of Szalit's other drawings for periodicals, her illustrations of her own short stories depict female (and male) protagonists, animals, children, and activities related to Jewish life. It is most probable that Szalit first composed the stories and then created accompanying illustrations. The two figures carrying Purim gifts appear in isolation, as simple character sketches of a young girl and an impoverished old man. Rowdy, costumed Purim players appear together with their billygoat, upon which Queen Esther rides (fig. 62). The story reminds us of the cross-dressing that took place on such occasions: Esther is played by Chaim, the cobbler's apprentice. This image of Purim players recalls an advertisement asking for Purim donations that Szalit published in both the *Jüdische Rundschau* and a Munich-based Zionist newspaper, *Das jüdische Echo* (The Jewish Echo), in 1928 (fig. 63).[51] Here, figures in costumes and masks carry flags and musical instruments, conveying the playful, humorous spirit of the holiday.

Similarly, the four drawings that accompany Szalit's Passover story are either character sketches or more complex scenes. Gitta the matzah-baker stands alone in the frame as she negotiates with the mayor. The brilliant line "You are the master of the city, I am the master of my oven" appears below Gitta's likeness as a caption. One vivid scene shows Leibe using the long wooden baker's peel to put matzah into the oven (fig. 64). Women are hard at work in the foreground; a woman also holds a child in the background, and a small lamp illuminates the cozy interior. In the most comical scene, we see chickens drunk on honey wine disrupting the matzah baking (fig. 65). The terrified women workers

Voran Königin Esther stolz auf einem Ziegenbock reitend . . .

FIGURE 62 | R. Szalit, *At the Front is Queen Esther, Riding Proudly on a Billy Goat*, illustration from Rahel Szalit's "Purim in a Small Town," in *Jüdische Rundschau*, 1930. Digitized by the University Library J. C. Senckenberg Frankfurt am Main.

FIGURE 63 | R. Szalit, *Before the Purim Festival Ends, Think of Your Purim Donation*, advertisement in *Jüdische Rundschau*, 1928. Digitized by the University Library J. C. Senckenberg Frankfurt am Main.

FIGURE 64 (*left*) | R. Szalit, *Leibe Slid the Matzahs in the Oven*, illustration from Rahel Szalit's "Baking Matzah in a Small Town," in *Jüdische Rundschau*, 1930. Digitized by the University Library J. C. Senckenberg Frankfurt am Main.

FIGURE 65 (*right*) | R. Szalit, *The Drunk Chickens*, illustration from Rahel Szalit's "Baking Matzah in a Small Town," in *Jüdische Rundschau*, 1930. Digitized by the University Library J. C. Senckenberg Frankfurt am Main.

flee the scene, scared that a dybbuk or possessing spirit has entered the chickens. In this image, *Die besoffenen Hühner* (The Drunk Chickens), Szalit again uses chickens to comical effect. Five boisterous chickens positioned front and center in the image demonstrate their prominence within the narrative. They are a regular presence in Jewish life, both for practical and for entertainment purposes.

Szalit's many contributions to newspapers and magazines led her to be part of some intriguing aspects of Berlin mass culture. Socially engaged cartoons intervened on behalf of unemployed female workers and women navigating a party scene that catered primarily to men. Portraits of prominent individuals demonstrate Szalit's ongoing connectedness to the theater world and its critics; they also helped establish her as a serious artist who could do more than literary illustration. Children appear in many works, offering glimpses of playful moments or a slower pace. Both wild and caged animals reflect her fascination with creatures not likely to appear randomly in the metropolis.

Yet despite this shift toward subject matter that held broad appeal, Szalit never abandoned her work as a Jewish artist. She contributed illustrations to Jewish periodicals with some frequency, most notably the Zionist *Jüdische Rundschau*. Her stories of Jewish village life, including the traditional cultures of East European shtetls, highlighted the roles of women and children as well as the proximity to animals. As we will see in the next chapter, other projects that Szalit embarked on in the late 1920s helped make stories of biblical Jewish women relevant amid the uniquely cosmopolitan environment of Weimar Berlin.

CHAPTER 8

Sexuality and the Bible

Berlin-Tiergarten, February 1929: It is not every day that Rahel meets with important scientists, but today she has been invited to the office of Dr. Magnus Hirschfeld at the Institute for Sexual Science. She has never seen anything like this fascinating place. As she walks through the institute, she sees posters protesting the antiabortion law, Paragraph 218. A display case in the corner of one room shows off a collection of contraception devices.

Dr. Hirschfeld is a friendly man of about sixty with white-and-gray hair, a large mustache, and small, scholarly spectacles. He explains that he has seen her illustrations in several magazines over the years ("My, you have been busy"), and he is interested in her East European background. Rahel tells him her story, noting that Berlin is a far better home for her now than Poland or Lithuania.

Hirschfeld is working on a new journal, Die Aufklärung (Enlightenment), and is looking for black-and-white images to enliven its pages. Additionally, he has a Bible-themed story lined up that would be well-suited to a Jewish artist. A friend has recommended Rahel as someone who could do some unconventional drawings. Rahel agrees: "Yes, this would interest me, though I must admit I haven't read much of the Bible. But it is never too late to start!" They determine that she will deliver twelve drawings in the next six months. At least half will serve as illustrations for installments of a new story, "Dina," by Thomas Mann, based on the biblical tale.

Rahel cannot believe this opportunity—she is being asked to prepare illustrations for Thomas Mann, the greatest German writer alive. Hirschfeld informs her that her drawings will be featured as prominently as Mann's story. He gives her the typed manuscript of "Dina." She should not hesitate to create vivid portrayals; no subject is off-limits. In fact, Hirschfeld ventures that, for some readers, Rahel's drawings will make an even greater impression than the text they illustrate.

Berlin was known for its sexual freedoms and pathbreaking approaches to sexuality, both in scientific circles and in its lavish nightlife. The homosexual rights movement got underway around the turn of the century, and the cultural scene soon followed. In 1914, there were forty bars in Berlin alone that catered primarily to homosexuals and lesbians.[1] Social hygiene films about sexuality, also called enlightenment films, were screened in German cinemas between 1918 and 1920. Many had Jewish directors, including *Anders als die Andern* (Different from the Others, 1919), a film that featured interviews with Magnus Hirschfeld and discussed the issue of suicide among homosexuals.[2] Gay establishments and social clubs rapidly expanded across Germany. Over 130 locales opened in Berlin by the mid-1920s, including about fifty clubs, bars, and cafés for women. A famous city guide to the lesbian scene indicated that it made a point of "satisfying every taste," and that women from all walks of life could find a place that suited them.[3] Some social clubs for women met in cafés and patisseries, including one group of Jewish lesbians who met in the afternoon to chat and play chess.[4] Finally, there was no shortage of journals that addressed topics related to sexuality for different audiences.

Weimar Berlin's vibrant gay scene attracted artists and writers from across Europe and beyond. In fact, its decadent offerings rivaled and perhaps even surpassed Paris's scene in some ways. British writer Christopher Isherwood, for one, joined his close friend W. H. Auden in Berlin in 1929. Isherwood later famously wrote of this time: "Berlin meant Boys." While in Berlin, Isherwood crossed paths with Hirschfeld and briefly lived next door to his Institute for Sexual Science; he later dubbed Hirschfeld one of the "heroic leaders" of his tribe.[5] Isherwood also got to know two of Thomas Mann's children: he became friends with Klaus Mann, and he arranged the marriage of convenience between Auden and Erika Mann to help her obtain a British passport in 1935.

It is unknown to what extent Rahel Szalit personally took part in the wilder sides of Berlin's nightlife, but she was no stranger to what we would call queer or LGBT circles by the late 1920s. Though we have few specifics, Szalit's surviving letters confirm that she had sexual and romantic relationships with both men and women. Perhaps this led her to frequent private women's social clubs such as the Violetta or the Pyramid, balls and dances held at other clubs, or smaller-scale gatherings at cafés. Many of these events took place in Schöneberg, only a short walk from Szalit's apartment.

Even if she was not tremendously active in gay nightlife as such, Szalit's involvement in the Association of Women Artists beginning in 1927 brought her into direct contact with Berlin's queer circles. Through this group, Szalit met numerous other women who identified as lesbian, bisexual, or nonconforming with respect to gender or sexuality.

A number are celebrated today as queer artists: Lotte Laserstein, Lene Schneider-Kainer, Renée Sintenis, Milly Steger, and Augusta von Zitzewitz.[6] Szalit's friendships with these women are discussed in the next chapter, but it is worth noting here that many artists involved in this association supported one another in different ways.

Some consider pioneering woman artist Käthe Kollwitz to have been a strong supporter of lesbian artists, including her student Gertrude Sandmann and the painter Gerda Rotermund. In fact, Kollwitz, who was married to a man, wrote in her memoirs that she felt attracted to both men and women, asserting: "As I look back upon my life I must make one more remark upon this subject: although my attraction toward the male sex was the dominant one, I also felt frequently drawn toward my own sex—an inclination which I could not correctly interpret until much later on. As a matter of fact, I believe that bisexuality is almost a necessary factor in artistic production; at any rate, the tinge of m.[asculinity] within me helped me in my work."[7] As was the case for many thinkers at this time, Kollwitz understood sexuality as closely linked to gendered attributes: women who are attracted to other women must have something "masculine" about them. Kollwitz's notion that masculine attributes could be artistically productive was applied to Szalit as well: one journalist described Szalit's literary illustrations of Heine, Sholem Aleichem, and Mendele as possessing an "almost masculine intellectuality, and on the other hand a completely feminine passionateness."[8]

Both gender and sexuality informed the work of many Weimar women artists who represented the human form. Julie Wolfthorn did many portraits of women, including nude and emancipated women, and was (like Szalit, Lasker-Schüler, and others) well acquainted with the work of Magnus Hirschfeld. Lotte Laserstein painted many nudes, and Renée Sintenis sculpted and drew some as well. Lene Schneider-Kainer and Jeanne Mammen became known for their open depictions of eroticism and sexuality; Mammen often depicted Berlin's gay and lesbian scenes.[9] The opposite was true for Szalit. In her case, works with nude or sexually explicit subjects received no mention in discussions of Szalit, possibly because they were more provocative than her other work. We recall that she was familiar enough with this genre to offer lessons in figure drawing and painting, though few of her own nudes survive. In the following, we examine material that has been neglected in the archive for over ninety years.

Dina as Cautionary Tale

Rahel Szalit's interests in Jewish subjects and sexuality found an unlikely intersection in her 1929 illustrations of Thomas Mann's "Dina," an account of Jacob's only daughter mentioned by name in the Bible. This story later became part of *Die Geschichten Jaakobs*

(The Stories of Jacob, 1933), the first book of Mann's four-volume novel *Joseph und seine Brüder* (Joseph and His Brothers, 1933–43). Mann began working on this project around 1926, and Szalit's illustrations accompanied one of the first publications, if not the very first, of Mann's "Dina."[10] The story garnered international attention as an independent work even before it was published as part of a book. An English translation by Ludwig Lewisohn appeared in the Paris-based modernist journal *This Quarter* in December 1930.[11] Even so, *The Stories of Jacob* was ultimately not the most successful of the four Joseph books, as two others later became best-sellers in the United States.[12] Although Thomas Mann was not Jewish (his wife came from a Jewish family that had converted to Protestantism), his monumental engagement with biblical figures reflects a strong interest in ancient Judaism and the role of religion in history. Some scholars understand the themes related to Jewish history and the history of religion in *Joseph and His Brothers* as a response to the growth of German fascism and the threat of anticivilized barbarism.[13]

Most intriguing about Mann's story and Szalit's eight accompanying illustrations, credited in large print directly under the title "Dina" as "Erzählung von Thomas Mann * Originalzeichnungen von R. Szalit" (Story by Thomas Mann * Original Drawings by R. Szalit), however, is their extraordinary publication history. They were featured in five installments from April to August 1929 in *Die Aufklärung* (Enlightenment), a journal coedited by anthropologist Maria Krische and sexologist Magnus Hirschfeld and affiliated with his institute.[14] Both its title and subtitle, *Monatsschrift für Sexual- und Lebensreform* (Monthly for Sexual and Life Reform), reflect the journal's broader aim of sex education. It seems likely that Szalit interacted with Magnus Hirschfeld directly in her work for this publication, though we have no evidence that they met. Hirschfeld lived with his partner, Karl Giese, at his Institute for Sexual Science overlooking the Tiergarten. Prominent intellectuals and artists, including André Gide, Gerhart Hauptmann, and Christian Schad, visited the institute.[15] If Szalit knew Hirschfeld well, the two might have remained in contact in exile several years later, though her name does not appear in his Paris guestbook.[16] (Might she have been wary of leaving a written record of a visit at that time?) Regardless of how Rahel Szalit came to place her drawings in *Die Aufklärung*, their publication demonstrates that Szalit was professionally active in queer Berlin.

Why was "Dina" first published in *Die Aufklärung*? The answer may lie in family history. Thomas Mann was widely known to be a closeted homosexual; his children, Klaus and Erika, were known for their same-sex relationships and openly gay or queer orientations. It is therefore not surprising that the Mann family's backing of Magnus Hirschfeld and his work began early. Already in 1900, Mann was among the prominent signatories of the Scientific Humanitarian Committee's unsuccessful petition to repeal Paragraph 175, the German statute that criminalized homosexual acts.[17] Hirschfeld had founded this committee in 1897 and chaired it until 1929. Thomas Mann's *Der Tod in Venedig* (Death in Venice, 1912) was targeted for its exploration of homoerotic desire between a middle-aged writer and a teenage boy; the writer's position as a sexual outcast is often read as a mirror of Mann's own status.[18] Klaus Mann's early novels from the mid-1920s also dealt with homosexuality, and both Klaus and Thomas Mann contributed to *Der Eigene*, one of the first gay journals. Finally, Thomas Mann's 1928 contribution to a volume for Magnus Hirschfeld's sixtieth birthday confirms that Mann continued to follow Hirschfeld's work.[19]

Yet the official reason given by *Die Aufklärung* for publishing "Dina" lies in the story's moral teachings about sex and intermarriage with outsiders. The prefatory remarks printed at the beginning of the first installment were authored by one P.K., probably Maria Krische's husband, Paul Krische, a long-time colleague of Hirschfeld's in the World League for Sexual Reform. These introductory comments suggested that the story also contained interesting material for research along "ethnological and national-psychological" lines.[20] They further cautioned the modern reader to avoid taking as an example the ethically dubious actions of primitive, patriarchal cultures, no matter how psychologically or artistically engaging.

The biblical story of Dina in Genesis 34 takes place in Shechem in the land of Canaan, which the children of Jacob, the biblical Israelites, first visit and later destroy. Thirteen-year-old Dina, the seventh child of Jacob and Leah and the only daughter alongside Jacob's twelve sons, goes out on her own to see the daughters of the land. Attractive and vulnerable, she catches the eye of Shechem (also: Sichem), the local Hivite prince, who immediately "lies with her." The prince's interest prompts Dina's father and brothers to try to negotiate a marriage, though her brothers, especially Simeon and Levi, ultimately conclude that Dina has been raped and decide to retaliate violently. Dina's name means "judgment" in Hebrew, and this is what she brings upon this outsider people. Her brothers first insist on the circumcision of all male Shechemites but subsequently decide to massacre them. No mention is made of the fate of Dina after she is retrieved from the prince's house. The result is a controversial avengement story that ultimately neglects its eponymous heroine.

Interpretations of the Dina story vary in terms of how they assign blame and victim status. In Genesis, the story is unclear on several points; most readers agree that Dina is a young victim who is subjected to both Sichem's desire and her brother's whims. Her story is interpreted as a cautionary tale that warns about the need to educate daughters and protect them from similarly compromised positions. One reading suggests that the biblical story in fact condemns the Israelites for labeling Dina as "defiled" and for violently overreacting to her situation.[21] Mann's version of Dina's story supports this interpretation in that he, too, implicates Jacob's sons. Today we also associate the biblical story with Jewish American writer Anita Diamant's best-selling women-centered novel *The Red Tent* (1997), written from Dina's perspective. Diamant portrays Dina's brothers as needlessly vengeful and violent and follows Dina's story beyond their horrific actions. Notably, Diamant also read and took inspiration from Mann's earlier version while producing her own work.[22] Szalit's illustrations similarly emphasize Dina's position and thus serve as a kind of feminist forerunner to Diamant's novel.

Mann and Szalit Portray Dina

Thomas Mann's "Dina" extends and rewrites Genesis 34 in several significant ways. Instead of immediately taking and lying with Dina upon first seeing her, Mann's Prince Sichem first sends his father, Hamor, to ask Jacob for permission to marry Dina. When circumcision is given as a condition, Sichem gladly complies but is then denied his prize. Only after this denial by her brothers does Sichem become angry and have his men kidnap Dina. Once Dina is in Sichem's house, she does not object to his advances but rather accepts them as necessary and natural. The rape of Dina thus becomes more of a fabrication by Dina's deceitful brothers than a straightforward violation of a young girl, and the brothers' quest for revenge becomes even more extreme. Jacob, who stands back and does nothing, is conveniently absent when his sons slaughter the Shechemites. But in its extension of the biblical story, Mann's story also does not end well for Dina, who, together with her mother Leah, is carried away by a camel, a scene depicted in Szalit's last illustration. Mann's final sentences suggest that Dina's own baby was left to die, and that "she herself grieved and withered away before her time. At fifteen her unhappy little face was that of an old woman."[23]

In Szalit's rendering, which builds on Mann's account, the young Dina initially appears proud, desirable, and even demure as she peeks out from behind a transparent veil (fig. 66). The side view of Dina and her facial features, especially the black kohl eyeliner extending her eyelid, evoke the type of beauty popularized by the iconic ancient Egyptian bust of Nefertiti. This bust was on display in Berlin museums beginning in the 1920s, and Szalit was undoubtedly familiar with it. The addition of a large neckpiece further recalls the colorful neckline of Nefertiti. Mann, too, had been greatly influenced by the discovery of King Tutankhamun's tomb in 1922 and had visited Egypt in 1925. The later books of *Joseph and His Brothers* take place mainly in Egypt.[24] Szalit's image is largely in line with Mann's description. According to Mann, Dina's tunic is not transparent but is revealing only when her arm is lifted, though Szalit's Dina lacks the pierced nose, painted fingernails, and hands adorned with rings that Mann discusses in detail. This is a notable omission, as Mann describes Sichem lusting after Dina's hands in particular. Szalit removes this aspect of how Dina is regarded by others as sexually alluring, though she remains a sexual figure.

SEXUALITY AND THE BIBLE

FIGURE 66 | R. Szalit, *Dina*, illustration from Thomas Mann's "Dina," in *Die Aufklärung*, 1929. Courtesy of the Magnus-Hirschfeld-Gesellschaft e.V.

Indeed, Szalit's illustrations of Dina and others are explicit and even racy. Women's breasts are visible in three of Szalit's eight illustrations. Szalit does not shy away from portraying the scene of Dina's kidnapping. Her image titled *Der Raub der Dina* (The Rape of Dina) shows Dina being lifted against her will by two soldiers; this is an image more of abduction than of sexual violation (fig. 67). The disconnect between the image's caption and what is pictured further underscores the hypocrisy of Dina's brothers, though the caption and general composition also recall famous paintings such as Rubens's *The Rape of the Sabine Women* (1635–40). Still, Szalit's abduction scene notably avoids the violence present in other visual representations of the Dina story. For example, Erich Büttner's lithographic illustration of *Dina und Sichem* (1917) obscures the partly nude figure of Dina behind a soldier who is actively plunging a sword into the neck of another man.[25]

Another Szalit illustration shows a wild dance scene at the autumn harvest festival (fig. 68). The caption, lifted from Mann's text, reads: "Men joined the dance as well; they were bearded and naked, with animal tails wrapped around them."[26] Here Szalit emphasizes the sexual, primal aspects of the Hivite or Shechemite culture while depicting a

FIGURE 67 | R. Szalit, *The Rape of Dina*, illustration from Thomas Mann's "Dina," in *Die Aufklärung*, 1929. Courtesy of the Magnus-Hirschfeld-Gesellschaft e.V.

scene that, except for public male near-nudity, does not seem entirely implausible in the context of Weimar Berlin. The dancing women's outfits are part Josephine Baker's banana skirt, part ancient Egypt.

This meeting of ancient Israelites and Shechemites produces the perfect storm for a culture clash. In Mann's version, however, it is difficult to muster sympathy for Dina's brothers, who turn out to be far less civilized in their excessive punishment of Sichem and

Männer kamen auch zu tanzen; sie waren bärtig und nackt, hatten Tierschwänze umgebunden

FIGURE 68 | R. Szalit, *Men Joined the Dance as Well*, illustration from Thomas Mann's "Dina," in *Die Aufklärung*, 1929. Courtesy of the Magnus-Hirschfeld-Gesellschaft e.V.

his people.[27] The Israelites are guilty of falling into barbaric patterns; they are certainly among the primitive, patriarchal cultures that *Die Aufklärung* warned against emulating.

In contrast to Mann's text, Szalit's illustrations do not show the Israelites in a negative light. For Szalit, it is the previously proud and later shamed Dina who is the victim, not the Shechemite people. In fact, Szalit refrains from depicting any scenes of slaughter or violence beyond Dina's abduction. To look only at Szalit's illustrations is to understand the story through Dina's eyes rather than to get the whole picture. Dina's father's word carries great authority, and Jacob is the focus of two images. But Dina's brothers, who only lurk in the background of those same images, are visually denied a chance to take their revenge.

Szalit further suggests a visible distinction between the Israelites and the Shechemites at the level of skin color. Although Mann describes Dina as having a "dark little face" and "golden-brown hands," Szalit's Dina appears pale white and contrasts sharply with the

FIGURE 69 | R. Szalit, *Sichem on a White Donkey*, illustration from Thomas Mann's "Dina," in *Die Aufklärung*, 1929. Courtesy of the Magnus-Hirschfeld-Gesellschaft e.V.

„Nach Ablauf der Frist aber kam Sichem selbst ins Lager hinaus auf einem weißen Esel . . ."

darker bodies of Sichem and his men, who are always shirtless, as in the image where Sichem rides in on a white donkey to discuss his intention to marry Dina (fig. 69). To be sure, Mann himself deployed what we would now consider racist stereotypes and language in his descriptions of Israelites and other peoples in *Joseph and His Brothers*, especially Egyptians, but he avoided describing the Israelites as pure.[28] Szalit's drawing of a white woman being abducted by men of color also alludes to other histories of racial and sexual violence. On one level, it reproduces the racist imagery of the German nationalist "Black Shame" campaign (1920–23), which accused colonial Black African soldiers of raping white German women during the French occupation of the Rhineland. In doing so, it depicts Dina as a "white" victim, notably claiming whiteness for a Middle Eastern Jewish woman.

Even as they challenge our understanding of how Szalit portrayed Jews and raise important questions about Jews and race, the "Dina" images also reflect many of Szalit's usual choices as an illustrator. They augment Mann's text by adding a new layer of content, thus creating a somewhat different narrative. In addition, Szalit's illustrations ensure that women are included in the visual record and foreground Jewish women characters. Animals remain front and center in over half of the illustrations: cats, a donkey, sheep, rams, and camels. The universal appeal of these animals is undeniable—their recurrence throughout different works by Szalit helps to connect past and present worlds. (We recall that camels also appear in her illustrations of Heine's "Jehuda ben Halevy" and Daudet's *Tartarin*, and the donkey that Sichem rides is the spitting image of the one ridden by Benjamin's sister in Tillier's *My Uncle Benjamin*.) Published in *Die Aufklärung*, Szalit's "Dina" illustrations opened the eyes of Weimar audiences to questions of how young women were treated and mistreated in biblical times, and, by extension, also in the 1920s.

Correctives to Social Mores

The story of Dina was not the only piece Szalit illustrated in Magnus Hirschfeld's journal. Four other images by "R. Szalit" appeared in *Die Aufklärung* in 1929: three accompanied short pieces of social criticism that seem to have been written by Hirschfeld himself, and a fourth illustrated a poem. As always, it is telling how and what Szalit chose to depict given the texts she was assigned. In one instance, Szalit's drawing of a breastfeeding woman appeared alongside Hirschfeld's article "Wegen Sittlichkeit" (Because of Morality, fig. 70).[29] This article pointed out that many people would not be sitting in jail for such offenses as same-sex sexual relations, incest, and children born out of wedlock if they had been born in locations that did not criminalize them. Szalit's illustration is thus not a perfect fit for this article, and it seems relevant only because of the brief references to mothers and children. But the placement of this image next to an article on morality implicitly references the taboo against breastfeeding openly in public, as well as the strides that women artists made in the late nineteenth and early twentieth centuries to overcome limitations on how women should be portrayed. This was not Szalit's first image of a breastfeeding mother; she also drew one in Jakob Steinhardt's guestbook (fig. 15).

Another socially conscious image by Szalit appeared as an illustration of Hermann Nöll's poem "Spaziergang der Sträflinge" (The Convicts' Walk, fig. 71).[30] Here we see another side of Szalit's engagement with the downtrodden, in this case an objective depiction of the poem's subject. Szalit's image shows three convicts walking in the prison courtyard, though she omits the strict guards who oversee this hour of exercise. Instead, she focuses on the beautiful flower bed toward which the men tilt their heads. By rendering only certain elements of the poem in this lone illustration, Szalit emphasized the quiet resistance of convicts who refused to concede their humanity to their captors.

FIGURE 70 | R. Szalit, *Because of Morality*, illustration from Magnus Hirschfeld's article in *Die Aufklärung*, 1929. Courtesy of the Magnus-Hirschfeld-Gesellschaft e.V.

Unsurprisingly, Szalit's illustrations of "Dina" and other images for *Die Aufklärung* are neither widely known nor regularly associated with the artist. Their depictions of sexually explicit content are anomalous within her known body of work. The journal itself did not have an especially large circulation, and we cannot be certain of how many readers encountered Szalit's images of Dina. On occasion, *Die Aufklärung* found itself embroiled in scandals related to the material it printed.[31]

The act of being associated with this journal or Hirschfeld's work could have been enough to mark or "out" Szalit publicly as queer; sexuality was something that she avoided mentioning in articles for Jewish publications. Jewish circles were generally conservative in their treatment of such topics as sex and sexuality, and Szalit, who was careful to avoid expressing even her political affiliation, would not have wanted to risk losing her favorable reception among one of her main audiences. Although it was by no means contradictory to be both Jewish and queer, there were plenty of Jews who did not see it that way. Today it is still very difficult to find concrete references to the queer lives that some Jewish artists led. The stories of lesbian activists such as Eve Adams, a Polish-Jewish

FIGURE 71 | R. Szalit, *The Convicts' Walk*, illustration from Hermann Nöll's poem in *Die Aufklärung*, 1929. Courtesy of the Magnus-Hirschfeld-Gesellschaft e.V.

contemporary of Szalit's who was deported from the United States in 1927 for obscenity and who was later murdered at Auschwitz, offer potential reasons why many Jews and others chose to conceal or downplay their sexualities.[32]

For Szalit, Jewish and queer identity were compatible, but being Jewish was far more significant, at least in her public life. Szalit's short autobiographical essay titled "I Am a Jewish [Woman] Artist" was published just one year after her final "Dina" illustration; tellingly, there is no mention whatsoever of sexuality in that essay. Despite her successful collaboration with *Die Aufklärung*, Szalit did not broadcast her involvement in queer circles, and we are left wondering if she agreed to the "Dina" illustrations largely because they focused on a Jewish woman. Throughout the late 1920s and early 1930s, Szalit never stopped exhibiting and publishing work through Jewish organizations and for Jewish audiences, though some of her most successful works from these years grappled with Jewishness in subtle ways.

CHAPTER 9

The Jewish Käthe Kollwitz

Berlin, Schöneberger Ufer, November 1929: The Association of Women Artists in Berlin is celebrating a major exhibition with ninety portraits of women, all created by women. Even the title is modern and sophisticated: Die Frau von heute, the woman of today. This woman has a new look. Male artists portray women differently; they simply do not see all that women see. Rahel is proud to have two paintings in this exhibition, and the one of a barmaid has been recognized with a prize. Her images look magnificent displayed alongside incisive portraits of New Women with stylish hats and daring short haircuts. Together, these artists have real momentum; they are changing the German art scene.

Every Thursday afternoon at five o'clock there's a special tea with a fashion show and short lecture to accompany this exhibition. Rahel arrives one Thursday as the sold-out event is winding down, with plans to meet several of her fellow artists afterward. They stroll in pairs, arm in arm, to a cozy nearby restaurant with candles on every table. With plentiful red wine, she forgets the pressing economic and political troubles of the moment. How liberating it feels to be among such cultured women.

Rahel and several other artists are also involved in Berlin's lesbian scene. She saw a few of them wearing pantsuits and neckties once while out with her former girlfriend. Some of these women are a bit older, well into their forties, and more established. In the exhibition, there is a striking portrait of her friend Eleonore Kalkowska, eyebrow raised. Eleonore's girlfriend is on the Association's board. With Eleonore, a writer from Warsaw, Rahel feels comfortable practicing her Polish. "Tonight we toast to my barmaid, Eleonore's portrait, and the success of the exhibition. Prost, na zdrowie, l'chaim!"

In the final years of the Weimar era, Rahel Szalit publicly embraced her identity as a woman artist and found new means of support and acclaim through women's organizations. The year 1927 was a crucial year for many women artists and photographers including Szalit.[1] Prior to becoming active in the Association of Women Artists in Berlin (Verein der Künstlerinnen zu Berlin, or VdBK) by early 1927, many of Szalit's known artist friends were men. Exposure to the current projects of other women artists would have a strong impact on Szalit's own style and choice of subject matter. It is unknown precisely what prompted her to gravitate toward groups of women artists, or what led to this major shift in her life and career, but her friendships with women surely played a role.

These friendships may have deepened during relaxing days at the beach. Like most Berliners, Szalit enjoyed getting out of the city, especially during the warmer months. In one letter from July 1927, Szalit noted that she was at the sea (*an der See*) for four weeks.[2] The use of the feminine article implies she was at the Baltic Sea, known in German as *die Ostsee*, a common destination for Berliners because of its location about 150 miles north of the city. There Szalit may have become better acquainted with the colony of painters who spent the summer months on the Baltic island of Hiddensee. In fact, two Jewish painters, Clara Arnheim and Henni Lehmann, founded a Hiddensoer Künstlerinnenbund (Hiddensee Alliance of Women Artists) in 1919. Prominent artist Käthe Kollwitz played an instrumental role in encouraging them to form this group.[3] Kollwitz, who turned sixty in July 1927, wrote of her time that year at "Hiddensee with my beloved people."[4] Szalit's friend Julie Wolfthorn also belonged to this group and loved to paint landscapes of the sea and dunes while working in the open air. Other artists who were affiliated with the Association of Women Artists had peripheral associations with the Hiddensee group, including Augusta von Zitzewitz and Martel Schwichtenberg. It seems more than a coincidence that Szalit summered at the sea the same year she joined forces with other women artists.

Thanks in part to her affiliation with the Association of Women Artists and to newfound recognition within Berlin's Jewish community, Szalit reached the peak of her career from 1927 to 1930. Her work was in highest demand during this period: she published countless illustrations in a variety of mainstream and Jewish periodicals, and her paintings and other work appeared in no fewer than twenty exhibitions. Most were not exhibitions of Jewish art; some focused on cars, portraits, or women as artists. Yet Szalit sometimes contributed works with Jewish themes to mainstream exhibitions, as was the case with *Thoraverhör* (Torah Examination), one of her paintings featured in the *Große Berliner Kunstausstellung* 1928, which was described as having an overall "green-yellow" tone and compared with a painting of musicians, likely *Die Dorfmusikanten*.[5] (Szalit also displayed still life paintings of flowers and fish.) Szalit's big break as a painter came in late 1929 when she won a prize for a painting. Until then, she was known primarily as a graphic artist, portraitist, and illustrator. But it was as a Jewish woman artist that

Szalit found greatest recognition. When compared with the work of other women artists in Germany, Szalit's art stood out because of its associations with Jewish, eastern, and other exotic subjects. In Jewish circles, she was considered exceptional because she was a talented female artist who could summon a mystical, soulful sensibility.

Two Art Historians, Different Canons

Some assessments of Rahel Szalit as a woman artist simply did not do her justice. Art historian Hans Hildebrandt's widely advertised and well-received book *Die Frau als Künstlerin* (Woman as Artist, 1928) makes plain that Hildebrandt regarded Szalit as a relatively insignificant eastern Jewish artist known mainly for her drawings. In this book, which features over 330 images, the one work by Szalit appears next to three images by Else Lasker-Schüler and one by Polish-Jewish artist Regina Mundlak. Though based mainly in Warsaw, Mundlak also studied and exhibited in Berlin. Szalit's image, one of her lithographic illustrations of Sholem Aleichem's *Motl* (titled "Drawing" by Hildebrandt), features a religious young man standing in front of an open book.[6] Mundlak's subject is very similar: a seated Jewish learned man is pictured reading. In stark contrast, drawings by Lasker-Schüler, who had a flair for the dramatic, show her ancient alter ego Prince Jussuf and a fakir. Of these three artists, only Lasker-Schüler is mentioned by name in Hildebrandt's main text, where he writes that her images embody a "fantastical oriental feeling" in a "dream world beyond all logic." Images of Chinese acrobats by Hedwig Pfizenmayer on the adjacent page suggest that Hildebrandt grouped Jewish-themed works with other eastern, exotic, or oriental subjects. In addition to the choice of image and its presentation in this context, the index further labels Szalit as a Polish artist.[7]

Szalit's detailed correspondence with Hans Hildebrandt and his wife, Lily, an artist, suggest that Szalit's assistance with *Die Frau als Künstlerin* was not properly repaid. Szalit sent them biographical information along with fifteen samples of her work, only one of which made it into the book, and the Hildebrandts also consulted her as a source of information about Russian women artists. She provided names and reached out to Parisian friends and to the Russian embassy in an attempt to locate the artists she knew. For her efforts, Szalit was rewarded with silence. She did not even receive the standard copy of Hildebrandt's book sent to the artists it discussed. In a letter to Hildebrandt from the early 1930s, Szalit pleaded with him to help: "All of my colleagues received a courtesy copy of this book at no cost—only I did not. I still have not seen this book even though it has already been so many years.... I would so very much like to have this work—unfortunately I cannot buy it for myself—the times are very difficult for us artists."[8] Hildebrandt may have forgotten, or perhaps he intentionally omitted Szalit from the courtesy list because the book did not feature her work as prominently as he had implied it would. For Hildebrandt, Szalit's primary contribution was her familiarity with Russian artists and her drawings of eastern-looking figures like those of other Jewish artists associated with the East. As of 1928, when Hildebrandt's book was published, Szalit had not yet achieved the status that she would soon earn as a painter.

Unlike Hildebrandt, who failed to give Szalit much of a platform among women artists, Karl Schwarz did everything he could in the 1920s to make room for Szalit among already canonical male Jewish artists. Schwarz's praise for Szalit exposed the sexist expectations harbored by many interested in Jewish art. In his book *Die Juden in der Kunst* (The Jews in Art, 1928), Schwarz lists key illustrators of the modern Jewish book (Joseph Budko, Jakob Steinhardt, Leo Michelson), noting, "And finally we must add to this list a female artist who had the exclusive claim to creating Jewish-novelistic illustrations [of Mendele and Sholem Aleichem]."[9] Elsewhere Schwarz wrote about Szalit: "It is astounding that the artistic-visual power that reveals itself in these full-of-character illustrations is a *woman* who far outshines all previous efforts of Jewish artists in this area. In her youth, she became acquainted with this tragic-grotesque milieu. She comes from a Polish Jewish small town and took from there the vitality that in her—despite hard strokes of fate—approaches the optimism of someone who stays cheerful by keeping busy."[10] It is certainly to Szalit's credit that Schwarz saw her as a force to be reckoned with. But it is also noteworthy that Szalit was the only woman included on such lists of Jewish illustrators, and that her success was considered astounding.

When Schwarz was hired in 1927 to work with the art collection of the Berlin Jewish community, of which he would later become curator and director, he had access to a special fund to purchase artworks by Jewish artists to support them during a time of economic crisis. The Jüdische Volkspartei (Jewish People's Party), an alliance of Zionists, Orthodox, East European, and lower-middle-class Jews, encouraged the Berlin Jewish community to support Jewish art, and a committee was established to help with acquisitions.[11] Volkspartei representative Aron Sandler, critic Adolph Donath, and sculptor Eugen Caspary were among the committee members, and all would join the Jüdisches Museumsverein (Jewish Museum Association) two years later.[12] Schwarz expanded the Berlin collection to include more modern art by such contemporary Jewish artists as Szalit, Steinhardt, Budko, Meidner, Struck, Lesser Ury, Samuel Hirszenberg, Leopold Pilichowski, Eugen Spiro, and Max Liebermann, and Schwarz also organized exhibitions of these works.[13] Szalit was one of few women, if not the only one, featured in these exhibitions.[14] Several of her works would later become part of the collection of the Berlin Jewish Museum, which eventually included art by many other women.[15]

Jewish Celebrity

Among Jews in Weimar Berlin, few Jewish women artists were better known than Rahel Szalit. Audiences of Jewish readers sought out examples of exceptional Jewish women, and Szalit's name reached more of these groups as her career reached its pinnacle. Journalists often learned about stars in the Jewish world from other Jewish publications, and one article could quickly lead to many. Three major profiles of Szalit appeared in Jewish journals in 1926: in the Viennese Zionist magazine *Menorah*, on the front page of *Die jüdische Frau*, and in the *Israelitisches Familienblatt*. Another by Karl Schwarz appeared in the *Jüdische Rundschau* in 1928, and the League of Jewish Women's newsletter published Szalit's autobiographical article a few years later.[16] Most articles reproduced multiple artworks by Szalit and introduced her to Jewish households across Germany and Austria.

Journalist Walter Kauders, writing for *Menorah*, instantly elevated Rahel Szalit's status by positioning her as a Jewish counterpart to Käthe Kollwitz. This comparison makes sense, though Szalit lacked the intense degree of social engagement that we now associate with Kollwitz. Still, Szalit's images of impoverished Jews and women naturally lent themselves to comparison with Kollwitz's many prints of women and the working class. Peasants, the unemployed, and mothers with children had figured prominently in Kollwitz's art since the 1890s. Her younger son died on the battlefield, and she became known for her depictions of suffering during and after the First World War, especially her pacifist print cycle *Krieg* (War, 1923).[17] Kollwitz was also extraordinarily successful for a German female artist: she was the first woman to be elected to the Preußische Akademie der Künste and to be named a professor there.

Kauders described Szalit as a force in the Jewish art world and beyond, and he exalted her in the highest terms for those familiar with Kollwitz. He suggested that while Szalit and Kollwitz were the only two female artists capable of depicting a given social moment and its corresponding figures of misery (*Elendsgestalten*), Szalit imbued her subjects with a type of Jewish "soul" missing from Kollwitz's works. Kauders asked, "But soul, where is soul? That is probably the gap between the safe, practiced drive of Kollwitz and the passionate pull of Szalit's hand. The one establishes, points to a circumstance; but the other lets her people and objects cry out, suffer, weep, laugh, decay."[18] He went on to suggest that the grotesque elements of Szalit's art should be attributed not to her but to the Jewish fate she depicted, which was itself grotesque given Jews' perpetual state of living in exile.

Kauders was far from the only critic to use the ambiguous notion of "soul" in describing work by a Jewish artist. Art historian Ernst Cohn-Wiener put it simply in his 1929 study: "Jewish art is always the art of the soul."[19] The term served as shorthand for the mystical and spiritual qualities that Central and West European Jews projected onto the more religious worlds of eastern Jewry. Other critics, too, described Szalit and her work as wistful and secretive, created from the "melancholic, mystical depths" of someone intimately familiar with the culture of East European Jews.[20] Kauders's opinion that Szalit's works were superior to Kollwitz's may not have been widely shared, and perhaps his comment was relevant only in Jewish circles that privileged a connection to eastern Europe. Yet even if unmerited, Kauders's comparison could only have helped Szalit earn additional recognition.

Two of Szalit's works featuring Jewish women found special resonance in Jewish circles. The first was her lithograph of a woman blessing Sabbath candles, *Sabbath*, an illustration of Heine's poem "Princess Sabbath" (fig. 41). The second, an eye-catching watercolor painting titled *Fahrt zur Hochzeit* (The Ride to the Wedding), was acquired by Karl Schwarz to become part of the Berlin Jewish community's collection and appeared in the first edition of Schwarz's book on Jewish art.[21] Both images were reproduced in the 1928 third annual calendar of the Jüdischer Frauenbund. This calendar brought together over four dozen artworks by Jewish artists across Europe, including Liebermann, Ury, Spiro, Steinhardt, and Meidner in Germany and Chagall, Mané-Katz, and Orloff in France.[22] Szalit's works were also included in later versions of the calendar.[23]

One great appeal of the League's calendar was it that it came with tear-out postcards featuring several artworks from the calendar. Szalit's *Fahrt zur Hochzeit* was printed on one of these cards and was thus seen by all who sent or received the postcard (fig. 72). This small watercolor uses thin brushstrokes to show a modest young woman, presumably the bride, riding with other women in a horse-drawn wagon reminiscent of transportation in small East European towns. Horse-drawn vehicles instantly recalled distant places or times gone by; in Berlin, automobile taxis had largely replaced horse-drawn carriages by this time. Aside from the driver and a small child, all of the subjects appear to be women. Their gazes face downward in anticipation; only the child, arms around its mother, stares straight out at the viewer.

Szalit sent a copy of the postcard bearing *Fahrt zur Hochzeit* to her friends Max and Charlotte Gollop to wish them a happy new year 1929.[24] German-Jewish dentist Max Gollop was an influential collector of modern art. Although we can guess from her many side jobs that Szalit, unlike some of her male counterparts, did not have official patrons who supported her on a regular basis, this postcard hints that the Gollops might have been collectors of Szalit's work.[25] Another collector, Siegbert Marzynski, a textile merchant and friend of artists Max Liebermann and Lovis Corinth, also purchased some of Szalit's works.[26] Postcards with the same image, though retitled *Fahrt zur Verlobung* (The Ride to the Engagement), would be reprinted in the 1930s.[27] Through these cards, many got to know Szalit as a Jewish artist.

The Berlin Jewish community continued its support for Szalit by awarding her the Helene Fischbein Endowment Fund prize in December 1930. The prize was named for an artist who had been a promising student of Lovis Corinth until her early death in 1919 from

FIGURE 72 | Rahel Szalit, *Fahrt zur Hochzeit* (The Ride to the Wedding), 1927, postcard from the 1928 Calendar of the Jüdischer Frauenbund (League of Jewish Women). Courtesy of Ute Luise Simeon.

influenza.[28] (Corinth himself was not Jewish, but his marriage to Jewish artist Charlotte Berend-Corinth had made him an honorary member of the Jewish community.) Rahel Szalit and two other artists, Ilse Weissmann and Hilde Bröder, each received the largest prize amount of five hundred Reichsmark (about two thousand in today's dollars). Adele Reifenberg, Ilse Häfner-Mode, and others received smaller amounts. The three judges were Karl Schwarz, Adolph Donath, and Käthe Kollwitz.[29] Winning this prize confirms that Szalit had strong backing among art historians, critics, and fellow artists.

It may come as a surprise that Kollwitz, a non-Jew, worked with the Berlin Jewish community on this award designed to champion up-and-coming Jewish women artists. Yet Kollwitz was unusually active in Jewish circles for a non-Jewish artist, and she clearly played an important role in the community.[30] Like Corinth, Kollwitz had Jewish connections in her immediate family: her sister Lisbeth Stern married a Jewish man, and Lisbeth's daughter Johanna Hofer (Kollwitz's niece) was married to Jewish actor Fritz Kortner, who was widely known for playing roles from Shylock to Dreyfus. This familial proximity surely helped Kollwitz play a role in Jewish public life.

In other Berlin Jewish circles, Kollwitz and Szalit were considered the leading women artists of the day. In the same month that Kollwitz voted for Szalit to receive the endowment prize, the Jüdische Altershilfe, an organization that cared for elderly Jews in Berlin, held several anniversary fundraising events. The main event was an opera performance followed by a society tea, which involved raffling off nearly a thousand signed books and original paintings by "Corinth, Kollwitz, Menkes, Szalit and others ... including Max Liebermann."[31] In this way, the Jüdische Altershilfe put culture at the center of its charitable efforts. But this list of major artists is also telling: Kollwitz and Szalit were the only two women included.

Though Szalit and Kollwitz were linked in many ways, we do not know to what extent Kollwitz actively supported Szalit beyond the 1930 Fischbein prize, or if the two were acquainted outside of mutual exhibitions and other professional occasions. Any letters or documents that might provide evidence of a friendship have not been preserved. The full story may well be complicated: Kollwitz was not always a fan of Ludwig Meidner, and Szalit's friendship with Meidner might have kept her at a distance from Kollwitz. But Kollwitz generously offered her mentorship to Ludwig's wife Else Meidner on several occasions, and Kollwitz must have served as a role model for Szalit as well.[32] By following in Kollwitz's footsteps, Szalit found her way to success in Jewish circles and to other women artists.

Women Artists of Berlin

Aside from Kollwitz, few women artists in early twentieth-century Germany achieved the same level of fame as their male contemporaries. Some were always overshadowed by male mentors, such as Gabriele Münter and many of the Bauhaus women.[33] The Association of Women Artists provided a chance to break this cycle. With 250 members by 1930, it regularly put on all-women exhibitions, and it arranged for work by members to be shown in special sections of larger Berlin exhibitions. Szalit participated in at least eight of the VdBK's exhibitions between 1927 and 1932. An exhibition catalog from 1928 indicates that she was a member of the Association of Women Artists at that time, and her name appears in the VdBK membership list for 1930, suggesting she was an official member for several key years.[34] In this way, Szalit came to show her work alongside many of Berlin's leading women artists, including Kollwitz, Annot (Annot Jacobi), Jeanne Mammen, Käthe Münzer-Neumann, Lotte Laserstein, and Julie Wolfthorn, to name but a few.

In some instances, critics perceived Kollwitz as a central highlight of VdBK exhibitions, whereas Szalit and others simply moved in orbit around Kollwitz. At least this was Adolph Donath's interpretation of *Die gestaltende Frau* (The Creating Woman), an exhibition of work by women artists at the Wertheim department store in October 1930.[35] In contrast, art critic Will Pless focused on the participating Jewish artists, noting that Szalit's oil painting *Musikanten* (Musicians) was one of her more poignant ghetto images.[36] The VdBK's exhibitions showcased a range of talents and earned Szalit regular mentions in reviews.

Szalit knew many of the artists in the Association of Women Artists personally, and through them she developed friendships and important connections. From one of her letters, we know Szalit was friends with Julie Wolfthorn, an older and more established artist who had helped found the Berlin Secession in 1898.[37] Both Wolfthorn and Münzer-Neumann contributed to Berlin exhibitions of Jewish art when Szalit first entered this scene in the early 1920s, and Szalit likely knew Münzer-Neumann socially as well. Indeed, the VdBK encouraged artists to gather at special social evenings that were often linked to exhibitions. For example, artists worked together to organize a festive artists' ball held in February 1927. In attendance at this ball were many artists affiliated with the VdBK (among them Schwichtenberg, Sintenis, Steger, Wolfthorn) as well as other well-known artists (Hofer, Orlik, Slevogt, Spiro) and prominent personalities (actresses Erna Morena, Gertrud Eysoldt, and Resi Langer; singer Claire Waldoff). Szalit helped with the decorations for this event, as the VdBK's newsletter reported: "Cool green dominated the primeval forest room [*Urwaldsaal*], adorned with eight giant paintings depicting primordial animals [*Urtiere*] from the hand of Frau Szalit."[38] Tragically, no images of these spectacular giant paintings of animals have been preserved.

Through her participation in the Association, Szalit also worked with Lotte Laserstein. In fact, they served together on a panel to select prize-winning paintings at the VdBK's spring exhibition in March 1930.[39] The two had much in common: they were not far apart in age, both experimented with same-sex relationships and intimacy, and both depicted androgynous, athletic, New Woman types. Nearly all of Laserstein's nudes portray her favorite model, Traute Rose, a short-haired athlete who was likely also her lover.[40] Laserstein, a baptized Protestant from an assimilated Jewish family, was not involved with Jewish art before 1933. But she had three Jewish grandparents, and the Nazis defined her as racially Jewish. She supposedly even took steps to convert back to Judaism to gain acceptance in the Jewish community in the mid-1930s.[41]

As in other mainstream German circles, Szalit's work as part of the Association of Women Artists was perceived as East European or foreign even when her Jewish identity was less relevant. This is evident through subtle comparisons in exhibition reviews. On multiple occasions, critics compared Szalit with Grete Csaki-Copony, who was born in Transylvania and lived in Hermannstadt (today Sibiu, Romania) in the 1920s. She spent winters in Berlin and was active in the VdBK during roughly the same years as Szalit.[42] Both artists worked in a variety of media and exhibited drawings and paintings.

Csaki-Copony's sketches of lively gypsies, peasants, and folklife were likened to Szalit's drawings—in one case, of chess players and animated children—which depicted another side of East European culture.[43] Paintings by Csaki-Copony from this period show barefoot women working in fields, harvesting potatoes or other crops, some carrying jugs on their heads. Seen through a mainstream frame of reference, the work of both Szalit and Csaki-Copony brought to life exotic aspects of East European folklore.

Either through these artists or through East European circles, Szalit also became close friends with Eleonore Kalkowska, a Polish-German writer from Warsaw.[44] Kalkowska was a politically engaged, independent-minded pacifist. She had made a name for herself with a 1916 collection of pacifist poetry written in response to the First World War. Her successful plays from the late Weimar years dealt with such topics as the death penalty, anti-Polish sentiments, unemployment, and the rash of suicides that resulted from the economic misery of the Great Depression. Having left her husband and children behind in another city, Kalkowska lived openly as a bisexual woman in Berlin. Milly Steger, a sculptor and Kalkowska's longtime girlfriend, was honorary chair (*Ehrenvorsitzende*) of the VdBK in 1930, and Steger also taught sculpture and figure drawing through its school. Steger lived on Nollendorfstrasse, quite close to Szalit. Kalkowska was close with many VdBK artists and at times participated in its events. She was the featured speaker at an "author's evening" held in conjunction with the Association's spring 1930 exhibition, which included works by Laserstein, Michaelis, Münzer-Neumann, Szalit, Steger, and others.[45] A famous photograph shows Kalkowska at a restaurant with Münzer-Neumann and Michaelis around this time.

Several of these women painted portraits or sculpted likenesses of each other, and they stayed in touch when some left Berlin for Paris and elsewhere. Eleonore Kalkowska would remain a confidante of Szalit's in exile until Kalkowska's death in Switzerland in 1937. Käthe Münzer-Neumann, too, would head to France and would survive the war. Lotte Laserstein would escape to Sweden. But not all were so fortunate: Alice Michaelis and Julie Wolfthorn would both perish in Theresienstadt, and several other artists active in the Association of Women Artists also would be murdered in the Holocaust.

A Prize-Winning Painting and the Artful Sport of Fencing

The exhibition *Die Frau von heute* (The Woman of Today), organized by the Association of Women Artists, brought Szalit further into the limelight when it opened on 10 November 1929. Politician Katharina von Kardorff oversaw the exhibition, and her presence guaranteed a certain amount of press. This month-long exhibition was conceived as an opportunity to display ninety new portraits of women by women and to demonstrate

FIGURE 73 | Photograph of *Die Frau von heute* (The Woman of Today) exhibition organized by the Verein der Künstlerinnen zu Berlin, 1929. Bundesarchiv, Bild 183-990-1015-503. Works displayed, from left: Julie Wolfthorn, *Frau Dr. Heller*; Käthe Münzer-Neumann, *Die bedeutende Frau* (Die Dichterin Eleonore Kalkowska) and *Die Berufstätige* (Kinoschauspielerin Aga v. Rosen; top row); Hanna Cauer, *Porträt der Tänzerin Anna Tesch* (sculpture); Ottilie Reyländer-Böhme, *Frau Dr. Waaser, Bildhauerin*; and Lotte Laserstein, *Porträt Polly Tieck*.

the talents of sixty-five contemporary female artists. It emerged in part as a response to "Das schönste deutsche Frauen-Porträt" (The Most Beautiful German Portrait of a Woman), a 1928 portraiture competition organized by the cosmetics company Elida and the Reichsverband Deutscher Künstler (National Organization of German Artists), which received more entries from male artists.[46] Fashion journalist Elsa Herzog noted in her opening remarks in the catalog that *Die Frau von heute*, in contrast, aimed to support the careers of women artists.[47] Reviews written by women praised the exhibition and emphasized the portraits' focus on working, career women.[48] One review suggested that the growing popularity of photography threatened to diminish the demand for painted portraits and that the exhibition doubled as a kind of propaganda for the art of painting.[49]

Along with the majority of works in this exhibition, Szalit's paintings were realistic portraits of career woman types in line with New Objectivity. A movement that emerged in reaction to Expressionism and focused on realistic, unsentimental portrayals, Neue

Sachlichkeit (which can be translated as either New Objectivity or New Sobriety) gained traction after 1925 and swept the German art scene in the late 1920s. Portraiture was common, especially portraits of specific social types. Several exhibitions in which Szalit participated in the late 1920s were linked to New Objectivity, including the Berliner Künstlerbund's exhibition *Der bildende Künstler als Reporter* (The Visual Artist as Reporter).[50]

Recent work by a broad array of women artists was on display in *Die Frau von heute*. Szalit, Csaki-Copony, Kollwitz, Laserstein, Michaelis, Münzer-Neumann, Schneider-Kainer, Schwichtenberg, Steger, Wolfthorn, von Zitzewitz, Elsa Haensgen-Dingkuhn, Marie Laurencin, Fanny Remak, Maria Slavona, and about fifty others were among the exhibitors. Their portraits showed women as writers, journalists, secretaries, doctors, actresses, dancers, artists, equestriennes, flower sellers, and more. Some of the best works were reproduced in the catalog, as well as in photographs of the exhibition (fig. 73): Wolfthorn's painting *Frau Dr. Heller* shows a chicly dressed woman in a hat with a cigarette holder; Münzer-Neumann's portrait of Kalkowska was exhibited under the title *Die bedeutende Frau* (The Remarkable Woman).

Szalit contributed two paintings to this exhibition. The first, *Fatma Karel*, depicted a Latin American dancer and film actress who visited Berlin and received considerable media attention around this time.[51] A portrait reproduced in an American Jewish magazine's article on Szalit is very likely her painting of Fatma Carell (fig. 74).[52] The woman

FIGURE 74 | Rahel Szalit, *Portrait*, in *B'nai B'rith Magazine: The National Jewish Monthly*, 1931. Courtesy of B'nai B'rith International.

in this image has the same center hair part, high eyebrow arches, long nose, and heavy makeup as Carell, whom Szalit could have met in person or painted based on photographs. But this was not the painting that exhibition-goers remembered.

The painting *Die Emigrantin als Bardame* (Emigrant Woman as Barmaid) was by far the more memorable and successful of Szalit's two contributions (fig. 75).[53] A portrait of a modish modern woman serving cocktails and pub fare, it was one of six paintings to win a prize of one hundred Reichsmark (about four hundred in today's dollars). Many incorrectly took this to mean that Szalit had won "first prize."[54] The other five prizewinners were Viktoria Boblenz, *Porträt Carmen Straus*; Grete Csaki-Copony, *Bildnis* (Portrait); Elsa Haensgen-Dingkuhn, *Selbstbildnis mit Sohn* (Self-Portrait with Son); Lotte Laserstein, *Porträt Polly Tieck*; and Augusta von Zitzewitz, *Barbara Kemp*.[55]

This prize-winning painting capitalized on Szalit's lived experience as an "emigrant": one who has left a country of origin, but who is still in transit and has not yet established permanent residence elsewhere. The dark hair and eye color of the woman in this painting enabled it to symbolize at once the Russian, Polish, and foreign, all elements that were seen as Jewish. The barmaid's downcast eyes suggest that her mind is elsewhere. Though the bar patrons behind her eat and drink merrily—a somewhat androgynous but likely male figure looks directly at the viewer, and two women seem to be eating directly from plates—the barmaid appears as a detached outsider who fits into this scene only because of her employee status. We can guess that Szalit knew East European women who indeed worked in restaurants or bars, as this was a profession open to those with limited language skills or without work permits.

The bar's interior is key because most paintings in *Die Frau von heute* featured only one central, female subject. Few showed women inhabiting populated public spaces. In Laserstein's *Polly Tieck*, a portrait of a well-known journalist, the central figure sports a monocle and cloche hat with cutouts. Behind her, a few sharply dressed people stand and are seated at tables against the back wall, as in a restaurant or nightclub. Elsa Haensgen-Dingkuhn's *Frau und Strasse* (Woman and Street) shows an elegant woman in the foreground with a busy street scene behind and below her.[56] Yet only Szalit's painting invites the viewer to consider the subject's complex positioning with respect to her immediate surroundings. It spotlights a low-paid worker in action, countering the tendency to portray women as seated, smoking, or otherwise acting as consumers in bars and cafés. This is alluded to in the background of *Die Emigrantin als Bardame*, where two patrons occupy themselves with plates of food. Drinks and bottles on a bar counter stand between the viewer and the barmaid, as in Édouard Manet's well-known painting *A Bar at the Folies-Bergère* (1882), where a barmaid likewise wears a flowerlike adornment and faces the viewer. Whereas Manet's title indicates his focus on the bustling space of the bar, Szalit's tells the story of an emigrant woman who must work.

FIGURE 75 | Rahel Szalit, *Die Emigrantin als Bardame* (Emigrant Woman as Barmaid), 1929. Akademie der Künste, Berlin, Verein der Berliner Künstlerinnen 1867, no. 5114. Photo © Knud Peter Petersen, Berlin, used with permission.

Indeed, Szalit's painting *Die Emigrantin als Bardame* caused quite a sensation. News of Szalit's prize and this Jewish woman artist's prominent role in a major Berlin exhibition traveled all the way to Poland and Lithuania via the Yiddish press.[57] Writing for the *Berliner Tageblatt*, Adolph Donath suggested that Szalit's barmaid had the *esprit* of a Parisian woman.[58] In contrast, Max Osborn, art critic for the *Vossische Zeitung* and the author of books on Jewish artists Emil Orlik, Nathan Altmann, and Irma Stern, concluded that Szalit's surprising and playfully composed painting had a social component, and that a certain "fate emerged from it."[59] (As it happens, Osborn and Szalit would share the fate of such emigrants ten years later in Paris, when Osborn would again have a chance to review Szalit's work.) Another review highlighted Szalit's painting as one of the best pieces in the exhibition and reached a similar conclusion about the "whole fate" it depicted—namely, that it "not only reflected, but rather relived and recreated a personality."[60] It was later considered to be one of only a few paintings that fully answered the call to employ current techniques and imagery of the 1920s, including images of the New Woman.[61] This may be another reason Szalit's emigrant woman found special resonance with many viewers.

Particularly strange is the fact that some Jewish audiences automatically assumed that Szalit's winning portrait depicted a "Russian" Jewish emigrant, though this was not an obvious implication. Jewish newspapers from Berlin, Frankfurt, Zurich, and even Warsaw added the word "Russian" to the painting's title, misquoting it as "Die russische Emigrantin als Bardame."[62] Szalit's portrait could have reminded some viewers of Laserstein's *Russisches Mädchen mit Puderdose* (Russian Girl with Compact, 1928), which had attracted attention as a finalist in the 1928 competition, "Das schönste deutsche Frauen-Porträt."[63] Wolfthorn's *Porträt einer Russin* (Painting of a Russian Woman) would have been known to many at the time as well; it adorned the cover of the VdBK's newsletter in September 1929.[64] Confusion about the Russianness of Szalit's subject also implies that a Russian emigrant woman was as likely to work as a barmaid as she was to apply makeup.

Whereas some reviewers understood the painting's subject as specifically Russian, one interpreted it as a broader story about the integration of migrants into German culture. Will Pless, the art editor of the *Israelitisches Familienblatt*, who had profiled Szalit several years earlier, noted that Szalit's more recent works depicted "the Jew of the western world," a subject that demanded a new means of expression. In Pless's view, Szalit achieved this through the execution, line, and color scheme of her latest works.[65] Key here is Pless's suggestion that even eastern "emigrant" Jews could be *of* the western world in which they resided.

If we compare *Die Emigrantin als Bardame* with Szalit's painting *Die Fechterin, Selbstbildnis* (The Fencer, Self-Portrait), it is possible to see that the emigrant barmaid in fact bears a strong resemblance to Rahel Szalit's own likeness, though *Die Emigrantin* was not a self-portrait. A photo of *Die Fechterin* appeared in the glossy fashion magazine *Die Dame*

THE JEWISH KÄTHE KOLLWITZ

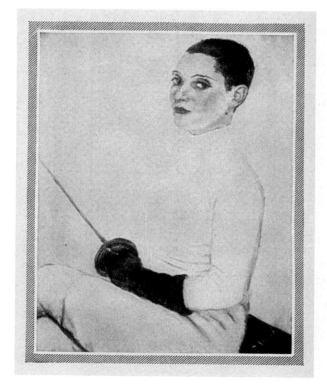

FIGURE 76 | Rahel Szalit, *Die Fechterin, Selbstbildnis* (The Fencer, Self-Portrait), in *Die Dame*, 1930. Kunstbibliothek, Staatliche Museen zu Berlin—Preußischer Kulturbesitz.

in January 1930, not long after Szalit became known as a prize-winning painter (fig. 76).[66] This sleek self-portrait, perhaps done with watercolors, shows Szalit in a high-necked white fencing uniform, with a black glove and épée in her left hand, indicating that she was either left-handed or used a mirror to create this portrait. She appears to be wearing makeup on her eyes, cheeks, and lips. As in other self-portraits from around this time, including paintings by Laserstein and Csaki-Copony, the artist's likeness steadily looks out to meet the viewer's gaze with an unsmiling, neutral expression. But Szalit's fencer offers an intervention into the woman-as-artist self-portrait genre: she painted herself not as an artist, holding a palette or paintbrush or at an easel, but as an athlete. Her weapon, even at rest, possesses a different kind of energy than a paintbrush or a cigarette holder. She is ready to rise, to engage her opponent, to fence, to prove herself.

Several months later, Szalit's illustrated article about "the artful sport of fencing" appeared in *die neue linie*. This magazine adopted Bauhaus notions of avant-garde typography and appealed to classy women readers, embodying "not just a fashion trend, but also a lifestyle, a way of life that is chiefly exemplified in travel, elegance, affluence and gaiety."[67] Titled "Parade Riposte" (Parry-Riposte/Retort) to spotlight the use of French fencing terms, Szalit's article drew on her extensive knowledge to pitch both the sport's

PARADE RIPOSTE

Die Malerin Rahel Szalit, selbst eine ausgezeichnete Fechterin, empfiehlt der eleganten Dame den kunstvollen Fechtsport

Parade riposte, Parade riposte, nicht die riposte vergessen, kommandiert der Fechtmeister. Leicht gesagt — man hat nicht nur den Angriff des Gegners abzuwehren, sondern a tempo ihm eins zu versetzen. Wieviel Geschicklichkeit, schnelles Denken und Intelligenz dazu gehört, um dies durchzuführen, merkt man erst, wenn man anfängt, frei zu fechten. Da hat man aber lange zu warten, bis dieser selige Augenblick kommt, denn es gibt kaum eine Sportart, die einer so langjährigen Ausbildung bedarf wie der Fechtsport. Tage, Wochen, Monate und Jahre vergehen in einem unermüdlichen Üben.

HELENE MAYER, die Meisterin

die blitzende, elegante Waffe auf den Gegner zu richten, durch das Drahtgeflecht der Masken einander von den Augen die Absicht des Vorhabens abzulesen. Wie eine Pantherkatze lauernd dazustehen, um dann blitzschnell auf den Gegner loszuschießen und alle seine schönen Absichten zu vereiteln. Nicht immer gelingt dies. Öfters bleibt man erstaunt mit dummem Gesicht an der gegnerischen Klinge aufgespießt hängen, und erst dann merkt man, daß man der Dumme war, denn der Gegner wollte man hinters Licht führen, tat so, als ginge er auf die Falle ein und lockte damit den anderen ins Verderben.

Mit gemischten Gefühlen, das heißt Bewunderung für den Gegner und Wut gegen sich selbst, gibt man den Treffer zu, indem man ansagt „touché moi". Denn es ist ein ritterlicher Sport, und man muß es sein, aber nicht selten merkt man dabei, wie wenig ritterlich die Menschen sind. Es existiert ein weiser Ausspruch zwischen den Fechtern: „Bloß 10 Minuten Fechten mit einem Menschen und sein Charakter ist dir bekannt." Das stimmt auch. Alle guten und schlechten Seiten des Gegners, seine Schwächen, Eitelkeiten, das geistige Niveau, Intelligenz, mit einem Worte, es ist keine Kleinigkeit, mit einem fremden Gegner einen Kampf aufzunehmen.

Es ist ein großer Genuß, einen Kampf zweier guter Fechter zu beobachten. Gleich ob es Florett, Säbel oder Degen ist, denn alle drei Waffen sind, jede in ihrer Art, herrlich. Eine Augenweide sind die schönen Bewegungen der Fechter, so stilvoll, so eigenartig. Der eng anliegende, elegante Fechtdreß, die Maske, die behandschuhte Hand beim Kampf, die blitzende Waffe, das alles ist etwas, was fasziniert. Und dann die ritterliche Höflichkeit, kaum ein anderer Sport besitzt so viele Höflichkeitsgesetze wie das Fechten. Jeder neue Gang beginnt mit einer Begrüßung des Gegners wie der Zuschauer, jeder Fehlschlag bedarf einer Entschuldigung, und es ist eine große Unhöflichkeit, die Fechtlinie zweier Kämpfer zu überschreiten, auch wenn sie im Moment ausruhen. Im Grunde genommen muß man das Fechten mehr zu den Künsten, denn zu den Sportarten zählen, gehört doch großes Talent dazu. Es trainiert wohl den Körper, macht ihn zäh und sehnig, hebt den Mut wie ein Sportart, entwickelt das Denken wie ein Schachspiel, aber die Hauptsache beim Fechten ist doch die Kunst der schönen Klingenführung, und das ist das Schwerste. Jahre, viele Jahre vergehen bis man es erreicht. Die Italiener, die Meister der Fechtkunst, fangen schon als

Kinder zu fechten an, mit dem Ergebnis, daß auf den internationalen Fechtturnieren vor allem die elegante Klingenkunst der Italiener auffällt. Nach der letzten Olympiade, nach den großen Siegen der deutschen Damen im Fechten, ist dieser Sportzweig hier in Mode gekommen. Es gehört nun zum guten Ton, Privatstunden im Fechten zu nehmen, sich einen Dreß à la Helene Mayer anzuschaffen und bei sich zu Haus Florette an der Wand hängen zu haben. Der Fechtmeister und die liebenswürdige Fechtmeisterin sind aber wirklich nicht zu beneiden, denn erreichen tun nur wirklich „arbeitende" Damen etwas, denn wie gesagt, das Fechten ist eine große Kunst und Ausdauer ist nicht jedermanns Stärke.

Aber es ist eine schöne Ablenkung vom grauen Alltag. Am Abend in hellerleuchteten Fechtsaal zu sitzen, vom Kampf ausruhend sich den Betrieb anzusehen, macht viel Freude.

Die Fechtklubs sind international. Man hört verschiedene Sprachen, und nirgends kann man die Temperamente der Völker so gut studieren wie hier. Dort kämpfen Italiener — man erkennt sie nicht nur an ihren schönen Bewegungen — sie sind laut, jeder angebrachte Treffer wird mit einem Jauchzen begleitet. Dort Ungarn — kraftvoll, vornehm und merkwürdig dezent. Und die Franzosen? Die bewegen sich kaum beim Fechten — sie führen fein mit winzigen Bewegungen ihre Waffe, und ihre Art ähnelt mehr einem Schachspiel, als einem Kampf. Ja so ein Abend ist wirklich lehrreich und schön — namentlich, wenn zum Schluß noch ein Wettkampf sämtlicher Fechter stattfindet, wo der Meister den Schiedrichter spielt — und der Sieger zum Lohn als erster unter die heiße Dusche gehen darf.

Text und Zeichnungen von **RAHEL SZALIT**

Kampf um die Meisterschaft zwischen SOMMER und CASMIR

Parade riposte — Parade riposte (Einladung— Antwort), hop — hop — hop — la — Stellung — Ausfall — Schritt vorwärts — hop — Schritt rückwärts — hop — la. Wie ein Zirkuspferd wird man trainiert und das Merkwürdige ist, daß man es keinen Moment als peinlich empfindet. Umgekehrt, dieses Fechten wird einem geradezu zur Leidenschaft. Man wird heiß und müde, man kriegt manchen blauen Fleck vom gegnerischen Treffer ab, aber das macht alles nichts. Man ist wie besessen, immer wieder zieht es einen in den Fechtsaal. Es ist ein Genuß,

Lehrerin und Schülerin in der Fechtstunde

Trotz seiner Wohlbeleibtheit ist der Italiener SCHIAVONI eine internationale Berühmtheit des Fechtsports

12

FIGURE 77 | Rahel Szalit, "Parade Riposte," in *die neue linie*, 1930. Getty Research Institute, Los Angeles (87-S446).

attire (tight-fitting clothes, mask, gloves, weapon) and its "chivalrous virtues" (fig. 77). Her dynamic drawings show fencers in action: an unnamed female student and instructor; Helene Mayer, famous for her gold medal at the 1928 Olympics; Robert Sommer and Erwin Casmir competing in the German Fencing Championship; and Italian fencing master Schiavoni, who taught at the Berliner Fechtklub. To stay on top of the trends, Szalit claims, one should "take private fencing lessons, purchase an outfit à la Helene Meyer, and have a foil hanging on the wall at home." Szalit's words further reveal her own love for the nuances of the sport: "It is as if one is obsessed, again and again one feels pulled into the fencing salle.... To stand there lurking like a panther cat, in order to then open fire on an opponent quick as lightning and thwart all of his good intentions."[68] This practiced athlete was as strategic in the fencing club as she was in the art world.

Szalit's "woman of today" was one like herself, a migrant who landed in the metropolis of Berlin to discover countless new opportunities. There were enough people in transit that the emigrant barmaid could be considered as valid a type for Weimar culture as the white-collar stenographer, shop girl, or athlete. But it is also significant that Szalit projected her own image and emigrant status onto an unspecified barmaid whose unknown fate is itself symbolic. The prize-winning painting accompanied Szalit four years later when she fled to Paris, where she found new circles of refugees, artists, partygoers, fencers, and women who loved freely.

Difficult Times for Artists

Despite the success she had recently found as a painter and regular contributor to periodicals, the early 1930s were not easy years for Rahel Szalit. We recall Szalit's remark in a letter from this period: "The times are very difficult for us artists." The worldwide Great Depression put her in a precarious financial situation even before things became politically untenable. In the early 1930s, Szalit found relatively few opportunities for paid work, with only a smattering of illustrations published in periodicals in 1931 and none in 1932. She thus returned to commercial illustration (she had already created an advertisement for Kantorowicz vodka several years earlier) and accepted a commission to illustrate a medical text.[69] A lexicon for natural medicine by Dr. Alfred Brauchle featured several drawings of Szalit's that resembled her other images of hunched, stricken women. One showed how to administer an increasing-temperature footbath to combat colds and infectious diseases (fig. 78).[70] This made good use of her skill in drawing the human form and helped pay the bills, though it was not the kind of work Szalit usually preferred.

The significant gap in Szalit's overall activity during these years suggests that something kept her away from her customary circles. There is no documentation of her

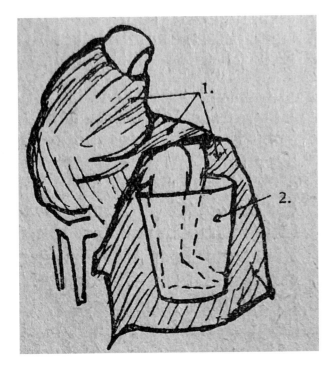

FIGURE 78 | Rahel Szalit, *Increasing-temperature Footbath*, illustration from Alfred Brauchle's *Lexikon für Naturheilkunde* (Lexicon for Natural Medicine), 1931.

participation in any exhibitions between January 1931 and February 1932, even though many groups continued to hold regular exhibitions. Szalit's name is conspicuously absent from these exhibition reviews.[71] Perhaps she was ill or away for an extended period, possibly visiting her sister, aging mother, and cousins in Poland. The endowment fund prize money she won in December 1930 would have funded a trip to Lodz, with enough left over to share with her family. Szalit also kept in touch with friends in Lodz, including pianist Maria Chazen, who would later visit her in Paris and would advise writer Bruno Schulz to contact Szalit when he visited Paris in 1938.[72] Szalit resumed public activities in Berlin by 1932, and she exhibited several times with the Association of Women Artists and other organizations.

When Berlin's first Jewish Museum in the Oranienburger Strasse finally opened on 24 January 1933 after a long delay and six days before Hitler's accession to power, Szalit's works may have been among those shown, possibly in its rotating graphic exhibitions.[73] Szalit later indicated that the Jewish Museum owned several of her paintings.[74] Museum records show that its collection included an original watercolor of Szalit's *Fahrt zur Hochzeit*, the chalk drawings *Rabbi und Schüler* (Rabbi and Pupil) and *Toralernen*, lithographs titled *Litauische Jüdin* (Lithuanian Jewish Woman) and *Der Rabbi*, and Szalit's illustrations of the stories of Reb Nachman of Breslov. Rachel Wischnitzer, a curator at the museum in the 1930s, donated her copy of Szalit's Reb Nachman illustrations to the museum in 1935.[75] The museum remained open through 1938, when it was shuttered by the Nazis; large parts of its collection, including some of Szalit's works, eventually made their way to the Jewish Historical Institute in Warsaw.

The rise of Nazism unleashed political and social turmoil. Jews were quickly shut out of mainstream circles. After Hitler was appointed chancellor on 30 January 1933 and the Nazi Party took power, only Jewish exhibitions and artistic circles remained open to Szalit. These included various print initiatives (especially calendars and postcards) aimed at Jews still living in Germany. That Jewish organizations after 1933 rose to the task of providing a space for Jewish culture to flourish is both wondrous and, viewed with the benefit of hindsight, highly controversial, as it played a role in convincing some Jews not to leave Germany in the early years of Nazi rule.

Remarkably, things came full circle for Szalit in the face of these new restrictions. In February 1933, she showed her work at the B'nai B'rith lodge in the Kleiststrasse—the very same location as her first exhibition in 1920, once again in an exhibition designed to help Jewish artists in need.[76] This space thus provided some of Szalit's first and last opportunities to see her work exhibited in Berlin. The 1933 exhibition coincided with the fiftieth anniversary celebration of B'nai B'rith in Germany. In a review, Rachel Wischnitzer extensively praised Szalit's watercolors, especially a bold sketch titled *Brücke* (Bridge). Wischnitzer also commented on Szalit's talent as a watercolor painter, noting, "We have become too accustomed to looking for Szalit the graphic artist, the interpretive illustrator, and we continue to be surprised to encounter such a rich talent for color and pictorial composition, above all this sensualism of form that contrasts with the deliberate meagerness of the means of expression."[77] Despite Szalit's success as a painter, many still thought of her primarily as an illustrator and graphic artist.

We do not know Szalit's exact departure date, but most sources suggest she fled to Paris in 1933. Even after she left, her work remained a prominent part of the German-Jewish art scene for another year or so. Along with Max Liebermann, Julie Wolfthorn, and Eugen Spiro, Szalit contributed artwork to the first *Kunst-Werk* initiative of the Jüdische Künstlerhilfe (Jewish Artists' Relief), which was undertaken in collaboration with the Kulturbund Deutscher Juden (Cultural Association of German Jews). This campaign to support Jewish artists distributed postcards featuring their art to over one hundred German-Jewish communities in December 1933 and January 1934.[78] Szalit further contributed to the Künstlerhilfe's tear-off calendar for the year 1934–35, though she could easily have arranged to do this in advance or by mail.[79] Two 1934 exhibitions of Jewish art in Berlin and Breslau also featured works by Szalit.[80] Although Szalit received considerable support as a well-known Jewish artist, there were not enough opportunities to keep her in Germany given the threat that loomed.

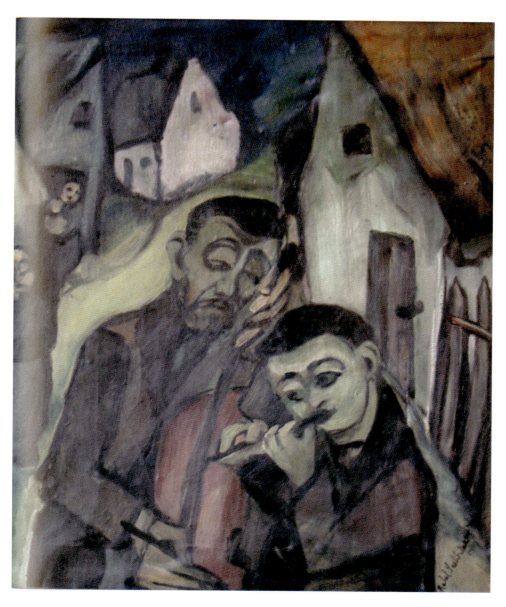

COLOR PLATE 1 | Rahel Szalit-Marcus, *Die Dorfmusikanten* (The Town Musicians), 1920. Oil on canvas, 56 × 50 cm. *Montparnasse déporté* exhibition catalog, 2005.

COLOR PLATE 2 | Marc Chagall, *The Fiddler*, ca. 1913. Oil on linen tablecloth, 196.5 × 166.5 cm, Stedelijk Museum, Amsterdam. © 2022 Artists Rights Society (ARS), New York / ADAGP, Paris.

COLOR PLATE 3 | Szalit's Berlin studio apartment, ca. 1921–33, Stübbenstrasse 3, Schöneberg. Sign across the street reads, "Promotionsverbot für Juden [Jews may not receive academic degrees], 15.4.1937." Orte des Erinnerns / Places of Remembrance—Memorial in the Bavarian Quarter (1993).

COLOR PLATE 4 | Cover of Hayim Nahman Bialik's *Ketina kol-bo*, with lithographs by Rahel Szalit-Marcus, Ernst Böhm, typography: Franziska Baruch (Berlin: Rimon-Verlag, 1923). Paper, bound, hand-colored, 30.50 × 23.5 × 1 cm; Jüdisches Museum Berlin, VIII.6. Biali 597. Photo: Jens Ziehe.

COLOR PLATE 5 | Cover of *Milgroym*, issue no. 1 (1922). Courtesy of the Leo Baeck Institute, call number q N 8 M5.

COLOR PLATE 6 | Ernst Böhm, *Crew of the Nutshell Boat*, illustration from Hayim Nahman Bialik's *Ketina kol-bo*, with lithographs by Rahel Szalit-Marcus, Ernst Böhm, typography: Franziska Baruch (Berlin: Rimon-Verlag, 1923). Paper, bound, hand-colored, 30.50 × 23.5 × 1 cm; Jüdisches Museum Berlin, VIII.6. Biali 597. Photo: Jens Ziehe.

COLOR PLATE 7 | Szalit's Paris studio apartment, late 1930s, 6bis rue Lecuirot, Montparnasse. Photo by Catherine Ellsberg.

COLOR PLATE 8 | Szalit's last known Paris address, 7 impasse du Rouet, Montparnasse. Photo by Catherine Ellsberg.

PART 4

Exile in Paris

(1933–1942)

CHAPTER 10

From Berlin to the School of Paris

Paris, June 1935: This is it: the solo exhibition in Paris that every modern artist dreams of. This is Rahel's first big break since arriving in Paris, where things have been very hard. She is a refugee again, cast out of Germany for the second time (the first was in 1914). But, with the help of some Polish acquaintances, she has managed to land an exhibition at Galerie Zborowski. Previously, it belonged to the famous dealer of Soutine and Modigliani. Rahel is sorry she didn't get to meet Monsieur Zborowski before he died. Originally from Warsaw, he was like a bridge from eastern Europe to Paris. The corner gallery with a white door, adorned with columns and white iron bars, is no longer what it once was—but it still bears his name and is located two blocks from the Seine, right across from the Louvre.

Almost every afternoon of her exhibition, Rahel walks over to the 6th arrondissement to visit the gallery. Some of these works traveled with her in suitcases; others are more recent paintings and drawings produced in her Paris studio apartment. At the gallery, Rahel often runs into Paulette Jourdain, the current owner, a slender woman with a long neck. Paulette is usually accompanied by her eleven-year-old daughter with Zborowski, Jacqueline. The radiant child is only a few years younger than Paulette was when she began posing for Modigliani. Rahel remembers what it was like to be this age, to gaze in wonder at the towns and cities around her.

The gallery is never full, but it usually has at least a few visitors. Several times Rahel has seen someone purchase a painting, yielding desperately needed income. Amid walls of elegant frames displaying her works, Rahel sees some faces she recognizes from Berlin. All who know her congratulate her warmly on this success: "Félicitations, c'est magnifique!" Practically all of

Berlin is in Paris now, or they have already passed through and moved on to London or New York.

But Rahel worries: what will become of her here in Paris?

Rahel Szalit made her way from Berlin to Paris soon after the Nazis came to power in January 1933. She was part of the first wave of emigration from Nazi Germany, well before the Nuremberg Laws of 1935 and the November Pogrom of 1938 (Kristallnacht) signaled to many others that it was time to leave.[1] For Szalit, the writing was on the wall: several of her friends fell victim to arrests or attacks in early 1933. Eleonore Kalkowska was imprisoned briefly before escaping from Germany. Jakob Steinhardt was arrested by the SA in March 1933, after which he promptly departed for Palestine. Also in March, the Nazi newspaper *Völkischer Beobachter* viciously took aim at the Jewish background of specific artists, including Käthe Münzer-Neumann and Else Lasker-Schüler. By April, Jewish artists Fanny Remak, Julie Wolfthorn, and Alice Michaelis were barred from serving on the board of the Association of Women Artists.[2]

The Nazi boycott of Jewish businesses on 1 April 1933 created a general climate of fear and intimidation among Jews, and many understood the boycott as a rupture.[3] For both liberal and Jewish writers, the book burning of 10 May served as a clear signal that it was time to pack their bags. The citizenship and denaturalization law of July 1933 targeted East European Jews by revoking German citizenship from anyone who had acquired it since 1918. This affected about one hundred and fifty thousand foreign or foreign-born Jews still living in Germany in mid-1933.[4]

The Nazi process of "Aryanization" looked somewhat different for artists, and many visual artists departed Germany slightly later than writers. Artists deemed unacceptable by the Nazis were excluded from public institutions in April 1933 and were not admitted into the Reichskulturkammer (Reich Chamber of Culture), founded that September, which effectively shut them out of their professions.[5] Rachel Wischnitzer observed in late 1934 that the "exodus of Jewish artists" from Germany was still ongoing.[6] The Chamber of the Fine Arts expressly forbade Julie Wolfthorn, Eugen Spiro, and others from practicing their profession in December 1934.[7] Over sixteen hundred visual artists were labeled as Jews and shut out of the Reichskulturkammer by 1938.[8] Many painters associated with Expressionism and New Objectivity were gradually expelled from art academies and banned from exhibiting. Szalit's non-Jewish friend Karl Hofer, for one, was personally attacked in *Deutsche Kultur-Wacht*, the journal of chief Nazi ideologue Alfred Rosenberg's Combat League for German Culture, though Hofer nevertheless chose to remain in Germany. His studio was later bombed and destroyed in 1943.[9]

The definitive warning event for artists, the *Entartete Kunst* (Degenerate Art) exhibition, opened in July 1937 in Munich. This particularly egregious form of Nazi propaganda targeted prominent modern artists including Oskar Kokoschka, Ernst Ludwig Kirchner, George Grosz, and Otto Dix; also Marc Chagall, Wassily Kandinsky, Paul Klee, and Pablo Picasso.[10] Still, many artists fled Germany even before 1937, and France was among the most popular destinations. Others left Nazi Germany for Czechoslovakia, Great Britain, and elsewhere.

Szalit must have sensed she was in personal danger early on. Did she take the time to put her affairs in order and obtain the necessary visas, or did she simply board a train bound for the French border? How much of her art was she able to bring with her to Paris, and what happened to the works she left behind? Who cleared out her Berlin studio? We do not know exactly when Szalit left, though most sources indicate it was in 1933. Any official records documenting her departure from Berlin and arrival in Paris have been destroyed. It is certain that she established herself in Paris before summer 1934. In any case, this was a transitional phase of Rahel Szalit's career. Her work was exhibited in Berlin, Breslau, and London while she made connections in Paris. Because she had been active in Germany before Hitler's rise to power, she soon became known as one of the many Jewish artists "from Germany." As the catalog for a 1934 London exhibition of works by German-Jewish artists put it, Szalit's geographical affiliation was "formerly Berlin, now Paris."[11]

Refugees in 1930s France

When Szalit arrived in France, land of liberty and equality, she was in very good company. In 1933 alone, approximately twenty-five thousand people headed from Germany to France, including over twenty thousand Jews, though many would later move on to other countries.[12] And, although obtaining an entry visa soon became more complicated, French officials continued to admit those who were at "evident, immediate risk" through 1936. Maintaining refugee status in France was another issue: once temporary visas expired, refugees needed to apply for a residence permit. Work permits were almost impossible to obtain.[13] Many refugees entered the country illegally, some under the pretense of visiting the 1937 World's Fair.[14] By the end of the 1930s, there were approximately three million foreigners in France; about one-third were refugees from fascist dictatorships.[15]

Paris was a natural choice for artists, writers, political activists, and others who fled Nazi Germany. It held special appeal because of its modernist movements, museums, educational institutions, and art market. France was a central destination for foreign artists well before the 1930s, and many German artists had spent time there before going into exile. Among those who fled to France circa 1933 were German-Jewish writers Hannah Arendt, Walter Benjamin, Alfred Döblin, Siegfried Kracauer, Lion Feuchtwanger, Joseph

Roth, and Anna Seghers. Photographers Robert Capa and Gisèle Freund and film critic Lotte Eisner were also in this first wave, as were novelist Heinrich Mann and actor Peter Lorre.

In total, about two hundred visual artists left Germany for France in the 1930s.[16] Jewish artists including Käthe Münzer-Neumann, Ludwig Wronkow, Jankel Adler, and J. D. Kirszenbaum all arrived in France around 1933. Münzer-Neumann, known in France as Kate Munzer, successfully joined the French art scene almost immediately upon arrival; she would survive the war and go on to become one of the more successful women émigré artists in Paris.[17] Many other Jewish artists and art historians arrived later in the 1930s. Eugen Spiro returned to Paris in 1935 (he had also lived there from 1906 to 1914). Art critic Max Osborn, a founding member of the Kulturbund in Berlin in 1933, arrived in Paris in 1938. Charlotte Salomon, then only twenty-one years old, fled Germany after the November Pogrom in 1938 and joined her grandparents in Villefranche-sur-Mer. Other artists such as Marc Chagall and surrealist Max Ernst had already spent considerable time living in France beginning in the 1920s. Only select émigrés such as Chagall were able to become French citizens.

On many levels, women artists had different experiences of immigration to or through France. Whereas many married couples ended up living in artists' colonies on the Mediterranean Coast between Marseille and Toulon, unmarried women were more likely to settle in Paris.[18] Yet women generally had less access to the opportunities, friendships, and connections that could have helped them succeed in Paris. They rarely lived in the famous artists' colonies such as La Ruche (the Beehive), and they did not receive the same offers of support from art dealers or potential patrons. Finally, most female refugees did not consider enlisting in the French Foreign Legion when thousands of their male counterparts did in 1939.[19]

Refugees fleeing Nazi Germany joined many other immigrants from eastern Europe who were already living in Paris. The wave of Russian-Jewish migration from the 1880s to the First World War brought over twenty thousand immigrants to Paris alone. Many other East Europeans arrived in the following decades, with the result that this city was home to about ninety thousand East European Jews on the eve of the Second World War (roughly 60 percent of the Jews in Paris). In all of France there were about one hundred and fifty thousand East European Jews in 1939, or about half of France's Jewish population. They had various backgrounds: Polish, Russian, Hungarian, Romanian, and Lithuanian. Several areas of the city housed most of these Jewish immigrants, especially the poorer eastern and central sections on the Right Bank.[20] In the interwar years, most Yiddish cultural organizations were located in the 10th arrondissement, for example the Communist-affiliated Paris *Kultur-Lige* and the Bundist Medem-Club and Medem Library.[21] Although Szalit found her rightful home among other foreign artists in Montparnasse, this did not put her in the vicinity of the largest communities of Jewish immigrants. Still, there were roughly one hundred thousand Yiddish speakers in Paris at the time, and Szalit knew some of them through the artists of the School of Paris (École de Paris), many of whom spoke Yiddish.[22]

Non-French citizens living in Paris faced constant challenges that intensified throughout the 1930s. They dealt with poor job prospects and extreme poverty, as well as endless bureaucratic paperwork and a society that was becoming increasingly xenophobic and anti-Jewish. Through 1935, material assistance was available for recent refugees from Germany. Upon arrival, Szalit was eligible for aid from relief organizations including the National Committee for the Welfare of German Refugees/Victims of Antisemitism, which helped fourteen thousand Jews by the end of 1934.[23] The Henri Heine Center was founded in June 1933 to provide both moral and material support to German-Jewish refugees, including meetings, concerts, and French classes. At other shelters throughout the city, bread and potatoes were distributed to Jewish and non-Jewish refugees alike, and hot meals were subsidized.[24] Dormitories housed many Jewish refugees. There was also a special committee that worked with the Polish consulate to help Polish-Jewish refugees who had escaped from Germany.[25] But even these extensive support networks could not do much to assuage refugees' feelings of isolation and displacement.

Place of origin soon held greater significance as French policies began to categorize refugees according to citizenship and legal status. In 1937, France began granting asylum only to political refugees who could demonstrate a reason for choosing France.[26] A policy of forced repatriation affected many Jews of East European origin. Some of Rahel Szalit's contemporaries held special Nansen passports, documents issued to stateless persons, which helped them remain in France as legal refugees.[27] In 1938, when new refugees flooded out of Austria and Czechoslovakia, the French government began issuing fines and prison sentences for foreigners with false papers or without visas, or who failed to comply with expulsion orders.[28] The situation became even more precarious for refugees and indeed for all foreign Jews in France in the years that followed.

Alone in Her Atelier

Ostracized by French society, Rahel Szalit found a home among émigrés and expatriates. Even so, she was profoundly lonely during her time in Paris, particularly after several love affairs fell apart in 1934. For one, Szalit split up with a woman she had been living with, whom she referred to as "the Swede" in a personal letter to her friend Eleonore Kalkowska from 14 August 1934. We have few other details about Szalit's lover except her nationality and gender. Szalit wrote that she "couldn't put up with her [the Swede] anymore," noting that she found out the Swede had "*some kind* of a disease" and was "a person who constantly walks around with a dark cloud over their head." Szalit further described the Swede's behavior that led to their breakup: "Last time, she woke me up at two A.M. and told me to get dressed. She arrived with some guy she had just met. They were drinking wine until five in the morning. And I, stunned by this meanness, couldn't open my mouth. The next day, I told her that I couldn't live with her anymore."[29] These lines reveal that Szalit was profoundly hurt by the Swede, whose brazenly offensive actions seemed intended to cause harm. They also offer a glimpse into the sexual fluidity of interwar Parisian artists' circles: although these two women were in a relationship and living together, one did not hesitate to bring home a man who was presumably a potential lover.

Another affair that Szalit had with an unnamed married man from Cuba came to a dramatic end around the same time. This man took a painting she had given him and disappeared, leaving only a false address when she asked him to return the painting. He further betrayed her by lying about his availability. Szalit lamented, "As it turns out, besides his wife . . . he's got another English woman that he introduces as his fiancée. And he told me that only I existed for him in this world. . . . This incident affected me greatly because I had never experienced anything like that before."[30] In addition to exposing her vulnerability, this account suggests that Szalit's love life was entangled with her art. It was common for artists who inspired each other to exchange works; in this instance, she lost both a painting and a lover.

This letter offers key evidence that Rahel Szalit had sexual and romantic relationships with both men and women. It further underscores that Szalit was a social person who sought the company of others, and that many of her friends were also foreigners. Filled with anxiety and loneliness in the wake of these emotionally devastating events, Szalit wrote to Kalkowska, who had recently left Paris for London:

> Sitting here makes no sense. I hate Paris right now. I've never had so many financial and emotional worries as here. I am alone in my atelier. . . . I'd like to escape this city—I don't like it here. . . . I am most curious how you have been, what your hopes are, and whether life is cheaper there than in Paris. Please, excuse my poor Polish—I have completely lost the habit of using this language. It seems to me now that the most horrible thing in the world is loneliness. If I could write well, I would describe the life of a person who is destined for solitude and suffering greatly because of it.[31]

Not long after her arrival, Szalit longed to leave Paris even though there were no viable alternatives. She was especially troubled because her relationships did not last, leaving her "destined for solitude." Szalit probably never felt as at home in Paris as she had in Berlin, though she would gain a stronger foothold in the Parisian art world just a year later.

The School of Paris in Montparnasse

Szalit eventually found a place among the artists who converged in the Left Bank neighborhood of Montparnasse. This group—termed the École de Paris or School of Paris circa 1925, though it had begun to form years earlier—consisted largely of foreign avant-garde artists who had come to Paris in search of opportunity and community. Around 150 artists are now considered to have been affiliated with this group. A large percentage were Jewish, many from eastern Europe. Montparnasse provided Szalit and her contemporaries with a bohemian, cosmopolitan support network, inexpensive studio space, art academies that welcomed foreigners, and cafés that brought artists together.[32] Chagall, for one, described the "world of richness, luxury, art, the play of life" that he found in Paris.[33] But even though the School of Paris to some extent represented Jewry to the French public, most artists did not participate in any Jewish communal or religious activities.[34]

When we think of the School of Paris, we think of Marc Chagall, Jacques Lipchitz, Amedeo Modigliani, Jules Pascin, and Chaim Soutine.[35] These core artists arrived in Montparnasse around 1910 and thus preceded Szalit by decades. Several first resided in the bohemian artists' colony La Ruche. Many reached their prime and achieved renown in the 1920s, when the art market boomed.[36] Though they lacked the unifying formal characteristics of some art movements, the foreign artists of the School of Paris were distinctive enough in background and aesthetics that they could be distinguished from other schools. The École de Paris did *not* include French-born artists of the French School (Fauvists such as Matisse; Cubists and post-Cubists including Picasso, Georges Braque, and Fernand Léger), Surrealists (Joan Miró, Salvador Dalí), or abstract artists (Piet Mondrian, Wassily Kandinsky). In contrast to these groups, most artists of the School of Paris tended toward figurative representation and avoided abstraction. The focus on the human figure and, in some cases, also on psychological study, is widely seen as characteristic of Jewish artists in this group.[37] New forms of portraiture were indeed central for Modigliani, Soutine, and others.[38]

Art historians agree that it is difficult to identify indications of Jewishness in works by most artists of the School of Paris, with a few exceptions, most notably Chagall, but also Mané-Katz, Issachar Ber Ryback, J. D. Kirszenbaum, Arthur Kolnik, and Abraham Weinbaum.[39] Some point to "Soutine's shudder" as a supposedly Jewish expressive force characterized by melancholia and negativity.[40] Paula Birnbaum has argued that the sculptor Chana Orloff engaged with questions of Jewishness and gender in her work, including through portrait busts of other Jewish artists.[41] To the extent that Szalit was affiliated with the School of Paris, Szalit constitutes another exception. Even though little is known about the work she created in Paris, she certainly published and exhibited work with Jewish themes during this period.

Many artists gathered at Café du Dôme, which was famous for attracting foreign artists and a key fixture of the Montparnasse café scene. The large café with numerous outdoor tables still exists at the intersection of Boulevard Raspail and Boulevard du Montparnasse, known as the Carrefour Vavin. Countless writers and artists have referenced Café du Dôme in memoirs, letters, and novels. When Picasso moved from Montmartre to Montparnasse in 1912, he lived just a few blocks from Le Dôme and its competitor, Café de la Rotonde. The Dôme changed owners and attracted a new generation of artists after World War I. In the 1920s and 1930s, it was frequented by the likes of Ernest Hemingway, Sinclair Lewis, Henry Miller, and Peggy Guggenheim. Walter Benjamin included Le Dôme on his list of waystations on a 1926 Paris trip, during which he described the area of "Montparnasse, where Russians have now established a new Bohemian quarter."[42] In an exile novel by Austrian writer Anna Gmeyner set in the mid-1930s, the protagonist, Nadia—who, like Szalit, left the Russian Empire for Germany and later France—orients herself in Paris thanks in part to Café du Dôme. Nadia's visits to this café provide "sudden and fleeting glimpses into the lives and destinies of all kinds of people."[43]

It is thus not surprising that Le Dôme was popular already in the early 1900s among the first Jewish émigrés who would become associated with the School of Paris. Walter Bondy and Rudolf Levy were some of the first "Dômiers," and they soon stood in the middle of a circle of other German artists.[44] Art dealers Alfred Flechtheim and Wilhelm Uhde, too, spent considerable time there, and Flechtheim even named a 1914 show in Düsseldorf after the Dômiers.[45] Eugen Spiro and Jules Pascin joined this crowd circa 1906. Modigliani was another regular. Chana Orloff, one of the best-known women artists in the School of Paris, could be found at Café du Dôme beginning around 1910. Moïse Kisling moved into a studio close to the Dôme, which he kept until 1940.[46] The cafés were an integral part of the neighborhood and the art scene.

Rahel Szalit, too, became a Montparnasse local who frequented the Café du Dôme. As a refugee living on savings and meager earnings, Szalit never had much money to spend at cafés. Even so, she connected with artists and other friends simply by joining them for conversation in the evenings. One source suggests that Szalit rarely sat at a table at the Dôme but instead stood around and schmoozed with friends and acquaintances that she encountered there.[47] Perhaps she ran into Mané-Katz, Kisling, Zadkine, Soutine, or other School of Paris artists who still visited Le Dôme in the 1930s. Yiddish writer Sholem Asch also frequented the café.[48] Szalit might even have rubbed elbows with Simone de Beauvoir and Jean-Paul Sartre, who sat and worked at Café du Dôme amid refugees who passed the time by reading newspapers and playing chess.[49] De Beauvoir famously learned from a waiter at the Dôme that Germany had declared war on Poland on 1 September 1939.[50] Szalit might also have found her way to the Triangle Bookstore just up the street, which served as a gathering spot for Jewish artists and Yiddish writers. Some of these contacts surely helped Szalit establish herself quickly in the Paris art scene.

Paris Exhibitions and Connections

Szalit lived in Paris's 14th arrondissement, near the heart of Montparnasse. The only surviving police record lists her address as 225 boulevard Raspail, then Hôtel de la Paix (today Hôtel Léopold).[51] This well-known residence for artists located steps from Café du Dôme was likely where Szalit stayed when she first arrived and needed to get her bearings. Its eighty beds were relatively inexpensive, with nightly prices ranging from fifteen to seventy francs, or roughly fourteen to sixty-five in today's dollars. However, Szalit stayed in this hotel only briefly—even as a recent transplant to a new city, she preferred her own apartment to a large, shared space.

By mid-1934, and until at least 1938, Szalit lived at 6bis rue Lecuirot, about a thirty-minute walk from Le Dôme. This two-story brick building can be found on a quiet side street just off rue d'Alésia, the southern border of Montparnasse (plate 7). Like many inexpensive artists' residences in this area, her apartment had multiple rooms and thus could serve as both living quarters and studio space. Szalit was content there for several years; the war must have forced her to downsize and relocate. Szalit's last known address before her arrest was 7 impasse du Rouet, a six-story building overlooking a small courtyard at the end of a narrow, dead-end alley off avenue Jean Moulin (plate 8). This was less than half a mile from her previous apartment, closer to the Alésia metro station. Her last home was smaller and more secluded, though hardly an effective space of wartime refuge, as Szalit was still required to register this address with the French police in October 1940.

Selling her artwork would have been critical for Szalit to support herself in Paris. Whereas many other émigré artists found work in journalism, publishing, or domestic work such as cleaning houses, it is possible that Szalit's only other source of income was teaching fencing, which she reportedly continued to do in Paris.[52] Still, selling paintings was no easy feat, particularly in a city where she was not especially well known. In 1934, Szalit wrote, "I keep painting, but so what—I have an atelier full of paintings but no one to buy them."[53] Her situation seems to have improved as she forged connections to local galleries and communities and found opportunities to exhibit her work.

The year 1935 was a banner year for Szalit's time as an artist in Paris. This was a good year for the French art market in general, and there was a perceptible increase of emigrant artists exhibiting in commercial galleries by late 1935.[54] Szalit participated in at least four exhibitions that year, including two solo exhibitions. This is especially impressive considering that few émigré artists managed to organize large-scale solo exhibitions at all.[55] Given Szalit's relative level of success as indicated in sources from the 1930s, it is strange that she receives almost no mention in the scholarship on German emigrant artists in France. She may have been overlooked because of her East European background or because she was a woman, or because she forged the strongest personal ties to people who did not survive the war.

In February 1935, two works by Szalit were shown in an exhibition of the Société des Artistes Indépendants (Society of Independent Artists) in the Grand Palais. This venue had historically been one that supported foreign artists, including Chagall. One of Szalit's exhibited works was titled *Portrait* and was priced at 2,000 francs. The other bore the French title *Intérieur de bar* and was priced at 3,000 francs (4,000 in today's dollars).[56] A review notes that one painting on display at the Société des Artistes Indépendants had won a prize in Berlin.[57] We therefore have good reason to believe that the painting renamed "Bar interior" was in fact *Die Emigrantin als Bardame* (fig. 75), suggesting that Szalit was able to transport her winning painting out of Germany, and that it was for sale in 1935, when she desperately needed funds. If Szalit was successful in selling it, we can remain hopeful that this extraordinary painting was not destroyed and is instead still hanging on the wall (or stored in the attic) of a French apartment.

That same month, Szalit held a small solo studio exhibition, presumably at her studio apartment at 6bis rue Lecuirot. It is uncertain whether this exhibition received much press in France, but a rave review appeared in the *Jüdische Rundschau* back in Berlin. From the review's vivid descriptions, we know that Szalit continued painting and made great progress with her work in Paris. One painting shown in her studio was a vibrantly colored garden landscape with three horses. Others depicted Jewish themes: klezmer musicians in village streets; praying with a *lulav* (palm branch) on Sukkot; and a child walking with its mother to a *cheder*, a traditional Jewish school. The Berlin review implies that the Paris Sephardic community was planning to establish a Jewish museum and had already acquired some of Szalit's paintings and illustrations for its museum.[58] Though it may sound odd that Szalit was adopted by a community of Jews with shared origins in the Iberian Peninsula, this makes more sense if we recall that a few works, such as her illustrations of Heine's "Hebrew Melodies," touched on subjects of particular interest to Sephardic Jewry.

At this juncture, Szalit seems to have taken this one step further by concocting an origin story for herself that included Sephardic heritage. It is unknown whether this was a complete fabrication or if it had factual underpinnings; before 1935, there is no mention whatsoever of Szalit having any Sephardic connections. Although it is difficult to reconcile her family's longstanding Lithuanian roots with Sephardic heritage, Szalit's family lore might have included ancestors who migrated eastward from Spain or other lands long ago. Or this may have been part of a broader ploy to call attention to herself—after all, if Else Lasker-Schüler could claim to be from ancient Thebes, why couldn't Rahel Szalit have Spanish ancestors? Regardless of whether Szalit's Sephardic ancestry was real or imagined, it brought her to the attention of the Paris Sephardic community at a critical moment when she needed publicity.

Szalit's "Sephardic origins" landed her a two-page write-up in the French-Jewish journal *Le Judaisme Sepharadi* in February 1935. Journalist and art critic Jacques Biélinky wrote about Szalit as one of many artists recently arrived from Germany. An immigrant himself, Biélinky—who, like Chagall, hailed from Vitebsk in the Russian Empire—recognized that exiles newly uprooted by Hitler's racist policies faced tremendous challenges as they attempted to integrate into the anonymous Paris multitudes. Biélinky commented on Szalit's sense of longing for the acclaim she had found in Germany, noting that she "melancholically leafs through the large collections of periodicals where her work is exalted by the best authors from across the Rhine." Evocative descriptions suggest Biélinky met Szalit and saw many of her works in person. He wrote of the "eternal Jewish breath of optimism" and "fresh colors" on "anemic and ravaged faces," as well as her "enormous and prodigious collection" of illustrations, displayed on various boards. Biélinky further commented on the "archaic" appearance of graphic art that lent itself perfectly to "outwardly grotesque and inwardly moving" characters.[59]

Two of Szalit's images appeared as illustrations of Biélinky's article: the Havdalah scene already discussed in chapter 6 (fig. 43), and *La leçon du Talmud* (The Talmud Lesson, fig. 79). Both works depict profoundly Jewish subjects and appear to have been created using chalk, pastels, or pencils. The lines in these 1930s sketches are noticeably thicker than those in Szalit's earlier lithographs. If we compare *La leçon du Talmud* with a print of a similar subject, *Der Rabbi und sein Schüler* (fig. 13), we again observe that Szalit borrowed the composition of her earlier works while updating them to look less stereotypically East European. Whereas the rabbi and his pupil from 1920 had visible *peyes*, the student and teacher in *La leçon du Talmud* wear more subtle head coverings, and their *peyes* are either absent or blend in against the background. The Talmud lesson image from 1935 foregrounds a candle not included in the otherwise similar 1920 lithograph; in the later image, the two men huddle together conspiratorially and pore over their books by candlelight. Their act of study is somehow more private, but no less important. In addition to praising and introducing his readers to Szalit's work by reproducing these two images, Biélinky's article anticipated Szalit's upcoming exhibition in June and concluded

FIGURE 79 | R. Szalit, *La leçon du Talmud* (The Talmud Lesson), in *Le Judaisme Sepharadi*, 1935, Jacques Biélinky papers. From the Archives of the YIVO Institute for Jewish Research, New York.

by strongly encouraging readers to visit this "exhibition that will be a milestone in the recent history of Jewish art."[60]

Indeed, Szalit reached the apex of her Paris career with a two week-long solo exhibition from 7–21 June 1935 at Galerie Zborowski, 26 rue de Seine. This widely known gallery had opened in 1927 with a top Left Bank location, and a solo show there was a very prestigious accomplishment. Léopold Zborowski, a Polish poet who came to Paris in 1910 and died in 1932, had made his name as a major art dealer and patron of Modigliani and Soutine. Galerie Zborowski was known to regularly exhibit works by Polish artists, and it was considered part of the Polish network in Paris.[61] Through this network, Szalit could have met such artists as Mela Muter, Alice Halicka, Frania Hart, and Alice Hohermann. After Zborowski's death, most of his paintings were sold to pay off his debts, and his assistant, Paulette Jourdain, ran the gallery for several more years. Because Jourdain had modeled for Modigliani, Soutine, Pascin, and Kisling, she was well connected in the Paris art scene.[62] Szalit's exhibition earned a brief mention in the *Pariser Tageblatt*, the foremost German-language exile newspaper in Paris, which reported that Galerie Zborowski was "currently showing a worthwhile exhibition of paintings by the well-known artist Rachel Szalit."[63] An address correction published two days later gave Szalit's exhibition additional publicity.⁶⁴ The newspaper's description confirms that Szalit's work was of interest to German-speaking emigrants in Paris. In late 1935, Szalit also found her way into mainstream French circles by exhibiting at the Salon Populiste.⁶⁵

In the years that followed, Szalit strengthened connections to other German émigré artists by joining the Free Artists' League (Freier Künstlerbund; Union des Artistes Libres), a professional organization of artists and critics. This group succeeded the short-lived Collective of German Artists (Kollektiv Deutscher Künstler), founded in 1936. It was formed in 1937 as the German Artists' League (Deutscher Künstlerbund) and reconstituted as the Free Artists' League in 1938. Perhaps Szalit attended the meeting at Café Mephisto on 20 April 1938, when the Freier Deutscher Künstlerbund was founded anew by Eugen Spiro, Gert Wollheim, Paul Westheim, and Heinz Lohmar.⁶⁶ Spiro was elected the League's official chair; Oskar Kokoschka's Prague-based group became affiliated with the Paris League as well.⁶⁷ Although we cannot determine the exact extent of Szalit's participation in the Free Artists' League, her name appears on its membership list from April 1938, and it is clear that she associated with leading German-speaking artists in Paris. Among the other members of this group were Hans Arp, J. D. Kirszenbaum, Max Lingner, Julius Schülein, Lilly Steiner, Wilhelm Uhde, and Willi Wolfradt.⁶⁸

The Free Artists' League aimed to counter the *Degenerate Art* exhibition that premiered in Munich in July 1937. It successfully organized a Paris exhibition, *Freie Deutsche Kunst* (Free German Art), from 4–18 November 1938 in the Maison de la Culture in the rue d'Anjou. This Paris exhibition featured works by seventy of Szalit's contemporaries (including Beckmann, Ernst, Grosz, Kirchner, Kirszenbaum, Klee, Kokoschka, Krauskopf, Münzer-Neumann, Schülein, Spiro, Tischler, Wollheim; also Felix Nussbaum, who would later become known for his wartime paintings of persecution), though it is unlikely that Szalit's work was included.⁶⁹ Even if it was not, she might have attended the opening or another cultural event paired with the exhibition. Lion Feuchtwanger, Egon Erwin Kisch, Joseph Roth, and Anna Seghers participated in these "German culture week" events.⁷⁰ In addition to cultural resistance, members of the Free Artists' League also shared news and their troubles with one another. In April 1939, Eugen Spiro wrote in the League's newsletter, "We have all experienced insane, unbelievably horrible things; we were torn away from our careers. We all, young and old, have been profoundly shaken to the core and battered by the world evil, the phenomenon of doom keeping humanity in suspense from Berlin, which forbids us to paint or 'dictates' painting to others, which chases us, incites, persecutes us—so that we perish [*verrecken*]!"⁷¹ For Szalit, joining the Free Artists' League constituted an act of political resistance, which she generally shied away from in Paris out of fear for her safety.⁷²

Rahel Szalit's last known participation in a major exhibition was in a show of Jewish art in June 1939. One of her paintings, a watercolor of an oriental rider, appeared alongside works by Marc Chagall, Eugen Spiro, Issachar Ber Ryback, Mané-Katz, Chana Orloff, and others. The subject of Szalit's painting links her to a long tradition of artists who depicted riders on horseback, from Dürer and Rembrandt to Rosa Bonheur, Edgar Degas, and Wassily Kandinsky. Including an animal was also typical for Szalit. This (now lost) painting further suggests that Szalit continued to embrace Jewish subjects through imaginary journeys to faraway places, even as she became unable to travel herself. Szalit was likely invited to participate in this 1939 art exhibition by Rachel Wischnitzer, one of many Berlin contacts with whom Szalit reconnected in Paris. The Wischnitzers moved from Berlin to Paris in spring 1938. Less than two years later, in January 1940, Rachel Wischnitzer left for the United States, where she would become a well-known scholar of Jewish art.

During her short time in Paris, one of Rachel Wischnitzer's accomplishments was organizing this sale exhibition of Jewish art as part of a larger Palestine exhibition at the Palmarium du Jardin d'Acclimatation. Proceeds went to the Zionist organization Keren Kayemeth L'Israel (Jewish National Fund). Although the exhibition was on display for only a few days in June 1939, it made a strong impression. If Szalit attended the exhibition opening on 17 June, she would have heard a concert with Hebrew, Yiddish, and Ladino songs, followed by dancing. Jewish newspapers reported on the exhibition in French, Yiddish, and German, affirming that Paris was home to a flourishing international Jewish art scene on the eve of the Second World War.[73] The German émigré paper *Pariser Tageszeitung*, successor to the *Tageblatt*, also published a short write-up.[74] Not only Jews in Paris but emigrants all over Europe were deeply invested in the question of Jewish immigration to Palestine at that precarious moment.

Most notably, Max Osborn's detailed review in the *Jüdische Welt-Rundschau* (Jewish World Review) specifically mentioned Szalit's oriental rider painting. Former editors of the *Jüdische Rundschau* who had relocated to Jerusalem created this German-language newspaper, which was printed in Paris from March 1939 to May 1940 and distributed internationally, including in Palestine. In his review, Osborn described the exhibition as a "highly interesting cross-section of the Jewish artists active in Paris." This included the "best names" (Chagall, Spiro, Viktor Tischler, Gert Wollheim) as well as others who were discussed according to their countries of origin or types of contribution. Osborn grouped Szalit with other "Russian" artists including Chagall, Ryback, Mané-Katz, Zygmunt Menkes, Jacques Chapiro, Nina Brodsky, Wladimir Segalowitsch, and S. Rachumowski. Contributions by other women artists, including Maxa Nordau and Chana Orloff, also earned brief mentions by Osborn.[75]

For some of the participants and organizers, this was their last exhibition in Paris prior to the outbreak of the Second World War. Within a year or two, many would manage to escape. Wischnitzer and Osborn stayed in contact after arriving in New York, providing a way for knowledge of Rahel Szalit's work in Berlin and Paris as well as memories of the artist herself to make their way across the Atlantic. Mané-Katz was drafted, imprisoned by the Germans, but then escaped to New York. Eugen Spiro, Marc Chagall, and Jacques Lipchitz were among those Varian Fry helped escape to the United States in 1941. Chana Orloff went into hiding and eventually escaped to Geneva, Switzerland, in December 1942. For those lucky enough to make it out, the art scene of 1930s Paris faded into memory, though some eventually returned to France after the war. A far worse end awaited Szalit and others who were left behind.

CHAPTER 11

Holocaust Fates

Paris, June 1942: Rahel sits at a table near the window of her tiny wartime apartment, overlooking a courtyard. She writes a letter to her sister, Szejna Michla, who has been confined to the Lodz ghetto in Poland for over two years:

> Dearest Sister!
> I hope these words reach you. It has been many months since I have heard from you. I hope you are all managing and do not starve. How is Herszek?
> It's hard to believe that I am still here—things are only getting worse in Paris. Food is in short supply even with ration cards. I rarely go out now—many friends have been arrested. No foreigners are safe anywhere!
> But I am stuck here—there is nowhere else to go. I am too old to risk travel without the right papers, and to get a visa is near impossible. I tried to get one for Switzerland—but this is out of the question now.
> I want to paint but cannot focus. All of life is a war. I cling to the hope that we will make it through to the other side. Please give the children big hugs from me.
>   With loving greetings
>   Your Rahel[1]

Here in Paris, Rahel has recently sewn a yellow star with the word *Juif* to the left side of her warm sweater and her worn gray coat. An unfinished watercolor painting of a woman and horse in the countryside sits atop a pile of artwork in the apartment's main room.

Outside, the streets are strangely quiet. Several French policemen are stationed at a major intersection just a block away. Rahel peers out from behind her curtain and catches a glimpse of an arrest. Despite the frequency of these arrests, each one is shocking and chills her.

France's Jewish population numbered over three hundred thousand in 1939, and three-quarters of these Jews survived the Holocaust. Most of those who were murdered—roughly fifty thousand of the seventy-five thousand Jews deported from France to Auschwitz-Birkenau and other Nazi killing centers in the East—were stateless or foreign nationals who had immigrated to France.[2] To put this a different way: almost 90 percent of French Jews survived the Holocaust, compared with only 60 percent of foreign Jews. Given these statistics, Rahel Szalit's experience is representative of what happened to foreign and especially East European Jews in France. Rahel Szalit was among the many murdered at Auschwitz. We are now ready to take a close look at the final years of Szalit's life in occupied France. We then return to Poland to learn more about the fate of Szalit's sister, Szejna Michla Kolp, and her family's experiences in Lodz, including Szalit's nephew's journey from the Lodz ghetto to a beach town near Tel Aviv.

War and Fear

Little is known about how Rahel Szalit spent the final years of her life prior to her arrest and deportation in summer 1942; she kept a low profile. This was a very challenging time to be in Paris, and it was increasingly threatening for foreign Jews. Antisemitism was not the only force at work here, for xenophobia was also rampant. When France declared war on Germany on 3 September 1939, circumstances changed rapidly for the Jews of France. Thousands of men from "Greater Germany" (including annexed territories such as Austria) were detained and eventually interned in camps. Politically suspect foreigners were arrested and likewise interned in detention camps that had much in common with Nazi concentration camps. About eight thousand men and women from Germany and its annexed lands were required to report to the camps Les Milles and Gurs in May 1940, including at least five thousand Jews.[3] This meant that many Jews were interned in French camps because they had once been German or Austrian nationals. Paradoxically, they were suspected of having loyalties to the German enemy even though they had come to France to flee Nazi Germany.

With the fall of Paris to the Germans on 14 June 1940, things got significantly worse for refugees and especially for foreign Jews. The armistice signed on 22 June included a provision that the French government "surrender upon demand" all Germans in France. This prompted many refugees to try to escape by heading south to the Unoccupied or

Free Zone. Once the Vichy government was established, foreign Jewish artists could no longer exhibit in Paris at all.[4] Jacques Biélinky, whose diary from this period is now well known, observed that Montparnasse was empty and deserted.[5] On 3 October 1940, five years after Nazi Germany enacted the Nuremberg Laws, the Vichy government passed a similar law (*Statut des Juifs*, Statute of the Jews) defining who was Jewish according to racial lines, rendering all Jews inferior in the eyes of the state. But the law of 4 October was even more consequential for foreign Jews. The Vichy government authorized prefects (local agents) to intern foreign Jews in camps or to force them to live under police surveillance in remote villages. All Jews in the Occupied Zone were required to register with their local police prefecture, and their identity papers were stamped *Juif* or *Juive*.[6]

Still, many prominent artists, writers, and intellectuals managed to escape France after June 1940, as did others who had connections or ample resources.[7] Varian Fry, working in Marseille on behalf of the Emergency Rescue Committee, persuaded the French police to release the recently arrested Chagall, who Fry argued was "one of the world's greatest living artists."[8] Chagall was fortunate to make it out of France via Spain and Lisbon. Other refugees who could not get to Lisbon through Spain traveled from Marseille across the Mediterranean to French Morocco, and then back to Lisbon, as in *Casablanca*.[9]

Despite having made a name for herself in Germany and to some extent also in France, Szalit had nowhere near the international renown of Chagall, Spiro, Lipchitz, and others rescued by the Emergency Rescue Committee. Szalit's name and the names of many other women artists simply did not appear on the lists given to the committee by the Museum of Modern Art and others in the United States. Without these connections, and without financial means, it would have been extremely difficult for her to secure the visas necessary to leave Europe for safer shores. Given these circumstances, Szalit still might have reached out to everyone who could have helped her escape. Did Szalit write to influential contacts such as Thomas Mann, who was able to pull strings for many others? Did she venture to Marseille to meet with Varian Fry and his associates? It is likely that, fearing arrest, she was not willing to risk such a dangerous trip through the Occupied Zone. We have no evidence that Szalit tried to leave Europe, and only anecdotal evidence that she was unsuccessful in escaping to Switzerland.[10]

This was a terrifying time for Rahel Szalit and other foreign Jews who were unable to get out. Fearing the regular roundups, many left Paris for the French countryside. Only because she had no better option, Szalit remained in occupied Paris. Like everyone in Paris, she would have covered her windows with blackout curtains at night. As a foreigner, she might not have been issued a gas mask. Food was rationed and many items were scarce and increasingly hard to come by. Starting on 7 June 1942, all Jews in France over the age of six were required to wear a yellow Star of David with the word *Juif* in mock Hebrew lettering.[11] A strict curfew required Jews to be indoors by eight o'clock in the evening. Szalit celebrated her last birthday when she turned fifty-four (or fifty, according to official French records) in early July 1942, just two weeks before she was arrested by the French police. Her birthday fell only a few days before German military authorities signed a new directive on 8 July banning Jews from all public places, including restaurants, cafés, cinemas, museums, and exhibitions.[12]

Vel d'Hiv Roundup, Drancy, Deportation

As a foreign Jew who stayed in Paris, Rahel Szalit did not have a good chance of surviving the events of 1942. Along with over thirteen thousand Jews from Germany, Austria, Poland, Czechoslovakia, and the Soviet Union, she was arrested by the French police in the massive raid to round up foreign and stateless Jews—anyone who did not hold French citizenship. Known as the Vel d'Hiv roundup, the raid took place in Paris on 16 and 17 July 1942. Having heard rumors of a raid from the Resistance, many men left their homes the day before, and police often found only women and children waiting for them. This was one of the first roundups to target women and children, and onlookers were particularly horrified by the highly visible arrests and public suicides and deaths.

Even if Szalit knew about the raid in advance, she might well have thought that she, as a woman, would be spared. But this was not the case: her luck in evading arrest had run out. Together with about five thousand other women and men, Szalit was taken directly to the internment camp at Drancy, northeast of Paris, the same day she was arrested. About eight thousand others, including over four thousand children, were incarcerated for nearly a week in the Vélodrome d'Hiver (Winter Velodrome), a covered stadium and sports arena, with no food or water, before being transferred to internment camps and then Auschwitz.[13]

The camp at Drancy consisted of makeshift barracks housed in a large horseshoe-shaped, multistory complex. By the time Szalit arrived, it had become a transit camp for those being deported to "unknown destinations" in the East. Its capacity at any given moment was five thousand prisoners; over sixty thousand Jews (two-thirds foreign, one-third French) passed through Drancy en route to Auschwitz-Birkenau from June 1942 to July 1944. Conditions in Drancy were filthy, bug-ridden, and overcrowded. The buildings were unfinished: straw was used on top of concrete floors; windows had no windowpanes. There were four stairwells reserved for women who arrived beginning on 16 July, and up to ninety-five women occupied one room. Many of these women were humiliated or abused by the gendarmes, and women also constituted the majority of suicides during this period. Food rations were insufficient, and many detainees suffered from malnutrition. Some died of hunger. Beginning on 19 July, three trains, each carrying one thousand people, departed every week for Auschwitz. The train that left Drancy on 19 July 1942 was the first whose passengers were nearly all murdered in the gas chambers upon arrival; prior to that, many deportees were registered and selected for slave labor.[14]

Szalit spent almost five weeks in the camp at Drancy before she, too, was sent to her death. In early August 1942, Szalit might have witnessed the arrival of Jews transferred from other locations in France to Drancy, including from the Southern Zone. On 15 August, a group of children arrived in Drancy from the camps in Le Loiret. These included unaccompanied children arrested in the Vel d'Hiv raid who had since been separated from their parents at camps in Pithiviers and Beaune-la-Rolande. Some of these children would end up in Szalit's convoy to Auschwitz. Prior to deportation, many internees at the camp in Drancy had their heads shaved and were subjected to brutal searches, then held in departure stairwells. Some received a postcard on which to jot their last words to loved ones.

French police deported Rahel Szalit from Le Bourget-Drancy station on 19 August 1942, in convoy no. 21 (Train 901-16), bound for Auschwitz. Official French deportation records spell her name as Rachel Schalit and list her age as fifty and her citizenship as Polish. In contrast to the records of other artists deported from France, records for Szalit describe her as *sans profession*, meaning she had "no occupation."[15] She may have intentionally concealed her profession to avoid having her artistic skills fall into the service of her captors, or perhaps she felt as if her career as an artist was irrelevant in the face of such inhumanity.

Szalit's convoy consisted of 1,000 Jews collected from several French camps. Among them were 237 German and Austrian Jews from Les Milles, 85 internees from Le Vernet, and 497 prisoners from the Vel d'Hiv who had been interned in Pithiviers and Drancy. There were more than 400 children under age twelve. All were packed into twenty overcrowded freight train cars for the nine-hundred-mile, three-day journey to Auschwitz. Benjamin Rapoport, one of only five people from this transport who survived the war, later recalled hearing the screams and cries of the children in other cars when the train made occasional stops.[16] Of the 1,000 people in this convoy, 817 met their deaths within a few days of 19 August, some en route in train cars, most in the gas chambers of Auschwitz-Birkenau. Only 5 men (and no women) from this transport survived the war and were still alive in 1945.[17] Szalit was never registered as a prisoner and was thus among those murdered on or around 22 August 1942.

The German freight train that brought Rahel Szalit to the East quickly reversed several decades of westward migration, taking her on a final journey through the countries where she had lived. Deportations from Drancy traveled through northern France into central Germany. Szalit's eastbound train would have passed through Dresden, about one hundred miles south of her former home in Berlin, before heading southeast toward Katowice and Auschwitz. Szalit spent part of her childhood in Lodz and possessed Polish citizenship, and it was in Nazi-occupied Poland that she died. The fate that befell her sister, who had remained in Lodz, and who would soon be murdered at Chelmno, was ultimately eerily similar to that of Szalit. But in August 1942, when Rahel Szalit's convoy turned southward toward Auschwitz, Szejna Michla Kolp was still in the Lodz ghetto, about 140 miles north of Szalit's final destination.

The Kolp Family in Lodz

Stories of other Markus family members give us a sense of what Szalit's life might have been like if she had never left Lodz. Sheina Machla Markus (1894–1942) was born several years after Rahel. Her Yiddish given name was Sheina Machla, though Polish public records usually spell her name as Szejna Michla, or, in several instances, as Zofja or Sophie. She adopted the Polish spelling Szejna Michla for use in everyday contexts, and we will refer to her this way. Among her Hebrew-speaking descendants, however, she is remembered as Michal, a variation of Machla.

After Rahel left for Germany in 1910 and her father Yudel Markus died in 1915, Szejna Michla and her mother Tsipa Markus continued to live together in Lodz. They made their home at Południowa 23 (today: Revolution of 1905 Street), close to the northern end of ulica Piotrkowska, a central street in a neighborhood with a large Jewish population. Another family of Markuses lived next door at Południowa 24, possibly cousins. This was a working-class area inhabited mainly by workers and members of the middle class, near the poorer Bałuty district (Yiddish: Balut) where the Lodz ghetto would later be established. Lodz was occupied by the German army during the First World War, and its factory production suffered. When Poland regained its independence in 1918, Lodz flourished and provided its residents with new opportunities for education and culture.[18]

Szejna Michla worked hard to build a life in interwar Lodz. Before getting married, she held a job as a typist. She married Herszek Kolp on 24 December 1922, when she was twenty-eight and he was thirty-eight. Rabbi Juszko Menachem Segał married them in a Jewish ceremony. (Perhaps Szalit traveled from Berlin to attend their wedding?) Herszek, a bookkeeper, was originally from Łaskarzew, a small Polish town about one hundred miles east of Lodz. Within five years of marrying, Szejna Michla and Herszek had two children: Juljusz (Polish for Yehuda) was born in 1924, and Esfira was born three years later.[19] Both would have been able to attend seven years of public school, and they probably had access to secondary education.

Around 1926, Szejna Michla Kolp opened a grocery store on the first floor of the same building where she lived.[20] It is likely that the entire Kolp family resided at Południowa 23 through the interwar period and lived together above their store. Archival records show that the grocery store was registered in Szejna Michla Kolp's name and did good business, with 1928 sales amounting to eight thousand zloty.[21] At that time, one zloty could buy a loaf of rye bread, a liter of milk, and several kilograms of potatoes. From these sales figures we can discern that Szalit's sister was a successful shopkeeper who helped support her family. It was very common for Jews in Lodz to be self-employed.[22] Especially telling is the fact that all paperwork for the store was in Szejna Michla Kolp's name, not her husband's. Men often earned about twice what women earned—but this store was Szejna Michla's opportunity to do her part. Perhaps Tsipa Markus also helped in the store or watched the children while Szejna Michla worked.

But the Great Depression brought hard times to everyone the world over, and Poland was no exception. Around 1934, when Rahel Szalit wrote to her sister about the situation in Paris, Szejna Michla encouraged Rahel to remain in France. Rahel pondered this in a letter: "What will become of me—I don't know. It makes no sense to go back to Poland. Utter poverty. My sister writes telling me not to go. She is also suffering greatly."[23] We can guess that Szejna Michla was hard-hit by the Depression and worked long hours in the store. Nearly 40 percent of Jewish women in Lodz held jobs in the 1930s.[24] Tsipa Markus, mother of Rahel and Szejna Michla, died in January 1938 and was buried in the New Jewish cemetery on Bracka Street, part of which would be enclosed within the Lodz ghetto several years later.

Rahel Szalit may have exchanged hundreds of letters with her family at Południowa 23 over the years, though not a single letter has survived. We do not know if they corresponded in Yiddish or Polish, though we can assume the Kolps knew and used both languages. Szejna Michla was still young when she arrived in Lodz, and it would have been easy for her to pick up the local language. As the owner of a neighborhood grocery store, she needed to be able to communicate with her customers. It was increasingly common for Jews in Poland to use Polish in their daily lives, and many read newspapers in both Yiddish and Polish. The Jewish world of interwar Lodz is described in detail in several novels, including I. J. Singer's *The Brothers Ashkenazi* (1936) and Chava Rosenfarb's *Of Lodz and Love* (2000). Arthur Szyk was perhaps the best-known Jewish artist active in Lodz around this time.

Misery in the Lodz Ghetto

This world came to an end when German forces occupied Lodz on 8 September 1939. The city was officially annexed as part of the Wartheland and was renamed Litzmannstadt. Jewish residents were required to wear a yellow Star of David badge bearing the word *Jude* and were forbidden from walking on Piotrkowska Street, renamed Adolf-Hitler-Strasse.

Plans were drafted to establish the ghetto in the Bałuty district; its southern edge was only a few blocks north of the Kolp residence and grocery store. The ghetto resembled a small city consisting of many wooden houses without windows or a proper sewer system. Local Jews were required to move into the ghetto in early 1940, and it was sealed as a kind of permanent prison on 30 April 1940, with about one hundred and sixty thousand inhabitants. In late 1941, nearly twenty thousand German, Austrian, and Czech Jews and five thousand Roma and Sinti were sent to the Lodz ghetto, and Jews from other ghettos followed in 1942. Through official paperwork, the Germans dissolved Jewish-owned businesses, including the grocery firm Szejna Michla Kolp had founded, which then ceased to exist even on paper.

Over four years, the Lodz ghetto had over two hundred and forty thousand residents. It eventually became a large factory dedicated to producing textiles and leather goods for the German war effort. The reopening of factories and workshops enabled the ghetto administration to organize its inhabitants into a workforce of slave labor, resulting in the Lodz ghetto being one of the last ghettos to be liquidated. Yet conditions in the Lodz ghetto remained brutal, and food in any form was scarce. Residents were entirely dependent on meager rations provided to them by the Germans: bread, soup, potatoes, and some vegetables. This was not the case in other ghettos, where smuggling was possible. People working in ghetto factories typically got a meal at work, but those without work positions did not have guaranteed access to food. A great number died of starvation. Malnutrition and exhaustion afflicted everyone. Most of those who could not work were deported in 1942, and the Lodz ghetto was liquidated in August 1944.[25]

The four members of the Kolp family were interned in the Lodz ghetto for several years. Three of them would perish by 1944. Records from the ghetto tell us a good bit about this period. The Kolp family was able to stay together at times, though they shared overcrowded rooms with other families. They lived at Honigweg Street 6 Flat 17 (ul. Miodowa), then relocated to Neben Gasse 6 (ul. Mroczna) in June 1942. Herszek and Szejna Michla Kolp both had "office worker" listed as their prewar occupations.[26] Szejna Michla might have found work in the ghetto, or she might have spent her time waiting in line for food rations or finding creative ways to prepare meals using whatever scraps she could find. Women were often responsible for feeding their families with very little. Diaries and literature written in the Lodz ghetto point to constant hunger as one of the biggest challenges. Writer Oskar Rosenfeld described hunger in the Lodz ghetto as "a new form of existence..., which we are expected to recognize as legal, predestined, even just."[27] Starvation was yet another punishment inflicted on Jews.

The other members of the Kolp family survived in the ghetto long enough that they must have been active in its workforce. Herszek Kolp, who was fifty-six in 1940, found work that helped him remain there for several years. Although Juljusz and Esfira were only teenagers upon entering the ghetto (ages sixteen and thirteen in 1940), they, too, were soon considered old enough to work. Girls often worked in sewing centers, boys in mechanical engineering workshops. Everyone worked long hours, from seven in the morning until seven in the evening. Around December 1942, Herszek, Juljusz, and Esfira relocated to an apartment at Neben Gasse 4. The fact that they survived the deportations of 1942 suggests all three were still able to work. The exact fates of Herszek and Esfira are not known, though both died by 1944, either in the Lodz ghetto or following deportation.

Szejna Michla Kolp was deported to Chelmno on or around 12 September 1942, at age forty-eight.[28] She was one of over seventy thousand Jews deported from the Lodz ghetto to Chelmno between January 1942 and March 1943. In fact, she was deported with over fifteen thousand Jews in a massive twelve-day deportation action in early September. This action was particularly brutal because it consisted of rounding up and removing those unable to work: children under ten, the elderly, and the sick.[29] To facilitate this, the Lodz ghetto leaders organized a weeklong curfew (*Gehsperre*), and doctors and nurses went from house to house to examine the residents. Shortly thereafter, German Gestapo units took over and arrested at random. The penalty for resisting arrest was death.

Journalist Josef Zelkowicz wrote at length about what it was like to experience this terrifying deportation action. His vivid descriptions are particularly moving: "People are sitting in their apartments, fettered like oxen waiting for the butcher, hands bound like *kapores*, the sacrificial hens. After being twirled overhead, they then sit and wait, all tied up, waiting for the slaughterer to come. The slaughterers move from apartment to apartment, and every hallway is marked by blood—Jewish blood. Every step of the way wrenches tears from more sets of eyes."[30] This passage offers a grim inversion of the usual roles in *kapores*, which we recall from the Sholem Aleichem tale about chickens on strike that Rahel Szalit illustrated (fig. 2). It also evokes the first line of the Hebrew prayer recited during *kapores*: "Children of man who sit in darkness and the shadow of death, bound in misery and chains of iron."

Whereas animals had previously appeared in many humorous stories and images by Jewish artists, they took on new symbolism in the 1940s. Twirling a chicken above one's head, leaving it disoriented and bewildered, was the poetic equivalent of confining already captive Jews to their ghetto residences to await arrest and imminent death. In the Holocaust, Germans and collaborating officials in Nazi-occupied lands regularly treated and murdered Jews as if they were animals. After the war, animal slaughter and slaughterhouses often served as metaphors for human suffering and unspeakable loss.[31]

The September 1942 deportations marked a turning point in the Lodz ghetto. Although there was only uncertain knowledge about the destinations of the deported, there was no hope that the sick, elderly, and children were being taken to a labor camp. Deportation certainly meant death. And indeed, Chelmno was a brutal, efficient killing center that did not make any pretense of housing prisoners. Nearly everyone deported to the village of Chełmno nad Nerem was murdered upon arrival, most in gas vans. After summer 1942, the bodies of victims were burned on open-air "ovens." There were no survivors from Szejna Michla Kolp's transport.

The two Markus sisters from Russian Lithuania led very different lives: Szejna Michla, a grocer and small business owner, stayed in eastern Europe, whereas Rahel worked as an artist in Germany for over two decades, and in France for close to a decade. Yet despite their divergent paths, both perished in Nazi killing centers in Poland during what is now considered the deadliest period of the Holocaust. Szejna Michla Kolp was murdered at Chelmno less than a month after Rahel Szalit was killed at (or en route to) Auschwitz-Birkenau. Their tragic paths were the same as those of many Polish Jews living in Lodz and Paris when the war broke out, and they were unable to evade the devastating fate that befell most of East European Jewry.

A Survivor's Journey

Of Szalit's immediate family members, only her nephew survived the Shoah. Ghetto records indicate that Juljusz Kolp was transferred in March 1944 from the Lodz ghetto to another ghetto or forced labor camp. In January 1945, Juljusz Kolp, then almost twenty-one years old, arrived at the Buchenwald concentration camp near the city of Weimar in Germany. His profession was registered as metalworker (*Schlosser*), and his parents were listed as "deported [*ausgewiesen*]."[32] He was among the twenty thousand or so prisoners liberated from Buchenwald by American troops on 11 April 1945. After the war, Juljusz/Yehuda Kolp immigrated to what would soon become the State of Israel, where he married a woman named Ester and went on to raise three sons. He completed a Page of Testimony about his aunt, Rahel Szalit, for Yad Vashem in 1999, suggesting that it was meaningful for him in his old age to remember his relatives from Europe.[33] Yehuda (Juljusz) Kolp, grandson of Yehuda (Yudel) Markus, died in 2004 at age eighty and was buried in Holon Cemetery in Bat Yam, a beach town just south of Tel Aviv.

Today, Yehuda Kolp's descendants live in Rishon LeZion and elsewhere in Israel. With the help of Yad Vashem and the Magen David Adom International Tracing Service, I was able to locate and interview one of Yehuda Kolp's three sons, Eliezer Kolp. Eliezer and his brothers did not learn many details from their father about his aunt. Even so, they knew Rahel Szalit tried to escape to Switzerland while living in Paris, and that this attempt was unsuccessful.[34] This confirms Szalit remained in contact with her family in Poland well into the 1930s and possibly the 1940s. Siblings in different countries often tried to stay in regular contact during the war, particularly if one was in a position to help the other.[35] Szalit's letters could have reached her sister in the Lodz ghetto, but it was difficult to send mail out of the ghetto to countries at war with Germany. Some mail was permitted to leave the ghetto through 1941, especially postcards written in German, which were easy to censor, but Szalit likely did not hear from her sister after that.[36] Did Rahel Szalit send a final postcard from Drancy on the eve of her deportation—and, if so, is there any chance someone in the Kolp family received it?

The Markus family started out in northwest Lithuania in the Russian Pale of Settlement and made their way to Poland, where they found a new home and Jewish community. Rahel Szalit succeeded at making a career for herself in Germany, though her time there was cut short, and France ultimately failed to provide asylum for foreign Jews. Nearly all members of the Markus family fell victim to the genocide of Europe's Jews. In the twenty-first century, the direct descendants of the nineteenth-century Markuses, like most other Jewish Israelis, speak Hebrew as a first language instead of Yiddish. They study English, and perhaps also Arabic, instead of German and Polish. And for many of the grandchildren and great-grandchildren of Yehuda Kolp, the artist's nephew, the eastern Europe depicted in Rahel Szalit's works has been replaced with views of the Mediterranean Sea.

Epilogue
Remembering Rahel Szalit

Like Rahel Szalit, many of the Jewish artists murdered by the Nazis and their collaborators have been forgotten—and many of their original works, too, have vanished, leaving art historians little to analyze. Memory politics, particularly as it relates to Jewish artists' legacies, can be oddly complicated and is often tied to nationality. If few or no family members survived, what countries or institutions are responsible for remembering these artists and their work? Who will grant these lost artists the appreciation and respect that they deserve but that was robbed from them?

It would be easier to do justice to Rahel Szalit's memory if more people had inscribed her into history in the first place. Yet we have few written traces by friends, relatives, and others who knew her personally. Why don't we have more memoirs or diary entries that contain references to Szalit, more surviving letters, more paintings, more evidence of her remarkable life? The Jewish communities in Szalit's many worlds were all obliterated: Telz, Lodz, Munich, Vienna, Berlin, Paris. As an East European who lived and worked outside of eastern Europe, she also had few regular connections to family members who knew her well. The fact is that we simply don't know about many of the people Szalit was close to or loved. In addition to the more famous acquaintances discussed here, Szalit had many friends who did not publish memoirs or leave known family archives.

Though some of Rahel Szalit's work survives, there is much we will never know about her as a person. So many questions remain. Who else should be counted among her artistic inspirations? What other aspects of life was she passionate about? How much did her working-class background inform her identity? Did she feel a true sense of belonging in Berlin? How well did she know French? These are but a few details we might find if we had more material from Szalit or those who knew her.

In the months and years following Szalit's arrest, a few of her acquaintances recorded what they knew about her fate. News about the mass murder of Jews began to emerge the same month that Szalit was arrested. On 2 July 1942, *The New York Times* ran a story about the slaughter of seven hundred thousand Jews in Poland, calling on Allied governments to save millions from destruction. The BBC and the *Times* reported in August that the arrests of foreign Jews in France amounted to a "virtual death sentence." But not everyone accepted this unthinkable news. Many later claimed total ignorance of the death camps prior to liberation, despite the evidence that existed during the war. Still, some believed: on 20 October 1942, one French Jewish publication, *J'accuse*, responding to suspicions about the "unknown destination" of deportations, announced that eleven thousand Jews deported from France had been gassed.[1] Four days later, Jacques Biélinky, who would be murdered at Sobibor in 1943, noted in a journal entry that he had just learned of Rahel Szalit's arrest and deportation.[2] Several years after the war ended, when far more was known, Ludwig Meidner wrote from London that he knew Szalit had perished, though "no one knows where and when."[3]

Others who were further removed from Europe were either uninformed or unable to engage with details about those who could not escape. Published in New York in 1943, the *Universal Jewish Encyclopedia* wrote about Szalit in the past tense but made no reference to her whereabouts after leaving Berlin.[4] Several of the encyclopedia's contributing editors (Hugo Bieber, David Ewen, Max Osborn, and Rachel Wischnitzer) had worked with Szalit directly and had written about her art in Berlin and Paris. Prompted to write about Szalit's contributions to Jewish culture, they composed a short entry on her that was easily comprehensible for English speakers. Yet why did this group of scholars and art historians not share more? Did they refrain from referencing Szalit's exile in France in case it could endanger her if she was still alive? Unfortunately, Rahel Szalit's name is nowhere to be found in subsequent surveys of Jewish art history published by Karl Schwarz and Rachel Wischnitzer in the late 1940s, nor does it appear in Schwarz's richly detailed memoirs.[5] This act of erasure is particularly tragic, as Schwarz and Wischnitzer were in ideal positions to lift up Szalit's memory.

To be sure, in the years immediately following the Holocaust, it was an overwhelming and near impossible task to tell the stories of all who had been murdered. Yiddish writer Hersh Fenster had the foresight to record everything he could learn about the Jewish artists of France who had perished. Originally from Baranów in Galicia, Fenster moved to Paris in 1922, and he organized gatherings of Jewish refugees in Paris in the late 1930s. After the war, he returned to Paris and started collecting materials about the eighty-four artists he wished to remember.[6] Fenster's *yizkor* book or memorial volume *Undzere farpaynikte kinstler* (Our Martyred Artists) was published in Yiddish in 1951; only 375 copies were printed. It was finally translated into French in 2021 (as *Nos artistes martyrs*), meaning that for seventy years, only those who could read Yiddish had access to this valuable information. As a foreword to Fenster's volume, Marc Chagall wrote a heartfelt poem, "For the Slaughtered Artists," which served as a Kaddish, a prayer of mourning. Chagall's poem opens, "Did I know them all? Did I visit their ateliers? Did I see their art close up or from afar?" Its vivid imagery further references the murdered "brothers of Israel, Pissarro and Modigliani, our brothers."[7] But of the "sisters"—indeed, of any women artists at all—Chagall makes no mention.

Fenster's volume includes a three-page account of Rahel Szalit's life that has long been the most important and reliable biographical account, though it, too, could contain inaccuracies. Fenster definitely had access to a copy of the 1922 portfolio of Szalit's *Motl* illustrations: the four images by Szalit reproduced in Fenster's book were taken from that portfolio, and Fenster appended Bal-Makhshoves's essay as well. Yet it is not clear from Fenster's account whether he ever met Szalit personally. To achieve this level of detail, Fenster must have been in contact with survivors who had known Szalit and her story. One possible lead could have been Henri Epstein's widow. Perhaps Chagall himself even offered Fenster details about Szalit, though it is doubtful that his knowledge of Szalit was this comprehensive.

Many of the murdered Jewish artists of the School of Paris were acquainted with Szalit. Among them were Henri Epstein and Marcel Słodki, the two artists from Lodz that Szalit knew in Munich. Some artists included in Fenster's book, such as Max Jacob, have recently gained new attention.[8] Of the seven other women discussed in Fenster's volume, most have been largely forgotten: Sophie Blum-Lazarus, Erna Dem, Frania Hart, Alice Hohermann, Chana Kowalska, Jane Levy, and Elisabeth Polak. Like Rahel Szalit, these artists hailed from all over Europe; they spoke Yiddish, Polish, German, French, as well as Russian and other languages. All spent time in France, a land that failed to provide them with the liberty it promised, and that today still struggles to preserve their memory.

Who Will Claim This Artist?

In these pages, I have sought to recover and bring to light as much as possible about Rahel Szalit and her work. As a well-known illustrator and a prize-winning painter, she earned a place in art history even though most of her paintings were destroyed. Not only paintings but also graphic artworks such as book illustrations can be exhibited and otherwise enjoyed by viewing publics, as Szalit's early career demonstrates. The problem remains that Szalit confounds those who seek to put her in a single category. We know now that Szalit can be celebrated as a bisexual and queer artist and that we can learn much about women's history and Jewish migration history from her story.

As a Jewish artist who lived in many places, Szalit has fallen through the cracks of national historical memory. There is much at stake in categorizing her as "German," "French," "Polish," or otherwise: doing so would help institutions in these countries take notice. Only a few German collectors and a handful of scholars in Germany, France, Poland, and the United States have demonstrated public interest in Szalit and her work in the past few decades. Szalit has been largely omitted from studies and exhibitions of interwar Jewish art and German-Jewish culture, in no small part because of her gender. One exception was a 1991 Berlin exhibition about the Jewish Renaissance, curated by Inka Bertz, now curator at the Jewish Museum Berlin.

On other occasions, found copies of Szalit's illustrated books have led to renewed interest in her work. Her illustrations of Heine's "Hebrew Melodies" were the subject of a small exhibition at the Jewish Museum Frankfurt in 2013, and they subsequently accompanied Heine exhibitions at other museums in Germany. The Akademie der Künste houses the papers of the Association of Women Artists in Berlin (now: Verein der Berliner Künstlerinnen 1867), which has included Szalit in a few of its exhibitions and publications. The Jewish Museum Berlin holds several of Szalit's works. One or more of these organizations would be perfectly situated to host a retrospective exhibition. After all, most of Szalit's surviving works were produced in or around Weimar Berlin.

By including Rahel Szalit in his Yiddish-language volume, Hersh Fenster remembered her as a Jewish artist of France. Some scholars of French art have followed Fenster's lead and continue to include Szalit in publications about the Jewish artists of the School of Paris. Her painting *Die Dorfmusikanten* (plate 1) was displayed as part of the exhibition *Montparnasse déporté* in 2005. The Paris Jewish Museum (Musée d'art et d'histoire du Judaïsme, or MahJ) contains a small file on Szalit as well, though her work was not featured in its 2021 exhibition on Hersh Fenster. Perhaps Szalit will be part of future exhibitions at MahJ. Despite recent interest in Fenster and the artists about whom he recovered so much, Szalit is not yet well known in France.

East European countries are of course not out of the question as possible claimants for Szalit's legacy. Some scholars consider Szalit a Polish artist because she possessed Polish citizenship. The Emanuel Ringelblum Jewish Historical Institute in Warsaw has several of Szalit's original lithographs, including some in the "Berlinka" collection that migrated over from the Jewish Museum Berlin during the Second World War.[9] Lithuanians, on the other hand, have thus far demonstrated no interest in Szalit. However,

I suggest it is more appropriate to consider Szalit as an artist "from" Germany: she left the Russian Empire at a young age and never lived in independent Poland but rather chose to live for over two decades in Germany, a country that did not readily grant citizenship to foreign Jews.[10]

Finally, a few institutions in the United States and Germany are becoming more invested in preserving her memory by digitizing their copies of Rahel Szalit's illustrated books. Among them are the Derfner Judaica Museum (a small museum in Riverdale near New York City), Leo Baeck Institute—New York|Berlin, the Jewish Museum Berlin, and the Judaica Division of University Library J. C. Senckenberg Frankfurt am Main. Israeli institutions, too, are likely to take an interest in Rahel Szalit in the future, not least because of her engagement with the Jewish Renaissance and Zionist subjects. Szalit's work is already known to some scholars and art dealers in Israel, and more of her works could be hiding there.

In the end, it does not matter which countries, institutions, or scholars decide that Rahel Szalit belongs to certain histories. Perhaps all those concerned should stake a partial claim to this artist and her extraordinary art; this would be far better than forgetting. We are at a pivotal moment for the rediscovery of Rahel Szalit and her work. The better known she becomes, the more lost paintings and drawings may reappear. In the meantime, it falls to us to remember Szalit's many contributions as an illustrator and a painter—and the fact that women artists played an active role in the creation of Jewish art. The destroyed Jewish worlds of eastern Europe are forever preserved in Szalit's works, and we now have a better picture of her life to help us interpret the art. We should remember Szalit not only out of a sense of obligation but also because the artworks themselves are unforgettable, just like the artist who created them.

Chronology

2 July 1888	Birth of Rahel Markus, to Yudel and Tsipa Markus in Telz
1894	Birth of Sheina Machla (Szejna Michla) Markus, Rahel's sister, in Šiauliai
1901	Death of Rahel's paternal grandfather, Yehuda Markus, in Telz
	Markus family moves to Lodz (year unknown)
June 1910	Rahel (now Marcus) moves to Munich to study art
Aug. 1914	First World War: Russian citizens expelled from Germany, flees to Innsbruck
Apr. 1915	Rahel marries Julius Szalit (Schalit) in Vienna
1916	Rahel and Julius Szalit take up residence in Berlin
27 July 1919	Suicide of Julius Szalit in Munich
1920	Articles about Rahel Szalit-Marcus begin to appear in the Jewish press
1921	Rahel Szalit has her own studio apartment at Stübbenstrasse 3 in Schöneberg
1921	First publication of a book with illustrations by Rahel Szalit-Marcus
1922	Solo exhibition at Gutenberg Buchhandlung in Berlin
1923	First illustrations appear in mainstream periodicals
1923/1924	Begins to sign work as Rahel Szalit, R. Szalit, and "R. Sz."
1925	Solo exhibition at Zinglers Kabinett in Frankfurt am Main
1927	Becomes active in Verein der Künstlerinnen zu Berlin
1929	Awarded one of six prizes at *Die Frau von heute* exhibition
Dec. 1930	Awarded Helene Fischbein Endowment Fund prize by Berlin Jewish community
1933	Exile in Paris; takes up residence in Montparnasse
1935	Solo exhibition at Galerie Zborowski
1938	Joins the Free Artists' League (Freier Künstlerbund)
16 July 1942	Arrested during the Vel d'Hiv roundup; interned in transit camp at Drancy
Aug. 1942	Deported to Auschwitz on 19 August; murdered on or around 22 August

Appendix 1
Rahel Szalit's Known Exhibitions and Works

Exhibitions During Szalit's Lifetime

Germany

1920	Exhibition of Jewish artists at the Berlin B'nai B'rith lodge (Logenhaus)
1921	*Schwarz-Weiß Ausstellung*, Akademie der Künste
1921	Exhibition of Jewish artists at the Berlin B'nai B'rith lodge
Nov. 1921	Works of Jewish Artists at the Lessing- und Heinrich Grätz-Loge, Breslau
1922	*Rahel Szalit-Marcus: Szenen aus dem jüdischen Kleinstadtleben*, Gutenberg Buchhandlung (solo exhibition)
Dec. 1923	Exhibition of graphic works by Jewish artists, Wiesbaden
1925	Watercolor exhibition, Berliner Secession
July 1925	Zinglers Kabinett, Frankfurt am Main (solo exhibition)
1926	Kunstsammlung der Bibliothek der Jüdischen Gemeinde zu Berlin
June 1926	*Berliner Bühnen-Bildner*, Berliner Secession (portraits)
1926	Herbstausstellung, Akademie der Künste
1927	Graphische Ausstellung/Herbstausstellung, Akademie der Künste
Nov. 1926	Sonderausstellung (Special exhibition), Berlin
1927	Reopening of the Jewish Community's Art Collection, Oranienburger Strasse
1927	*Kunstschau des Rheins und des Weins*, Koblenz
May 1928	*Große Berliner Kunstausstellung*, Landesausstellungsgebäude, Lehrter Bahnhof (as member of VdBK)
July 1928	International *Pressa* Exhibition, Cologne (graphic art, "Jüdische Sonderschau")
Sept. 1928	*Humor in der Malerei*, Neue Kunsthandlung, Berliner Secession
Nov. 1928	*Der bildende Künstler als Reporter*, Berliner Künstlerbund

APPENDIX 1

Dec. 1928	Kunstkammer Wasservogel, Leipziger Strasse
Nov. 1928	Porza Kunstgemeinschaft
1929	*Große Berliner Kunstausstellung*, Schloss Bellevue (as member of VdBK)
1929	Porträtausstellung, Kunstgruppe des Lyceumklubs
Feb. 1930	*Das Auto im Bild*, Berliner Künstlerbund
Jan. 1931	*Die Tombola des Presseballs: Eine Kunstausstellung im Zoo*
May 1932	*Gemälde, Aquarelle und Plastiken lebender deutscher Künstler*, Paul Graupe
Feb. 1933	Exhibition of Jewish artists at the Berlin B'nai B'rith lodge
1934	*Jüdische Künstler aus Deutschland*, Berlin Jewish Museum in April 1934; Breslau Jewish Museum from 21 October through November 1934

Exhibitions of the Verein der Künstlerinnen zu Berlin (VdBK)

Feb. 1927	Artists' Festival (*Urtiere*)
Dec. 1927	Verein der Künstlerinnen (*Strassenausschnitte*)
Mar. 1928	Verein der Künstlerinnen (*Naturausschnitte*)
Dec. 1928	Aquarelle, Graphik, Zeichnungen (lithographs: *Disputation, Jahrmarkt, Mutter und Kind, Die Strasse niest*; watercolors: *Junges Mädchen, Der Reigen*)
Nov. 1929	*Die Frau von heute* (two paintings: *Die Emigrantin als Bardame, Fatma Karel*)
Mar. 1930	Frühjahrsausstellung 1930 (painting: *Frühling*)
Oct. 1930	*Die gestaltende Frau*, Deutscher Staatsbürgerinnen-Verein im Haus Wertheim (oil painting: *Musikanten*)
Feb. 1932	Frühjahrsausstellung (*Die Schachspieler*, drawings of children)
Oct. 1932	*Rund ums KaDeWe*, Herbstausstellung (painting: *Herbst im Zoo*)

Norway and Sweden

1923	Exhibitions in Christiania and Stockholm (unconfirmed; see *Milgroym*, Jan. 1923)

Switzerland

July 1929	*Jüdische Künstler unserer Zeit*, Salon Henri Brendlé, Zurich

United Kingdom

June 1934	*Exhibition of German Jewish Artists' Work: Sculpture—Painting—Architecture*, Parsons' Galleries, London, 5–15 June 1934

France

Feb. 1935	Studio exhibition (solo exhibition)
Feb. 1935	Société des Artistes Indépendants, Grand Palais (*Portrait, Intérieur de bar*)
June 1935	Galerie Zborowski (solo exhibition)
Dec. 1935	Salon Populiste (illustrations)
June 1939	Exhibition of Jewish Art, Palmarium du Jardin d'Acclimatation, Paris

Exhibitions Since Szalit's Death

1968	*Jewish Artists Who Perished in the Holocaust*, Tel Aviv Museum
1982	*Frühjahrsausstellung* (VdBK), Berlin
1991	*Eine neue Kunst für ein altes Volk: Die Jüdische Renaissance in Berlin*, Jüdisches Museum, Berlin
2005	*Montparnasse déporté*, Musée du Montparnasse, Paris
2011–12	*Zwischen Bedrängnis und Widerstand: Grafiken und Gemälde der Jahre 1933 bis 1945 aus der Sammlung Gerd Gruber*, Cranach-Stiftung, Wittenberg
2011	Derfner Judaica Museum, Riverdale, New York
2013	Jüdisches Museum Frankfurt (Heine illustrations)
2016–17	*Fortsetzung folgt! 150 Jahre Verein der Berliner Künstlerinnen 1867 e.V.*, Berlin
2021	Derfner Judaica Museum, Riverdale, New York (online exhibition: https://derfner.org/rahel-szalit-marcus-solomon-gershov)

Illustrations of Literary Works

Print Portfolios

Szalit-Marcus, Rahel. *Fischke der Krumme* [by S. Y. Abramovitsh (Mendele Moykher Sforim)]. Sixteen lithographs by Rahel Szalit-Marcus. Introduction by Julius Elias. Berlin: Propyläen-Verlag, 1922. [Derfner Judaica Museum; Jüdisches Museum Berlin; Klau Library, Cincinnati; University Library J. C. Senckenberg Frankfurt am Main]

Markus-Shalit, Fr. *Menshelakh un stsenes. Zekhtsen tseykhenungen tsu Sholem Aleykhems verk: "Motl Peysi dem hazens yingel"* (People and scenes. Sixteen illustrations to Sholem Aleichem's work *Motl, Peysi the Cantor's Son*). Accompanying text by Bal-Makhshoves. Berlin: Klal-Farlag, 1922. [Yiddish] [Derfner Judaica Museum; Leo Baeck Institute, New York (LBINY); YIVO]

Heine, Heinrich. *Hebräische Melodien*. Twelve lithographs by Rahel Szalit-Marcus. Edited and with an introduction by Hugo Bieber. Berlin: Für die literarische Vereinigung Hesperus, 1923. [Stanford University Libraries]

Books

Dostoyevsky, Fyodor. *Das Krokodil*. Translated by Edith Ziegler. Potsdam: Kiepenheuer Verlag, 1921. Twenty-one illustrations by Rahel Szalit-Marcus. [Hathitrust; LBINY]

Tolstoy, Leo. *Die Kreutzersonate*. Translated by August Scholz. Berlin: Sebastian Löwenbuck Akademischer Verlag, 1922. With seven original lithographs by R. Szalit-Markus. [LBINY]

Bialik, Hayim Nahman. *Ketina kol-bo*. Berlin: Rimon-Verlag, 1923. Two illustrations. [Hebrew] [Jüdisches Museum Berlin; MahJ, Paris]

Dickens, Charles. *Londoner Bilder*. Translated by Ernst Sander. Berlin: Hans Heinrich Tillgner Verlag, 1923. Sixteen lithographs by Rahel Szalit-Marcus. [Deutsches Literaturarchiv Marbach; LBINY]

Tillier, Claude. *Mein Onkel Benjamin*. Translated and with an afterword by Ludwig Pfau. Berlin: Volksverband der Bücherfreunde / Wegweiser-Verlag in Berlin, 1927. Eight illustrations. [LBINY]

Unpublished and Lost Illustrations

Zangwill, Israel. *Der König der Schnorrer*. Eighteen graphite and ink drawings signed R. Szalit-Marcus and dated 1921. Likely never published in book form. Previously presumed lost; original drawings sold at auction in New York in 2023.

Buber, Martin. *Kindergeschichten* (ca. 1922) (lost)

Nahman Bratslaver, R. [Reb Nachman of Breslov], *Sipure maysies*. Fun tekst bearbet durkh Moshe Kleinman. Zekhtsen litografyes fun Rachel Szalit-Marcus. Berlin: Rimon, 1923. [Yiddish] (lost)

Literary Illustrations in Periodicals

Daudet, Alphonse. *Tartarin of Tarascon* (before 1922). Illustrations in *Die Schaffenden*, 1923, and *Der Querschnit*, 1925–26. Lithographs.

Zollikofer, Fred von. "Harfe," *Der Feuerreiter: Blätter für Dichtung, Kritik, Graphik* 2, no. 2 (1923). Two lithographs.

Gorelik, Shemarya. "Ein jüdischer Schriftsteller reist nach Canada," *Jüdische Rundschau*, 1928. Three drawings.
Mann, Thomas. "Dina," *Die Aufklärung*, 1929. Eight drawings. [Magnus-Hirschfeld-Gesellschaft e.V., Berlin]
Aleichem, Sholem. "Chanukkah=Geld. Eine lustige Geschichte," *Israelitisches Familienblatt*, 1930. Three drawings.
Aleichem, Sholem. "Streik der Hühner: Eine lustige Jom-Kippur-Geschichte," *Israelitisches Familienblatt*, 1931. Two drawings.

Paintings (originals mostly lost)

Die Dorfmusikanten / Zwei musizierende Juden in einem Dorf (oil on canvas, 1920; 56 × 50 cm; French: *Les musiciens du village*; 2005 Paris exhibition)
In der Kälte (*Ost und West*, 1920)
Leipziger Platz (*Ost und West*, 1920)
Leipziger Strasse (*Ost und West*, 1920)
Schneelandschaft (*Ost und West*, 1920)
Interieur (*Ost und West*, 1920)
Fahrt zur Hochzeit (watercolor, ca. 1927; also *Fahrt zur Verlobung*; reprint at JHI Warsaw)
Five paintings in Große Berliner Kunstausstellung 1928: *Blumenstilleben; Die Musikanten; Das Thoraverhör; Darwintulpen; Stilleben mit Flundern*
Wasserbock (1928 Porza exhibition)
Der Reigen (watercolor, 1928 Porza exhibition, VdBK)
Junges Mädchen (watercolor, 1928 VdBK)
Portrait of a modern young man (1929 Lyceumklub)
Jahrmarkt (1929 Große Berliner Kunstausstellung)
Selbstportrait (oil, 1929 Zurich Henri Brendlé exhibition, 21 × 26 cm)
Im Cheder (watercolor, 1929 Zurich exhibition, 60 × 48 cm)
Erster Schulgang (watercolor, 1929 Zurich exhibition, 48 × 60 cm)
Nacht auf dem alten Markt (1929 Zurich exhibition)
Die Emigrantin als Bardame (1929 *Die Frau von heute*)
Fatma Karel (1929 *Die Frau von heute*)
Die Fechterin, Selbstbildnis (*Die Dame*, 1930)
Portrait of a woman (*B'nai B'rith Magazine*, 1931)
Jewish Neighborhood (*B'nai B'rith Magazine*, 1931)
Bäuerinnen (watercolor, before 1932, 48 × 59 cm)
Herbst im Zoo (1932 Rund ums KaDeWe)

APPENDIX 1

Brücke (watercolor, 1933 B'nai B'rith lodge)

Individual Lithographs

Altes Paar auf der Strasse (1921, sold at auction in Switzerland in 1994)
Der Rabbi und sein Schüler (*Schlemiel*, 1920; Beck Archives)
The Drive to the Rabbi (*Milgroym/Rimon*, 1922)
Jahrmarkt (ca. 1922, *Menorah* 1926; JHI Warsaw)
Girl with a Headscarf (1922, LBINY)
Litauische Jüdin (ca. 1927, Kunstsammlung der Jüdischen Gemeinde Berlin, lost)
Der Rabbi (ca. 1927, Kunstsammlung der Jüdischen Gemeinde Berlin; 1968 Tel Aviv exhibition)
Mutter und Kind (before 1928, lost)

Lost Drawings

Sitzende Pinscher (colored chalk drawings; 1923)
Portraits of Alexander Granach and Walter Frank (1926 Berliner Bühnen-Bildner)
Herbst im Tiergarten (pastel; 1926 Akademie der Künste Herbstausstellung)
Der arme Schneider (1926 Akademie der Künste Herbstausstellung)
Brautfahrt in Litauen (1926 Akademie der Künste Herbstausstellung)
Zwei Kinder (pastel; 1927 Akademie der Künste Herbstausstellung)
Rabbi und Schüler (chalk, ca. 1927; Kunstsammlung der Jüdischen Gemeinde Berlin)
Toralernen (chalk, ca. 1927; Kunstsammlung der Jüdischen Gemeinde Berlin)

Works Likely Created in 1930s France

Garden Landscape with Three Horses (Red, Blue, Brown)
Klezmer in the Village Street
Lulav Prayer (Lulew-Benschen)
Child Going to School (Cheder) with Its Mother
Painting of an Oriental Rider
Young Woman in her Garden (oil on panel, 27 × 22 cm; resurfaced in France in 2021; sold as *Jeune femme dans son potager*)
Landscape (oil on canvas, 51 × 64 cm; included in Paris auctions in 2022 and 2023 as *Paysage*)

Appendix 2
Translations of Short Stories by Rahel Szalit

Rahel Szalit, "Purim in a Small Town: A Children's Tale in Word and Image"
Jüdische Rundschau, 14 March 1930

"And with the greatest glee (*Gedille*), they go to the Megillah [Book of Esther], tralalala, tralalala." Old Chane sings, standing in the middle of the kitchen, clapping her hands and keeping the rhythm with her head. Today is Purim and Chane is merry. She teaches us children that one must be joyous on holidays, and especially on Purim. The March sun shines in through the open window, and it smells of spring and freshly baked Hamantaschen. We children are in a state of great excitement, for one must send *Schalachmones* [Purim gifts; also called *mishloach manot*] to all friends. We count how many we must give and become convinced that we don't have enough money. What to do? We can't forget about anyone. We consider at length, and when we don't get anywhere, we ask Chane for advice. Chane is smart and always knows a solution. She is our best friend. Chane is poor and she has no one in the whole world. On every holiday she comes over, bringing great joy. No one knows as many stories and no one is as helpful as she is. Now, too, she has good advice. "Wait until the other children send you *Shalachmones*, then you buy something as well, switch around the gifts, and send them along to the others." How easy—yet such a brilliant idea would never have occurred to us on our own! We are reassured and go to buy our *Schalachmones* treasures.

Old Leiser's store is totally transformed, everywhere there are chickens, pretzels, and all kinds of fantastic animals made of sugar standing around. Those are the sought-after things that we want to buy for our friends. We look for a while, count our pennies again and again. Finally we have everything. As a parting gift the old Leiser gives us a Hamangrogger, a thing made of wood that makes a terrible racket once put into motion; we run home to this music.

In the meantime, a *Schalachmones* has arrived. The small six-year-old Rose brought it. "My sister sends you *Schalachmones*," she chirps. She stands there bashfully, her little head bent to the side, clasping the gift tightly with both hands. It is a small plate covered with a napkin. We gently open the treasure and find an orange, three sugar chickens, and a pretzel. Exactly the same things we bought just a minute ago. What to do? The same gift certainly can't be sent back to her as *Schalachmones*. We must wait for other incoming gifts. Maybe there will be something different. Right, soon the door opens and the small neighbor's son arrives with a whole load of dolls, sugar fruits, and chocolate. Now it's a simple task. We mix our gifts with the purchased sweets and arrange them on colorful small plates. In the middle there is an apple or orange, and around that are dolls, chickens, chocolate. My younger sister is the messenger. She takes the small plate with the white napkin in her hands and carries it away carefully. "My sister sends you *Schalachmones*," she will say, and turn red.

So it goes the whole day. The *Schalachmones* comes and goes again. Sometimes it is difficult to part with the beautiful sweets. My little sister's eyes often fill with tears when we must send gifts out again. But the day is fine, and it's fun to play the messenger. The kinds of things one witnesses! With red cheeks and beaming eyes, she comes back and tells us. Schlojme, the *Schalachmones* carrier, brought the rich woman Pesche a chocolate cake from someone. Schlojme told her himself; Schlojme is earning lots of money today. From early to late he delivers *Schalachmones* for the grown-ups and is well paid for it. The whole year he's hard up, often he's hungry, only on Purim does he become rich and proud. He bustles about with an absent-minded face. In one hand the plate of *Schalachmones*, with the other he gathers up his extra long caftan. "Schlojme, come to us soon, too," everyone calls to him from all sides. He rarely answers, for he must hurry. What's more, he is proud today. Only on Purim does he feel so glad to be seen and sought-after. But he truly has not much time, for he has another great thing planned for today.

The Purim players have determined that Schlojme should play Haman. He is very pleased about this, even if it is no honor to be a Haman. But Schlojme knows how to make the best of the situation: he will play Haman in such a way that everyone will see he is ridiculing himself. At four o'clock in the afternoon he is finally done with his *Schalachmones* carrying, and now he runs to the barn at the end of the small town where the costuming is taking place. Everything there is already in full swing. Busily the costumes are put together. Abraham, the butcher's assistant, is Achaschverosch, and Chaim, the cobbler's apprentice, is Queen Esther; both are dressed whimsically. Achaschverosch has a long goatee and a cardboard crown, and a yellow quilt is his royal cloak. Queen Esther is also beautiful. Chaim has affixed long flaxen braids to his crown, his upper body is wrapped in a linen sheet, and his high boots peek out below. Schlojme, the Haman, gets a mask for his face, bulging eyes, gigantic nose, tongue sticking out, and as clothing he wears his caftan upside down. In addition, from time to time he uses a frightening voice to hurl out terrible curses. Mordechai, the meek one, is our neighbor's son; he has a nice white beard and a green-and-red-striped cloak.

At sundown the whole company is on the move. It goes from house to house with song, play, and dance. At the front is Queen Esther, riding proudly on a billy goat with the whole company behind her (fig. 62). A stop is made in front of every house. "Vasti, Vasti will come soon," sing the Purim players. Their strange songs are accompanied by grotesque dances; through the rattling of the Haman-groggers they express their rage toward Haman. The poor Haman twists and strains his limbs and hurls out dreadful curses. The audience is thrilled, laughs, is excited and guesses who could be hiding under the masks.

Only we children are in on the secret, only we alone know who the actors are. We follow them everywhere and feel connected to them. We rattle our Haman-groggers together and perform the whole comedy with them. In exchange, we must collect donations. Bags are draped onto us, which the spectators fill with apples, Hamantaschen, and other treats to nosh. The poor Purim players divide these amongst themselves. The amusement continues late into the night until the billy goat refuses to cooperate and, unobserved for the blink of an eye, runs away to ponder the strange events of the day in his stall. He probably came to no good realizations, for our otherwise very gentle playmate avoided us from then on for a long time.

The night has begun, and from all sides one hears mothers calling for their children. One is reluctant to return home, for the Purim players are still not finished, and for a while their singing can still be heard from a distance. "Just a little, just one more time, Mother, can we see it only one more time," we beg, "after all, it's only Purim once a year." Our good mother cannot say no. Jubilantly we run from there, "Vasti, Vasti is coming," we sing, running until we are out of breath. We have forgotten our promise to return home soon. Totally entranced, we go around with the Purim players, until our worried mother locates us after a long search and transports us home. We can't fall asleep until late into the night, despite great weariness. We can still hear the festivities in our minds, and we see the Purim players before us. Until good Chane comes in and hums us to sleep with a soothing little song.

"Baking Matzah in a Small Town." Text and Drawings by Rahel Szalit
Jüdische Rundschau, 11 April 1930

"You are the master of the city, I am the master of my oven," so speaks Gitta to the mayor. She stands before him, undaunted, combative. Her eyes emit sparks, with a final sense of desperation she fights for her rights. She must prevail. The mayor must release the oven.

Otherwise, she and her family will be ruined. Gitta is in fact the owner of a large baking oven. This treasure is located in her pitiful little room, where she lives with her husband, the carpenter Leibe, and eight children. Gitta has eleven children, but the other three have long since emigrated to America. To feed and satisfy these eight hungry mouths is no small feat. The old workbench that stands in the living room is mostly unused, for who has money to order anything from a carpenter. And so one waits the whole year longing for Hanukkah, for one begins already at that time to bake matzah for Pesach. Anyone who owns a large oven is a lucky devil, assuming that the mayor has given permission for matzah to be baked in the oven. Gitta had until now always been lucky: until Hanukkah she baked her black bread in it. Around this time, she would clean it with glowing hot stones and boiling water, and the poor carpenter's home along with the oven transformed for several months into a matzah factory. Gone was the hunger; the thin, tiny arms of the children slowly began to grow round. For Sabbath they could even afford a little fish. But of course, the jealousy of some angry neighbor erupted. Enough: the mayor found out that Gitta was baking matzah for others in her oven without permission—and gone was the bliss. One beautiful morning, a fat gendarme came with jingling sword and other policemen into the room, which smelled of matzah. With a threatening voice he screamed at scared-to-death Gitta, sealed the opening of the oven, and put several thick official seals on top. The mayor has forbidden Gitta to bake any more matzah. Poor Gitta stood there hopelessly. In front of her pained eyes, she could already see the starving children, her heart clenched up, what to do? Suddenly, a thought shot through her head. She jumped up, put on her Sabbath dress, smoothed her sheitel with some water, slung a shawl over her shoulders, and disappeared through the door. Across the marketplace she walked with firm steps to the house of the mayor; she put her last ruble into the hand of the soldier on duty, and then she stood before the mayor. For one minute she felt herself get weak; with effort, she pulled herself together. Her fear for the children gave her the courage, and in broken Russian she began to explain to the mayor his injustice.

"You are the master of the city, I am the master of my oven." This sentence, belted out frantically in despair, was so unexpected, so grotesque, and at the same time so strangely logical that the mayor looked up from his papers for the first time. He saw in front of him a face tormented with suffering that still carried traces of past beauty. He must have read something in her eyes, probably the despair of a mother, for he said nothing to her, but beckoned to a gendarme and whispered something to him. The gendarme then went with Gitta back across the marketplace to her house, removed the seals from the oven, and Gitta had won. Again, one could hear the rattling of the buckets of the water carrier Schmuel, who brought the water for baking matzah. With rolled up sleeves, the women stood in rows at the tables and kneaded and rolled the dough. The fire crackled merrily in the oven; equipped with a long wooden peel, the carpenter Leibe slid the raw matzahs into the oven and took them out after a short while, crisp again (fig. 64).

When night comes, the kerosene lamps are lit, a cozy heat streams out of the oven. The children, washed clean, in pristine shirts, romp about between the women working and watch every matzah that goes into the large hamper with eager eyes. Sometimes one falls onto the ground to the great delight of the children since they get that one. Such a matzah is chametz and may not be eaten on Pesach. Day and night, alternating teams of workers are busy baking, for there is lots to do. Gitta bakes not only for all the neighbor women, but also for the Jewish women from the villages who come to her in the city. They bring their small children with them and stay in the nearby houses for only a few pennies. Their small farm carts stand in the courtyard, and the scraggly little horses find shelter in Gitta's goat shed. Outside, the snow falls. The windows are covered with frost patterns, and the people who walk by in the street press their noses curiously to the windows and try to peer into the matzah factory. Gitta runs busily to and fro, her face reddened by the heat of the oven. She's got her hands full: she takes over from her husband at the oven, looks after the children, milks the goats, cooks the food, chats with the customers, shouts at the dog, and encourages the workers. No one knows when she sleeps, for she's on her feet day and night. In the time from Hanukkah to Pesach she knows no rest. Whenever she feels her strength failing her, she begins to sing, and when she sings, everyone sings with her.

Jossel, the *badchen* (jester), also comes over often. He is a sought-after guest, for Jossel can do many things. He writes poems, sings, dances, tells jokes, and does it all jumbled up at the same time. In between he makes eyes at the rosy-cheeked Mierele, who bashfully lowers her eyelids every time. He is a secret employee of Gitta, for when she notices that the workers are beginning to roll out the dough more slowly and open their mouths again and again to yawn, she sends a child over to Jossel straight away, and all are awake in an instant. Jossel puts on a woman's skirt, ties a cloth around his head, imitates the voice of Gitta, and makes everyone laugh. For the time that Jossel is there, Gitta can leave without worry and take care of all her other duties. Jossel pays close attention, and every completed matzah is received with a joke. In order to hear these over and over, the women hurry and produce three times as many amid unrestrained laughter. With a friendly nod, Gitta expresses her satisfaction to him and promises him as thanks that she will become his mother-in-law, which Jossel accepts with a terrible grimace. "I would rather have a few bottles of your Pesach mead than one of your daughters as a wife"— and everyone laughs again.

Gitta is not at all insulted, though, for she is at least as proud of her mead as she is of her daughters. She brews it just before Purim, by which time she has forty bottles full of sweet mead standing in her cellar. Yet by Pesach there is not much left, because for some reason half of them explode even before then. Repeatedly one hears a bang coming from under the ground, there is one bottle fewer, and Gitta is sad for a moment. Often her chickens come up from the cellar behaving strangely: they cackle, crow without reason, and roll around comically in confusion (fig. 65). In the beginning everyone got a fright: their behavior was so uncanny, so unlike the usual behavior of chickens, and some even believed that a dybbuk [possessing spirit] had entered them. The rosy-cheeked Mierele was the first one to say that, and everyone let out a scream. The worker women ran horror-stricken, and poor Gitta ran in her desperation to the rabbi to seek advice. The rabbi inquired specifically about her mead bottles and whether she didn't also keep the chickens in her cellar, and he explained to her then that the animals simply drank from her mead and were probably drunk. Relieved, she came home, and the soothed women went about their work again. From then on, they only looked forward to the "chicken theater" whenever they heard an explosion in the cellar.

These lovely diversions like chicken theater and Jossel cease when the day comes on which the matzah is baked for the pious Talmud scholar Reb Mendele. The oven is freshly cleaned, the children are sent over to the neighbor, the workers put on fresh aprons. Reb Mendele supervises the baking himself. After every matzah they must wash their hands, and not a piece of dough can remain on the roller, the water for preparation is brought a day earlier, for so the law requires it. Everyone feels festive and blessed. It is quiet, yet the tired women do not yawn; they feel honored to bake the matzahs for Reb Mendele. His handsome, sad face with the long white beard, his quiet voice, his kind words fill all hearts. To bake a matzah for Reb Mendele is something entirely different, for Reb Mendele will eat this, the great scholar who sits day and night with the Talmud and fasts every other day. Everything that he has, he distributes among the poor, and the Lord continues to give him riches. This is what the women tell each other, and everyone blesses him.

Gitta herself operates the oven. Her face beams, her frowns smooth themselves out, and she quietly mumbles a prayer of thanks for the honor that the dear God has sent to her. Although Reb Mendele allows her to bake his matzahs every year, Gitta is intoxicated by her luck every time. The old Esther, Reb Mendele's wife, stands next to Gitta and takes the matzah from the wooden peel. Every time, she says a kind word to her; every time, she smiles at her; she finds everything to be good and fine. And when Gitta's youngest child, little Chazkele, takes a piece of matzah from the basket and Gitta turns pale from shame, for no matzah may be eaten before Pesach, Esther simply nods and smiles in response. "He is still just a small child, just leave him be, he doesn't know the law yet," she comforts Gitta. Reb Mendele, however, places his hand on the child's head in blessing, and Gitta beams again.

With Reb Mendele's matzahs, which are baked right before Pesach, the hard and wonderful time comes to an end. Gitta still has only the matzahs for herself left to bake, and then Pesach will arrive. While engrossed in the difficult work, none of them noticed how the winter faded and spring swept in with all its beauty. Everywhere the doors and windows are open, the houses are being cleaned of chametz, the children are having a jumping contest with the calves, and everyone is looking forward to and waiting with joy for the first Seder evening.

Notes

INTRODUCTION

1. Fictional scenes at the beginning of each chapter are set off with italics. In the introduction only, part of this scene is based on an actual birthday party for Ludwig Meidner that Szalit and the others mentioned here attended. Unpublished manuscript, Ludwig Meidner Nachlass, Bestand 45/67, no. 1517, Stadtarchiv Darmstadt.

2. There has been little written about Rahel Szalit outside of encyclopedia and lexicon entries. One scholar has written about Szalit's *Motl* illustrations: Sabine Koller, "*Mentshelekh un stsenes*: Rahel Szalit-Marcus illustriert Sholem Aleichem," in *Leket: Jiddistik heute / Yiddish Studies Today*, ed. Marion Aptroot, Efrat Gal-Ed, Roland Gruschka, and Simon Neuberg (Düsseldorf: Düsseldorf University Press, 2012), 207–31. See also Kerry Wallach, *Passing Illusions: Jewish Visibility in Weimar Germany* (Ann Arbor: University of Michigan Press, 2017), 48–50; and Kerry Wallach, "Art Without Borders: Artist Rahel Szalit-Marcus and Jewish Visual Culture," in *German-Jewish Studies: Next Generations*, ed. Kerry Wallach and Aya Elyada (New York: Berghahn Books, 2023), 149–70.

3. All translations are mine unless noted otherwise. Ger Trud, "Rahel Szalit: Eine jüdische Malerin," *Die jüdische Frau* 2, nos. 11–12 (1926): 1; and Will Pless, "Die jüdische Malerin Rahel Szalit-Marcus," *Aus alter und neuer Zeit*, no. 63, *Illustrierte Beilage zum Israelitischen Familienblatt* 28, no. 48 (1926): 498. Most German-Jewish periodicals cited in this book have been digitized and can be found in the database Compact Memory, http://www.compactmemory.de.

4. See Margaret Olin, *The Nation Without Art: Examining Modern Discourses on Jewish Art* (Lincoln: University of Nebraska Press, 2001); and Larry Silver and Samantha Baskind, "Looking Jewish: The State of Research on Modern Jewish Art," *Jewish Quarterly Review* 101, no. 4 (2011): 631–52.

5. See Adolf Sennewald, *Deutsche Buchillustratoren im ersten Drittel des 20. Jahrhunderts: Materialien für Bibliophile* (Wiesbaden: Harrassowitz, 1999); and Lothar Lang, *Expressionist Book Illustration in Germany, 1907–1927*, trans. Janet Seligman (Boston: New York Graphic Society, 1976). Other women artists remembered as book illustrators include Ida Berisch, Charlotte Christine Engelhorn, Christine von Kalckreuth, Else Lasker-Schüler, Fritzi Löw, Renée Sintenis, Lilly Steiner, and Ines Wetzel.

6. One exception is a brief reference to Szalit in Trude Maurer, *Ostjuden in Deutschland, 1918–1933* (Hamburg: Hans Christians, 1986), 721. But there is no mention of Szalit in numerous other studies where one might hope to find a discussion of her work: for example, Michael Brenner, *The Renaissance of Jewish Culture in Weimar Germany* (New Haven: Yale University Press, 1996); Andrea von Hülsen-Esch and Marion Aptroot, *Jüdische Illustratoren aus Osteuropa in Berlin und Paris: Eine Ausstellung des Instituts für Jüdische Studien und des Seminars für Kunstgeschichte der Heinrich-Heine-Universität Düsseldorf*, exh. cat. (Düsseldorf: Heinrich-Heine-Universität Düsseldorf, 2008); and Todd M. Endelman and Zvi Gitelman, eds., *The Posen Library of Jewish Culture and Civilization*, vol. 8, *Crisis and Creativity Between World Wars, 1918–1939* (New Haven: Yale University Press, 2020).

NOTES TO PAGES 5–8

7. Rahel Szalit, "Ich bin eine jüdische Künstlerin," *Blätter des jüdischen Frauenbundes* 6, no. 9 (1930): 2–3. Digitized by the University Library J. C. Senckenberg Frankfurt am Main: https://sammlungen.ub.uni-frankfurt.de/cm/id/4805666.

8. Letter from Rahel Szalit to Felix Weltsch, 9 February 1930, "Antworten auf 'Selbstwehr' Rundfrage zum Judentum," ARC. Ms. Var. 418 3 168 Felix Weltsch Archive, National Library of Israel, Jerusalem.

9. Many Jewish women artists from eastern Europe eventually ended up in Paris. Both Alice Halicka and Erna Dem (Ernestine Wolfson née Davidoff) studied in Munich in the early 1910s; Chana Kowalska moved to Berlin briefly in 1922, then Paris. Others found great success in Paris, including Chana Orloff, Sonia Delaunay (born Sarah Stern), and Mela Muter (Maria Melania Mutermilch, née Klingsland).

10. The *Yidishe Ilustrierte Tsaytung* (1924), for example, featured articles on fourteen visual artists, all male. See Marion Neiss, *Presse im Transit: Jiddische Zeitungen und Zeitschriften in Berlin von 1919 bis 1925* (Berlin: Metropol, 2002), 153.

11. See Inka Bertz, *"Eine neue Kunst für ein altes Volk": Die Jüdische Renaissance in Berlin 1900 bis 1924* (Berlin: Jüdisches Museum, Berlin Museumspädagogischer Dienst, 1991); and Inka Bertz, "Jewish Renaissance—Jewish Modernism," in *Berlin Metropolis: Jews and the New Culture, 1890–1918*, ed. Emily D. Bilski (Berkeley: University of California Press, 1999), 164–87. See also Brenner, *Renaissance of Jewish Culture*.

12. Moritz Goldstein, "Rahel Szalit: Die Schöpferin unserer Bilder," *Der Schild* 3, 1 September 1924. Moritz Goldstein Nachlass, Institut für Zeitungsforschung, Dortmund.

13. Frances S. Connelly, "Grotesque," in *Encyclopedia of Aesthetics*, 2nd ed., ed. Michael Kelly (Oxford: Oxford University Press, 2014), https://doi:10.1093/acref/9780199747108.001.0001.

14. J[acques] Biélinky, "Les artistes sepharadim: Rachel Szalit," *Le Judaisme Sepharadi* 4, no. 26 (1935): 27. Jacques Biélinky Papers, YIVO Institute for Jewish Research. Translated from the French by Esther-Lilith Melchior.

15. Scholem Alejchem (Sholem Aleichem), "Streik der Hühner: Eine lustige Jom-Kippur-Geschichte, illustriert von Rahel Szalit," *Israelitisches Familienblatt* 33, no. 38 (1931): 7. Digitized by the University Library J. C. Senckenberg Frankfurt am Main: https://sammlungen.ub.uni-frankfurt.de/cm/id/11343138.

16. See especially Joseph Roth, *The Wandering Jews*, trans. Michael Hofmann (New York: W. W. Norton, 2001).

17. See Bella Lown, *Memories of My Life: A Personal History of a Lithuanian Shtetl* (Malibu, CA: Joseph Simon / Pangloss Press, 1991), 12. Artist Chana Orloff notably kept a rooster as a childhood pet for many years. Paula J. Birnbaum, *Sculpting a Life: Chana Orloff Between Paris and Tel Aviv* (Waltham, MA: Brandeis University Press, 2022), 10–12.

18. See Avram Kampf, *Chagall to Kitaj: Jewish Experience in 20th Century Art* (New York: Praeger, 1990), 16–21; and Samantha Baskind and Larry Silver, *Jewish Art: A Modern History* (London: Reaktion Books, 2011), 8–11, 241–57.

19. Vicki Caron, *Uneasy Asylum: France and the Jewish Refugee Crisis, 1933–1942* (Stanford: Stanford University Press, 2003), 14. See also Greg Burgess, *Refuge in the Land of Liberty: France and Its Refugees, from the Revolution to the End of Asylum, 1787–1939* (New York: Palgrave Macmillan, 2008).

20. Several of these escapes were retold in fictionalized form in Julie Orringer's novel *The Flight Portfolio* (New York: Alfred A. Knopf, 2019), which has its basis in Varian Fry's *Surrender on Demand* (New York: Random House, 1945). See also Rosemary Sullivan, *Villa Air-Bel: World War II, Escape, and a House in Marseille* (New York: HarperCollins, 2006).

21. Others managed to escape to Palestine via India, Tehran, or Turkey, or to destinations as far-flung as South Africa, Australia, and Shanghai. See Marion Kaplan, *Hitler's Jewish Refugees: Hope and Anxiety in Portugal* (New Haven: Yale University Press, 2020); Noah Isenberg, *We'll Always Have Casablanca: The Life, Legend,*

and Afterlife of Hollywood's Most Beloved Movie (New York: W. W. Norton, 2017); and Mark Wischnitzer, *To Dwell in Safety: The Story of Jewish Migration Since 1800* (Philadelphia: Jewish Publication Society of America, 1949).

22. Kenneth E. Silver, "Jewish Artists in Paris, 1905–1945," in *The Circle of Montparnasse: Jewish Artists in Paris, 1905–1945*, ed. Kenneth E. Silver and Romy Golan (New York: Universe Books, 1985), 53. See also Hersh Fenster's memorial volume and Nadine Nieszawer's work on the École de Paris.

23. Encyclopedia entries with useful biographical information on Szalit include Isaac Landman et al., eds., *The Universal Jewish Encyclopedia: An Authoritative and Popular Presentation of Jews and Judaism Since the Earliest Times* (New York: Universal Jewish Encyclopedia, 1943), 10:139; Hersh Fenster, *Undzere farpaynikte kinstler* (Paris: H. Fenster, 1951), 231–35, and the French translation: Hersh Fenster, *Nos artistes martyrs* (Paris: Hazan, 2021), 254–57; Hedwig Brenner, *Jüdische Frauen in der bildenden Kunst*, vol. 2, *Ein biographisches Verzeichnis*, ed. Erhard Roy Wiehn (Constance: Hartung-Gorre Verlag, 2004), 331–32; Serge Klarsfeld, *Mémorial de la Déportation des Juifs de France* (Paris: FFDJF Fils et Filles des Déportés Juifs de France, 2012), 583; Nadine Nieszawer, ed., *Artistes Juifs de L'École de Paris, 1905–1939 / Jewish Artists of the School of Paris, 1905–1939*, trans. Deborah Princ (Paris: Somogy éditions d'art, 2015), 322, 453; Nadine Nieszawer, ed., *Histoires des Artistes Juifs de L'École de Paris 1905–1939 / Stories of Jewish Artists of the School of Paris*, trans. Deborah Princ (Paris: Les Étoiles, 2020), 387–88, 590; and Gerd Gruber, "Szalit, Rahel," *Allgemeines Künstlerlexikon: Die Bildenden Künstler aller Zeiten und Völker*, ed. Andreas Beyer et al. (Berlin: De Gruyter, 2020), 107:329. Many sources on Szalit include incorrect information, such as that she knew Sholem Aleichem personally, which is likely the result of mistranslating previous lexicon entries.

24. The following journalistic profiles of Szalit include useful biographical information: Karl Schwarz, "Rahel Szalit-Marcus," *Ost und West*, nos. 3–4 (1920): 74–77; Ger Trud, "Rahel Szalit: Eine jüdische Malerin," 1; Karl Schwarz, "Die Malerin Rahel Szalit," *Jüdische Rundschau* 33, no. 36 (1928): 259–60; David Ewen, "Rahel Szalit Portrays Soul of Israel: Artist Who Won Coveted German Honor Is Uniquely Gifted," *American Hebrew*, 19 September 1930, 472, 496; and David Ewen, "A Great Painter of the Jew," *B'nai B'rith Magazine* 45 (May 1931): 267–68.

25. Known articles and stories written by Szalit include Szalit, "Ich bin eine jüdische Künstlerin"; Rahel Szalit, "Purim im Städtchen: Eine Kinderidylle in Wort und Bild," *Jüdische Rundschau* 35, no. 21 (1930): 141; Rahel Szalit, "Mazzebacken im Städtchen: Text und Zeichnungen von Rahel Szalit," *Jüdische Rundschau* 35, no. 29 (1930): 203; and Rahel Szalit, "Parade Riposte: Text und Zeichnungen von Rahel Szalit," *die neue linie* 2, no. 10 (1930): 12. She also likely authored "Schönheitspflege der Tiere," *Zeitbilder: Beilage zur Vossischen Zeitung*, no. 1 (1930): 4.

26. Rahel Szalit, "Selbstporträt," *Menorah* 4, no. 2 (1926): 90. Digitized by the University Library J. C. Senckenberg Frankfurt am Main: https://sammlungen.ub.uni-frankfurt.de/cm/id/2916896.

27. See Ewen, "Great Painter of the Jew," 267–68, and Ewen, "Rahel Szalit Portrays Soul," 472, 496.

28. In 1897, 99.4 percent (over 2.6 million) of Jews in the Pale of Settlement claimed Yiddish as their first language. Joshua D. Zimmerman, *Poles, Jews, and the Politics of Nationality: The Bund and the Polish Socialist Party in Late Tsarist Russia, 1892–1914* (Madison: University of Wisconsin Press, 2004), 15.

29. Walter Kauders, "Rahel Szalit," *Menorah* 4, no. 2 (1926): 87–94.

30. The oil painting that resurfaced in 2021 was sold at auction in Tours for 370 EUR under the title *Jeune femme dans son potager*. The painting's subject wears a white headscarf, yellow-brown sweater, and lavender skirt with red trim. She is seated and working in a garden with a chicken by her side; flowers are visible in the background. The landscape painting, titled

simply *Paysage*, was included in a Paris auction in December 2022 (but not sold) and then sold at another Paris auction in April 2023. Also an oil painting, it uses muted greens, browns, and pinks to show a small figure, likely a woman with a brown headscarf and skirt, standing on a tree-lined path; slanted roofs of country houses peek out from behind the trees. Both *Jeune femme dans son potager* and *Paysage* are signed "R. Szalit" and were likely produced in France in the 1930s.

31. See Hartman's theory of critical fabulation. Saidiya Hartman, "Venus in Two Acts," *small axe* 26 (June 2008): 1–14; and Saidiya Hartman, *Wayward Lives, Beautiful Experiments: Intimate Histories of Riotous Black Girls, Troublesome Women, and Queer Radicals* (New York: W. W. Norton, 2019).

CHAPTER 1

1. Szalit's painting *Die Dorfmusikanten* was deposited at an auction house in Paris circa 2017; its current location is unknown. See Jean Digne and Sylvie Buisson, eds., *Montparnasse déporté: Artistes d'Europe* (Paris: Musée du Montparnasse, 2005), 153.

2. See Mirjam Rajner, "Chagall's Fiddler," *Ars Judaica* 1 (2005): 119.

3. Jizchok-Leib Perez, *Musikalische Novellen*, trans. Alexander Eliasberg, with five original lithographs by Jakob Steinhardt (Berlin: Fritz Gurlitt, 1920).

4. Ruth Morold, "Jüdische Kunst auf der Großen Berliner Kunstausstellung," *Jüdische Rundschau* 33, no. 45 (1928): 325.

5. Ewen, "Great Painter of the Jew," 268.

6. Zimmerman, *Poles, Jews*, 14.

7. Benjamin Nathans and Gabriella Safran, introduction to *Culture Front: Representing Jews in Eastern Europe*, ed. Benjamin Nathans and Gabriella Safran (Philadelphia: University of Pennsylvania Press, 2008), 11.

8. See Yuri Slezkine, *The Jewish Century*, new ed. (Princeton: Princeton University Press, 2019), 117.

9. Robert Jan van Pelt, *Lodz and Getto Litzmannstadt: Promised Land and Croaking Hole of Europe* (Toronto: Art Gallery of Ontario, 2015), 14.

10. Aelita Ambrulevičiūtė, "Economic Relations Between Jewish Traders and Christian Farmers in the Nineteenth-Century Lithuanian Provinces," in *POLIN: Studies in Polish Jewry* 25: *Jews in the Former Grand Duchy of Lithuania Since 1772*, ed. Šarūnas Liekis, Antony Polonsky, and ChaeRan Freeze (Oxford: Littman Library of Jewish Civilization, 2013), 72–73.

11. Šarūnas Liekis and Antony Polonsky, introduction to Liekis, Polonsky, and Freeze, *POLIN* 25, 13.

12. On Užventis, see Nancy Schoenburg and Stuart Schoenburg, *Lithuanian Jewish Communities* (New York: Garland, 1991), 323.

13. According to genealogical records, Yankel Markus (ca. 1816–1901) married Leah (1816–1895, daughter of Leyzer) sometime before 1842.

14. Antony Polonsky, *The Jews in Poland and Russia: A Short History* (Oxford: Littman Library of Jewish Civilization, 2013), 81–82.

15. See Benjamin Nathans, *Beyond the Pale: The Jewish Encounter with Late Imperial Russia* (Berkeley: University of California Press, 2002), 69–72.

16. Darius Staliūnas, *Enemies for a Day: Antisemitism and Anti-Jewish Violence in Lithuania under the Tsars* (Budapest: Central European University Press, 2015), 19, 126.

17. Polonsky, *Jews in Poland and Russia*, 89.

18. Staliūnas, *Enemies for a Day*, 18, 93, 129–69, 186.

19. Dov Levin, *The Litvaks: A Short History of the Jews in Lithuania* (Jerusalem: Yad Vashem, 2000), 74.

20. Staliūnas, *Enemies for a Day*, 123–24.

21. Eli Lederhendler, "Democracy and Assimilation: The Jews, America, and the Russian Crisis from Kishinev to the End of World War I," in *The Revolution of 1905 and Russia's Jews*, ed. Stefani Hoffman and Ezra Mendelsohn (Philadelphia: University of Pennsylvania Press, 2008), 245.

22. See Sigalit Meidler-Waks, "Die Pogromserie von Issachar Ber Ryback," in *Berlin Transit: Jüdische Migranten aus Osteuropa in den 1920er*

Jahren, published by Stiftung Jüdisches Museum Berlin (Göttingen: Wallstein, 2012), 22–33, 37–41.

23. See ChaeRan Y. Freeze and Jay M. Harris, eds., *Everyday Jewish Life in Imperial Russia: Selected Documents, 1772–1914* (Waltham: Brandeis University Press, 2013), 32–33; Israel Bartal, *The Jews of Eastern Europe, 1772–1881*, trans. Chaya Naor (Philadelphia: University of Pennsylvania Press, 2005), 151; and Zvi Gitelman, *A Century of Ambivalence: The Jews of Russia and the Soviet Union, 1881 to the Present* (Bloomington: Indiana University Press, 2001).

24. Tsipa's maiden name is given as Gerszonowicz in the 1922 marriage record of Rahel's sister. Varniai had a Jewish population of 1,226 in 1897 (39 percent of the total population). Schoenburg and Schoenburg, *Lithuanian Jewish Communities*, 375.

25. Ezra Mendelsohn, *Class Struggle in the Pale: The Formative Years of the Jewish Workers' Movement in Tsarist Russia* (New York: Cambridge University Press, 1970), 73–75.

26. In later documents, the birthdate for Sheina Machla Markus is listed as 5 April 1894 (also 8 March 1896); her birthplace is usually listed as "Szawle," Polish for Šiauliai or Shavli/Shavel. According to the Lithuanian State Historical Archives, birth records for Šiauliai have not been preserved for years prior to 1910.

27. In her memoirs, Rebecca Himber Berg explains that the births of girls in her part of Russian Lithuania (ca. 1878) were not recorded, in contrast to those of boys, which were both recorded and celebrated. Rebecca Himber Berg, "Childhood in Lithuania," in *Memoirs of My People: Jewish Self-Portraits from the 11th to the 20th Centuries*, ed. Leo W. Schwarz (New York: Schocken Books, 1963), 269–80.

28. Ewen, "Rahel Szalit Portrays Soul," 496.

29. Benjamin Harshav, *Marc Chagall and His Times: A Documentary Narrative* (Stanford: Stanford University Press, 2004), 65.

30. Both Rahel Szalit's marriage record and deportation record list her birthdate as 3 July 1892; Munich police records list 1 July 1892.

31. Staliūnas, *Enemies for a Day*, 27–32.

32. Polonsky, *Jews in Poland and Russia*, 155.

33. *Jahrmarkt* was reproduced in *Menorah* 4, no. 2 (1926): 94, and exhibited in 1928.

34. Ewen, "Rahel Szalit Portrays Soul," 496. David Ewen was born in Lemberg and immigrated to the United States as a child. Details of his interview with Szalit may have gotten lost in translation, as some of Ewen's information differs radically from other sources.

35. Szalit, "Ich bin eine jüdische Künstlerin," 2.

36. Ewen, "Rahel Szalit Portrays Soul," 496.

37. Robert Jan van Pelt, "Łódź/Lodz/Lodsch/לאדזש and Getto Litzmannstadt: A Historical Introduction," in *Memory Unearthed: The Lodz Ghetto Photographs of Henryk Ross*, ed. Maia-Mari Sutnik (New Haven: Yale University Press, 2015), 206; Theodore R. Weeks, "Jews in the Kingdom of Poland, 1861–1914: Changes and Continuities," in *POLIN: Studies in Polish Jewry*, vol. 27, *Jews in the Kingdom of Poland, 1815–1918*, ed. Glenn Dynner, Antony Polonsky, and Marcin Wodzinski (Oxford: Littman Library of Jewish Civilization, 2015), 305–19.

38. Wiesław Puś, "The Development of the City of Łódź (1820–1939)," in *POLIN: Studies in Polish Jewry*, vol. 6, *Jews in Łódź 1820–1939*, ed. Antony Polonsky (Oxford: Littman Library of Jewish Civilization, 1991), 9. See also Heiko Haumann, *A History of East European Jews*, trans. James Patterson (Budapest: Central European University Press, 2002), 126–27.

39. Zimmerman, *Poles, Jews*, 12.

40. Puś, "Development of the City of Łódź," 9.

41. Van Pelt, *Lodz and Getto Litzmannstadt*, 14.

42. Fenster, *Undzere farpaynikte kinstler*, 231.

43. Ibid.

44. Szalit, "Ich bin eine jüdische Künstlerin," 2; and Erna Stein, "Das jüdische Haus in der Kunst," *Der Orden Bne Briss: Mitteilungen der Großloge für Deutschland VIII U.O.B.B.* 14, nos. 6–7 (1934): 86–87.

45. Ewen, "Rahel Szalit Portrays Soul," 496.

CHAPTER 2

1. Annemarie H. Sammartino, *The Impossible Border: Germany and the East, 1914–1922* (Ithaca: Cornell University Press, 2010), 25.

2. Rogers Brubaker, *Citizenship and Nationhood in France and Germany* (Cambridge, MA: Harvard University Press, 1992), 118.

3. Jack Wertheimer, *Unwelcome Strangers: East European Jews in Imperial Germany* (New York: Oxford University Press, 1987), 14–15.

4. Kenneth Moss has demonstrated that there was a parallel focus on creating a "new Jewish culture" in Russia and Ukraine circa 1917–1920. See Kenneth B. Moss, *Jewish Renaissance in the Russian Revolution* (Cambridge, MA: Harvard University Press, 2009), 2.

5. See Hermann Struck and Herbert Eulenberg, *Skizzen aus Litauen, Weissrussland und Kurland* (Berlin: Verlag von Georg Stilke, 1916); and Arnold Zweig, *The Face of East European Jewry*, with drawings by Hermann Struck, ed. and trans. Noah Isenberg (Berkeley: University of California Press, 2004).

6. File on Rahel Marcus at the Munich Stadtarchiv, Bestand Polizeimeldebögen, Signatur: DE-1992-PMB M 42.

7. Marion A. Kaplan, *The Making of the Jewish Middle Class: Women, Family, and Identity in Imperial Germany* (New York: Oxford University Press, 1991), 158.

8. Letter from Rachela Szalitowa to Eleonore Kalkowska, 14 August 1934, archive of Tomasz Szarota, courtesy of Anna Dżabagina. Translated from the Polish by Karolina Hicke.

9. On German women artists in Paris, see Kathrin Umbach, *Die Malweiber von Paris: Deutsche Künstlerinnen im Aufbruch* (Berlin: Gebr. Mann Verlag, 2015). See also Diane Radycki, *Paula Modersohn-Becker: The First Modern Woman Artist* (New Haven: Yale University Press, 2013).

10. "Breslau. Ausstellung von Werken jüdischer Künstler," *Der Gemeindebote* 85, no. 24 (1921): 3.

11. Robin Lenman, "A Community in Transition: Painters in Munich, 1886–1924," *Central European History* 15, no. 1 (1982): 4.

12. Incidentally, Franz Marc may have descended from Jewish ancestors with the last name Markus. Franz Landsberger, *A History of Jewish Art* (Cincinnati: Union of American Hebrew Congregations, 1946), 302, 360n71.

13. See Dorothy Price, ed., *German Expressionism: Der Blaue Reiter and Its Legacies* (Manchester: Manchester University Press, 2020).

14. Starr Figura, *German Expressionism: The Graphic Impulse*, with an essay by Peter Jelavich (New York: Museum of Modern Art, 2011), 10.

15. Shulamith Behr, "Performing the Wo/man: The 'Interplay' Between Marianne Werefkin and Else Lasker-Schüler," in *Marianne Werefkin and the Women Artists in Her Circle*, ed. Tanja Malycheva and Isabel Wünsche (Leiden: Brill Rodopi, 2017), 92–105.

16. Fenster, *Undzere farpaynikte kinstler*, 231. See also "Henryk Epstein," in Jerzy Malinowski and Barbara Brus-Malinowska, *W kręgu École de Paris: Malarze żydowscy z Polski* (Warsaw: Wydawnictwo DiG, 2007), 118–26.

17. Gudrun Schury, *Ich Weltkind: Gabriele Münter, die Biografie* (Berlin: Aufbau Verlag, 2012), 46.

18. See Shulamith Behr, "Jewish Women and Expressionism: Artists, Patrons and Dealers," *Issues in Architecture, Art and Design* 5, no. 1 (1996): 99–114.

19. On Berlin as a collection point of Jewish art, see Ruth Morold, "Von jüdischen Künstlern," *Menorah* 6, nos. 11–12 (1928): 612. See also Celka Straughn, "Jewish Expressionism: The Making of Modern Art in Berlin" (PhD diss., University of Chicago, 2007), 2:290.

20. Alfred Kerr, "Früher Schluß," in *Berlin wird Berlin: Briefe aus der Reichshauptstadt, 1897–1922*, ed. Deborah Vietor-Engländer (Göttingen: Wallstein Verlag, 2021), 4:181.

21. Marsha L. Rozenblit, *Reconstructing a National Identity: The Jews of Habsburg Austria During World War I* (New York: Oxford University Press, 2004), 66.

22. File on Julius Szalit at the Munich Stadtarchiv, Bestand Polizeimeldebögen, Signatur: DE-1992-PMB S 467.

23. File on Julius Schalit [*sic*] at the Wiener Stadt- und Landesarchiv, Meldeunterlagen.

24. "Theater und Kunst," *Arbeiter-Zeitung: Zentralorgan der Deutschen Sozialdemokratie in Österreich*, 21 May 1913, 12.

25. "Die Saison des Innsbrucker Stadttheaters," *Innsbrucker Nachrichten*, 22 September 1913, 17; "Theater: Die Zarin," *Allgemeiner Tiroler Anzeiger*, 20 December 1913, 6; "Theater: 'Der Teufel,'" *Allgemeiner Tiroler Anzeiger*, 10 January 1913; and "Aus Stadt und Land: Julius Szalit," *Allgemeiner Tiroler Anzeiger*, 9 May 1914, 4.

26. Cited in Schury, *Ich Weltkind*, 144. On Münter, Werefkin, and other women artists active around the fin de siècle, see Katja Behling and Anke Manigold, *Die Malweiber: Unerschrockene Künstlerinnen um 1900* (Munich: Elisabeth Sandmann Verlag, 2009).

27. Stadtarchiv Innsbruck confirmed the absence of records for Rahel Marcus and Julius Szalit.

28. File on Rahel Schalit [sic] at the Wiener Stadt- und Landesarchiv, Meldeunterlagen.

29. On the Leopoldstadt, see Lisa Silverman, *Becoming Austrians: Jews and Culture Between the World Wars* (New York: Oxford University Press, 2012), 103–40.

30. Roth, *Wandering Jews*, 55.

31. Marriage record of Rahel Marcus and Julius Schalit, 1915, TB_IKG-WienII_1915_236. Courtesy of the Archive of the Jewish Community of Vienna.

32. Ewen, "Rahel Szalit Portrays Soul," 472.

33. See Daniela L. Caglioti, *War and Citizenship: Enemy Aliens and National Belonging from the French Revolution to the First World War* (Cambridge: Cambridge University Press, 2021), 90–91.

34. "Theater, Kunst und Literatur: Julius Szalit," *Neues Wiener Tagblatt*, 31 July 1915, 18.

35. Charlotte Ashby, "The Cafés of Vienna: Space and Sociability," in *The Viennese Café and Fin-de-siècle Culture*, ed. Charlotte Ashby, Tag Gronberg, and Simon Shaw-Miller (New York: Berghahn Books, 2015), 9–31.

36. See Julie M. Johnson, *The Memory Factory: The Forgotten Women Artists of Vienna 1900* (West Lafayette: Purdue University Press, 2012).

37. "Aus Berlin wird uns telegraphiert," *Neues Wiener Journal*, 5 October 1916.

38. Landesarchiv Berlin confirmed the absence of records for Rahel and Julius Szalit in the Berliner Einwohnermeldekartei.

39. Julius Szalit's address is listed in the Berlin address book for 1918. Rahel Szalit was not listed under her own name until 1921. See the Berliner Adressbücher online, http://adressbuch.zlb.de.

40. Schwarz, "Rahel Szalit-Marcus," 74–77. See also David A. Brenner, *Marketing Identities: The Invention of Jewish Ethnicity in* Ost und West (Detroit: Wayne State University Press, 1998).

41. See Celka Straughn, "Reviewing the Weimar Jewish Renaissance: Exhibition Reviews in the German-Jewish Press," in *Deutsch-jüdische Presse und jüdische Geschichte: Dokumente, Darstellungen, Wechselbeziehungen*, ed. Eleonore Lappin and Michael Nagel (Bremen: edition lumière bremen, 2008), 1:354–55.

42. Otto Friedrich, *Before the Deluge: A Portrait of Berlin in the 1920's* (New York: Harper and Row, 1972), 122. See also Donna Rifkind, *The Sun and Her Stars: Salka Viertel and Hitler's Exiles in the Golden Age of Hollywood* (New York: Other Press, 2020), 34.

43. Julius Szalit appeared in at least two films (*Der 10. Pavillon der Zitadelle* and *In den Krallen der Ochrana*, both 1916) and numerous plays at the Residenz-Theater (*Die Warschauer Zitadelle, Der junge Zar, Hotel Stadt Lemberg, Barbara Stossin, Die Spur*, and *Raskolnikow*).

44. On Schildkraut and art, see Celka Straughn, "'A Substratum of Unprejudiced Art History': The Critical Discourse of Jewish Art in Early Twentieth-Century Germany," *Journal of Modern Jewish Studies* 15, no. 1 (2016): 29–46.

45. Curt Moreck, "Berliner Theater in München," *Allgemeine Zeitung*, 25 August 1918, 385.

46. Kerr, "Früher Schluß," 183.

47. Siegfried Jacobsohn, *Das Jahr der Bühne* (Berlin: Oesterheld, 1918), 7:26.

48. Alfred Kerr, "Rudolf Leonhard, Die Vorhölle," in *"Ich sage, was zu sagen ist": Theaterkritiken, 1893–1919*, ed. Günther Rühle (Frankfurt am Main: S. Fischer, 1998), 797.

49. Oskar Maria Graf, *We Are Prisoners: A Confession*, trans. Ed Walker (Sandpoint, ID: RedLines Press, 2020), 342.

50. See files on Julius Szalit at the Munich Stadtarchiv: Sterberegistereintrag (Standesamt Mü. IV, Registernummer C 1523/1919) and

Sterbefallanzeige (Signatur: DE-1992-STANM-6455).

51. See "Julius Szalit," obituary in *Vossische Zeitung*, Abend-Ausgabe, 29 July 1919; and "Julius Szalit," obituary in *Berliner Tageblatt*, 30 July 1919.

52. Nora Zepler, "Bühnen Kunst," *Sozialistische Monatshefte* 25, no. 15 (1919): 944.

53. Kerr, "Früher Schluß," 181.

54. Moriz Seeler, "Offener Brief an Julius Szalit," *Das junge Deutschland, 1918–1920* (Berlin: Kraus Reprint, 1969), 20:360.

55. See, for example, "Julius Szalit," obituary in *Vossische Zeitung*, 29 July 1919.

56. The name Iser Weissberg appears mainly in brief biographical accounts of Julius Szalit, for example his entry in IMDb (Internet Movie Database), but there is no evidence that there was an actual painter by this name, nor that Rahel had any kind of interaction with him. There was, however, a painter named Leon Weissberg whom Szalit might have known.

57. Kerr, "Früher Schluß," 183.

58. See Heike Bauer, *The Hirschfeld Archives: Violence, Death, and Modern Queer Culture* (Philadelphia: Temple University Press, 2017), 39–44, 47; and Laurie Marhoefer, *Racism and the Making of Gay Rights: A Sexologist, His Student, and the Empire of Queer Love* (Toronto: University of Toronto Press, 2022), 120–23.

59. On suicide in German-Jewish contexts, see Darcy C. Buerkle, *Nothing Happened: Charlotte Salomon and an Archive of Suicide* (Ann Arbor: University of Michigan Press, 2013), 163–72.

60. Letter from Rachela Szalitowa to Eleonore Kalkowska, 14 August 1934.

CHAPTER 3

1. See Elizabeth Otto, *Haunted Bauhaus: Occult Spirituality, Gender Fluidity, Queer Identities, and Radical Politics* (Cambridge, MA: MIT Press, 2019), 98–104.

2. Julius Rosenbaum, "Das Studium der Malerei und Bildhauerei: Ein Mahnwort an jüdische junge Leute," *Israelitisches Familienblatt* 12, no. 26 (1910): 11. See also Straughn, "Jewish Expressionism," 1:186–87.

3. Werner Bab, "Neue jüdische Kunst," *Israelitisches Familienblatt* 25, no. 30 (1923): 2.

4. Ewen, "Great Painter of the Jew," 268.

5. Fenster, *Undzere farpaynikte kinstler*, 231.

6. Schwarz, "Rahel Szalit-Marcus," 75.

7. Ida Katherine Rigby, *An alle Künstler! War—Revolution—Weimar: German Expressionist Prints, Drawings, Posters and Periodicals from the Robert Gore Rifkind Foundation* (San Diego: San Diego State University Press, 1983), 1.

8. Cited in Figura, *German Expressionism*, 30; see also 12, 24, 28.

9. See the Berliner Adressbücher online, http://adressbuch.zlb.de.

10. Anne-Christin Saß, *Berliner Luftmenschen: Osteuropäisch-jüdische Migranten in der Weimarer Republik* (Göttingen: Wallstein Verlag, 2012), 14.

11. Translation taken from the multilingual app created to guide visitors through this memorial. See Renata Stih and Frieder Schnock: *Orte des Erinnerns / Places of Remembrance*, https://www.stih-schnock.de/remembrance.html.

12. Ger Trud, "Rahel Szalit: Eine jüdische Malerin," 1.

13. Ewen, "Great Painter of the Jew," 267.

14. "Mal- und Zeichenunterricht erteilt Rahel Szalit (Portrait, Akt, Landschaft, Komposition), Graphik, Kunstgewerbe," advertisement in *Jüdische Rundschau* 33, no. 71 (1928): 511; and "Rahel Szalit erteilt Unterricht in Zeichnen und Malen," advertisement in *Blätter des jüdischen Frauenbundes* 6, no. 11 (1930): 16.

15. Max Osborn, "Jüdische Künstlerinnen in ihrer Werkstatt," *Gemeindeblatt der jüdischen Gemeinde zu Berlin*, 13 October 1935, 18. Akademie der Künste, Berlin, Verein der Berliner Künstlerinnen 1867, no. 1598 (BG-VdBK 424-38).

16. Szalit, "Parade Riposte," 12.

17. Katie Sutton, *The Masculine Woman in Weimar Germany* (New York: Berghahn Books, 2011), 137.

18. Letter from Rahel Szalit to Hans Hildebrandt, undated (probably early 1930s), Hans and Lily Hildebrandt Papers, Getty Research Institute, Los Angeles, box 42, folder 35.

19. Tobias Brinkmann, "Ort des Übergangs—Berlin als Schnittstelle der jüdischen Migration

aus Osteuropa nach 1918," in *Transit und Transformation: Osteuropäisch-jüdische Migranten in Berlin, 1918–1939*, ed. Verena Dohrn and Gertrud Pickhan (Göttingen: Wallstein Verlag, 2010), 25–44. See also Verena Dohrn, Gertrud Pickhan, and Anne-Christin Saß, "Einführung," in Stiftung Jüdisches Museum Berlin, *Berlin Transit*, 14.

20. Saß, *Berliner Luftmenschen*, 21–22.

21. See Karl Schlögel, *Berlin Ostbahnhof Europas: Russen und Deutsche in ihrem Jahrhundert* (Berlin: Siedler Verlag, 1998), 84–86, 99–102, 104–5.

22. Robert C. Williams, *Culture in Exile: Russian Emigrés in Germany, 1881–1941* (Ithaca: Cornell University Press, 1972), 111–12, 116, 131.

23. Jackie Wullschlager, *Chagall: A Biography* (New York: Alfred A. Knopf, 2008), 285–86.

24. Letter from Rahel Szalit to Hans Hildebrandt, undated (probably 1927), and letter from Rahel Szalit to Lily Hildebrandt, 26 July 1927, Hans and Lily Hildebrandt Papers, Getty Research Institute, Los Angeles, box 42, folder 35. On Boguslawskaja, see Fritz Mierau, ed., *Russen in Berlin: Literatur, Malerei, Theater, Film, 1918–1933* (Leipzig: Reclam Verlag, 1991), 338–39.

25. Mierau, *Russen in Berlin*, 340–45.

26. Lowenstein Family Papers, Beck Archives, Special Collections, University of Denver Libraries.

27. On the Romanisches Café, see Shachar M. Pinsker, *A Rich Brew: How Cafés Created Modern Jewish Culture* (New York: New York University Press, 2018); Shachar M. Pinsker, *Literary Passports: The Making of Modernist Hebrew Fiction in Europe* (Stanford: Stanford University Press, 2011), 121–25; Shachar M. Pinsker, "Spaces of Hebrew and Yiddish Modernism—The Urban Cafés of Berlin," in Dohrn and Pickhan, *Transit und Transformation*, 56–76; and Sarah Wobick-Segev, *Homes Away from Home: Jewish Belonging in Twentieth-Century Paris, Berlin, and St. Petersburg* (Stanford: Stanford University Press, 2018), 29–30.

28. Fenster, *Undzere farpaynikte kinstler*, 233.

29. Rachel Seelig, *Strangers in Berlin: Modern Jewish Literature Between East and West, 1919–1933* (Ann Arbor: University of Michigan Press, 2016), 4.

30. Cited in Gennady Estraikh, introduction to *Yiddish in Weimar Berlin: At the Crossroads of Diaspora Politics and Culture*, ed. Gennady Estraikh and Mikhail Krutikov (London: Legenda, 2010), 14. On YIVO, see also Brenner, *Renaissance of Jewish Culture*, 195–97.

31. Wullschlager, *Chagall: A Biography*, 286.

32. Fritz Stahl, "Schwarz-Weiß-Ausstellung. In der Akademie der Künste," *Berliner Tageblatt*, 4 May 1921.

33. See Schwarz, "Rahel Szalit-Marcus," 74–77; Karl Schwarz, "Die Malerin Rahel Szalit," *Jüdische Rundschau* 33, no. 36 (1928): 259; Karl Schwarz, *Die Juden in der Kunst* (Berlin: Welt, 1928), 170–71; and K. Sch., "Rahel Szalit," *Jüdisches Lexikon: Ein enzyklopädisches Handbuch des jüdischen Wissens in vier Bänden*, vol. 4.2, S–Z (1930), 822.

34. Karl Schwarz was coeditor of *Der Cicerone* from 1919 to 1922. See "Der Graphiksammler," *Der Cicerone* 14, no. 17 (1922): 739; and "Die Zeit und der Markt—Ausstellungen," *Der Cicerone* 14, no. 20 (1922): 843.

35. R[uth] M[orold], "Die jüdische Familie in der Kunst," *Jüdische Rundschau* 33, no. 90 (1928): 630.

36. See Katharina S. Feil, "Art Under Siege: The Art Scholarship of Rachel Wischnitzer in Berlin, 1921–1938," *Leo Baeck Institute Year Book* 44 (1999): 167–90.

37. Rahel Wischnitzer-Bernstein, "Eine Selbst-Anzeige," *Soncino-Blätter: Beiträge zur Kunde des Jüdischen Buches* 1 (1925–26): 95–96.

38. Letter from Euphorion Verlag to members of the Soncino Gesellschaft, 3 December 1930, Jüdisches Museum Berlin. Inv.-Nr. DOK 93/502/201. On the Soncino Society, see Brenner, *Renaissance of Jewish Culture*, 174–77.

39. "Kunstausstellungen—Berlin," *Der Kunstwanderer* 3–4 (December 1921): 185.

40. Letter from Rahel Szalit to Hans Hildebrandt, undated (probably 1927).

41. "Rahel Szalit-Marcus: Szenen aus dem jüdischen Kleinstadtleben," *Die Weltbühne* 18, no. 41 (1922): 401. See also "Gerhart Hauptmann

über Tolstoi," *Neues Wiener Journal* 30, no. 10.368 (1922): 7; and "Rahel Szalit-Marcus," *Berliner Tageblatt*, 3 November 1922.

42. "Kunstausstellungen—Berlin," *Der Kunstwanderer* 4–5 (October 1922): 58.

43. Several of Szalit's Zangwill illustrations can be viewed on the website of the auction house where they resurfaced in January 2023: https://us.bidspirit.com/ui/lotPage/kestenbaum/source/search/auction/29147/lot/119803/MARCUS-SZALIT-RAHEL?lang=en.

44. Willi Wolfradt, "Ausstellungen," *Das Kunstblatt* 6, no. 11 (1922): 503.

45. "Rahel Szalit-Marcus," *Berliner Tageblatt*, 3 November 1922.

46. Małgorzata Stolarska-Fronia, "Jewish Expressionism—A Quest for Cultural Space," in *Jewish Artists and Central-Eastern Europe: Art Centers—Identity—Heritage from the 19th Century to the Second World War*, ed. Jerzy Malinowski, Renata Piątkowska, and Tamara Sztyma-Knasiecka (Warsaw: Polish Society of Oriental Art and Wydawnictwo DiG, 2010), 316.

47. Rahel Szalit, "Der Rabbi und sein Schüler," *Schlemiel: Jüdische Blätter für Humor und Kunst*, no. 14 (1920): 191. The print reproduced here belonged to Maria Lowenstein and is now part of the Beck Archives, Special Collections, University of Denver Libraries.

48. Letter from Rahel Szalit to Felix Weltsch, 9 February 1930.

49. Artists who engaged with Expressionism did not always identify as Expressionist artists; Chagall, for example, explicitly rejected this label. See Harshav, *Marc Chagall and His Times*, 162. See also Richard D. Sonn, "Jewish Expressionists in France, 1900–1940," in *The Routledge Companion to Expressionism in a Transnational Context*, ed. Isabel Wünsche (New York: Routledge, 2019), 332–47.

50. Ernst Cohn-Wiener, *Die jüdische Kunst: Ihre Geschichte von den Anfängen bis zur Gegenwart* (Berlin: Martin Wasservogel Verlag, 1929), 257, 260; and Ernst Cohn-Wiener, *Jewish Art: Its History from the Beginning to the Present Day*, trans. Anthea Bell (Yelvertoft Manor, Northamptonshire: Pilkington Press, 2001), 255, 257.

51. Landsberger, *History of Jewish Art*, 280.

52. On Hermann Struck's students, see Jane Rusel, *Hermann Struck (1876–1944): Das Leben und das graphische Werk eines jüdischen Künstlers* (Frankfurt am Main: Peter Lang, 1997), 44–52. See also Bertz, "Jewish Renaissance—Jewish Modernism," 181.

53. Hermann Struck, *Die Kunst des Radierens: Ein Handbuch* (Berlin: Paul Cassirer, 1920).

54. See, for example, Heinrich Berl, "Die Juden in der bildenden Kunst der Gegenwart," *Der Jude* 8, nos. 5–6 (1924): 323–38. On Lene Schneider-Kainer's graphic work, see Sabine Dahmen, *Leben und Werk der jüdischen Künstlerin Lene Schneider-Kainer im Berlin der zwanziger Jahre* (Dortmund: Ed. Ebersbach, 1999), 67–85.

55. For example, around 1921 Meidner shifted from drypoint etching to using nitric acid to make his lines broader and more powerful. Thomas Grochowiak, *Ludwig Meidner* (Recklinghausen: Verlag Aurel Bongers, 1966), 150.

56. On Meidner, Steinhardt, and the Pathetiker, see Bertz, "Jewish Renaissance—Jewish Modernism," 183–84; Emily D. Bilski, "Images of Identity and Urban Life: Jewish Artists in Turn-of-the-Century Berlin," in Bilski, *Berlin Metropolis*, 102–45; Straughn, "Jewish Expressionism," 1:181–82; and Baskind and Silver, *Jewish Art*, 108–9. The name "Pathetiker" further showed solidarity with Expressionist writers of the Neo-Pathetic Cabaret who had been inspired by Stefan Zweig's notion of a "new pathos." See Donald E. Gordon, *Expressionism: Art and Idea* (New Haven: Yale University Press, 1987), 101.

57. Rachel Wischnitzer-Bernstein, "Some Aspects of Jewish Art in Europe Before 1939," manuscript draft from spring 1944, 2, in Rachel Wischnitzer Collection (AR 25657), Leo Baeck Institute, Series 1: Subseries 2.

58. Heinrich Berl, "Die Juden in der bildenden Kunst der Gegenwart," *Der Jude* 8, nos. 5–6 (1924): 333.

59. Jakob Steinhardt, "Erinnerungen," in *Jakob Steinhardt: Der Prophet. Ausstellungs- und Bestandskatalog, Jüdisches Museum im Berlin Museum*, ed. Dominik Bartmann (Berlin: Berlin Museum, 1995), 18–19.

60. On Steinhardt's gatherings, see Małgorzata Stolarska-Fronia, "The Centenary of Polish Avant-Garde in Berlin," in *Polish Avant-Garde in Berlin*, ed. Małgorzata Stolarska-Fronia (Berlin: Peter Lang, 2019), 18–19.

61. See Michael A. Meyer, "Ludwig Meidner (1884–1966)—Künstler und Jude," in *Vorträge aus dem Warburg-Haus* (Berlin: Akademie Verlag, 2001), 5:131.

62. Grochowiak, *Ludwig Meidner*, 119.

63. Cited in Wullschlager, *Chagall: A Biography*, 291.

64. Erik Riedel and Mirjam Wenzel, eds., *Ludwig Meidner: Expressionismus, Ekstase, Exil / Expressionism, Ecstasy, Exile* (Berlin: Gebr. Mann Verlag, 2018).

65. Ludwig Meidner, *Dichter, Maler und Cafés*, ed. Ludwig Kunz (Zurich: Die Arche, 1973), 18–22, 145–56.

66. On Ludwig Meidner and homosexuality, see Joseph Paul Hodin, *Aus den Erinnerungen von Else Meidner* (Darmstadt: Justus von Liebig Verlag, 1979), 35; Philipp Gutbrod, ed., *Ludwig Meidner: Begegnungen/Encounters* (Munich: Hirmer, 2016), 129; and Meyer, "Ludwig Meidner," 145.

67. "Wiesbaden. Ausstellung von Graphik jüdischer Kunstler," *Jüdische Rundschau* 28, no. 104 (1923): 605.

68. See, for example, Helga Kliemann, *Die Novembergruppe* (Berlin: Gebr. Mann Verlag, 1969), 50–52; and Berlinische Galerie Museum für Moderne Kunst, "Beteiligung von Künstler*innen und Architekt*innen an Ausstellungen der Novembergruppe, 1919–1932," 29 October 2019, https://berlinischegalerie.de/assets/downloads/K%C3%BCnstler_innenarchive/berlinische-galerie_beteiligung-an-ausstellungen-der-novembergruppe-1919-1932.pdf.

69. On Stern, see LaNitra M. Berger, *Irma Stern and the Racial Paradox of South African Modern Art: Audacities of Color* (London: Bloomsbury Visual Arts, 2020), 23–24.

70. Unpublished manuscript, Ludwig Meidner Nachlass, Bestand 45/67, no. 1517, Stadtarchiv Darmstadt. In addition, a letter from Meidner to poet Wolf Bergmann, whom Meidner first met in 1925, suggests Bergmann knew Szalit through Meidner as well. Letter from Ludwig Meidner to Wolf Bergmann, 29 April 1950, Ludwig Meidner Nachlass, Bestand 45/67, no. 114, Stadtarchiv Darmstadt. See also Sonja Sikora, "Wolf Bergmann (1904–1972)," in Gutbrod, *Ludwig Meidner*, 245–47.

71. For an example of a work by Chagall that incorporates German, see *Erinnerung 1914*. Harshav, *Marc Chagall and His Times*, 162, viii, 9–12.

72. On Chagall and Eliashev, see Wullschlager, *Chagall: A Biography*, 204, 276, 285; and Emily D. Bilski, "Images of Jewish Men: Marc Chagall in the Pre-War Berlin Jewish Museum," in *Auf der Suche nach einer verlorenen Sammlung: Das Berliner Jüdische Museum (1933–1938)*, ed. Chana Schütz and Hermann Simon (Berlin: Hentrich & Hentrich, 2011), 168–74.

73. See, for example, the review of Boris Aronson, *Marc Chagall* (Berlin: Razum-Verlag, 1924) in *Die Wahrheit* 40, no. 24 (1924): 10; and Eduard Fuchs, *Die Juden in der Karikatur: Ein Beitrag zur Kulturgeschichte* (Munich: Albert Langen, 1921), 310.

74. See Brenner, *Jüdische Frauen in der bildenden Kunst*, 332.

CHAPTER 4

1. On B'nai B'rith lodge exhibitions, see Straughn, "Reviewing the Weimar Jewish Renaissance," 355; and Straughn, "Jewish Expressionism," 2:290–306.

2. "Jüdische Künstler," *Israelitisches Familienblatt* 22, no. 51 (1920): 2–3.

3. Paul Zucker, "Ausstellung jüdischer Künstler," *Jüdische Rundschau*, no. 87 (7 December 1920): 651–52. Feiga (Yuli) Blumberg was based in Berlin only briefly; she moved to New York by 1925.

4. Rosy Lilienfeld, *Bilder zu der Legende des Baalschem* (Leipzig: R. Löwit Verlag, 1935). See Eva Atlan, "Rosy Lilienfeld—Discovering a Nearly Forgotten Expressionist Artist," https://www.juedischesmuseum.de/blog/rosy

-lilienfeld-expressionist; and Eva Sabrina Atlan and Mirjam Wenzel, eds., *Zurück ins Licht: Vier Künstlerinnen—Ihre Werke. Ihre Wege. Rosy Lilienfeld, Amalie Seckbach, Erna Pinner, Ruth Cahn*, exh. cat. (Bielefeld: Kerber Verlag, 2022), 23–64.

5. Jonathan Wilson, *Marc Chagall* (New York: Schocken Books, 2007), 95.

6. Szalit, "Ich bin eine jüdische Künstlerin," 3.

7. Susan Hagan, "Illustrators: Collaborative Problem Solvers in Three Environments," in *A Companion to Illustration*, ed. Alan Male (Hoboken, NJ: John Wiley and Sons, 2019), 170–71.

8. Franziska Walther, "Shifting Authorship: The Illustrator's Role in Contemporary Book Illustration: Decision-Making with Depictive Augmenting, and Appropriational Strategies: Illustration: Concept of Diffusion vs. Innovation," in Male, *Companion to Illustration*, 313, 324.

9. Marjet Brolsma, "Dostoevsky: A Russian Panacea for Europe," in *European Encounters: Intellectual Exchange and the Rethinking of Europe, 1914–1945*, ed. Carlos Reijnen and Marleen Rensen (Amsterdam: Brill, 2014), 192, 194.

10. "Dostojewski-Mappe. Mit einer Dichtung von Johannes R. Becher," *Die Schaffenden* 2, no. 2 (1919).

11. See Rusel, *Hermann Struck*, 214–21. Karl Rössing's illustrations appeared in a German version of *Weiße Nächte*, trans. A. Eliasberg (Munich: Orchis Verlag, 1923). See also Andreas Hüneke, *"Dostojewski ist mein Freund": Graphiken, Gemälde und Buchillustration zu Dostojewski in der deutschen Kunst zwischen 1900 und 1950* (Altenburg: Lindenau-Museum, 1999).

12. "Das Weihnachtsgeschenk! Die graphischen Bücher," *Das Kunstblatt* 5 (1921): 572.

13. "Gerhart Hauptmann über Tolstoi," *Neues Wiener Journal*, 7.

14. Jewish artist Leonid Pasternak, a close friend of Tolstoy's, illustrated *War and Peace* in 1892. See Baskind and Silver, *Jewish Art*, 78–79.

15. Margareta Friesen, *Bruno Krauskopf (1892–1960): Ich lebe noch und male weiter* (Darmstadt: Kunsthalle Darmstadt, 1992), 28–30, 58n32.

16. Ger Trud, "Rahel Szalit: Eine jüdische Malerin," 1.

17. An estimated three hundred total copies were printed of each book in the series Das Prisma. Sennewald, *Deutsche Buchillustratoren*, 267.

18. Dickens created several problematic Jewish characters, most notably Fagin in *Oliver Twist*. Elsewhere in *Sketches by Boz*, Dickens describes secondhand clothes shopping on Holywell Street: "Red-headed and red-whiskered Jews who forcibly haul you into their squalid houses, and thrust you into a suit of clothes, whether you will or not." Charles Dickens, *Sketches by Boz* (London: Chapman and Hall, 1903; Project Gutenberg, 1997), chap. 6, https://www.gutenberg.org/files/882/882-h/882-h.htm.

19. Goldstein, "Rahel Szalit: Die Schöpferin unserer Bilder."

20. On Szalit's Dickens illustrations, see Michael Hollington, ed., *The Reception of Charles Dickens in Europe* (London: Bloomsbury, 2013); and Ulrich von Kritter, "Illustration im Umfeld des Expressionismus," in *Literatur und Zeiterlebnis im Spiegel der Buchillustration, 1900–1945: Bücher aus der Sammlung v. Kritter* (Bad Homburg: Ulrich von Kritter, 1989), 115.

CHAPTER 5

1. See Leo Fuks and Renate Fuks, "Yiddish Publishing Activities in the Weimar Republic, 1920–1933," in *Leo Baeck Institute Year Book* 33 (1988): 423; and Saß, *Berliner Luftmenschen*, 18.

2. See Estraikh, introduction to *Yiddish in Weimar Berlin*, 5–6; and Brenner, *Renaissance of Jewish Culture*, 191–92.

3. See Glenn S. Levine, "Yiddish Publishing in Berlin and the Crisis in Eastern European Jewish Culture, 1919–1924," in *Leo Baeck Institute Year Book* 42 (1997): 85–108; and Fuks and Fuks, "Yiddish Publishing Activities."

4. On perceptions of eastern Jews, see Saß, *Berliner Luftmenschen*; Maurer, *Ostjuden in Deutschland*; Wertheimer, *Unwelcome Strangers*; and Steven E. Aschheim, *Brothers and*

Strangers: The East European Jew in German and German Jewish Consciousness, 1800–1923 (Madison: University of Wisconsin Press, 1982).

5. Max Osborn, "Abraham Palukst: The Jewish Goya," *Yidishe Ilustrierte Tsaytung*, 16 May 1924. English translation from Natan Gross, ed., *Avraham Palukst: The Rediscovered Artist* (Tel Aviv: Eked, 1982), 15.

6. R. Inbar, "The Lithograph, A Chapter from the History of Graphic Art," *Milgroym* 1, no. 2 (1922): 21.

7. Ibid.

8. On right-to-left orientation, see Sara Blair, *How the Other Half Looks: The Lower East Side and the Afterlives of Images* (Princeton: Princeton University Press, 2018), 149.

9. Michèle Hannoosh, "Caricature," in Kelly, *Encyclopedia of Aesthetics*.

10. Szalit, "Ich bin eine jüdische Künstlerin," 2.

11. Letter from Rahel Szalit to Felix Weltsch, 9 February 1930. Sholem Aleichem notably borrowed this phrase from Ukrainian writer Nikolai Gogol. On the origins of "laughter through tears," see Amelia M. Glaser, *Jews and Ukrainians in Russia's Literary Borderlands: From the Shtetl Fair to the Petersburg Bookshop* (Evanston: Northwestern University Press, 2012), 108.

12. Jeremy Dauber, *The Worlds of Sholem Aleichem: The Remarkable Life and Afterlife of the Man Who Created Tevye* (New York: Schocken Books, 2013), 197.

13. Louis Kaplan has suggested that Berlin Rabbi Lippmann Moses Büschenthal's joke book from 1812 already understood Jewish humor as something that involved the transformation of suffering into laughter. Louis Kaplan, *At Wit's End: The Deadly Discourse on the Jewish Joke* (New York: Fordham University Press, 2020), 16, 241n46. See also Elliott Oring, ed., *The First Book of Jewish Jokes: The Collection of L. M. Büschenthal*, trans. Michaela Lang (Bloomington: Indiana University Press, 2018), 51.

14. Fenster, *Undzere farpaynikte kinstler*, 232.

15. See Jeffrey Veidlinger, ed., *Going to the People: Jews and the Ethnographic Impulse* (Bloomington: Indiana University Press, 2016); Andreas Kilcher and Gabriella Safran, eds., *Writing Jewish Culture: Paradoxes in Ethnography* (Bloomington: Indiana University Press, 2016); and Samuel J. Spinner, *Jewish Primitivism* (Stanford: Stanford University Press, 2021).

16. On Soutine and Jewishness, see Stanley Meisler, *Shocking Paris: Soutine, Chagall and the Outsiders of Montparnasse* (New York: St. Martin's Press, 2015), 92–94; and Donald Kuspit, "Jewish Naiveté? Soutine's Shudder," in *Complex Identities: Jewish Consciousness and Modern Art*, ed. Matthew Baigell and Milly Heyd (New Brunswick, NJ: Rutgers University Press, 2001), 87–99.

17. Szalit, "Ich bin eine jüdische Künstlerin," 3.

18. Marcus Moseley, "Bal-Makhshoves," *YIVO Encyclopedia of Jews in Eastern Europe*, 2017, https://yivoencyclopedia.org/article.aspx/Bal-Makhshoves.

19. Rahel Szalit-Marcus, *Menshelakh un stsenes: Zekhtsen tseykhenungen tsu Sholem Aleykhems verk "Motl Peysi dem hazens yingel"* (Berlin: Klal-Farlag, 1922). On Bal-Makhshoves and the Klal-Farlag, see Estraikh, introduction to *Yiddish in Weimar Berlin*, 8. This short essay by Bal-Makhshoves was reprinted in Fenster, *Undzere farpaynikte kinstler*, 234–35.

20. Koller, "Mentshelekh un stsenes," 225.

21. Compare with the scene at the end of *Motl*, part one, chapter 19. See Sholem Aleichem, *Tevye the Dairyman and Motl the Cantor's Son*, trans. Aliza Shevrin (New York: Penguin Books, 2009), 264–65.

22. Wallach, "Art Without Borders," 160.

23. Magnus Hirschfeld, "Prügelpädagogen," *Die Aufklärung* 1, no. 4 (1929): 97. See also Bauer, *Hirschfeld Archives*, 72–74.

24. Schwarz, "Die Malerin Rahel Szalit," 259. This image is also referred to as *A gas nist* (Yiddish) or *Die Strasse niest* (German).

25. Ruth Morold, "Ausstellungsstreife," *Jüdische Rundschau* 33, no. 100 (1928): 707. The examples given of primitive Russian grotesques include those created by the agitprop theater troupe Die blaue Bluse and by director Alexander Granowsky.

26. Scholem Alejchem [Sholem Aleichem], "Chanukkah=Geld: Eine lustige Geschichte mit Illustrationen von R. Szalit," *Israelitisches Familienblatt* 32, no. 51 (1930): 9.

27. The original Yiddish caption is "Mir forn keyn Amerika." In Fuchs's *Die Juden in der Karikatur*, the image bears the German title *Die Amerikafahrer: Die Sonne geht im Westen auf* (The America Travelers: The Sun Rises in the West). Whether Fuchs or someone else provided this title is unclear. See Wallach, "Art Without Borders," 162, 168n60; and Wallach, *Passing Illusions*, 48–50.

28. Fuchs, *Juden in der Karikatur*, 266 (image no. 271). Original titles: *Di frume yidene* (Yiddish) and *Die Agentin* (German; Fuchs). In fact, the image retitled "The Agent" was further misconstrued as a depiction of someone involved in soliciting young women for sex trafficking. See Edward J. Bristow, *Prostitution and Prejudice: The Jewish Fight Against White Slavery, 1870–1939* (New York: Schocken Books, 1983), 244–45.

29. Kaplan, *At Wit's End*, 92–94. See also Wallach, "Art Without Borders," 162.

30. Kaplan, *At Wit's End*, 72.

31. Fuchs, *Juden in der Karikatur*, 310.

32. Walter Benjamin, "Eduard Fuchs, Collector and Historian," in *Walter Benjamin: Selected Writings*, vol. 3, *1935–1938*, ed. Howard Eiland and Michael W. Jennings, trans. Edmund Jephcott, Howard Eiland, and others (Cambridge, MA: Belknap Press of Harvard University Press, 2002), 271. For Benjamin, Fuchs and other collectors served as ciphers for "the material economy of memory." Michael P. Steinberg, "The Collector as Allegorist: Goods, Gods, and the Objects of History," in *Walter Benjamin and the Demands of History*, ed. Michael P. Steinberg (Ithaca: Cornell University Press, 1996), 115.

33. "Der Graphiksammler," *Der Cicerone*, 739.

34. Rahel Szalit-Marcus, *Fischke der Krumme: Sechzehn Lithographien* (Berlin: Propyläen-Verlag, 1922).

35. Julius Elias, *Graphiker der Gegenwart: Max Liebermann* (Berlin: Verlag Neue Kunsthandlung, 1921).

36. Dan Miron, introduction to S. Y. Abramovitsh (Mendele Moykher Sforim), *Tales of Mendele the Book Peddler: Fishke the Lame and Benjamin the Third*, ed. Dan Miron and Ken Frieden, trans. Ted Gorelick and Hillel Halkin (New York: Schocken Books, 1996), xxvii.

37. Abramovitsh, *Tales of Mendele*, 55.

38. L.G., "Literarische Mitteilungen: Mendele Mocher-Sforim, *Fischke der Krumme*," *Allgemeine Zeitung des Judentums* 83, no. 27 (1919): 299–300. Translation of Geiger quote from Delphine Bechtel, "Babylon or Jerusalem: Berlin as Center of Jewish Modernism in the 1920s," in *Insiders and Outsiders: Jewish and Gentile Culture in Germany and Austria*, ed. Dagmar C. G. Lorenz and Gabriele Weinberger (Detroit: Wayne State University Press, 1994), 122.

39. Julius Elias, "Erläuterung," in Szalit-Marcus, *Fischke der Krumme*, 2r.

40. Uriel Birnbaum, *Album* (Vienna: Kval Farlag, 1920–21).

41. Wallach, "Art Without Borders," 161.

42. Abramovitsh, *Tales of Mendele*, 150.

43. Rahel Szalit, "Erste Talmudprüfung," *Menorah* 4, no. 2 (1926): 92. Another reproduction in the *Jüdische Rundschau* made clear that it was taken from Szalit's book of *Fishke* illustrations. Rahel Szalit, "Aus Mendele Mocher Sforim, *Fischke der Krumme*," *Jüdische Rundschau* 33, no. 36 (1928): 259.

44. "Der Graphiksammler," *Der Cicerone*, 739.

45. See Ewen, "Rahel Szalit Portrays Soul," 472; and Landman, *Universal Jewish Encyclopedia*, 139.

46. See Peter Gay, *Weimar Culture: The Outsider as Insider* (New York: W. W. Norton, 2001).

CHAPTER 6

1. On Bialik and Hebrew culture in Berlin, see Brenner, *Renaissance of Jewish Culture*, 186–211; and Pinsker, *Literary Passports*, 105–43.

2. See Jonathan Skolnik, *Jewish Pasts, German Fictions: History, Memory, and Minority Culture in Germany, 1824–1955* (Stanford: Stanford University Press, 2014), 105–46.

3. See Mark H. Gelber, "Heine, Herzl, and Nordau: Aspects of the Early Zionist Reception," in *The Jewish Reception of Heinrich Heine*, ed. Mark H. Gelber (Tübingen: Niemeyer, 1992), 139–52.

4. "Heinrich Heine: Romanzero. Eine Einleitung von Alfred Kerr," *Jüdische Rundschau* 28, no. 48 (1923): 288.

5. Hugo Bieber, "Die 'Hebräischen Melodien,'" *Vossische Zeitung*, 19 June 1923 (Abend-Ausgabe), 2–3.

6. Rahel Szalit-Marcus, *Girl with a Headscarf*, 1922, Leo Baeck Institute, call number 78.582. This print is dated "Weihnachten 1922" and bears the inscription "Dr. Michel gewidmet."

7. All illustrations of Heinrich Heine's "Hebrew Melodies" are courtesy of Stanford University Libraries. Rahel Szalit-Marcus, *Hebräische Melodien* (Berlin: Für die literarische Vereinigung Hesperus, 1923), Department of Special Collections, Stanford University Libraries, call number PT2304.A2 H4 1923 FF.

8. Ewen, "Rahel Szalit Portrays Soul," 496.

9. This image was reprinted as *Hawdala* in *Blätter des jüdischen Frauenbundes*. See Szalit, "Ich bin eine jüdische Künstlerin," 3. Elsewhere it bears the title *Sabbath II*.

10. Biélinky, "Les artistes sepharadim," 26.

11. "Kunst un literatur khronik [Art and Letters]," *Milgroym*, no. 6 (June 1924), 38–39.

12. See, for example, Kauders, "Rahel Szalit"; Schwarz, "Die Malerin Rahel Szalit"; and Rachelle Szalit [*sic*], "Die Disputation," *Der Querschnitt* 9, no. 10 (1929): 713.

13. Ruth Morold, "Jüdische Künstler und jüdische Kunst: Die Ausstellungen gelegentlich des XVI. Zionistenkongresses in Zürich," *Jüdische Rundschau* 34, no. 65 (1929): 420. See also Karl Baum, "Eine Ausstellung moderner jüdischer Kunst in der Schweiz," *Aus alter und neuer Zeit*, no. 49, *Illustrierte Beilage zum Israelitischen Familienblatt* 31, no. 34 (1929): 386–87.

14. See B[ertha] B[adt]-St[rauss], "Der Schabbat in der jüdischen Kunst," *Jüdische Rundschau* 41, no. 7 (1936): 19; and "Vorträge über Kunst: Dr. Irmgard Schüler: Sabbat im Spiegel der jüdischen Kunst," *C.V.-Zeitung* 15, no. 5 (1936).

15. See, for example, *Exhibition of German Jewish Artists' Work: Sculpture—Painting—Architecture*, exh. cat. (London: Parsons' Galleries, 1934), 8, Leo Baeck Institute, Microfilm x MfW S116.

16. Heinrich Heine, *Hebrew Melodies*, illustrated by Mark Podwal, trans. Stephen Mitchell and Jack Prelutsky (University Park: Penn State University Press, 2019).

17. Avner Holtzman, *Hayim Nahman Bialik: Poet of Hebrew*, trans. Orr Scharf (New Haven: Yale University Press, 2017), 158–59.

18. Ibid., 147.

19. On Szalit's lost illustrations of Reb Nachman of Breslov's Hasidic tales, see Maria Kühn-Ludewig, *Jiddische Bücher aus Berlin (1918–1936): Titel, Personen, Verlage* (Nümbrecht: Kirsch-Verlag, 2006), 31; Levine, "Yiddish Publishing in Berlin," 102; and Fuks and Fuks, "Yiddish Publishing Activities," 134.

20. See *Milgroym/Rimon*, no. 3 (January 1923). Both hinted at *Ketina kol-bo*'s upcoming publication in their first issues in September 1922, using the listing "Ch. N. Bialik, Ktina Kolbo, ein Gedicht für Kinder. Mit Illustrationen u. Schmuck. Hebräischer Originaltext."

21. Ada Wardi, ed., *New Types: Three Pioneers of Hebrew Graphic Design* (Jerusalem: Israel Museum, 2016), 172–245. Franziska Baruch immigrated to Palestine in 1933 and became an influential Hebrew typography designer.

22. On Ernst Böhm and Charlotte Salomon, see Griselda Pollock, *Charlotte Salomon and the Theatre of Memory* (New Haven: Yale University Press, 2018), 285.

23. The copies I consulted belong to Jüdisches Museum Berlin (hardbound and paper) and Musée d'art et d'histoire du judaïsme in Paris (paper only). The copy at Yeshiva University Museum in New York was altered by someone (perhaps a child) who added color to some of the book's black-and-white images. See Jean Moldovan, "Letters Dipped in Honey: An Introduction by the Collector," in *Letters Dipped in Honey: Jewish Children's Literature from the Moldovan Family Collection* (New York: Yeshiva University Museum, 1995), 3–5.

24. Hayim Nahman Bialik, *Ketina kol-bo* (Berlin: Rimon-Verlag, 1923), 1. Translated from the Hebrew by Asaph Levy.

25. Soncino-Gesellschaft der Freunde des jüdischen Buches, communication regarding publications of the Rimon-Verlag, Berlin, 1924, Jüdisches Museum Berlin, Inv.-Nr. DOK 93/502/81.

26. See Dina Stern, "Godlo Ezba U'Vechor Satan—A Study of Ch. N. Bialik's 'Ketina Kol-Bo,'" *Jerusalem Studies in Jewish Folklore* 9 (1986): 67–88 (in Hebrew).

27. "Der Bialik-Ehrenabend," *Jüdische Rundschau* 28, no. 6 (1923): 26.

28. See Michael Berkowitz, *The Jewish Self-Image in the West* (New York: New York University Press, 2001).

29. Letter from Rahel Szalit to Felix Weltsch, 9 February 1930.

30. Letter from Joseph Budko to Felix Weltsch, 30 January 1930, "Antworten auf 'Selbstwehr' Rundfrage zum Judentum," ARC. Ms. Var. 418 3 168 Felix Weltsch Archive, National Library of Israel, Jerusalem.

CHAPTER 7

1. Konrad Dussel, *Pressebilder in der Weimarer Republik: Entgrenzung der Information* (Berlin: LIT Verlag Dr. W. Hopf, 2012), 43.

2. Nathan Diament, ed., *J. D. Kirszenbaum (1900–1954): The Lost Generation* (Paris: Somogy éditions d'art, 2013), 53. Kirszenbaum, too, was acquainted with Jakob Steinhardt in the early 1920s.

3. Fred Hildenbrandt, "Goldener Sonntag," *Berliner Tageblatt*, 22 December 1924.

4. "Entlassen! Zeichnung von Rahel Szalit," *Lachen links: Das republikanische Witzblatt* 1, no. 43 (1924): 529. Universitätsbibliothek Heidelberg, https://doi.org/10.11588/diglit.8803#0537. See also Udo Achten, ed., *Lachen links: Das republikanische Witzblatt 1924 bis 1927* (Berlin: J. H. W. Dietz, 1985), 191.

5. See Karl Hofer, *Aus Leben und Kunst* (Berlin: Rembrandt Verlag, 1952).

6. Renate Hartleb, *Karl Hofer* (Leipzig: Reclam, 1987), 35–39.

7. "Kostümball. Zeichnung von Rahel Szalit," *Ulk: Wochenbeilage zum Berliner Tageblatt* 59, no. 9 (1930): 68. Universitätsbibliothek Heidelberg, https://doi.org/10.11588/diglit.2343#0068.

8. Ernst Hoferichter, "Auf dem Bal paré: Eine Münchener Faschingsstudie. Zeichnungen von Rahel Szalit," *Lachen links: Das republikanische Witzblatt* 3, no. 6 (1926): 68.

9. Several portraits (Becher, Brecht, George, Ihering) are held at the Akademie der Künste, Berlin; others can be found in *Die literarische Welt*, no. 10 (1925), Deutsches Literaturarchiv Marbach. Szalit's portraits of Alexander Granach and Walter Frank are referenced in *Berliner Bühnen-Bildner*, exh. cat. (Berlin: Berliner Secession, 1926), 22.

10. Meidner, *Dichter, Maler und Cafés*, 18.

11. Gutbrod, *Ludwig Meidner*, 25, 158–65. See also Herbert Ihering, *Regisseure und Bühnenmaler* (Berlin: Bibliophiler Verlag O. Goldschmidt-Gabrielli, 1921).

12. Ludwig Meidner, *Im Nacken das Sternemeer* (Leipzig: Kurt Wolff Verlag, 1918), 61–63. English translation from *The Silverman Collection*, exh. cat. (London: Richard Nagy, 2012), 103.

13. Rahel Szalit's portrait of Johannes Becher was reprinted in *Die neue Bücherschau* 6, no. 10 (1928): 493.

14. Letter from Rahel Szalit to Herbert Ihering, 2 April 1928, Akademie der Künste, Berlin, Herbert Ihering Archive, no. 2441.

15. Letter from Theodor Däubler to Toni Sussmann, 10 July 1924, Akademie der Künste, Berlin, Theodor-Däubler-Archiv, no. 268. Däubler noted that he was unable to help Rolf Stein find a position at a publishing house because of Stein's minimal training and urgent need to earn money.

16. "Kunstausstellungen—Frankfurt a.M.," *Der Kunstwanderer* 6–7 (July 1925): 396.

17. Pless, "Die jüdische Malerin Rahel Szalit-Marcus," 498.

18. Rahel Szalit, "Kinder beim Frühstück. Pastell," in Szalit, "Ich bin eine jüdische Künstlerin," 2. Image courtesy of Institut für die Geschichte der deutschen Juden, Hamburg.

19. Rahel Szalit, "Kinder mit Katze (Pastell)," in *Kunst-Spiegel: Illustrierte Wochenschrift des Berliner Tageblatts*, 25 October 1927, 24.

20. Szalit, "Ich bin eine jüdische Künstlerin," 3.
21. Fenster, *Undzere farpaynikte kinstler*, 233.
22. L. Heck, *Führer durch den Zoologischen Garten Berlin* (Berlin: Actien-Verein des Zoologischen Gartens zu Berlin, 1931), 3.
23. Gary Bruce, *Through the Lion Gate: A History of the Berlin Zoo* (New York: Oxford University Press, 2017), 136–37.
24. "Die Tombola des Presseballs: Eine Kunstausstellung im Zoo," *Vossische Zeitung*, 31 January 1931 (Morgen-Ausgabe, Erste Beilage), 1.
25. See Paul Reitter, *Bambi's Jewish Roots and Other Essays on German-Jewish Culture* (New York: Bloomsbury Academic, 2015), 91–92.
26. Walter Benjamin, *Berlin Childhood Around 1900*, in *Selected Writings*, 3:365–66.
27. See Yuliya Komska's ongoing research on Margret and H. A. Rey.
28. August Macke, "Aus einem Brief an Bernhard Koehler: 30. März 1913," in *Künstlerbekenntnisse: Briefe / Tagebuchblätter / Betrachtungen heutiger Künstler*, ed. Paul Westheim (Berlin: Propyläen Verlag, 1925), 166.
29. See, for example, Uriel Birnbaum, *Allerlei absonderliche Tiere* (Peculiar Animals of All Kinds, 1926).
30. On Erna Pinner, see Justin Howes and Pauline Paucker, "German Jews and the Graphic Arts," *Leo Baeck Institute Year Book* 34 (1989): 459; and Atlan and Wenzel, *Zurück ins Licht*, 113–45, especially 120–25.
31. It is possible that Szalit met Vishniac through Jakob Steinhardt. Steinhardt and Vishniac were neighbors and acquaintances, and they shared an interest in Jewish art. See James H. Fraser, Mara Vishniac Kohn, and Aubrey Pomerance, eds., *Roman Vishniacs Berlin* (Berlin: Jüdisches Museum Berlin, 2005), 10.
32. Paul Raabe, "Illustrated Books and Periodicals," in *German Expressionist Prints and Drawings: The Robert Gore Rifkind Center for German Expressionist Studies*, by Stephanie Barron et al. (Los Angeles: Los Angeles County Museum of Art, 1989), 1:129.
33. R. Szalit, *Cats* (untitled drawing), *Der Querschnitt* 7, no. 7 (1927): 542.
34. R. Szalit, *Bird* (untitled drawing), *Der Querschnitt* 11, no. 6 (1931): 409.

35. The camel illustration of Daudet's *Tartarin of Tarascon* reproduced here appeared in *Die Schaffenden* 4, no. 3 (1923), Gerd Gruber Collection, Wittenberg. Szalit's four lithographs that likely illustrate *Tartarin of Tarascon* appeared in *Der Querschnitt* 5, no. 5 (1925): 391; no. 7 (1925): 622; and no. 9 (1925): 775; and *Der Querschnitt* 6, no. 2 (1926): 103. The last Querschnitt image, elsewhere titled *Dromedar in der Wüste* (Dromedary in the Desert), is identical to figure 56.
36. Alphonse Daudet, *Die Abenteuer des Herrn Tartarin aus Tarascon*, trans. Klabund, illustrated by George Grosz (Berlin: Erich Reiss Verlag, 1921).
37. Rahel Szalit, "Elefanten-Pediküre" and "Morgentoilette der Giraffen," illustrations of "Schönheitspflege der Tiere," *Zeitbilder: Beilage zur Vossischen Zeitung*, no. 1 (5 January 1930): 4. Staatsbibliothek zu Berlin—Preußischer Kulturbesitz, https://zefys.staatsbibliothek-berlin.de/list/title/zdb/26373300.
38. "Brunnenkur im Zoo: Zeichnungen von Rahel Szalit," *Ulk: Wochenbeilage zum Berliner Tageblatt* 59, no. 24 (1930): 190. Universitätsbibliothek Heidelberg, https://doi.org/10.11588/diglit.2343#0190.
39. On the ethnographic showcases or "human zoo" shows held at the Berlin Zoo, see Bruce, *Through the Lion Gate*, 137–42.
40. For this exhibition, artists were limited to displaying works that depicted the area from "Wittenbergplatz bis Bahnhof Zoo, Zoo bis Kurfürstendamm und Zoologischer Garten." "Rund um's KaDeWe," *Deutscher Lyceum-Club / Mitteilungen des Vereins der Künstlerinnen zu Berlin* 27, no. 3 (1932), AdK, Berlin, VdBK 1867, no. 4198 (BG-VdBK 1266-3).
41. Reviews from Akademie der Künste, Berlin, Verein der Berliner Künstlerinnen 1867, no. 4198: A[dolph] D[onath], "Künstlerinnen stellen aus: 'Rund um's Ka De We,'" *Berliner Stadtblatt*, no. 250 (23 October 1932), BG-VdBK 1266-21; and V.J., "'Rund ums KaDeWe': Herbst-Ausstellung des Vereins der Künstlerinnen," newspaper unknown, BG-VdBK 1266-23.
42. Szalit, "Ich bin eine jüdische Künstlerin," 3.
43. R. Sz., illustration of "Sport Schild," *Der Schild* 4, no. 1 (1925): 15.

44. See Goldstein, "Rahel Szalit: Die Schöpferin unserer Bilder."

45. Todd Samuel Presner, *Muscular Judaism: The Jewish Body and the Politics of Regeneration* (New York: Routledge, 2007), 200.

46. Letter from Rahel Szalit to Felix Weltsch, 9 February 1930.

47. Drawing of vacationers by R. Szalit, *Jüdische Rundschau* 33, no. 51 (1928): 372. Digitized by the University Library J. C. Senckenberg Frankfurt am Main: https://sammlungen.ub.uni-frankfurt.de/cm/id/2678016.

48. R. Szalit, "Ich machte auch mit Mr. Stone meinen ersten Spaziergang," illustration from Sch. Gorelik, "Ein jüdischer Schriftsteller reist nach Canada," *Jüdische Rundschau* 33, no. 5 (1928), Unterhaltungs-Beilage no. 3, 34. Digitized by the University Library J. C. Senckenberg Frankfurt am Main: https://sammlungen.ub.uni-frankfurt.de/cm/id/2677578. See also issues no. 13 (14 February 1928) and no. 21 (13 March 1928).

49. See letter from Rachela Szalitowa to Eleonore Kalkowska, 14 August 1934.

50. See Rahel Szalit, "Purim im Städtchen: Eine Kinderidylle in Wort und Bild," *Jüdische Rundschau* 35, no. 21 (1930): 141; and "Mazzebacken im Städtchen: Text und Zeichnungen von Rahel Szalit," *Jüdische Rundschau* 35, no. 29 (1930): 203. Digitized by the University Library J. C. Senckenberg Frankfurt am Main: https://sammlungen.ub.uni-frankfurt.de/cm/id/2679535 and https://sammlungen.ub.uni-frankfurt.de/cm/id/2679613.

51. Rahel Szalit, "Eh' das Purimfest zu Ende / Denkt an Eure Purimspende," *Jüdische Rundschau* 33, no. 18 (1928): 129. Digitized by the University Library J. C. Senckenberg Frankfurt am Main: https://sammlungen.ub.uni-frankfurt.de/cm/id/2677703. See also *Das Jüdische Echo* 15, no. 9 (1928): 145.

CHAPTER 8

1. Robert Beachy, *Gay Berlin: Birthplace of a Modern Identity* (New York: Alfred A. Knopf, 2014), 59.

2. See Valerie Weinstein, "Homosexual Emancipation, Queer Masculinity, and Jewish Difference in *Anders als die Andern* (Different from the Others, Richard Oswald, 1919)," in *Rethinking Jewishness in Weimar Cinema*, ed. Barbara Hales and Valerie Weinstein (New York: Berghahn Books, 2020), 152–77.

3. Ruth Roellig, introduction to *Berlins Lesbische Frauen* (1928), in *Lila Nächte: Die Damenklubs im Berlin der zwanziger Jahre*, ed. Adele Meyer (Berlin: Ed. Lit. Europe, 1994), 13–26. See also Clayton J. Whisnant, *Queer Identities and Politics in Germany: A History, 1880–1945* (New York: Harrington Park Press, 2016), 96.

4. See Ilse Kokula's research as cited in B. Ruby Rich, *Chick Flicks: Theories and Memories of the Feminist Film Movement* (Durham: Duke University Press, 1998), 203.

5. Christopher Isherwood, *Christopher and His Kind* (New York: Farrar, Straus and Giroux, 1976), 120.

6. These and other artists were included in a 2018 exhibition, *Lesbisches Sehen / Lesbian Visions: Artistic Positions from Berlin*, Schwules Museum, Berlin. To the list of queer artists Szalit might have encountered in Berlin—though not active in VdBK at that time—we could add Hannah Höch.

7. This is a modified version of the translation in *The Diary and Letters of Kaethe Kollwitz*, ed. Hans Kollwitz, trans. Richard and Clara Winston (Evanston: Northwestern University Press, 1988), 23. See also Käthe Kollwitz, *"Ich will wirken in dieser Zeit": Auswahl aus den Tagebüchern und Briefen, aus Graphik, Zeichnungen und Plastik* (Berlin: Gebr. Mann Verlag, 1981), 26; and Ilse Kokula, "Lesbisch leben von Weimar bis zur Nachkriegszeit," in Meyer, *Lila Nächte*, 105, 122n6.

8. Ger Trud, "Rahel Szalit: Eine jüdische Malerin," 1.

9. On Jeanne Mammen, see Annelie Lütgens, "The Conspiracy of Women: Images of City Life in the Work of Jeanne Mammen," in *Women in the Metropolis: Gender and Modernity in Weimar Culture*, ed. Katharina von Ankum (Berkeley: University of California Press,

1997), 89–105; Marsha Meskimmon, *We Weren't Modern Enough: Women Artists and the Limits of German Modernism* (Berkeley: University of California Press, 1999); and Jill Suzanne Smith, *Berlin Coquette: Prostitution and the New German Woman, 1890–1933* (Ithaca: Cornell University Press, 2013).

10. William E. McDonald, *Thomas Mann's Joseph and His Brothers: Writing, Performance, and the Politics of Loyalty* (Rochester, NY: Camden House, 1999), 99. Thomas Mann is believed to have been working on the sixth and seventh final chapters of *The Stories of Jacob* in April 1929; "Dina" is the third chapter of this volume.

11. Thomas Mann, "Dina: Authorized Translation from the German by Ludwig Lewisohn," *This Quarter* 3 no. 2 (1930): 204–36.

12. Tobias Boes, *Thomas Mann's War: Literature, Politics, and the World Republic of Letters* (Ithaca: Cornell University Press, 2019), 73–75, 295n80. Both *Joseph in Egypt* (1938) and *Joseph the Provider* (1944) were released as part of the Book-of-the-Month Club in the United States, and *Joseph in Egypt* sold over two hundred thousand copies.

13. See Wolf-Daniel Hartwich, "Religion and Culture: *Joseph and His Brothers*," in *The Cambridge Companion to Thomas Mann*, ed. Ritchie Robertson (Cambridge: Cambridge University Press, 2002), 151–67; Todd Kontje, *The Cambridge Introduction to Thomas Mann* (New York: Cambridge University Press, 2011), 78–85; and Boes, *Thomas Mann's War*, 83.

14. "Dina: Erzählung von Thomas Mann; Originalzeichnungen von R. Szalit," *Die Aufklärung* 1, nos. 3–7 (1929): 76, 78, 109, 158, 159, 187, 188, 221.

15. Ralf Dose, *Magnus Hirschfeld: The Origins of the Gay Liberation Movement*, trans. Edward H. Willis (New York: Monthly Review Press, 2014), 28, 57.

16. See Marita Keilson-Lauritz, "Magnus Hirschfeld und seine Gäste: Das Exil-Gästebuch, 1933–1935," in *Der Sexualreformer Magnus Hirschfeld: Ein Leben im Spannungsfeld von Wissenschaft, Politik und Gesellschaft*, ed. Elke-Vera Kotowski and Julius H. Schoeps (Berlin: be.bra wissenschaft verlag, 2004), 71–92.

17. Elena Mancini, *Magnus Hirschfeld and the Quest for Sexual Freedom: A History of the First International Sexual Freedom Movement* (New York: Palgrave Macmillan, 2010), 92.

18. On *Death in Venice*, see Robert Tobin, *Peripheral Desires: The German Discovery of Sex* (Philadelphia: University of Pennsylvania Press, 2015), 185–210.

19. Thomas Mann, "Für Magnus Hirschfeld zu seinem 60. Geburtstage," in *Essays*, vol. 3, *Ein Appell an die Vernunft*, ed. Hermann Kurzke and Stephan Stachorski (Frankfurt am Main: S. Fischer Verlag, 1994).

20. P.K., "Wir veröffentlichen diese Novelle...," *Die Aufklärung* 1, no. 3 (1929): 76. The terms used here are "völkerkundlich[e]" and "völkerpsychologisch[e] Forschung."

21. See, for example, Rachel Adelman, "Dinah: Bible," in *Jewish Women: A Comprehensive Historical Encyclopedia*, Jewish Women's Archive, 23 June 2021, https://jwa.org/encyclopedia/article/dinah-bible.

22. Anita Diamant confirmed that she read Thomas Mann's Joseph novels while conducting research for *The Red Tent* (New York: St. Martin's Press, 1997). Anita Diamant, email to author, 19 June 2022.

23. Thomas Mann, *Joseph and His Brothers*, trans. John E. Woods (New York: Alfred E. Knopf, 2005), 146.

24. Kontje, *Cambridge Introduction to Thomas Mann*, 79.

25. Arthur Kahane, ed., *Novellen aus der Bibel*, with colorized original lithographs by Erich Büttner (Berlin: Verlag Erich Reiß, 1917).

26. English translation from Mann, *Joseph and His Brothers*, 132.

27. See Kontje, *Cambridge Introduction to Thomas Mann*, 82.

28. Todd Kontje, *Thomas Mann's World: Empire, Race, and the Jewish Question* (Ann Arbor: University of Michigan Press, 2011), 132–34.

29. "Querschnitt durch die sexuelle Zeitgeschichte mit Randbemerkungen von M. H.:

18. Wegen Sittlichkeit," *Die Aufklärung* 1, no. 5 (1929): 160.

30. Hermann Nöll, "Spaziergang der Sträflinge," *Die Aufklärung* 1, no. 4 (1929): 149.

31. On the publication history of *Die Aufklärung*, see Ralf Dose, "Aufklärungen über 'Die Aufklärung'—Ein Werkstattbericht," *Mitteilungen der Magnus-Hirschfeld-Gesellschaft* 2, no. 15 (1991): 31–43.

32. See Jonathan Ned Katz, *The Daring Life and Dangerous Times of Eve Adams* (Chicago: Chicago Review Press, 2021).

CHAPTER 9

1. Ute Eskildsen, "A Chance to Participate: A Transitional Time for Women Photographers," in *Visions of the 'Neue Frau': Women and the Visual Arts in Weimar Germany*, ed. Marsha Meskimmon and Shearer West (Aldershot, UK: Scolar Press, 1995), 65.

2. Letter from Rahel Szalit to Lily Hildebrandt, 26 July 1927.

3. Behling and Manigold, *Die Malweiber*, 42–44.

4. Kollwitz, *"Ich will wirken in dieser Zeit,"* 107.

5. Morold, "Jüdische Kunst auf der Großen Berliner Kunstausstellung," 325. A photograph of *Thoraverhör* was reproduced in *Grosse Berliner Kunstausstellung 1928*, exh. cat. (Berlin: Otto Elsner, 1928), 27.

6. Szalit's title for this drawing is *Meyn bruder Eliyahus khavr Pinye* (My Brother Elyahu's Friend Pinye). On Szalit's illustrations of Sholem Aleichem, see chapter 5.

7. Hans Hildebrandt, *Die Frau als Künstlerin* (Berlin: Rudolf Mosse Buchverlag, 1928), 124, 130–31, 186.

8. Letter from Rahel Szalit to Hans Hildebrandt, undated (probably early 1930s).

9. Schwarz, *Juden in der Kunst*, 170–71. This line appears in the 1936 edition published in Vienna and Jerusalem as well. See also Karl Schwarz, "Die Juden und die graphischen Künste," *Gemeindeblatt der israelitischen Religionsgemeinde zu Leipzig* 5, no. 1 (1929): 1–3.

10. Schwarz, "Die Malerin Rahel Szalit," 259.

11. On the Volkspartei's cultural initiatives, see Brenner, *Renaissance of Jewish Culture*, 51–52.

12. Jewish Telegraphic Agency (JTA), "European Jewish Life Losing Art Because of Economic Crisis," *Jewish Daily Bulletin*, 24 January 1927, 1, 4; and "Berlin: Ankauf jüdischer Kunstwerke," *Jüdisch-liberale Zeitung*, 7 January 1927, 14.

13. See Brenner, *Renaissance of Jewish Culture*, 177–81; Katharina Rauschenberger, *Jüdische Tradition im Kaiserreich und in der Weimarer Republik: Zur Geschichte des jüdischen Museumswesens in Deutschland* (Hanover: Verlag Hahnsche Buchhandlung, 2002), 138; and Tobias Metzler, "Collecting Community: The Berlin Jewish Museum as Narrator Between Past and Present, 1906–1939," in *Visualizing and Exhibiting Jewish Space and History*, ed. Richard I. Cohen (New York: Oxford University Press, 2012), 55–79.

14. See Ruth Morold, "Jüdisches Museum," *Jüdische Rundschau* 32, no. 96 (1927): 680; and Rahel Wischnitzer-Bernstein, "20 Jahre Jüdisches Museum," *Jüdische Rundschau* 42, no. 12 (1937): 16.

15. Chana Schütz and Hermann Simon, eds., *Bestandsrekonstruktion des Berliner Jüdischen Museums in der Oranienburger Strasse* (Berlin: Hentrich & Hentrich, 2011), 58, 82. Other women artists whose works were part of the Berlin Jewish community's collection in the 1930s include Susanne Carvallo-Schülein, Käthe Ephraim-Marcus, Else Meidner, Helene Mises, Regina Mundlak, Anita Rée, Adele Reifenberg-Rosenbaum, Käthe Wilczynski, Grete Wolf-Krakauer, and Julie Wolfthorn.

16. Kauders, "Rahel Szalit," 87–88; Ger Trud, "Rahel Szalit: Eine jüdische Malerin," 1; Pless, "Die jüdische Malerin Rahel Szalit-Marcus," 498; Schwarz, "Die Malerin Rahel Szalit," 259–60; and Szalit, "Ich bin eine jüdische Künstlerin," 2–3.

17. See Claire C. Whitner, "Käthe Kollwitz and the *Krieg* Cycle: The Genesis, Creation, and Legacy of an Iconic Print Series," in *Käthe Kollwitz and the Women of War: Femininity, Identity, and Art in Germany During World Wars I and II*, ed. Claire C. Whitner (New Haven: Yale University Press, 2016), 101–11.

18. Kauders, "Rahel Szalit," 88.

19. Cohn-Wiener, *Jewish Art*, 260.

20. *Jüdische Künstler unserer Zeit*, exh. cat. (Zurich: Salon Henri Brendlé, 1929).

21. Schwarz, *Juden in der Kunst*, 170–71.

22. Karl Schwarz, "Die Künstler des J. F. B. Kalenders," *Blätter des jüdischen Frauenbundes* 4, no. 7 (1928): 2–3.

23. See, for example, Bertha Badt-Strauss, "Das Jahr des Jüdischen Frauenbundes," *Jüdische Rundschau* 37, no. 78 (1932): 379.

24. Postcard from Rahel Szalit to Max and Charlotte Gollop, 29 December 1928. Courtesy of Ute Luise Simeon.

25. Jakob Steinhardt, for example, was supported by a stipend from "a group of wealthy Posen Jews" from 1906 until World War I. Straughn, "Jewish Expressionism," 1:190.

26. Items from the collection of Siegbert Marzynski (later Marcy) have since been auctioned off, including an original lithograph of *Die Strasse niest* (1920) from Szalit's *Motl* illustrations (fig. 35).

27. A postcard titled *Fahrt zur Verlobung* (*Jüd. Mus.*) was printed by Herbert Loewenstein (later Hanoch Avenary), Berlin, possibly as part of the Kalender der jüdischen Künstlerhilfe.

28. Karl Schwarz, *Führer durch das jüdische Museum: Sammlungen der jüdischen Gemeinde zu Berlin* (Berlin: Aldus, 1933), 5.

29. "Aus der Kunstwelt," *Der Kunstwanderer* 12–13 (December 1930): 123–24.

30. Darcy Buerkle has suggested that "Kollwitz's life was intertwined with Jewishness at a time in German history when this was not a given for a non-Jew." Darcy C. Buerkle, "Käthe Kollwitz and 'Boasting Virility' at Smith College's Museum of Art," in Whitner, *Käthe Kollwitz and the Women of War*, 31.

31. "Die Jüdische Altershilfe Groß-Berlin," *Jüdische Rundschau* 35, no. 95 (1930): 644.

32. Hodin, *Aus den Erinnerungen von Else Meidner*, 36.

33. See Elizabeth Otto and Patrick Rössler, *Bauhaus Women: A Global Perspective* (London: Herbert Press, 2019).

34. The catalog of the *Grosse Berliner Kunstausstellung* (May to July 1928) indicates that Szalit was a VdBK member at that time. Although she was active in the VdBK already in 1927, Szalit's name is not on the 1927 membership list. Membership lists from 1928, 1929, 1931, and 1932 have not been preserved. Akademie der Künste, Berlin, VdBK 1867 archives. See also Birgit Möckel, ed., *Fortsetzung folgt! 150 Jahre Verein der Berliner Künstlerinnen 1867 e.V.: 1867–2017* (Berlin: Vice Versa Verlag, 2016), 144–45; Dietmar Fuhrmann and Carola Muysers, eds., *Profession ohne Tradition: 125 Jahre Verein der Berliner Künstlerinnen; Ein Forschungs- und Ausstellungsprojekt der Berlinischen Galerie in Zusammenarbeit mit dem Verein der Berliner Künstlerinnen* (Berlin: Kupfergraben, 1992), 267–68, 446; and Carola Muysers and Dietmar Fuhrmann, eds., *Käthe, Paula, und der ganze Rest* (Berlin: Kupfergraben, 1992), 168.

35. Adolph Donath, "Kunst der Frau: Ausstellung bei Wertheim," *Berliner Tageblatt*, 17 October 1930. Organized by the Deutscher Staatsbürgerinnenverband, this exhibition included painting, sculpture, and graphic art as well as architecture, handicrafts, and photography.

36. Will Pless, "Jüdische Künstlerinnen in der Ausstellung 'Die gestaltende Frau,'" *Israelitisches Familienblatt* 32, no. 37 (1930): 12. It is unknown whether the exhibited painting was *Die Dorfmusikanten* or a different one with a similar subject.

37. Letter from Rahel Szalit to Hans Hildebrandt, undated (probably early 1930s). See also "Kunstausstellungen—Berlin," *Der Kunstwanderer* 3–4 (December 1921), 185.

38. G. Sp., "Vom Fest der tanzenden Palette," *Deutscher Lyceum-Club / Mitteilungen des Vereins der Künstlerinnen zu Berlin* 22, no. 3 (1927): 20, AdK, Berlin, VBdK 1867, no. 4193.

39. Else Hertzer, "Unsere Frühjahrsausstellung 1930," *Deutscher Lyceum-Club / Mitteilungen des Vereins der Künstlerinnen zu Berlin* 25, no. 4 (1930): 12, AdK, Berlin, VBdK 1867, no. 4196 (BG-VdBK 1264-9).

40. Alexander Eiling and Elena Schroll, eds., *Lotte Laserstein: Face to Face* (Munich: Prestel, 2018).

41. Chana Schütz, "Die Künstlerhilfe der Jüdischen Gemeinde zu Berlin," in Schütz and Simon, *Auf der Suche*, 225.

42. Marius Joachim Tataru, *Grete Csaki-Copony, 1893–1993* (Munich: Verlag Südostdeutsches Kulturwerk, 1994).

43. See the following exhibition reviews: *Der Tag*, 23 December 1928, AdK, Berlin, VdBK 1867, no. 4194 (BG-VdBK 1262-12); W.G., "Frühjahrskunst am Schöneberger Ufer," *Berliner Lokalanzeiger*, 5 March 1932, AdK, Berlin, VdBK 1867, no. 4198 (BG-VdBK 1266-14); and Adolph Donath, "Kunstausstellungen," *Berliner Tageblatt*, 30 March 1932, AdK, Berlin, VBdK 1867, no. 4198 (BG-VdBK 1266-17).

44. On Kalkowska, see Anna Dżabagina, "Berlin's Left Bank? Eleonore Kalkowska in Women's Artistic Networks of Weimar Berlin," in *Polish Avant-Garde in Berlin*, ed. Małgorzata Stolarska-Fronia (Berlin: Peter Lang, 2019), 151–70; and Anna Dżabagina, *Kalkowska: Biogeografia* (Gdańsk: Fundacja Terytoria Książki, 2020).

45. Hertzer, "Unsere Frühjahrsausstellung 1930," 12.

46. See Eva Züchner, "Frauenfreunde und Kunstfreundinnen: Zwei Porträt-Ausstellungen am Ende der Zwanziger Jahre," in Fuhrmann and Muysers, *Profession ohne Tradition*, 268; Susanne Meyer-Büser, *Das schönste deustche Frauenporträt: Tendenzen der Bildnismalerei in der Weimarer Republik* (Berlin: Reimer, 1994); and Darcy C. Buerkle, "Real Women: Missing Women," in *Mirror or Mask? Self-Representation in the Modern Age*, ed. David Blostein and Pia Kleber (Berlin: VISTAS Verlag, 2003), 93–107.

47. *Die Frau von heute Ausstellung: Gemälde, Graphik, Plastik*, exh. cat. (Berlin: Verein der Künstlerinnen zu Berlin, 1929). See also Carola Muysers, ed., *Die bildende Künstlerin: Wertung und Wandel in deutschen Quellentexten, 1855–1945* (Dresden: Verlag der Kunst, 1999), 196–97.

48. Buerkle, "Real Women: Missing Women," 101.

49. Dora Landau, "Kunstausstellungen—Berlin," *Der Kunstwanderer* 11–12 (December 1929): 147.

50. A[dolph] D[onath], "Der Künstler als Reporter," *Berliner Tageblatt*, 7 November 1928.

51. Photographs of Fatma Carell appeared in *Der Querschnitt*, *Revue des Monats*, and *Scherl's Magazin* in 1928. Other photos appeared in the early 1930s in several American newspapers.

52. Ewen, "Great Painter of the Jew," 268.

53. Rahel Szalit, *Die Emigrantin als Bardame*, in *Die Frau von heute*, exh. cat., Staatsbibliothek zu Berlin—Preußischer Kulturbesitz, Signatur Nr. 1282/694. Photo courtesy of Akademie der Künste, Berlin, Verein der Berliner Künstlerinnen 1867, no. 5114.

54. See, for example, W[ill] P[less], "Berliner Ausstellungen jüdischer Künstler," *Israelitisches Familienblatt* 32, no. 8 (1930): 14.

55. "Die Frau von heute," *Deutscher Lyceum-Club / Mitteilungen des Vereins der Künstlerinnen zu Berlin* 24, no. 12 (1929): 17. AdK, Berlin, VdBK 1867, no. 4195 (BG-VdBK 1263-12).

56. See Elinor Beaven, "Regional Women Artists and the Artist as Mother: Elsa Haensgen-Dingkuhn," *Art History* 42, no. 4 (2019): 735–36; and Meskimmon, *We Weren't Modern Enough*, 31–33.

57. "Yudishe Kinstlerin," *Unzer Express* (Warsaw), 24 February 1930, 7; and "Nayes in 2–3 Shures," *Folksblat* (Kaunas), 27 February 1930.

58. Adolph Donath, "Pressezeichner und Malerinnen: Galerie Wertheim—Verein der Künstlerinnen," *Berliner Tageblatt*, 12 November 1929. See also Muysers, *Die bildende Künstlerin*, 198–200.

59. Max Osborn, "Die Frau von heute," *Vossische Zeitung*, 11 November 1929 (Abend-Ausgabe), 3. Osborn's review of the exhibition was not entirely favorable; see Buerkle, "Real Women: Missing Women," 101.

60. "Frauen, von Frauen gemalt: Die Ausstellung des Künstlerinnen-Vereins," *Berliner Morgenpost*, 11 November 1929. AdK, Berlin, VdBK 1867, no. BG-VdBK 1263-18.

61. Züchner, "Frauenfreunde und Kunstfreundinnen," 268.

62. See "Vermischtes," *Jüdische Rundschau* 35, no. 14 (1930): 96; "Yudishe Kinstlerin," *Unzer*

Express, 24 February 1930, 7; "Erfolg von Rahel Szalit," *Jüdische Pressezentrale Zürich* 13, no. 585 (1930): 11; "Der erste Preis," *Der Orden Bne Briss: Mitteilungen der Großloge für Deutschland VIII U.O.B.B.* 10, no. 3 (1930): 60; and "Aus den Gemeinden," *Frankfurter Israelitisches Gemeindeblatt* 8, no. 8 (1930): 328.

63. See Meyer-Büser, *Das schönste deustche Frauenporträt*; Dorothy Rowe, "Representing Herself: Lotte Laserstein Between Subject and Object," in *Practicing Modernity: Female Creativity in the Weimar Republic*, ed. Christiane Schönfeld (Würzburg: Königshausen & Neumann, 2006), 77; and Kristin Schroeder, "A New Objectivity: Fashionable Surfaces in Lotte Laserstein's New Woman Pictures," *Art Bulletin* 101, no. 4 (2019): 105.

64. Julie Wolfthorn, *Porträt einer Russin, Deutscher Lyceum-Club / Mitteilungen des Vereins der Künstlerinnen zu Berlin* 24, no. 9 (September 1929), 1, AdK, Berlin, VdBK 1867, no. 4195 (BG-VdBK 1263-9).

65. Will Pless, "Jüdisches auf Kunst-Ausstellungen: Die Frau von heute," *Israelitisches Familienblatt* 32, no. 13 (1930): 14.

66. Rahel Szalit, *Die Fechterin, Selbstbildnis*, *Die Dame* 57, no. 9 (1930): 38.

67. Patrick Rössler, *The Bauhaus at the Newsstand / Das Bauhaus am Kiosk: die neue linie 1929–1943* (Bielefeld: Kerbert Verlag, 2009), 13, 54.

68. Szalit, "Parade Riposte," 12.

69. R. Szalit, *Kantorowicz Wodka, Der Querschnitt* 5, no. 5 (1925): 463.

70. Alfred Brauchle, *Lexikon für Naturheilkunde*, mit Zeichnungen von Rahel Szalit (Leipzig: Reclam, 1931), 9.

71. See, for example, Will Pless, "Jüdische Künstler auf Berliner Kunstausstellungen," *Jüdische Rundschau* 36, no. 79 (1931): 479.

72. It seems unlikely that Bruno Schulz took Chazen's suggestion and met with Szalit. Schulz's correspondence suggests he mainly sought access to prominent artists and writers while visiting Paris from Drohobycz. Bruno Schulz, *Księga listów* (Gdańsk: Słowo/obraz terytoria, 2002), 276–79. See also Anna Kaszuba-Dębska, *Bruno: Epoka genialna* (Krakow: Wydawnictwo Znak, 2020), 55–58.

73. Schwarz, *Führer durch das jüdische Museum*, 27.

74. Biélinky, "Les artistes sepharadim," 26.

75. "Vom Jüdischen Museum," *Jüdische Rundschau* 40, no. 55 (1935): 9. See also Schütz and Simon, *Bestandsrekonstruktion des Berliner Jüdischen Museums*, 82.

76. "Kunstausstellungen der Berliner Logen," *Israelitisches Familienblatt* 35, no. 7 (1933): 12; and E.P., "50 Jahre Großloge Bne Brith," *C.V.-Zeitung* 12, no. 7 (1933): 53.

77. Rahel Wischnitzer-Bernstein, "Kunstausstellung der Berliner B.B.-Logen," *Jüdische Rundschau* 38, no. 14 (1933): 68.

78. See, for example, "'Das Kunst-Werk,' eine Aktion jüdischer Künstlerhilfe," *Jüdisch-liberale Zeitung* 13, no. 30 (1933): 232; and "Neue Bilderserie des 'Kunst-Werks,'" *Jüdisch-liberale Zeitung* 14, no. 16 (1934): 89.

79. Lutz Weltmann, "Ein Kalendar für das jüdische Haus," *Bayerische Israelitische Gemeindezeitung* 10, no. 17 (1934): 349.

80. See L. V. Aschheim, "Die jüdische Kunst-Ausstellung," *Breslauer Jüdisches Gemeindeblatt* 11, no. 16 (1934): 1–4.

CHAPTER 10

1. On the different waves of emigration in the 1930s, see Mark Wischnitzer, "Jewish Emigration from Germany, 1933–1938," *Jewish Social Studies* 2, no. 1 (1940): 23–44; and Wischnitzer, *To Dwell in Safety*.

2. F.B., "Zwei Ausstellungen," *Völkischer Beobachter*, 18 March 1933, 2, AdK, Berlin, VdBK 1867, no. 4199. See also Darius Cierpialkowski and Carina Keil, "Der Verein Berliner Künstlerinnen in der Zeit zwischen 1933 und 1945," 2, AdK, Berlin, VdBK 1867, no. 4198.

3. Marion A. Kaplan, *Between Dignity and Despair: Jewish Life in Nazi Germany* (New York: Oxford University Press, 1998), 18, 21–22; and Debórah Dwork and Robert Jan van Pelt, *Flight from the Reich: Refugee Jews, 1933–1946* (New York: W. W. Norton, 2009), 13–15.

4. John C. Torpey, *The Invention of the Passport: Surveillance, Citizenship and the State*, 2nd ed. (New York: Cambridge University Press, 2018), 163.

5. Hélène Roussel, "German-Speaking Artists in Parisian Exile: Their Routes to the French Capital, Activities There, and Final Flight—a Short Introduction," in *Echoes of Exile: Moscow Archives and the Arts in Paris, 1933–1945*, ed. Ines Rotemund-Reynard (Berlin: De Gruyter, 2014), 7.

6. Rahel Wischnitzer-Bernstein, "Kunst und Kunstpflege im jüdischen Haus," *Der Orden Bne Briss: Mitteilungen der Großloge für Deutschland VIII U.O.B.B.* 14, nos. 6–7 (1934): 85.

7. Heike Carstensen, *Leben und Werk der Malerin und Graphikerin Julie Wolfthorn (1864–1944): Rekonstruktion eines Künstlerinnenlebens* (Marburg: Tectum Verlag, 2011), 138.

8. Schütz, "Die Künstlerhilfe," 215.

9. Jean-Michel Palmier, *Weimar in Exile: The Antifascist Emigration in Europe and America*, trans. David Fernbach (New York: Verso, 2006), 26 and 667n12.

10. Wullschlager, *Chagall: A Biography*, 374–78.

11. *Exhibition of German Jewish Artists' Work*, 8.

12. Caron, *Uneasy Asylum*, 14.

13. Burgess, *Refuge in the Land of Liberty*, 167–69, 195–96.

14. Caron, *Uneasy Asylum*, 163.

15. Sullivan, *Villa Air-Bel*, 435n2.

16. Palmier, *Weimar in Exile*, 215; and Hélène Roussel, "Die emigrierten deutschen Künstler in Frankreich und der Freie Künstlerbund," *Exilforschung: Ein internationales Jahrbuch* 2 (1983–84): 174.

17. See, for example, Madeleine Israël, "Le Salon d'Automne 1933," *L'Univers Israélite* 89, no. 12 (1933): 349–50.

18. Rita Thalmann, "Jewish Women Exiled in France After 1933," in *Between Sorrow and Strength: Women Refugees of the Nazi Period*, ed. Sibylle Quack (New York: Cambridge University Press, 1995), 54–55.

19. Caron, *Uneasy Asylum*, 242.

20. The largest immigrant Jewish neighborhoods were the *Pletzl* (3rd and 4th arr.), Belleville (20th, 11th, 19th arr.), and Montmartre. David H. Weinberg, *A Community on Trial: The Jews of Paris in the 1930s* (Chicago: University of Chicago Press, 1977), 4–5, 105.

21. Paula Hyman, *From Dreyfus to Vichy: The Remaking of French Jewry, 1906–1939* (New York: Columbia University Press, 1979), 84.

22. See Nick Underwood, *Yiddish Paris: Staging Nation and Community in Interwar France* (Bloomington: Indiana University Press, 2022).

23. See Thalmann, "Jewish Women Exiled in France After 1933," 53; Caron, *Uneasy Asylum*, 22; and Burgess, *Refuge in the Land of Liberty*, 173.

24. Jacques Biélinky, "Paris Hospitalier," *L'Univers Israélite* 89, no. 10 (1933): 286.

25. Jacques Biélinky, "La situation des 'Ostjuden' réfugiés en France," *L'Univers Israélite* 89, no. 7 (1933): 186–87.

26. Burgess, *Refuge in the Land of Liberty*, 195–200.

27. Caron, *Uneasy Asylum*, 34–35; Dwork and Van Pelt, *Flight from the Reich*, 52–68.

28. Caron, *Uneasy Asylum*, 114, 174.

29. Letter from Rachela Szalitowa to Eleonore Kalkowska, 14 August 1934. Emphasis in original.

30. Ibid.

31. Ibid.

32. Richard D. Sonn, "Jewish Modernism: Immigrant Artists of Montparnasse, 1905–1914," in *Foreign Artists and Communities in Modern Paris, 1870–1914: Strangers in Paradise*, ed. Karen L. Carter and Susan Waller (Burlington, VT: Ashgate, 2017), 125–40.

33. Wullschlager, *Chagall: A Biography*, 298.

34. Hyman, *From Dreyfus to Vichy*, 21.

35. Silver, "Jewish Artists in Paris," 12–59. Of these core artists, only Soutine still lived in Montparnasse in the late 1930s, though Chagall was not far away in the 16th arrondissement.

36. Sonn, "Jewish Modernism," 126.

37. Ibid., 129.

38. Meisler, *Shocking Paris*, 24, 41, 85, 197.

39. Nieszawer, *Artistes Juifs*, 22.

40. Sonn, "Jewish Modernism," 127–29. See also Kuspit, "Jewish Naivete," 87–99.

41. Paula J. Birnbaum, "Chana Orloff: A Modern Jewish Woman Sculptor of the School of Paris," *Journal of Modern Jewish Studies* 15, no. 1 (2016): 65–87. See also Birnbaum, *Sculpting a Life*, 135–46.

42. Letter from Walter Benjamin to Jula Radt, 22 March 1926, in *The Correspondence of Walter Benjamin, 1910–1940*, ed. and annotated Gershom Scholem and Theodor W. Adorno, trans. Manfred R. Jacobson and Evelyn M. Jacobson (Chicago: University of Chicago Press, 1994), 292.

43. Anna Gmeyner, *Café du Dôme*, ed. Birte Werner, with contributions by Birte Werner and Deborah Vietor-Engländer (Bern: Peter Lang, 2006), 144. Only the English translation of this novel, published in London in 1941, has been preserved.

44. See Friedrich Ahlers-Hestermann, "Der deutsche Künstlerkreis des Café du Dôme," in Westheim, *Künstlerbekenntnisse*, 267–78.

45. Billy Klüver and Julie Martin, "Carrefour Vavin," in Silver and Golan, *Circle of Montparnasse*, 68–79; and Nieszawer, *Artistes Juifs*, 15.

46. Billy Klüver and Julie Martin, *Kiki's Paris: Artists and Lovers, 1900–1930* (New York: Harry N. Abrams, 1989), 80. Pascin lived in this same apartment building briefly, and because Zborowski also lived at this address for many years, Modigliani often came there to paint.

47. Fenster, *Undzere farpaynikte kinstler*, 233.

48. Jacques Biélinky claims that Sholem Asch influenced Szalit's work, though it is unknown if Szalit ever met Asch. Biélinky, "Les artistes sepharadim," 27.

49. Herbert R. Lottman, *The Left Bank: Writers, Artists, and Politics from the Popular Front to the Cold War* (San Francisco: Halo Books, 1991), 37, 125.

50. Simone de Beauvoir, *The Prime of Life*, trans. Peter Green (Cleveland: World, 1962), 303.

51. Archives de la Préfecture de Police, Paris: Fichier des demandes d'autorisation de séjour des etrangers, document coté 328 W.

52. Roussel, "German-Speaking Artists," 15; and Fenster, *Undzere farpaynikte kinstler*, 233.

53. Letter from Rachela Szalitowa to Eleonore Kalkowska, 14 August 1934.

54. Keith Holz, *Modern German Art for Thirties Paris, Prague, and London: Resistance and Acquiescence in a Democratic Public Sphere* (Ann Arbor: University of Michigan Press, 2004), 117.

55. Roussel, "Die emigrierten deutschen Künstler," 177. Max Lingner and John Heartfield were among the few artists who managed successful large-scale solo exhibitions.

56. Jacques Rochvarger (Treasurer for the Société des Artistes Indépendants), email to author, 12 December 2018. For reference, Hilla Rebay bought four Chagall paintings for sixty thousand francs in September 1936. Harshav, *Marc Chagall and His Times*, 453.

57. F.G., "Rahel Szalit-Ausstellung in Paris," *Jüdische Rundschau* 40, no. 35 (1935): 9.

58. Ibid.

59. Biélinky, "Les artistes sepharadim," 27.

60. Ibid.

61. Marek Bartelik, *Early Polish Modern Art: Unity in Multiplicity* (Manchester: Manchester University Press, 2005), 19, 33n16.

62. Billy Klüver and Julie Martin, "Paulette Jourdain," in *Dictionary of Artists' Models*, ed. Jill Berk Jiminez and Joanna Banham (Chicago: Fitzroy Dearborn, 2001), 290. Modigliani's 1919 portrait of Jourdain sold for $38 million ($42.8 million with fees) in 2015.

63. "Ausstellung Rachel Szalit," *Pariser Tageblatt*, 12 June 1935, 3.

64. "Ausstellung Rachel Szalit," *Pariser Tageblatt*, 14 June 1935, 3.

65. Gustave Kahn, "Le troisième Salon populiste (Galerie de Paris)," *Le Quotidien* 13, no. 4694 (23 December 1935): 4; and Gustave Kahn, "Salon populiste," *Mercure de France* 47, no. 904 (14 February 1936): 188–89.

66. Gisela Josten and Friedegund Weideman, eds., *Max Lingner, 1888–1959: Gemälde, Zeichnungen, Pressegraphik*, exh. cat. (Berlin: Staatliche Museen zu Berlin, 1888), 33.

67. "Der Freie Künstlerbund," *Freie Kunst und Literatur* 1, no. 1 (1938): 6. See also Roussel, "Die emigrierten deutschen Künstler," 182, 189.

68. Membership list of the Freier Künstlerbund, Paris, April 1938. Reproduced in Josten and Weideman, *Max Lingner*, 35.

69. Holz, *Modern German Art*, 229–37; and Roussel, "German-Speaking Artists," 22–24.

70. "Deutsche Kulturwoche in Paris," *Freie Kunst und Literatur* 1, no. 2 (1938): 10.

71. Eugen Spiro, "Selbstbetrachtung," *Freie Kunst und Literatur* 1, no. 6 (1939): 3.

72. Fenster, *Undzere farpaynikte kinstler*, 233. Hersh Fenster suggests Szalit led a lonely, withdrawn life in Paris.

73. On the 1939 exibition, see Max Osborn, "Jüdische Kunstausstellung in Paris," *Jüdische Welt-Rundschau* 1, no. 19 (1939): 6; "La Vente-Exposition Palestinienne du Kéren-Kayémeth Leisraël," *L'Univers Israélite* 94, no. 38 (1939): 697; "Une exposition d'art juif," *L'Univers Israélite* 94, no. 41 (1939): 740; and "A l'exposition d'art juif," *L'Univers Israélite* 94, no. 42 (1939): 765. The exhibition was also reviewed in the Yiddish *Naye Prese* and *La Terre Retrouvée*, the monthly magazine of the French Jewish National Fund. See also Rachel Wischnitzer, "From My Archives," *Journal of Jewish Art* 6 (1979): 12.

74. "Zugunsten des Palaestina-Siedlungsfonds," *Pariser Tageszeitung*, 20 June 1939, 3.

75. Osborn, "Jüdische Kunstausstellung," 6. See also Birnbaum, *Sculpting a Life*, 230.

CHAPTER 11

1. This is a fictional letter. No correspondence between Rahel Szalit and her sister Szejna Michla Kolp is known to have survived.

2. Laura Jockusch, *Collect and Record! Jewish Holocaust Documentation in Early Postwar Europe* (Oxford: Oxford University Press, 2012), 46.

3. Caron, *Uneasy Asylum*, 242–44, 259.

4. Silver and Golan, *Circle of Montparnasse*, 87.

5. See Jacques Biélinky's journal entries dated 19 July 1940 and 12 August 1941. Jacques Biélinky, *Journal, 1940–1942: Un journaliste juif à Paris sous l'Occupation*, ed. Renée Poznanski (Paris: Cerf, 1992), 37, 137.

6. Michael R. Marrus and Robert O. Paxton, *Vichy France and the Jews* (New York: Basic Books, 1981), 3–4, 7.

7. Between fourteen hundred and seven thousand refugees were able to emigrate successfully between July 1940 and May 1941. Caron, *Uneasy Asylum*, 337.

8. Fry, *Surrender on Demand*, 207.

9. Esti Freud (Sigmund Freud's daughter-in-law), for example, later returned from Casablanca to Lisbon to secure passage across the Atlantic. Meredith Hindley, *Destination Casablanca: Exiles, Espionage, and the Battle for North Africa in World War II* (New York: PublicAffairs, 2017), 165–70. See also Kaplan, *Hitler's Jewish Refugees*.

10. Phone interview with Eliezer Kolp on 17 June 2019.

11. Marrus and Paxton, *Vichy France*, 236.

12. David Drake, *Paris at War, 1939–1945* (Cambridge, MA: Belknap Press of Harvard University Press, 2015), 261.

13. Renée Poznanski, *Jews in France During World War II*, trans. Nathan Bracher (Hanover, NH: Brandeis University Press, 2001), 260–65; and Susan Zuccotti, *The Holocaust, the French, and the Jews* (New York: Bison Books, 1999), 103f.

14. Poznanski, *Jews in France*, 260–67, 287.

15. See the entry for "Rachel Schalit née Marcus" in deportation list no. 21, Arolsen Archives, digital file number 11180725. See also Klarsfeld, *Mémorial de la Déportation*, IX.

16. Benjamin Rapoport, *Ma vie et mes camps* (Paris: Harmattan, 2002), 88.

17. Klarsfeld, *Mémorial de la Déportation*, IX; and Zuccotti, *Holocaust*, 126.

18. Puś, "Development of the City of Łódź," 13–14.

19. Lodz Ghetto records, United States Holocaust Memorial Museum.

20. This was their home address according to Lodz census records, 1916–1921.

21. The grocery store was registered to Szejna Mechla Kolp in 1928–29. File 39/221/0/4.19/125697, Akta miasta Łodzi, Archiwum Państwowe w Łodzi (State archives in Lodz).

22. Jerzy Tomaszewski, "Jews in Łódź in 1931 According to Statistics," in Polonsky, *POLIN* 6, 182.

23. Letter from Rachela Szalitowa to Eleonore Kalkowska, 14 August 1934.

24. Michal Unger, "The Status and Plight of Women in the Lodz Ghetto," in *Women in the*

Holocaust, ed. Dalia Ofer and Lenore J. Weitzman (New Haven: Yale University Press, 1998), 123–42, here 127–28.

25. Isaiah Trunk, *Łódź Ghetto: A History*, trans. and ed. Robert Moses Shapiro (Bloomington: Indiana University Press, 2006); and Unger, "Status and Plight of Women," 123, 129.

26. Lodz Ghetto records, United States Holocaust Memorial Museum.

27. Oskar Rosenfeld, "Golem and Hunger," cited in Sven-Erik Rose, "Oskar Rosenfeld, the Lodz Ghetto, and the Chronotope of Hunger," in *The Aesthetics and Politics of Global Hunger*, ed. Manisha Basu and Anastasia Ulanowicz (New York: Palgrave Macmillan, 2017), 41. See also Oskar Rosenfeld, *In the Beginning Was the Ghetto: Notebooks from Łódź*, ed. Hanno Loewy, trans. Brigitte M. Goldstein (Evanston: Northwestern University Press, 2002).

28. Record for Szejna Michla Kolp, Holocaust Survivors and Victims Database, United States Holocaust Memorial Museum.

29. Trunk, *Łódź Ghetto*, 267, table 17; and Unger, "Status and Plight of Women," 126.

30. Josef Zelkowicz, "In Those Nightmarish Days," in *In Those Nightmarish Days: The Ghetto Reportage of Peretz Opoczynski and Josef Zelkowicz*, ed. Samuel D. Kassow and David Suchoff, trans. David Suchoff (New Haven: Yale University Press, 2015), 262.

31. The slaughterhouse photographs of Madame d'Ora from the early 1950s provide one example. Lisa Silverman, "Art of Loss: Madame d'Ora, Photography, and the Restitution of Haus Doranna," *Leo Baeck Institute Year Book* 60 (2015): 173–90.

32. Records for Juljusz Kolp, Arolsen Archives.

33. Yehuda Kolp, contributor, "Page of Testimony," Yad Vashem, *The Central Database of Shoah Victims' Names*.

34. Phone interview with Eliezer Kolp on 17 June 2019.

35. For example, see the correspondence between photographer Dora Kallmus (in Paris) and her sister Anna Kallmus (in Austria) between 1938 and 1941. Silverman, "Art of Loss."

36. See Andrea Löw, *Juden im Getto Litzmannstadt: Lebensbedingungen, Selbstwahrnehmung, Verhalten* (Göttingen: Wallstein, 2006), 146–52; and Lucjan Dobroszycki, ed., *The Chronicle of the Łódź Ghetto, 1941–1944*, trans. Richard Lourie, Joachim Neugroschel, and others (New Haven: Yale University Press, 1984), 66.

EPILOGUE

1. Zuccotti, *Holocaust*, 149.
2. Biélinky, *Journal*, 262.
3. Letter from Ludwig Meidner to Wolf Bergmann, 29 April 1950.
4. Landman, *Universal Jewish Encyclopedia*, 139.
5. Karl Schwarz, *Jüdische Kunst—Jüdische Künstler: Erinnerungen des ersten Direktors des Berliner Jüdischen Museums*, ed. Chana C. Schütz and Hermann Simon (Berlin: Hentrich & Hentrich, 2001). An unpublished German draft of Karl Schwarz's *Jewish Artists of the 19th and 20th Centuries* (New York: Philosophical Library, 1949) briefly discusses Szalit in its section on graphic artists. Yet it seems that Szalit, along with several other women artists mentioned in the draft (Charlotte Berend-Corinth, Regina Mundlak, Chana Orloff, and Irma Stern), did not make the cut for the published version. ARC. 4* 1623 01 3.1 Karl Schwarz Archive, National Library of Israel, Jerusalem.
6. On Hersh Fenster, see the 2021 French edition of *Nos artistes martyrs*. See also Nieszawer, *Histoires des Artistes Juifs*, 34, 459; and Rachel E. Perry, "Inserting Hersh Fenster's *Undzere farpainikte kinstler* into Art History," *Images* 14 (2021): 109–35.
7. Fenster, *Undzere farpaynikte kinstler*, 11. Chagall poem translated from the Yiddish by Barbara and Benjamin Harshav, cited in Perry, "Inserting Hersh Fenster," 135.
8. See Rosanna Warren, *Max Jacob: A Life in Art and Letters* (New York: W. W. Norton, 2020).
9. Jakob Hübner, "Auf der Suche nach Objekten des Berliner Jüdischen Museums in Polen: Funde und Hypothesen," in Schütz and Simon, *Auf der Suche*, 73–85.
10. See Wallach, "Art Without Borders."

Selected Bibliography

LIBRARIES AND ARCHIVAL COLLECTIONS

Austria
Israelitische Kultusgemeinde Wien (Archive of the Jewish Community of Vienna)
Stadtarchiv Innsbruck
Wiener Stadt- und Landesarchiv

France
Alliance Israélite Universelle, Paris
Archives de la Préfecture de Police, Paris
Bibliothèque Polonaise de Paris / Biblioteka Polska w Paryżu
Musée d'art et d'histoire du judaïsme, Paris

Germany
Akademie der Künste (AdK), Berlin
Arolsen Archives, Bad Arolsen
Deutsches Literaturarchiv Marbach, Marbach am Neckar
Eva-Maria Thimme Collection, Berlin
Gerd Gruber Collection, Wittenberg
Institut für Zeitungsforschung, Stadt Dortmund
Jüdisches Museum Berlin
Jüdisches Museum Frankfurt
Landesarchiv Berlin
Magnus-Hirschfeld-Gesellschaft e.V., Berlin
Staatsbibliothek zu Berlin—Preußischer Kulturbesitz, Berlin
Stadtarchiv Darmstadt
Stadtarchiv München
University Library J. C. Senckenberg Frankfurt am Main (and CompactMemory.de)

Israel
National Library of Israel, Jerusalem
Yad Vashem: The World Holocaust Remembrance Center, Jerusalem

Lithuania
Lietuvos valstybės istorijos archyvas (Lithuanian State Historical Archives)

Poland
Archiwum Państwowe w Łodzi (State Archives in Łódź)
Emanuel Ringelblum Jewish Historical Institute, Warsaw

United States
Beck Archives, Special Collections, University of Denver Libraries
Derfner Judaica Museum, Riverdale
Getty Research Institute, Los Angeles
Hebrew Union College, Cincinnati
Leo Baeck Institute, New York
Metropolitan Museum of Art, New York
Stanford University Library
United States Holocaust Memorial Museum, Washington DC
YIVO Institute for Jewish Research, New York

UNPUBLISHED PAPERS AND INTERVIEWS OF INDIVIDUALS

Konrad Bieber, Oral History Interview, United States Holocaust Memorial Museum
Jacques Biélinky, YIVO Institute for Jewish Research, New York
Theodor Däubler, Akademie der Künste, Berlin
Moritz Goldstein, Institut für Zeitungsforschung, Stadt Dortmund
Hans Hildebrandt, Getty Research Institute, Los Angeles
Herbert Ihering, Akademie der Künste, Berlin
Eleonore Kalkowska, Tomasz Szarota Collection, Warsaw

SELECTED BIBLIOGRAPHY

Eliezer Kolp, Phone Interview, Rishon LeZion, Israel
Maria Lowenstein, Beck Archives, Special Collections, University of Denver Libraries
Ludwig Meidner, Stadtarchiv Darmstadt
Karl Schwarz Archive, National Library of Israel, Jerusalem
Jakob Steinhardt, Jüdisches Museum Berlin
Felix Weltsch Archive, National Library of Israel, Jerusalem
Rachel Wischnitzer-Bernstein, Leo Baeck Institute, New York

PERIODICALS

Jewish Periodicals in Germany
Bayerische Israelitische Gemeindezeitung
Blätter des jüdischen Frauenbundes
Breslauer Jüdisches Gemeindeblatt
C.V.-Zeitung
Frankfurter Israelitisches Gemeindeblatt
Gemeindeblatt der israelitischen Religionsgemeinde zu Leipzig
Gemeindeblatt der jüdischen Gemeinde zu Berlin
Israelitisches Familienblatt
Das jüdische Echo
Die jüdische Frau
Jüdische Rundschau
Jüdisch-liberale Zeitung
Menorah
Milgroym/Rimon
Der Orden Bne Briss: Mitteilungen der Großloge für Deutschland VIII U.O.B.B.
Ost und West
Der Schild
Schlemiel: Jüdische Blätter für Humor und Kunst
Soncino-Blätter: Beiträge zur Kunde des Jüdischen Buches
Yidishe Ilustrierte Tsaytung

Periodicals in Germany
Berliner Tageblatt
Der Cicerone
Die Dame
Deutscher Lyceum-Club / Mitteilungen des Vereins der Künstlerinnen zu Berlin
Der Feuerreiter
Das Kunstblatt
Der Kunstwanderer
Lachen links: Das republikanische Witzblatt
Die literarische Welt
Die neue Bücherschau
die neue linie
Der Querschnitt
Die Schaffenden
Ulk: Wochenbeilage zum Berliner Tageblatt
Vossische Zeitung
Die Weltbühne
Zeitbilder: Beilage zur Vossischen Zeitung

Periodicals in France
Freie Kunst und Literatur: Liberté pour l'art et la littérature. Revue mensuelle en langue allemande
Le Judaisme Sepharadi
Jüdische Welt-Rundschau
Mercure de France
Pariser Tageblatt (later: *Pariser Tageszeitung*)
Le Quotidien
This Quarter
L'Univers Israélite

Periodicals in Other Locations
Allgemeiner Tiroler Anzeiger, Innsbruck
American Hebrew, New York
Arbeiter-Zeitung: Zentralorgan der Deutschen Sozialdemokratie in Österreich, Vienna
B'nai B'rith Magazine: The National Jewish Monthly, Chicago
Folksblat, Kaunas, Lithuania
Innsbrucker Nachrichten, Innsbruck
Jewish Daily Bulletin, Jewish Telegraphic Agency (JTA), New York
Jüdische Pressezentrale Zürich
Neues Wiener Journal, Vienna
Unzer Express, Warsaw

SELECTED PUBLISHED SOURCES

Abramovitsh, S. Y. (Mendele Moykher Sforim).
 Tales of Mendele the Book Peddler: Fishke the Lame and Benjamin the Third. Edited by Dan Miron and Ken Frieden. Translated by Ted Gorelick and Hillel

SELECTED BIBLIOGRAPHY

Halkin. New York: Schocken Books, 1996.

Aleichem, Sholem. *Tevye the Dairyman and Motl the Cantor's Son*. Translated by Aliza Shevrin. New York: Penguin Books, 2009.

Aschheim, Steven E. *Brothers and Strangers: The East European Jew in German and German Jewish Consciousness, 1800–1923*. Madison: University of Wisconsin Press, 1982.

Atlan, Eva Sabrina, and Mirjam Wenzel, eds. *Zurück ins Licht: Vier Künstlerinnen—Ihre Werke. Ihre Wege. Rosy Lilienfeld, Amalie Seckbach, Erna Pinner, Ruth Cahn*. Bielefeld: Kerber Verlag, 2022. Exh. cat.

Baskind, Samantha, and Larry Silver. *Jewish Art: A Modern History*. London: Reaktion Books, 2011.

Bauer, Heike. *The Hirschfeld Archives: Violence, Death, and Modern Queer Culture*. Philadelphia: Temple University Press, 2017.

Behling, Katja, and Anke Manigold. *Die Malweiber: Unerschrockene Künstlerinnen um 1900*. Munich: Elisabeth Sandmann Verlag, 2009.

Benjamin, Walter. *Walter Benjamin: Selected Writings*. Vol. 3, *1935–1938*. Edited by Howard Eiland and Michael W. Jennings. Translated by Edmund Jephcott, Howard Eiland, and others. Cambridge, MA: Belknap Press of Harvard University Press, 2002.

Bertz, Inka. *"Eine neue Kunst für ein altes Volk": Die Jüdische Renaissance in Berlin 1900 bis 1924*. Berlin: Jüdisches Museum, Berlin Museumspädagogischer Dienst, 1991.

Biélinky, Jacques. *Journal, 1940–1942: Un journaliste juif à Paris sous l'Occupation*. Edited by Renée Poznanski. Paris: Cerf, 1992.

Bilski, Emily D., ed. *Berlin Metropolis: Jews and the New Culture, 1890–1918*. Berkeley: University of California Press, 1999.

Birnbaum, Paula J. *Sculpting a Life: Chana Orloff Between Paris and Tel Aviv*. Waltham, MA: Brandeis University Press, 2022.

Boes, Tobias. *Thomas Mann's War: Literature, Politics, and the World Republic of Letters*. Ithaca: Cornell University Press, 2019.

Brenner, Michael. *The Renaissance of Jewish Culture in Weimar Germany*. New Haven: Yale University Press, 1996.

Bruce, Gary. *Through the Lion Gate: A History of the Berlin Zoo*. New York: Oxford University Press, 2017.

Buerkle, Darcy C. *Nothing Happened: Charlotte Salomon and an Archive of Suicide*. Ann Arbor: University of Michigan Press, 2013.

———. "Real Women: Missing Women." In *Mirror or Mask? Self-Representation in the Modern Age*, edited by David Blostein and Pia Kleber, 93–107. Berlin: VISTAS Verlag, 2003.

Burgess, Greg. *Refuge in the Land of Liberty: France and Its Refugees, from the Revolution to the End of Asylum, 1787–1939*. New York: Palgrave Macmillan, 2008.

Caron, Vicki. *Uneasy Asylum: France and the Jewish Refugee Crisis, 1933–1942*. Stanford: Stanford University Press, 2003.

Cohen, Richard I., ed. *Visualizing and Exhibiting Jewish Space and History*. New York: Oxford University Press, 2012.

Cohn-Wiener, Ernst. *Jewish Art: Its History from the Beginning to the Present Day*. Translated by Anthea Bell. Yelvertoft Manor, Northamptonshire: Pilkington Press, 2001.

Dohrn, Verena, and Gertrud Pickhan, eds. *Transit und Transformation: Osteuropäisch-jüdische Migranten in Berlin 1918–1939*. Göttingen: Wallstein Verlag, 2010.

Dose, Ralf. *Magnus Hirschfeld: The Origins of the Gay Liberation Movement*. Translated by Edward H. Willis. New York: Monthly Review Press, 2014.

Dwork, Debórah, and Robert Jan van Pelt. *Flight from the Reich: Refugee Jews, 1933–1946*. New York: W. W. Norton, 2009.

Estraikh, Gennady, and Mikhail Krutikov, eds. *Yiddish in Weimar Berlin: At the

SELECTED BIBLIOGRAPHY

Crossroads of Diaspora Politics and Culture. Oxford: Legenda, 2010.

Exhibition of German Jewish Artists' Work: Sculpture—Painting—Architecture. London: Parsons' Galleries, 1934. Exh. cat.

Fenster, Hersh. *Undzere farpaynikte kinstler*. Paris: H. Fenster, 1951. French translation: *Nos artistes martyrs*. Paris: Hazan, 2021.

Figura, Starr. *German Expressionism: The Graphic Impulse*. With an essay by Peter Jelavich. New York: Museum of Modern Art, 2011.

Die Frau von heute Ausstellung: Gemälde, Graphik, Plastik. Berlin: Verein der Künstlerinnen zu Berlin, 1929. Exh. cat.

Fuchs, Eduard. *Die Juden in der Karikatur: Ein Beitrag zur Kulturgeschichte*. Munich: Albert Langen, 1921.

Fuhrmann, Dietmar, and Carola Muysers, eds. *Profession ohne Tradition: 125 Jahre Verein der Berliner Künstlerinnen; Ein Forschungs- und Ausstellungsprojekt der Berlinischen Galerie in Zusammenarbeit mit dem Verein der Berliner Künstlerinnen*. Berlin: Kupfergraben, 1992.

Fuks, Leo, and Renate Fuks. "Yiddish Publishing Activities in the Weimar Republic, 1920–1933." *Leo Baeck Institute Year Book* 33 (1988): 417–34.

Gay, Peter. *Weimar Culture: The Outsider as Insider*. New York: W. W. Norton, 2001.

Gitelman, Zvi. *A Century of Ambivalence: The Jews of Russia and the Soviet Union, 1881 to the Present*. Bloomington: Indiana University Press, 2001.

Gross, Natan, ed. *Avraham Palukst: The Rediscovered Artist*. Tel Aviv: Eked, 1982.

Gutbrod, Philipp, ed. *Ludwig Meidner: Begegnungen/Encounters*. Munich: Hirmer, 2016.

Harshav, Benjamin. *Marc Chagall and His Times: A Documentary Narrative*. Stanford: Stanford University Press, 2004.

Hartman, Saidiya. *Wayward Lives, Beautiful Experiments: Intimate Histories of Riotous Black Girls, Troublesome Women, and Queer Radicals*. New York: W. W. Norton, 2019.

Hildebrandt, Hans. *Die Frau als Künstlerin*. Berlin: Rudolf Mosse Buchverlag, 1928.

Hodin, Joseph Paul. *Aus den Erinnerungen von Else Meidner*. Darmstadt: Justus von Liebig Verlag, 1979.

Holtzman, Avner. *Hayim Nahman Bialik: Poet of Hebrew*. Translated by Orr Scharf. New Haven: Yale University Press, 2017.

Holz, Keith. *Modern German Art for Thirties Paris, Prague, and London: Resistance and Acquiescence in a Democratic Public Sphere*. Ann Arbor: University of Michigan Press, 2004.

Howes, Justin, and Pauline Paucker. "German Jews and the Graphic Arts." *Leo Baeck Institute Year Book* 34 (1989): 443–73.

Hülsen-Esch, Andrea von, and Marion Aptroot. *Jüdische Illustratoren aus Osteuropa in Berlin und Paris*. Düsseldorf: Heinrich-Heine-Universität Düsseldorf, 2008. Exh. cat.

Hyman, Paula E. *From Dreyfus to Vichy: The Remaking of French Jewry, 1906–1939*. New York: Columbia University Press, 1979.

Johnson, Julie M. *The Memory Factory: The Forgotten Women Artists of Vienna, 1900*. West Lafayette: Purdue University Press, 2012.

Josten, Gisela, and Friedegund Weidemann, eds. *Max Lingner, 1888–1959: Gemälde, Zeichnungen, Pressegraphik*. Berlin: Staatliche Museen zu Berlin, 1888. Exh. cat.

Kampf, Avram. *Chagall to Kitaj: Jewish Experience in 20th Century Art*. New York: Praeger, 1990.

Kaplan, Louis. *At Wit's End: The Deadly Discourse on the Jewish Joke*. New York: Fordham University Press, 2020.

Kaplan, Marion A. *Between Dignity and Despair: Jewish Life in Nazi Germany*. New York: Oxford University Press, 1998.

———. *Hitler's Jewish Refugees: Hope and Anxiety in Portugal*. New Haven: Yale University Press, 2020.

Kelly, Michael, ed. *Encyclopedia of Aesthetics*. 2nd ed. Oxford: Oxford University Press,

2014. doi: 10.1093/acref/9780199747108.001.0001.

Kerr, Alfred. *Berlin wird Berlin: Briefe aus der Reichshauptstadt, 1897–1922*. Vol. 4. Edited by Deborah Vietor-Engländer. Göttingen: Wallstein Verlag, 2021.

Klarsfeld, Serge. *Mémorial de la Déportation des Juifs de France*. Paris: FFDJF Fils et Filles des Déportés Juifs de France, 2012.

Koller, Sabine. "*Mentshelekh un stsenes*: Rahel Szalit-Marcus illustriert Sholem Aleichem." In *Leket: Jiddistik heute / Yiddish Studies Today*, edited by Marion Aptroot, Efrat Gal-Ed, Roland Gruschka, and Simon Neuberg, 207–31. Düsseldorf: Düsseldorf University Press, 2012.

Kollwitz, Käthe. *The Diary and Letters of Kaethe Kollwitz*. Edited by Hans Kollwitz. Translated by Richard and Clara Winston. Evanston: Northwestern University Press, 1988.

——. *"Ich will wirken in dieser Zeit": Auswahl aus den Tagebüchern und Briefen, aus Graphik, Zeichnungen und Plastik*. Berlin: Gebr. Mann, 1981.

Kontje, Todd. *The Cambridge Introduction to Thomas Mann*. New York: Cambridge University Press, 2011.

——. *Thomas Mann's World: Empire, Race, and the Jewish Question*. Ann Arbor: University of Michigan Press, 2011.

Kritter, Ulrich von, ed. *Literatur und Zeiterlebnis im Spiegel der Buchillustration, 1900–1945: Bücher aus der Sammlung v. Kritter*. Bad Homburg: Ulrich von Kritter, 1989.

Kühn-Ludewig, Maria. *Jiddische Bücher aus Berlin (1918–1936): Titel, Personen, Verlage*. Nümbrecht: Kirsch-Verlag, 2006.

Landsberger, Franz. *A History of Jewish Art*. Cincinnati: Union of American Hebrew Congregations, 1946.

Lang, Lothar. *Expressionist Book Illustration in Germany, 1907–1927*. Translated by Janet Seligman. Boston: New York Graphic Society, 1976.

Levine, Glenn S. "Yiddish Publishing in Berlin and the Crisis in Eastern European Jewish Culture, 1919–1924." *Leo Baeck Institute Year Book* 42 (1997): 85–108.

Liekis, Šarūnas, Antony Polonsky, and ChaeRan Freeze, eds. *POLIN: Studies in Polish Jewry*. Vol. 25, *Jews in the Former Grand Duchy of Lithuania Since 1772*. Oxford: Littman Library of Jewish Civilization, 2013.

Male, Alan, ed. *A Companion to Illustration*. Hoboken, NJ: John Wiley and Sons, 2019.

Malinowski, Jerzy, Renata Piątkowska, and Tamara Sztyma-Knasiecka, eds. *Jewish Artists and Central-Eastern Europe: Art Centers—Identity—Heritage from the 19th Century to the Second World War*. Warsaw: Polish Society of Oriental Art and Wydawnictwo DiG, 2010.

Mann, Thomas. *Joseph and His Brothers*. Translated by John E. Woods. New York: Alfred E. Knopf, 2005.

Marrus, Michael R., and Robert O. Paxton. *Vichy France and the Jews*. New York: Basic Books, 1981.

Meisler, Stanley. *Shocking Paris: Soutine, Chagall and the Outsiders of Montparnasse*. New York: St. Martin's Press, 2015.

Meskimmon, Marsha. *We Weren't Modern Enough: Women Artists and the Limits of German Modernism*. Berkeley: University of California Press, 1999.

Meskimmon, Marsha, and Shearer West, eds. *Visions of the "Neue Frau": Women and the Visual Arts in Weimar Germany*. Aldershot, UK: Scolar Press, 1995.

Meyer, Adele, ed. *Lila Nächte: Die Damenklubs im Berlin der zwanziger Jahre*. Berlin: Ed. Lit. Europe, 1994.

Mierau, Fritz, ed. *Russen in Berlin: Literatur, Malerei, Theater, Film, 1918–1933*. Leipzig: Reclam Verlag, 1991.

Möckel, Birgit, ed. *Fortsetzung folgt! 150 Jahre Verein der Berliner Künstlerinnen 1867 e.V.: 1867–2017*. Berlin: Vice Versa Verlag, 2016.

SELECTED BIBLIOGRAPHY

Montparnasse déporté: Artistes d'Europe. Edited by Jean Digne and Sylvie Buisson. Paris: Musée du Montparnasse, 2005. Exh. cat.

Muysers, Carola, ed. *Die bildende Künstlerin: Wertung und Wandel in deutschen Quellentexten, 1855–1945.* Dresden: Verlag der Kunst, 1999.

Muysers, Carola, and Dietmar Fuhrmann, eds. *Käthe, Paula, und der ganze Rest.* Berlin: Kupfergraben, 1992.

Nathans, Benjamin, and Gabriella Safran, eds. *Culture Front: Representing Jews in Eastern Europe.* Philadelphia: University of Pennsylvania Press, 2008.

Neiss, Marion. *Presse im Transit: Jiddische Zeitungen und Zeitschriften in Berlin von 1919 bis 1925.* Berlin: Metropol, 2002.

Nieszawer, Nadine, ed. *Artistes Juifs de L'École de Paris, 1905–1939 / Jewish Artists of the School of Paris, 1905–1939.* Translated by Deborah Princ. Paris: Somogy éditions d'art, 2015.

———, ed. *Histoires des Artistes Juifs de L'École de Paris 1905–1939 / Stories of Jewish Artists of the School of Paris.* Translated by Deborah Princ. Paris: Les Étoiles, 2020.

Ofer, Dalia, and Lenore J. Weitzman, eds. *Women in the Holocaust.* New Haven: Yale University Press, 1998.

Olin, Margaret. *The Nation Without Art: Examining Modern Discourses on Jewish Art.* Lincoln: University of Nebraska Press, 2001.

Otto, Elizabeth. *Haunted Bauhaus: Occult Spirituality, Gender Fluidity, Queer Identities, and Radical Politics.* Cambridge, MA: MIT Press, 2019.

Otto, Elizabeth, and Patrick Rössler. *Bauhaus Women: A Global Perspective.* London: Herbert Press, 2019.

Palmier, Jean-Michel. *Weimar in Exile: The Antifascist Emigration in Europe and America.* Translated by David Fernbach. New York: Verso, 2006.

Perry, Rachel E. "Inserting Hersh Fenster's *Undzere farpainikte kinstler* into Art History." *Images: A Journal of Jewish Art and Visual Culture* 14 (2021): 109–35.

Pinsker, Shachar M. *Literary Passports: The Making of Modernist Hebrew Fiction in Europe.* Stanford: Stanford University Press, 2011.

———. *A Rich Brew: How Cafés Created Modern Jewish Culture.* New York: New York University Press, 2018.

Polonsky, Antony. *The Jews in Poland and Russia: A Short History.* Oxford: Littman Library of Jewish Civilization, 2013.

———, ed. *POLIN: Studies in Polish Jewry.* Vol. 6, *Jews in Łódź, 1820–1939.* Oxford: Littman Library of Jewish Civilization, 1991.

Poznanski, Renée. *Jews in France During World War II.* Translated by Nathan Bracher. Hanover: Brandeis University Press, 2001.

Price, Dorothy, ed. *German Expressionism: Der Blaue Reiter and Its Legacies.* Manchester: Manchester University Press, 2020.

Riedel, Erik, and Mirjam Wenzel, eds. *Ludwig Meidner: Expressionismus, Ekstase, Exil / Expressionism, Ecstasy, Exile.* Berlin: Gebr. Mann Verlag, 2018.

Roth, Joseph. *The Wandering Jews.* Translated by Michael Hofmann. New York: W. W. Norton, 2001.

Roussel, Hélène. "Die emigrierten deutschen Künstler in Frankreich und der Freie Künstlerbund." *Exilforschung: Ein internationales Jahrbuch* 2 (1983–84): 173–211.

———. "German-Speaking Artists in Parisian Exile: Their Routes to the French Capital, Activities There, and Final Flight—A Short Introduction." In *Echoes of Exile: Moscow Archives and the Arts in Paris, 1933–1945,* edited by Ines Rotemund-Reynard, 1–26. Berlin: De Gruyter, 2014.

Rozenblit, Marsha L. *Reconstructing a National Identity: The Jews of Habsburg Austria During World War I.* New York: Oxford University Press, 2004.

Saß, Anne-Christin. *Berliner Luftmenschen: Osteuropäisch-jüdische Migranten in der*

Weimarer Republik. Göttingen: Wallstein Verlag, 2012.

Schlögel, Karl. *Berlin Ostbahnhof Europas: Russen und Deutsche in ihrem Jahrhundert*. Berlin: Siedler Verlag, 1998.

Schütz, Chana, and Hermann Simon, eds. *Auf der Suche nach einer verlorenen Sammlung: Das Berliner Jüdische Museum (1933–1938)*. Berlin: Hentrich & Hentrich, 2011.

———, eds. *Bestandsrekonstruktion des Berliner Jüdischen Museums in der Oranienburger Strasse*. Berlin: Hentrich & Hentrich, 2011.

Schwarz, Karl. *Führer durch das jüdische Museum: Sammlungen der jüdischen Gemeinde zu Berlin*. Berlin: Aldus, 1933.

———. *Jewish Artists of the 19th and 20th Centuries*. New York: Philosophical Library, 1949.

———. *Die Juden in der Kunst*. Berlin: Welt-Verlag, 1928.

———. *Jüdische Kunst—Jüdische Künstler: Erinnerungen des ersten Direktors des Berliner Jüdischen Museums*. Edited by Chana C. Schütz and Hermann Simon. Berlin: Hentrich & Hentrich, 2001.

Seelig, Rachel. *Strangers in Berlin: Modern Jewish Literature Between East and West, 1919–1933*. Ann Arbor: University of Michigan Press, 2016.

Sennewald, Adolf. *Deutsche Buchillustratoren im ersten Drittel des 20. Jahrhunderts: Materialien für Bibliophile*. Wiesbaden: Harrassowitz Verlag, 1999.

Silver, Kenneth E., and Romy Golan, eds. *The Circle of Montparnasse: Jewish Artists in Paris, 1905–1945*. New York: Universe Books, 1985.

Silver, Larry, and Samantha Baskind, "Looking Jewish: The State of Research on Modern Jewish Art." *Jewish Quarterly Review* 101, no. 4 (2011): 631–52.

Silverman, Lisa. *Becoming Austrians: Jews and Culture Between the World Wars*. New York: Oxford University Press, 2012.

Skolnik, Jonathan. *Jewish Pasts, German Fictions: History, Memory, and Minority Culture in Germany, 1824–1955*. Stanford: Stanford University Press, 2014.

Slezkine, Yuri. *The Jewish Century*. New ed. Princeton: Princeton University Press, 2019.

Spinner, Samuel J. *Jewish Primitivism*. Stanford: Stanford University Press, 2021.

Staliūnas, Darius. *Enemies for a Day: Antisemitism and Anti-Jewish Violence in Lithuania Under the Tsars*. Budapest: Central European University Press, 2015.

Steinhardt, Jakob. "Erinnerungen." In *Jakob Steinhardt: Der Prophet; Ausstellungs- und Bestandskatalog, Jüdisches Museum im Berlin Museum*, edited by Dominik Bartmann, 17–20. Berlin: Berlin Museum, 1995.

Stiftung Jüdisches Museum Berlin. *Berlin Transit: Jüdische Migranten aus Osteuropa in den 1920er Jahren*. Göttingen: Wallstein, 2012.

Stolarska-Fronia, Małgorzata, ed. *Polish Avant-Garde in Berlin*. Berlin: Peter Lang, 2019.

Straughn, Celka. "Jewish Expressionism: The Making of Modern Art in Berlin." PhD diss. University of Chicago, 2007.

———. "Reviewing the Weimar Jewish Renaissance: Exhibition Reviews in the German-Jewish Press." In *Deutsch-jüdische Presse und jüdische Geschichte: Dokumente, Darstellungen, Wechselbeziehungen*, edited by Eleonore Lappin and Michael Nagel, 1:351–58. Bremen: edition lumière bremen, 2008.

———. "'A Substratum of Unprejudiced Art History': The Critical Discourse of Jewish Art in Early Twentieth-Century Germany." *Journal of Modern Jewish Studies* 15, no. 1 (2016): 29–46.

Sutton, Katie. *The Masculine Woman in Weimar Germany*. New York, Berghahn Books, 2011.

Trunk, Isaiah. *Łódź Ghetto: A History*. Translated and edited by Robert Moses Shapiro. Bloomington: Indiana University Press, 2006.

Underwood, Nick. *Yiddish Paris: Staging Nation and Community in Interwar France*.

Bloomington: Indiana University Press, 2022.

Wallach, Kerry. "Art Without Borders: Artist Rahel Szalit-Marcus and Jewish Visual Culture." In *German-Jewish Studies: Next Generations*, edited by Kerry Wallach and Aya Elyada, 149–70. New York: Berghahn Books, 2023.

———. *Passing Illusions: Jewish Visibility in Weimar Germany*. Ann Arbor: University of Michigan Press, 2017.

Westheim, Paul, ed. *Künstlerbekenntnisse: Briefe / Tagebuchblätter / Betrachtungen heutiger Künstler*. Berlin: Propyläen Verlag, 1925.

Whisnant, Clayton J. *Queer Identities and Politics in Germany: A History, 1880–1945*. New York: Harrington Park Press, 2016.

Whitner, Claire C., ed. *Käthe Kollwitz and the Women of War: Femininity, Identity, and Art in Germany During World Wars I and II*. New Haven: Yale University Press, 2016.

Wischnitzer, Mark. *To Dwell in Safety: The Story of Jewish Migration Since 1800*. Philadelphia: Jewish Publication Society of America, 1949.

Wobick-Segev, Sarah. *Homes Away from Home: Jewish Belonging in Twentieth-Century Paris, Berlin, and St. Petersburg*. Stanford: Stanford University Press, 2018.

Wullschlager, Jackie. *Chagall: A Biography*. New York: Alfred A. Knopf, 2008.

Zimmerman, Joshua D. *Poles, Jews, and the Politics of Nationality: The Bund and the Polish Socialist Party in Late Tsarist Russia, 1892–1914*. Madison: University of Wisconsin Press, 2004.

Zuccotti, Susan. *The Holocaust, the French, and the Jews*. New York: Bison Books, 1999.

Index

Italicized page references indicate illustrations. Endnotes are referenced with "n" followed by the endnote number.

Abramovitsh, S. Y. (Mendele Moykher Sforim), 18
   Fischke der Krumme (Fishke the Lame), 55, 89, 94, 102–9, 155, 225, 250n43
abstract artists, 195
Academy of the Arts, 53
Adalbert, Max, 137
Adams, Eve, 164–65
Adler, Jankel, 5, 192
advertisements, 147, 149, 183
Akademie der Künste (Academy of Arts), 130, 170, 218
Aleichem, Sholem, 18, 155, 239n23
   "Chickens on Strike," 6–7, *7*, 99, 212
   on Jewish humor, 93, 249n11
   Motl, the Cantor's Son, 63, 93–102, 109, 144, 168, 217, 225
Alexander II, Tsar of Russia, 21
Altmann, Nathan, 180
American Hebrew (magazine), 24
Anders als die Andern (Different from the Others, 1919), 154
animals
   at Berlin Zoo, 125, 132, 138–44, 151
   birds, 140–41
   camels, 117, 139, 140–41, 163
   cats, 140, 163
   chickens, 6–7, 70, 99, 140, 144, 149–51
   crocodiles, 71–74
   donkeys, 139, 162, 163
   elephants, 139, 143
   Expressionism and, 32, 139–41
   giraffes, 139, 143, 144
   goats, 70
   horses, 70, 91–92, 140, 171, 202
   insects, 123
   interactions with people, 70, 138–40
   lions, 141, 144
   monkeys, 73–74, 139, 144
   primordial, 174
   rats, 98
   sheep, 163
   symbolism of, 105, 212
Annot (Annot Jacobi), 173
anti-Jewish violence
   in Nazi Germany, 190, 192
   in Russian Empire, 19, 21–22, 26
   See also Holocaust
antisemitism
   in Austria-Hungary, 36
   caricature and, 101–2
   in France, 8, 193, 205
   in Germany, 30, 105, 108
   Jewish humor and, 105, 108
   in Lithuania, 19–20
   self-defense against, 146
   See also persecution of Jews
Antwerp, 36, 96
Arendt, Hannah, 8, 191
Arnheim, Clara, 167
Arp, Hans, 201
art academies, 31–33, 47, 53, 130, 170
Asch, Sholem, 196, 261n48
assimilation, 6, 79, 139, 174
Association of Women Artists in Berlin. *See* Verein der Künstlerinnen zu Berlin
athleticism, 9, 146
   See also fencing
Auden, W. H., 154
Auschwitz-Birkenau (death camp), 12, 165, 205, 207–8, 221
Austria, 193
Austria-Hungary, 34
Austrian citizenship, 38–39, 45
avant-garde
   in Berlin, 52
   international, 32
   Jewish difference and, 94
   School of Paris, 195–97
   Yung Yiddish, 57
awards and prizes, 167, 171–73, 221

INDEX

Baeck, Leo, 61–63
Ball, Hugo, 62
Bal-Makhshoves (Man of Thoughts). *See* Eliashev, Isidor
Bambi (Salten), 139
Barney, Natalie, 44
Baruch, Franziska, 121, 251n21
Baudelaire, Charles, 92
Bauhaus, 47, 130, 173, 181
BBC, 216
Beaune-la-Rolande (French detention camp), 208
Becher, Johannes, 62, 134–35
Beckmann, Max, 48, 133, 136, 201
beggars, Jewish, 103–5
Belgium, 36
ben Halevy, Jehuda, 117
Benjamin, Walter, 52, 102, 139, 191, 196, 250n32
Berend, Alice, 133
Berend-Corinth, Charlotte, 58, 172, 263n5
Berg, Rebecca Himber, 241n27
Bergelson, Dovid, 52
Bergmann, Wolf, 247n70
Berlin, 3, 7–8, 11, 39–42, 49, 221, 243n39
    artists, 51–53
    cafés, 49–52, 60, 139, 154
    celebrity culture, 42
    East Europeans and Russians, 7–8, 51–53, 89
    Expressionist artists, 46–63
    Hebrew writers, 111
    Jewish community, 7–8, 22, 33, 48–49, 89, 215
    lesbian and gay scene, 154 (*see also* LGBT/queer history)
    nightlife, 132–34, 151–52, 154, 174
    portraits of Berliners, 134–38
    Schöneberg neighborhood, 39–40, 48–49, 54, 62, 154, 221
    Weimar-era milieu, 131–34
    Zoologischer Garten, 125, 132, 138–44, 151
Berlin Artists Association, 147
Berliner Börsen-Courier (newspaper), 134–35
Berliner Secession, 47, 50, 174, 223
    exhibitions, 130, 137, 223
Berliner Tageblatt (newspaper), 54, 55, 131–33, 180
Berlin Jewish Museum (1930s), 169, 184
Bershter Bund (union), 22
Bertz, Inka, 218
Bialik, Hayim Nahman, 111
    Ketina kol-bo, 63, 120–25, 226, 251n20
Bieber, Hugo, 83, 110, 112, 216
Biélinky, Jacques, 5, 6, 199, 206, 216, 261n48

Bingham, Hiram "Harry," 8
Birnbaum, Paula, 195
Birnbaum, Uriel, 105, 139
"Black Shame" campaign (1920–23), 162
Blumberg, Feiga (Yuli), 68, 247n3
Blum-Lazarus, Sophie, 217
B'nai B'rith lodge, exhibitions at, 53–54, 68, 185, 1920
B'nai B'rith Magazine, 17, 17, 177, 227
Boblenz, Viktoria, 178
Boguslawskaja, Xenia, 51
Böhm, Ernst, 121, 123, 251n22
Bondy, Walter, 196
Bonheur, Rosa, 202
Braque, Georges, 195
Brauchle, Alfred, 183
Brecht, Bertolt, 52, 134–35
Breslau, exhibitions in, 53, 191, 223
Bröder, Hilde, 172
Brodsky, Nina, 202
Buber, Martin, 5–6, 30, 54, 58, 67, 129, 226
Buchenwald (concentration camp), 213
Budko, Joseph, 5, 6, 58, 69, 112, 113, 120, 121, 125, 169
Buerkle, Darcy, 257n30
Bundist Medem-Club, 192
Büschenthal, Lippmann Moses, 249n13
Büttner, Erich, 159

Cabaret (musical and film), 49
cafés
    in Berlin, 49–52, 60, 139, 154
    lesbian, 154
    in Paris, 196–97, 201
Capa, Robert, 192
Carell, Fatma, 177–78, 224, 227, 258n51
caricatures, 92–93, 101–2, 131
cartoons, 11, 131–32, 134, 144, 151
Carvallo-Schülein, Susanne, 256n15
Casablanca (film), 8, 206, 262n9
Casmir, Erwin, 183
Caspary, Eugen, 169
Cassatt, Mary, 59
Cauer, Hanna, 176
Cézanne, Paul, 132
Chagall, Bella, 61
Chagall, Marc, 1, 7–8, 32, 171, 191, 199, 261n56
    birthdate, 23
    book illustrations, 69
    encounter with Szalit, 62–63
    Expressionism and, 57, 246n49
    The Fiddler, 16

"For the Slaughtered Artists" (poem), 217
Jewish subjects, 102
  Meidner and, 60–61
  migration to US, 203, 206
  in Paris, 192, 195, 198, 202, 260n35
  Romanisches Café and, 51–52
chalk drawings, 3, 58, 116, 130, 132, 184, 199, 228
  See also works by Szalit
Chapiro, Jacques, 202
Charney, Daniel, 52
Chazen, Maria, 184, 259n72
Chelmno (killing center), 209, 212–13
children
  corporal punishment, 97, 98–99
  impoverished, 59, 170
  Jewish traditions and, 22–23, 149
  as subjects, 3, 7, 47, 59, 84–85, 91, 95–99, 113, 123–25, 136–38, 149–52, 198
citizenship. *See* nationality and citizenship
Cohn-Wiener, Ernst, 57, 170
Collective of German Artists, 201
color
  Expressionist style and, 16, 32
  Szalit's use of, 144, 167, 174, 185
  See also paintings; watercolors
Corinth, Lovis, 57, 58, 103, 171–73
corporal punishment, 97, 98–99
costume balls, 132–34
cross-dressing, 149
Csaki-Copony, Grete, 174–75, 177, 178, 181
Cubism, 31, 195
Curious George stories, 139
Czechoslovakia, 193

Dadaism, 94
Dalí, Salvador, 195
Das jüdische Echo (The Jewish Echo), 149
Das Prisma, 248n17
Däubler, Elena, 136
Däubler, Theodor, 135–36, 252n15
Daudet, Alphonse, 54, 67
  Tartarin of Tarascon, 78, 141–43, 142, 163, 226
Daumier, Honoré, 68, 91
Davringhausen, Heinrich Maria, 42, 70
de Beauvoir, Simone, 196–97
Degas, Edgar, 202
Degenerate Art (*Entartete Kunst*) exhibition, 190–91, 201
Delaunay, Sonia, 238n9
Dem, Erna (Ernestine Wolfson née Davidoff), 217, 238n9

Der Blaue Reiter (the Blue Rider), 32–33
Der Blaue Vogel (cabaret), 51–52
Der Cicerone (magazine), 53, 108, 245n34
Der Eigene (journal), 157
Der Feuerreiter (The Fire Rider, journal), 62
Derfner Judaica Museum, 219, 225
Der Jude (journal), 129
Der Kunstwanderer (The Art Wanderer, journal), 54
Der Marschall (play), 37
Der Querschnitt (The Cross Section, journal), 103, 131, 139, 140–41
Der Schild (The Shield, journal), 146
Der Sturm (gallery), 58
Deutsch, Ernst, 75
Deutsche Kultur-Wacht, 190
Diamant, Anita, 157–58, 255n22
Dickens, Charles, 54–55, 63, 67, 69, 78–83, 87, 118
  problematic Jewish characters, 79–80, 248n18
  Sketches by Boz (*Londoner Bilder*), 31, 79–83, 226, 248n18
Die Aufklärung (Enlightenment), 156–65
Die blaue Bluse (theater troupe), 249n25
Die Brücke (the Bridge, artist group), 32
Die Dame (The Lady, magazine), 52, 180–81
Die Frau als Künstlerin (Woman as Artist, 1928), 168–69
Die Frau von heute exhibition, 166, 175–78, 176, 221, 224
Die gestaltende Frau (The Creating Woman) exhibition, 173–74, 224
Die Juden in der Kunst (The Jews in Art), 169
Die jüdische Frau (The Jewish Woman, magazine), 49, 170
Die Kreutzersonate (film), 75
die neue linie (the new line, magazine), 9, 50, 181–83
Die Schaffenden (The Creators, magazine), 70, 141
Die Schaubühne (magazine), 42
Dietrich, Marlene, 44, 49
Die Weltbühne (magazine), 42, 245n41
Dix, Otto, 48, 94, 131, 191
Döblin, Alfred, 52, 62, 191
Dodo (Dörte Clara Wolff), 130
Dôme, Café du, 196–97
Donath, Adolph, 5, 54, 169, 172, 173, 180
d'Ora, Madame, 263n31
Dostoyevsky, Fyodor, 53, 54, 63, 67, 70–74, 87
  Crime and Punishment, 42
  The Crocodile, 70–74, 226
Drancy (internment camp), 12, 207–8, 214, 221

INDEX

Dresden, 32, 39, 208
Dürer, Albrecht, 57, 202
dybbuk, 151, 234

East European Jewish communities, 16–28
    authenticity and, 7, 30, 42, 57, 59, 89, 107–9, 120, 144–46
    émigrés from, 2–3, 7–8, 30, 51, 180, 192 (see also Jewish migration patterns)
    markets, 24
    migration, 192
    as mystical, 170–71
    religious observance, 26
    See also shtetls
economic conditions
    Great Depression, 175, 183, 210
    hardships after First World War, 41, 48
    hyperinflation in 1920s Germany, 11, 68, 79, 111
    stability in mid-1920s, 130
    See also poverty
Edschmid, Kasimir, 139
Edzard, Dietz, 70
Egypt, 158–60
Ehrenburg, Ilya, 51
Einstein, Albert, 49
Eisner, Lotte, 192
Elder, Lissy (Alice Newman), 130
Elias, Julie, 103
Elias, Julius, 103, 105
Eliasberg, Alexander, 103
Eliashev, Isidor (Bal-Makhshoves), 63, 88, 95, 217
Emanuel Ringelblum Jewish Historical Institute, Warsaw, 185, 218
Emergency Rescue Committee, 206
emotion, 32, 48, 55, 63, 75, 91, 112, 194
Ephraim-Marcus, Käthe, 256n15
Epstein, Henri (Chaim), 33, 217
Ernst, Max, 192, 201
etchings, 48, 59, 103, 115, 139
    techniques, 57–58, 246n55
ethnic identities, 3, 30, 42, 146
Europe, map of, 4
Ewen, David, 24–25, 27, 49–50, 113, 216, 241n34
exhibitions, 223–25
    in Berlin, 167, 169, 184, 191
    Berliner Secession, 130, 137, 223
    B'nai B'rith lodge, 53–54, 68, 185, 1920
    in Breslau, 53, 191, 223
    Die Frau von heute, 166, 175–78, 176, 221, 224
    Die gestaltende Frau (The Creating Woman), 173–74, 224
    at Galerie Zborowski, 189, 200–201, 221, 225
    at Gutenberg Buchhandlung, 54–55, 67, 74, 221, 223
    Jewish, 53, 54, 62, 185
    on Jewish Renaissance, 218
    at KaDeWe, 144, 224, 227, 253n40
    in London, 191
    Montparnasse déporté, 218, 225
    New Objectivity and, 177
    in Paris, 198–203, 225
    Rund ums KaDeWe, 144, 224
    Salon Henri Brendlé, 120, 224
    solo (Szalit), 54, 89, 136–37, 198
    at Wertheim, 40, 174, 224
    in Wiesbaden, 53, 62, 223
    at Zinglers Kabinett, 136–37, 221, 223
exotic subjects, 56, 74, 144, 168, 175
Expressionism, 3–6, 16, 94
    animals and, 32, 139–41
    artists' groups and, 32–33
    artists' identification with, 246n49
    in Berlin, 55–63
    birth of, 32
    graphic works and printmaking, 48
    Jewish style, 55–57
    Jewish subjects, 105, 107
    language and, 45
    Nazism and, 190
    New Objectivity and, 176
    pathos and, 246n56
    popularity of, 63
    in Szalit's work, 55–57, 68, 94, 107
    in Vienna, 39
Eysoldt, Gertrud, 174

Fasching (holiday), 133–34
fashion illustration, 4, 130–31
Fauvism, 31, 195
fencing, 9, 50–51, 125, 180–83, 197
Fenster, Hersh, 9, 93, 216–18, 262n72, 263n6
Feuchtwanger, Lion, 8, 191, 201
Fiddler on the Roof (musical), 6, 16
films, 8, 41, 43, 49, 59, 75, 93, 105, 154, 243n43
Flechtheim, Alfred, 196
folk traditions, eastern Jewish, 6–7, 16, 63, 83, 91, 174–75
France
    foreign or stateless Jews in, 8, 12, 193, 205–8
    Holocaust and detention camps, 205–9
    Jewish refugees in, 8, 191–93
    See also Paris

Free Artists' League (Freier Künstlerbund Union des Artistes Libres), 201, 221
Freier Deutscher Künstlerbund, 201
Freier Künstlerbund. *See* Free Artists' League
French Foreign Legion, 192
French language, 33, 216, 217
French School, 195
Freud, Esti, 262n9
Freund, Gisèle, 192
Friedlaender, Lieselotte, 130
Fromm, Erich, 49
Fry, Varian, 8, 203, 206, 238n20
Fuchs, Eduard, 99, 101–2, 250n32, 250nn27–28

Galerie Zborowski exhibition, 189, 200–201, 221, 225
Galicia, 34
Geiger, Ludwig, 103
General Jewish Encyclopedia, 52
George, Heinrich, 134
George, Stefan, 34
German books, 3, 54, 69, 110–20
German Expressionism. *See* Expressionism
German-Jewish press, 40
German Jews, 89, 99, 105, 146
    culture, 5, 191, 218
    press, 111
German language, 31, 33, 44–45, 48
Germany
    citizenship, 30, 190
    fascism, 156
    Paragraph 175 (statute criminalizing homosexuality), 156
    See also Berlin; Nazi Germany; Weimar Germany
ghettos, 6, 37, 174
    Lodz, 28, 209–14
Gide, André, 156
Giese, Karl, 156
Gleichmann, Otto, 70
Gmeyner, Anna, 196
Goethe, Johann Wolfgang von, 57
Goldenring, Stefania, 41
Goldstein, Moritz, 6, 83
Gollop, Charlotte, 171
Gollop, Max, 171
Gordon, Yehuda Leib, 24
Gorelik, Shemarya, 147–48, 227
Goya, Francisco, 91
Graf, Oskar Maria, 42
Granach, Alexander, 61, 134, 137

Granowsky, Alexander, 249n25
Graphic Books (series), 71
graphic design, 130–31, 185
Great Yeshiva (Telz), 24
Greenberg, Uri Zvi, 52
Große Berliner Kunstausstellung, 167
Großmann, Rudolf, 139
Grosz, George, 48, 62, 94, 133, 143, 191, 201
grotesque figures, 6, 88–109, 170
Guggenheim, Peggy, 196
Gurlitt, Fritz, 240n3
Gurs (French detention camp), 205
Gustav Kiepenheuer Verlag, 70–71
Gutenberg Buchhandlung exhibition, 54–55, 67, 74, 221, 223
gypsies, 175
    "Jewish gypsies," 87, 105

Haensgen-Dingkuhn, Elsa, 177, 178
Häfner-Mode, Ilse, 172
Halicka, Alice, 200, 238n9
Hans Heinrich Tillgner Verlag, 78
Hart, Frania, 200, 217
Hartman, Saidiya, 12
Hauptmann, Gerhart, 75, 156
Heartfield, John, 261n55
Hebrew books, 3, 53–54, 63, 111, 120–25
Hebrew language, 48, 149, 214
Heckel, Erich, 70
Heine, Heinrich, 63, 93, 132, 155
    Der Rabbi von Bacherach (The Rabbi of Bacherach), 111–12
    "Hebrew Melodies," 109, 110–20, 198, 218, 226
    "Jehuda ben Halevy," 163
    "Princess Sabbath," 111–12, 171
Helene Fischbein Endowment Fund prize, 171–73, 221
Hemingway, Ernest, 196
Hennings, Emmy, 62
Henri Heine Center, 193
Herrmann-Neisse, Max, 62
Herzfelde, Wieland, 62
Herzog, Elsa, 176
Hiddensoer Künstlerinnenbund (Hiddensee Alliance of Women Artists), 167
Hildebrandt, Hans, 51, 54, 168–69
Hildenbrandt, Fred, 132
Hirschfeld, Magnus, 43, 97, 99, 153, 154, 156–57, 163
Hirszenberg, Samuel, 169
Hitler, Adolf, 3, 144, 184–85, 191, 199, 210

INDEX

Höch, Hannah, 62, 254n6
Hofer, Johanna, 172, 174
Hofer, Karl, 1, 52, 62, 70, 132–33, 135, 190
Hohermann, Alice, 200, 217
Holitscher, Arthur, 1, 62
Holocaust, 8, 12, 19, 40, 175, 204–14, 216, 221
    See also Nazi Germany
Holz, Arno, 49
Holz, Paul, 70
Hotel Eden, 133
"human zoos," 144
Hungarian-Jewish refugees, 192
hunger, 26, 41, 207, 211
Huxley, Julian, 139
hyperinflation, 11, 68, 79, 111
    See also inflation

Ihering, Herbert, 134–35
illustrations, 2–4, 185, 225–27
    commercial, 183
    literary, 3–4, 11–12, 54, 63, 67–87
    literary interpretation and, 69–70
    memory politics and, 217–18
    in periodicals, 11–12, 53–54, 130, 167
    See also chalk drawings; lithographs; newspaper illustrations; pastels; pencil drawings; works by Szalit
Inbar, R., 91
inflation, 41, 68, 89, 125
Innsbruck, 35–36
Institute for Sexual Science, 154
    See also Hirschfeld, Magnus
Ischgenty (Ichjenty), 20
    See also Užventis
Isherwood, Christopher, 49, 154
Israel, 12, 24, 111, 125, 202, 213, 214, 219
Israelitisches Familienblatt (Israelite Family Paper), 6, 7, 99, 131, 144, 170, 180

J'accuse (periodical), 216
Jacob, Max, 217
Jacobsohn, Siegfried, 42
Jaeckel, Willy, 61, 133
Janthur, Richard, 58, 70, 139
Jawlensky, Alexej von, 36
Jerusalem, 63, 111, 117, 202
Jewish art and artists
    in Berlin, 47, 168–73
    defined, 7
    escaping the Holocaust, 206
    exhibitions in Paris, 201–2, 225

    German-Jewish press and, 40
    refugees in France, 192
    scholarship on Szalit and, 216, 218
    School of Paris and, 195–96
    women, 168–73, 192
    See also Jewish subject matter; *specific artists*
Jewish Diaspora, 7, 51
Jewish difference
    antisemitic responses to, 105 (*see also* antisemitism)
    "soul of the Jew," 50, 170
    stereotypes about, 42, 93, 102, 116
    visibility of eastern Jews and, 89, 116, 199
    See also East European Jewish communities
Jewish history, 9, 111, 120, 156
Jewish humor, 63, 105, 108, 120
    "laughter through tears," 89–95, 109, 249n11, 249n13
Jewish identity, 6, 10, 27, 125, 198–99
Jewish migration patterns, 2–3, 7–8, 19, 30, 34, 51, 96, 180, 190–92, 202, 203
    See also Berlin; Palestine; Paris; United States
Jewish Museum Berlin (founded 2001), 218, 219
Jewish Museum Frankfurt, 218
Jewish press
    articles on Szalit, 2–3, 131, 221
    Jewish artists and, 40, 120
    queer identity and, 164–65
    Szalit's illustrations for, 8, 115–16, 116, 131, 144–48, 152
    See also *specific periodicals*
Jewish relief organizations, 173, 185, 193
Jewish Renaissance
    exhibition on, 218
    Hebrew writers and, 111, 120
    in Russia and Ukraine, 242n4
    Szalit and, 4–6, 30, 48, 219
    Zionism and, 125
Jewish subject matter, 2–3, 16–18, 152, 198
    in Berlin Expressionism, 55–63
    caricatures, 101–2
    depictions of eastern Jews, 6, 30, 89, 109, 120, 144–46, 170–71, 174–75, 178
    as exotic, 168
    Expressionism and, 59
    folkloric characters, 6–7, 16, 63, 83, 91, 174–75
    grotesque Yiddish figures, 6, 87–109, 170
    holidays, 26, 99, 132, 148–51, 229–35
    Jewish Renaissance and, 5–6
    traditions and rituals, 110–20, 171, 199
Jourdain, Paulette, 189, 200, 261n62

INDEX

Jüdische Altershilfe (organization), 173
Jüdische Künstlerhilfe (Jewish Artists' Relief), 185
Jüdischer Frauenbund (League of Jewish Women), 26, 51, 170, 171
Jüdische Rundschau (Jewish Review, newspaper), 68, 98, 112, 120, 131, 146–47, 149, 152, 170, 198, 202, 229, 231, 250n43
Jüdisches Museumsverein (Jewish Museum Association), 169
Jüdische Volkspartei (Jewish People's Party), 169
Jüdische Welt-Rundschau (Jewish World Review), 202

KaDeWe department store, 67
  exhibition at, 144, 224, 227, 253n40
Kafka, Franz, 52, 129
  Metamorphosis, 139
Kaléko, Mascha, 52
Kalkowska, Eleonore, 44, 175, *176*, 177, 190, 193–94
Kandinsky, Wassily, 32, 34, 36, 191, 195, 202
Kaplan, Louis, 249n13
Karel, Fatma. *See* Carell, Fatma
Kästner, Erich, 52
Kauders, Walter, 170–71
Kaufhaus des Westens. *See* KaDeWe department store
Keren Kayemeth L'Israel (Jewish National Fund), 202
Kerr, Alfred, 42–43, 112
Kesten, Hermann, 52
Kipling, Rudyard, 139
Kirchner, Ernst Ludwig, 16, 191, 201
Kirszenbaum, J. D., 131, 192, 195, 201, 252n2
Kisch, Egon Erwin, 49, 201
Kishinev pogroms, 22
Kisling, Moïse, 196, 200
Klal-Farlag publishing house, 88, 89, 95, 121
Klee, Paul, 32, 136, 191, 201
Kleinman, Moshe, 121
Klimt, Gustav, 39
Kogan, Moissey, 55, 133
Kokoschka, Oskar, 39, 191, 201
Koller, Sabine, 96, 237n2
Kollwitz, Käthe
  Berlin Jewish community and, 172–73, 257n30
  education, 32, 33
  exhibitions, 177
  renown, 58
  sexual identity, 155

  social commentary, 48, 59, 131, 170
  Szalit and, 11, 172–73
  women artist groups and, 167
Kolnik, Arthur, 195
Kolp, Herszek, 209, 211–12
Kolp, Juljusz (Yehuda), 209, 211–14
Kolp, Sheina Machla (née Markus; also Szejna Michla), 19, 23, 28, 138, 205, 209–13, 241n26
Kortner, Fritz, 41, 172
Kovno Province (Kaunas Gubernia), 19, 23
Kowalska, Chana, 217, 238n9
Kracauer, Siegfried, 191
Krakow, 34, 96
Krauskopf, Bruno, 46, 70, 75, 201
Krauss, Werner, 137
Kreutzer, Rudolf, 74–75
Krische, Maria, 156–57
Krische, Paul, 157
Kubin, Alfred, 70
Kulbak, Moyshe, 52
Kulturbund Deutscher Juden (Cultural Association of German Jews), 185, 192
Kultur-Lige (organization), 192
Kunstschule für Frauen und Mädchen (Art School for Women and Girls), 39
Kunst-Werk, 185

Lachen links (Laughter on the Left, magazine), 132, 134
landscapes, 3, 12, 47, 49–50, 136, 144, 198, 228, 239n30
Langer, Resi, 174
languages
  linguistic identities, 3, 20
  Szalit's skills in, 3, 11, 31, 33, 44–45, 51–52, 62, 69–70, 194
  See also specific languages
La Ruche (the Beehive), 192, 195
Laserstein, Lotte, 155, 173–75, *176*, 177, *178*, *180*, *181*
Lasker-Schüler, Else, 5, 33, 49, 52, 57, 111, 155, 168, 190, 199, 237n5
La Terre Retrouvée (magazine), 262n73
"laughter through tears." *See* Jewish humor
Laurencin, Marie, 177
Léger, Fernand, 195
Lehmann, Henni, 167
Le Judaisme Sepharadi (journal), 116, 199, *200*
Le Loiret (French detention camp), 208
Lenya, Lotte, 61
Leo Baeck Institute, 219, 225–26
Les Milles (French detention camp), 205

INDEX

Levy, Jane, 217
Levy, Rudolf, 196
Lewis, Sinclair, 196
Lewisohn, Ludwig, 156
LGBT/queer history, 11, 43–45, 153–55, 164–66, 175
Liberal Jewish organizations, 146
Liebermann, Max, 47, 57, 58, 103, 112, 121, 169, 171, 173, 185
Lilien, Ephraim Moses, 6, 125
Lilienfeld, Rosy, 69
Lingner, Max, 201, 261n55
Lipchitz, Jacques, 195, 203, 206
Lisbon, 206, 262n9
Lissitzky, El, 51, 112
literary illustrators, 3–4
    See also German books; Hebrew books; illustrations; world literature; Yiddish books; *specific authors*
lithographs, 3–4, 11–12, 33, 67–87
    German Expressionism and, 48
    Jewish approach to, 91
    techniques, 58
    See also illustrations; works by Szalit
Lithuania, 3, 11, 16, 19–26, 214, 218–19
    birth records and gender, 241n27
    during First World War, 59
    Jewish communities in, 16 (*see also* East European Jewish communities; shtetls)
    Lithuanian-Jewish refugees, 192
Lodz, 11, 19, 22, 26–27, 33, 184, 205, 208, 209–10, 215
    ghetto (during Second World War), 28, 210–14
Loewenstein, Herbert, 257n27
Lohmar, Heinz, 201
London, 79–83, 96
    Jewish migration to and exile in, 22, 48, 139, 191, 216
    Szalit's visits to, 30–31
Lorre, Peter, 192
Lowenstein, Maria (née Baetge; also, Maria Steinberg), 52, 246n47
lower classes, 59
    See also poverty; working class

Macke, August, 32, 139
magazines. *See* periodicals; *specific magazines*
Mammen, Jeanne, 130, 155, 173
Mané-Katz, 16, 57, 171, 195, 196, 202, 203
Manet, Édouard, 58, 178
Mann, Erika, 154, 156

Mann, Heinrich, 192
Mann, Klaus, 154, 156–57
Mann, Thomas, 31, 34, 154, 206, 255n10, 255n12, 255n22
    Der Tod in Venedig (Death in Venice), 156–57
    "Dina" illustrations, 83, 125, 139, 153, 155–65, 227
    Joseph and His Brothers books, 155–56, 158
Marc, Franz, 16, 32–34, 129, 242n12
Markus, Tsipa (née Gerszonowicz), 19, 22, 28, 209, 210, 241n24
Markus, Yankel, 20–21, 24, 240n13
Markus, Yudel (Yehuda), 19–22, 27–28, 209, 213
Markus family, 11, 19–28, 209–14, 242n12
Marseille, 8, 192, 206
Marxism, 101–2
Marzynski, Siegbert (later Marcy), 171, 257n26
masculinity
    Jewish athleticism and, 146
    lesbians and, 51, 155
mass culture, 130
Matisse, Henri, 31, 195
Mayer, Helene, 50, 183
May Laws (1882), 21
Medem Library, 192
Meidner, Else, 63, 173, 256n15
Meidner, Ludwig, 1, 8, 12, 52, 57, 60–63, 91, 94, 135, 169, 171, 173, 216, 237n1, 246n55, 247n70
    Apokalyptische Landschaft (Apocalyptic Landscape, 1912), 58
memorials, 9, 49
memory politics, 215, 250n32
Mendele Moykher Sforim (Mendele the Book Peddler). *See* Abramovitsh, S. Y.
Menkes, Zygmunt, 173, 202
Menorah (magazine), 10, 107, 170
Menschheitsdämmerung (Twilight of Humanity, 1920), 133
Michaelis, Alice, 175, 177, 190
Michel, Artur, 112
Michelson, Leo, 5, 169
Middle East, 111, 125
migration. *See* Jewish migration patterns
Milgroym (Pomegranate, magazine), 5, 53–54, 91, 118, 121, 251n20
    See also *Rimon*
military service, 21, 30, 42, 146
Miller, Henry, 196
Miró, Joan, 195
Miron, Dan, 103
Mises, Helene, 256n15

modern art movements, 31
    See also avant-garde; Expressionism; New Objectivity
Modersohn-Becker, Paula, 32, 59
Modigliani, Amedeo, 62, 189, 195, 196, 200, 217, 261n46, 261n62
Mondrian, Piet, 195
Montparnasse, 195–97, 206
Montparnasse déporté exhibition, 218, 225
morality, 8, 157, 163
Moreck, Curt, 41
Morena, Erna, 174
Morisot, Berthe, 59
Morocco, 206
Morold, Ruth, 16, 98, 120
Moss, Kenneth, 242n4
Motl illustrations, 63, 89, 91, 93–102, 109, 168, 217, 225, 257n26
Münchner Künstlertheater (Munich Art Theater), 36
Mundlak, Regina, 5, 57, 168, 256n15, 263n5
Munich, 11, 29–45, 215, 221
Munich Art Academy, 33
Münter, Gabriele, 32, 33, 36, 173
Münzer-Neumann, Käthe, 173–75, 176, 177, 190, 192, 201
Museum of Modern Art, 206
Muter, Mela, 200, 238n9
Mynona, 62

Nabokov, Vladimir, 51
Nachman, Reb (of Breslov), 67, 95, 121, 184–85, 226
Nadel, Arno, 46
National Committee for the Welfare of German Refugees/Victims of Antisemitism, 193
nationality and citizenship, 3, 8, 28, 38–39, 45, 208, 218–19
Naye Prese (magazine), 262n73
Nazi Germany, 3
    Jewish organizations in, 185
    Lodz ghetto, 28, 210–14
    modern art and, 190–91
    persecution of Jews, 49, 185, 190–92, 199
    See also Holocaust
Nefertiti, 158
New Objectivity, 4, 6, 141, 176–77, 190
newspaper illustrations, 129–52
    for Berlin Jewish press, 144–48
    captions, 131, 143
    weekly papers, 130

New Woman, 38, 51, 166, 174, 180
New York Times, 216
Nicholas I, Tsar of Russia, 21
Nöll, Hermann, 163
non-Jewish subjects, 87, 118, 132, 136
Nordau, Maxa, 202
nostalgia, 93, 113
Novembergruppe (radical socialist artist group), 62
November Pogrom (1938, Kristallnacht), 190, 192
Nowak, Willi, 136
nudes, 155, 174
Nuremberg Laws (1935), 190, 206
Nussbaum, Felix, 201

Odessa, 22
oppression. See Holocaust; persecution of Jews
Orlik, Emil, 103, 174, 180
Orloff, Chana, 59, 171, 195, 196, 202, 203, 238n9, 238n17, 263n5
Orte des Erinnerns (Places of Remembrance), 49
Osborn, Max, 5, 91, 180, 192, 202, 216, 258n59
Ostjuden (East European Jews), 5, 30, 89
Ost und West (magazine), 6, 40, 47, 53

paintings, 17–18, 185, 227–28
    in Berlin, 47
    destroyed, 217
    Expressionist forms, 41
    gouache, 47
    oil, 47, 130, 239n30
    of street scenes, 40–41, *40–41*
    See also watercolors; works by Szalit
Palestine, 125, 190, 202, 251n21
Palmarium du Jardin d'Acclimatation, 202
Palukst, Abraham, 5, 46, 52, 91
Paris
    cafés in, 196–97, 201
    as cultural capital of Europe, 31–32
    exile in, 3, 7–8, 12, 185, 189–91, 193–95, 221, 262n72
    Jewish community in, 7–8, 189–93, 215, 260n20
    Szalit's visits to, 30–32
Pariser Tageblatt (newspaper; later, *Pariser Tageszeitung*), 200, 202
Paris Jewish Museum, 218
Pascin, Jules, 195–96, 200, 261n46
pastels, 3, 116, 123, 130, 132, 138, 199, 228
Pasternak, Leonid, 248n14
Pathetiker (Pathetic Ones, or Artists of Pathos), 58, 91, 246n56

INDEX

pathos, 58, 91
Pechstein, Max, 75, 103
pencil drawings, 3, 58, 59, 130, 132, 199
PEN Club, 51
Peretz, I. L., 16
periodicals
    illustrations in, 11, 12, 53–54, 167
    increase in numbers of, 130
    See also German-Jewish press; Jewish press; newspaper illustrations; *specific periodicals*
persecution of Jews
    allegories of, 139
    humor as defense against, 93, 102
    in Nazi Germany, 49, 185, 190–92, 199 (*see also* Holocaust)
    in Russian Empire, 19–22
    See also anti-Jewish violence; antisemitism
Pfau, Ludwig, 83
Pfizenmayer, Hedwig, 168
philology, 33
photography, 176
Picasso, Pablo, 31, 132, 191, 195, 196
Pilichowski, Leopold, 169
Pinner, Erna, 139
Pissarro, Camille, 58, 217
Pithiviers (French detention camp), 208
Pless, Will, 174, 180
Podwal, Mark, 120
pogroms, 21–22, 26
    See also anti-Jewish violence
Polak, Elisabeth, 217
Poland, 3, 16, 26, 209, 214
    citizenship, 28, 208, 218
    Polish-Jewish refugees, 192
    See also Lodz
Polgar, Alfred, 52
Polish language, 3, 11, 28, 45, 48, 194
portraits
    of Berliners, 134–38
    New Objectivity and, 177
    School of Paris and, 195
    of Szalit, 59, *60*
    See also self-portraits
poverty, 19, 59, 93, 103–5, 170, 193, 210
    See also economic conditions
printmaking
    costs of, 48
    popularity of, 63, 68
    techniques, 57–58
    See also lithographs; *specific techniques*

Propyläen-Verlag (publisher), 102–3
Puni, Iwan, 51
Pyramid (club), 154

queer history. See LGBT/queer history

Rabinovich, Sholem. See Aleichem, Sholem
Rachumowski, S., 202
racist stereotypes, 162
radical literary journals, 48
Radierklub der Wiener Künstlerinnen (Print Club of Viennese Women Artists), 39
Rapoport, Benjamin, 208
Rebay, Hilla, 261n56
Rée, Anita, 256n15
refugees
    during First World War, 36
    from Nazi Germany, 8, 189–93, 262n7, 262n9
    See also Holocaust; statelessness
Reichsbund jüdischer Frontsoldaten (National Union of Jewish War Veterans), 146
Reichskulturkammer (Reich Chamber of Culture), 190
Reifenberg, Adele, 172, 256n15
Reimann School, 130
Remak, Fanny, 177, 190
Rembrandt, 57, 202
Renoir, Pierre-Auguste, 58
Residenz-Theater (Berlin), 41
Rey, H. A., 139
Rey, Margret, 139
Reyländer-Böhme, Ottilie, *176*
Rilke, Rainer Maria, 139
Rimon (magazine), 53–54, 251n20
    See also *Milgroym*
Rimon Publishing Company, 53–54, 95, 120–21, 124
Ringelnatz, Joachim, 61, 133
Robert, Eugen, 36, 39
Rodin, Auguste, 31, 58
Romanian-Jewish refugees, 192
Romanisches Café (Berlin), 49, 52, 60, 139
Rose, Traute, 174
Rosenbaum, Julius, 47
Rosenberg, Alfred, 190
Rosenfarb, Chava, 210
Rosenfeld, Oskar, 211
Rössing, Karl, 70, 248n11
Rotermund, Gerda, 155
Roth, Joseph, 6, 7, 37, 52, 69, 147, 191–92, 201
Rubens, Peter Paul, 159

Rund ums KaDeWe exhibition, 144, 224
Russian culture, 70–78
Russian Empire, 3
    Jewish life in, 96–98
    Pale of Settlement, 11, 19–26, 214, 239n28 (*see also* Lithuania)
    Yiddish language in, 18
Russian-Jewish migration, 19, 22, 51, 180, 192, 199
Russian language, 48, 51–52, 232
Ryback, Issachar Ber, 22, 195, 202

Salomon, Charlotte, 121, 192
Salon Henri Brendlé exhibition, 120, 224
Salon Populiste, 201
Salten, Felix, 139
Sandler, Aron, 169
Sandmann, Gertrude, 155
Sartre, Jean-Paul, 196–97
satire, 7, 56, 68, 71–74, 83, 92, 94, 101–2, 111, 124–25, 132–34
Schad, Christian, 156
Schiavoni, 183
Schiele, Egon, 39
Schildkraut, Rudolph, 41
Schlemiel (magazine), 56
Schneider-Kainer, Lene, 58, 155, 177
Scholz, August, 74
School of Paris (École de Paris), 8, 193, 195–97, 217, 218
Schülein, Julius, 201
Schulz, Bruno, 184, 259n72
Schwarz, Karl, 5, 40, 47–48, 53, 108, 169, 170, 172, 216, 245n34, 263n5
Schwichtenberg, Martel, 61, 167, 174, 177
Scientific Humanitarian Committee, 156
Sebastian Löwenbuck Akademischer Verlag, 74
Seeler, Moriz, 43
Segal, Arthur, 55
Segall, Lasar, 5, 55
Segalowitsch, Wladimir, 202
Seghers, Anna, 192, 201
Selbstwehr (Self-Defense, journal), 125, 146
self-portraits
    genre of, 181
    by Szalit, 9, *10*, 50, *181*
Sephardic Jewry, 198
Serebriakova, Zinaida, 51–52
sexuality
    in the Bible, 155–63
    same-sex relationships, 11, 43–45, 153–55, 164–66, 175

shtetls, 16–22, 24, 107, 146, 152
Šiauliai district, Lithuania, 20–22, 241n26
Singer, I. J., 210
Sintenis, Renée, 133, 139, 155, 174
slaughterhouses, 212, 263n31
Slavona, Maria, 32, 177
Slevogt, Max, 58, 174
Słodki, Marcel, 33, 217
Sobibor (killing center), 216
social hygiene films, 154
Société des Artistes Indépendants (Society of Independent Artists), 198
Sommer, Robert, 183
Soncino-Blätter (journal), 54
Soncino Society, 124
Soutine, Chaim, 94, 129, 189, 195, 196, 200, 260n35
Spain
    medieval, 111, 117, 118
    migration through, 8, 199, 206
Spiro, Eugen, 8, 47, 69, 169, 171, 174, 185, 190, 192, 196, 201–3, 206
statelessness, 8, 12, 193, 205–8
Statut des Juifs (Statute of the Jews), 206
Steger, Milly, 155, 174, 175, 177
Stein, Gertrude, 44
Stein, Otto Th. W., 136
Stein, Rolf, 135–36, 252n15
Steiner, Lilly, 201
Steinhardt, Jakob, 6, 8, 46, 91, 113, 120, 121, 169, 171, 252n2, 253n31
    animal paintings, 139
    Berlin Expressionism and, 57–60
    book illustrations, 69
    Dorfstrasse mit Frau (Village Street with Woman), 17–18, *18*
    guestbook drawing, 59, *61*, 163
    income, 257n25
    migration to Palestine, 190
    painting style and motifs, 16–18
    Portrait of Rahel Szalit-Marcus, 59, *60*
    Sabbatausgang (The Departure of the Sabbath), 115
    Szalit compared to, 55
    Zionism, 125
Steinrück, Albert, 36
Stencl, Avrom Nokhum, 52
Stern, Irma, 55, 62, 180, 263n5
Stern, Lisbeth, 172
Stolarska-Fronia, Małgorzata, 55
Straub, Agnes, 137
Straughn, Celka, 40

INDEX

Struck, Hermann, 6, 30, 47, 54, 69, 70, 120, 125, 169
    Die Kunst des Radierens (The Art of Etching, 1908), 57–58
    Hawdala, 115
suicide
    homosexuality and, 43, 154
    Julius Szalit's, 11, 42–45, 211
    rates of, 43
    during Vel d'Hiv roundup, 207
Surrealists, 195
Switzerland, 12, 36, 203, 206, 213
Szalit, Julius
    Austrian citizenship, 38
    in Berlin, 243n39
    career, 34–37, 39, 41–42, 134, 243n43, 244n56
    marriage, 11, 34–45, 37, 48, 221
    photograph of, 35
    sexuality, 43–44
    suicide, 11, 42–45, 211
Szalit, Rahel (née Markus; also Szalit-Marcus)
    in academic scholarship and historical memory, 2–5, 215–19
    artistic identity, 6, 27, 167–68
    awards and artistic success, 11, 47, 167, 171–73, 185
    birthdate, 11, 23–24, 30, 207, 221, 241n30
    deportation and death, 8, 12, 205, 207–8, 214, 216, 221
    early life and family, 11, 15–28, 209–14
    education, 11, 27, 33, 39
    income, 11, 50, 197
    Jewish identity, 6, 10, 27, 198–99
    love affairs with men and women, 43–44, 193–94
    marriage, 11, 34–45, 37, 48, 134, 221
    nationality and citizenship, 3, 8, 28, 38–39, 45, 208, 218–19
    personality, 9–10
    photograph of, 2, 2, 9
    physical appearance, 38, 49–50
    portrait of, 59, *60*
    renown, 8–9, 69, 89, 170, 217
    self-portraits, 9, *10*, 50, *181*
    sexuality, 43–44, 51, 164–65, 218
    See also works by Szalit
Szyk, Arthur, 210

Tarnopol, 34
Telz (Telšiai), 11, 21, 24, 215
Tevye stories, 6
theater, 36–37, 41–42, 89, 134–35
Theresienstadt (ghetto), 175
This Quarter (journal), 156
Tietz department store, 40
Tietze, Hans, 48
Tillier, Claude, 69, 139
    My Uncle Benjamin, 83–87, 163, 226
Tischler, Viktor, 201, 202
Tolstoy, Leo, 53, 54–55, 67, 70, 87, 118
    Die Kreutzersonate (The Kreutzer Sonata), 74–78, 226
    War and Peace, 248n14
translations, 69–70
travel and transportation, 27, 36, 40, 49, 147, 171
Triangle Bookstore, 197
Tucholsky, Kurt, 49, 52
Tutankhamun, King, 158

Uhde, Wilhelm, 196, 201
Ukraine, 22, 34
Ulk (magazine), 131, 143, 144
Ullstein (publisher), 102
Undzere farpaynikte kinstler (Our Martyred Artists), 9, 93, 217, 239n23, 263n6
Union des Artistes Libres. *See* Free Artists' League
United States
    Jewish migration to, 8, 22, 96, 202–3, 206, 241n34
    lesbians deported from, 165
    Mann's works in, 156, 255n12
    scholarship in, 218–19
Universal Jewish Encyclopedia, 216
University Library J. C. Senckenberg, Frankfurt am Main, Judaica Division, 219
Ury, Lesser, 47, 49, 54, 57, 169, 171
Užventis, 20–21

Valetti, Rosa, 36
van Hoboken, Anthony, 42
van Hoddis, Jakob, 61, 133
Varniai, 22, 241n24
Veidt, Conrad, 44
Vel d'Hiv roundup, 12, 207–8, 221
Verein der Künstlerinnen zu Berlin (VdBK, Association of Women Artists in Berlin), 11, 51, 103, 144, 154–55, 166–67, 173–75, 184, 190, 218, 221, 224, 257n34
Vereinigte Staatsschulen für Freie und Angewandte Kunst (United State Schools for Free and Applied Arts), 133

Vienna, 34–39, 42, 96, 215
Viertel, Salka, 41
Vilna, 22, 89
Violetta (club), 154
Vishniac, Roman, 139, 253n31
Vitebsk, 7, 199
Völkischer Beobachter, 190
Volksverband der Bücherfreunde (National Association of Bibliophiles), 83
von Kardorff, Katharina, 175
von Molo, Walter, 134
von Zitzewitz, Augusta, 155, 167, 177, 178
Vossische Zeitung (newspaper), 110, 112, 131, 135, 143, 180

Walden, Herwarth, 58
Waldoff, Claire, 174
Wandering Jew figure, 83
Warsaw, 22, 24, 168, 175, 180, 185, 218
Wartheland, 210
watercolors, 47, 130, 171, 181, 184, 185, 201–2, 228
    See also paintings; works by Szalit
Wedekind, Frank, 34
Wegener, Paul, 75
Wegweiser-Verlag, 83
Weimar Germany, 2–3
    equal rights in, 47
    See also Berlin
Weinbaum, Abraham, 195
Weissberg, Iser, 43, 244n56
Weissberg, Leon, 244n56
Weissmann, Ilse, 172
Weltsch, Felix, 125, 146
Weltsch, Robert, 146
Wendriner, Richard, 37
Werefkin, Marianne von, 32–33, 36
Werfel, Franz, 62, 133
Wertheim department store exhibition, 40, 174, 224
Westheim, Paul, 70, 201
Wiesbaden, exhibitions in, 53, 62, 223
Wilczynski, Käthe, 256n15
Wilder, Billy, 49
Wischnitzer, Mark, 53, 239n21, 259n1
Wischnitzer-Bernstein, Rachel, 5, 53–54, 95, 121, 184–85, 190, 202, 216
Wolfenstein, Alfred, 133
Wolf-Krakauer, Grete, 256n15
Wolfradt, Willi, 55, 201
Wolfthorn, Julie, 32, 44, 47, 50, 155, 167, 173–74, 176, 177, 180, 185, 190, 256n15

Wollheim, Gert, 201, 202
women
    in art academies, 31–32
    breastfeeding mothers, 59, 163
    employment, 31, 132, 151, 178, 180, 209–10
    in "human zoos," 144
    impoverished, 59, 170
    Jewish traditions and, 113, 149
    modern love affairs and, 78, 84
    in public spaces, 178
    as subjects, 5, 6, 59, 70, 76, 84–86, 91, 125, 132, 138, 148, 151–52, 171
women artists
    in Berlin, 166–75, 256n15
    in European Jewish art history, 5
    gender-bending activities, 33
    groups of, 167 (*see also* Verein der Künstlerinnen zu Berlin)
    illustrators, 4
    immigration to France, 192
    in Paris, 191–92, 238n9
    self-portraits, 181
    in Weimar Germany, 47
    See also specific artists
woodcuts, 17, 48, 58
working class, 19, 33, 62, 132, 170, 178, 209, 216
works by Szalit
    Arabella Minxit, Benjamin's Intended, 84, 86
    Because of Morality, 163, 164
    Benjamin Rathery and His Sister on a Donkey, 83, 84
    Bird, 141, *141*
    Blowing a Sailboat, 122, 123
    Brücke (Bridge), 185
    Brunnenkur im Zoo (Spa Cure at the Zoo), 144, *145*
    Cats, 140, 141
    The Convicts' Walk, 163, 165
    Das Auto im Bild (Images of Cars), 147
    In der Kälte (In the Cold), 41, *41,* 132, 227
    Der Rabbi, lithograph, 184
    Der Rabbi und sein Schüler (The Rabbi and His Pupil, 1920), lithograph, 56, *56,* 199, 228
    Der Raub der Dina (The Rape of Dina), 159, 160
    Die Dorfmusikanten (The Town Musicians), 16, 167, 218, 227, 240n1, 257n36
    Die Emigrantin als Bardame (Emigrant Woman as Barmaid), 9, 166, 178–80, *179, 183,* 198, 227

INDEX

works by Szalit (*continued*)
   Die Fechterin, Selbstbildnis (The Fencer, Self-Portrait), 9, 180–81, *181*, 227
   Die Musikanten (Musicians), 174, 227, 257n36
   Dina, 158, *159*
   Disputation, 118, *119*
   The Drive to the Rabbi, 91, *92*, 228
   The Drunk Chickens, 149, *151*
   Elena Ivanovna Studies the Monkeys, 72
   Elephant Pedicure, 143, *143*
   In the Emigration Office / Miss Zaichik from "Ezra," 90, *91*
   Entlassen! (Laid Off!), 132, *133*
   Fahrt zur Hochzeit (The Ride to the Wedding), 171, *172*, 184, 227
   Fatma Karel, 177–78, 224, 227, 258n51
   Fischke der Krumme (Fishke the Lame), 18, 55, 89, 94, 102–9, 155, 225, 250n43
   At the Front is Queen Esther, Riding Proudly on a Billy Goat, 149, *150*
   Group of Boys, 123, *124*
   Havdalah, 113–15, *115*
   Herbst im Zoo (Autumn at the Zoo), 144, 227
   I also Took My First Walk with Mr. Stone, 147–48, *148*
   Increasing-temperature Footbath, 183, *184*
   Interieur, 47, *47*–48, 227
   Jahrmarkt (1929), painting, 227
   Jahrmarkt (Annual Fair, 1922), lithograph, 24, *25*, 224, 228, 241
   Jehuda Halevi in Heaven, 117, *118*
   Jerusalem, 117, *117*
   Jeune femme dans son potager, 239n30
   Jewish Neighborhood, 17, *17*, 227
   Kinder beim Frühstück (Children Eating Breakfast), 138, *138*
   Kostümball (Costume Ball), 133, *134*
   La leçon du Talmud (The Talmud Lesson), 199, *200*
   La prière dite "Havdalah" (The Prayer Called Havdalah), 115–16, *116*, 199
   Leibe Slid the Matzahs in the Oven, 149, *151*
   Leipziger Platz, 40, *40*, 227
   Litauische Jüdin (Lithuanian Jewish Woman), 184
   Men Joined the Dance as Well, 159–60, *161*
   Moishe the Bookbinder Whacks the Children with a Board, 97, *98*
   Mrs. Tibbs Faints, 81, *82*
   The Narrator's Grandmother, 84, *85*
   Painting of an Oriental Rider, 201–2, 228
   "Parade Riposte," 181–83, *182*
   Paysage, 240n30
   Peering into the Crocodile's Mouth, 71
   Perk Number Two ("Chickens on Strike"), 6–7, *7*, 99, 212
   Portrait, 198
   Portrait, in *B'nai B'rith Magazine*, 177
   Portrait of Herbert Ihering, 135, *137*
   Portrait of Johannes Becher, 135, *136*
   Pozdnyshev Sitting by His Wife's Coffin, 78
   Prügelpädagogen (Abusive Pedagogues), 97, 99
   Before the Purim Festival Ends, Think of Your Purim Donation, 149, *150*
   Rabbi Pöckelhering, illustration for Zangwill, 55, 226, 246n43
   Rabbi und Schüler (Rabbi and Pupil), chalk drawing, 184
   Reb Mendele and the Innkeeper's Son, 107, *108*
   Reb Mendele and the Moon, 104, *105*
   Ritt auf dem Camel (Riding on the Camel), 141, *142*
   Sabbath, 113, *114*, 171
   Self-Portrait, 10
   Sichem on a White Donkey, 161–62, *162*
   Sport Schild (Sport Shield), 146, *146*
   Steinhardt Guestbook entry, 59, *61*
   A Street Sneezes, 98, *100*, 249n24
   Thoraverhör (Torah Examination), 167, 227
   The Three Briggs Sisters, 79, *80*
   Three Monkeys, 74
   Toralernen, 184
   The Traveling Band of Beggars, 105, *107*
   Tuggs and Belinda Waters, 80, *81*
   Two Men Surrounded by Women, 76
   Vacationers, 147, *147*
   Watching the Crocodile, 73
   We're Going to America, 101, *101*
   We Say Goodbye to Our Loved Ones at the Ship, 96, *97*
   Wife Anticipating Her Murder, 77
   Woman Sitting with Children, 95, *95*
   See also chalk drawings; exhibitions; illustrations; landscapes; lithographs; paintings; pastels; pencil drawings; portraits; watercolors
World League for Sexual Reform, 157
world literature, 67–87
World War, First, 11, 30, 42, 59, 170, 175, 209
World War, Second. See Holocaust; Nazi Germany
Wronkow, Ludwig, 192

xenophobia
    in France, 8, 69, 193, 205
    in Germany, 30

Yad Vashem, 213
Yiddish books, 3, 6, 53–54, 88–109, 111, 118–20
Yiddish culture, 18, 192
Yiddish language, 11, 18, 20, 48, 51, 62, 121, 148–49, 214, 239n28
Yiddish press, 5, 180
    See also specific publications
YIVO (Yiddish Scientific Institute), 52
Yung Yiddish avant-garde movement, 57

Zadkine, Ossip, 196
Zangwill, Israel, 54–55, 246n43
    The King of Schnorrers, 12, 54–55, 67, 226
Zapolska, Gabriela, 41
Zborowski, Léopold, 189, 200, 221, 225, 261n46
Zeitbilder (magazine), 143
Zelkowicz, Josef, 212
Zinglers Kabinett exhibition, 136–37, 221, 223
Zionism
    cultural, 5–6, 120, 124–25
    Expressionism and, 57
    Heine and, 112
    Jewish masculinity and, 146
    Markus family and, 24
    in Paris, 202
    Szalit and, 111, 120, 125, 146, 152, 219
Zoologischer Garten, Berlin, 125, 132, 138–44, 151
Zucker, Paul, 68
Zweig, Arnold, 30, 52
Zweig, Stefan, 52, 246n56